The Pursuit of Certaint

The peoples of the world are now facing economic integration and social interaction on a wider scale than ever before. But has this produced a greater sense of common reason, or shared world citizenship? Contemporary global communication, itself celebrating diversity, has paradoxically stimulated local commitments to exclusive ethnic, cultural and religious identity. The chapters in this book explore the ways in which anthropology can throw light on these diverging new 'certainties', often possessive of place, bodily substance or cultural heritage and often claiming divine justification.

The contributors are leading anthropologists from the world-wide Commonwealth, the UK and Europe. One is at present teaching in the USA, where several others have also held posts. They present a dozen original case studies which provide a valuable critical perspective on recent religious and ethno-cultural movements. Two chapters show how displaced African communities have had to reorient themselves to current definitions of politico-cultural identity (and an epilogue discusses the dilemma this concept poses for the Greeks, to whom we owe an older and more accommodating notion of civilization). An analysis of current discourse about 'diversity' in the influential setting of an American campus is followed by studies of the acceptance of a Pakistani Sufi cult in Britain, and of intensifying religious fundamentalism among Madras Christians, Israeli Jews and Malaysian Muslims. Concluding contributions focus on responses which the proselytizing religions have provoked within the complexities of traditional communities: they consider debates between Christians and Buddhists in Sri Lanka, ecumenical musings of the Yoruba diviners, and vernacular /Islamic interactions in Benin and off the East African coast.

The Pursuit of Certainty is a convincing demonstration of anthropology's relevance to the contemporary world and its turbulence. It offers ground-level insights into a growing global consensus about the primacy of cultural difference; into the shrill new certainties which are spreading in some areas – though being resisted in others; and into the 'post-Enlightenment' rise of religious justification in human affairs.

Wendy James is University Lecturer in Social Anthropology and a Fellow of St Cross College, Oxford.

ASA Decennial Conference Series

The Uses of Knowledge: Global and Local Relations
Series editor: Marilyn Strathern

The Pursuit of Certainty
Religious and Cultural Formulations

Edited by Wendy James

London and New York

First published 1995
by Routledge
11 New Fetter Lane, London EC4P 4EE

Simultaneously published in the USA and Canada
by Routledge
29 West 35th Street, New York, NY 10001

Typeset in Times by Florencetype Ltd, Stoodleigh, Devon
Printed and bound in Great Britain by Biddles Ltd,
Guildford and King's Lynn

British Library Cataloguing in Publication Data
A catalogue record for this book is available from the
British Library

Library of Congress Cataloguing in Publication Data
A catalogue record for this book has been requested

ISBN 0-415-10790-3 (hbk)
ISBN 0-415-10791-1 (pbk)

Contents

vi   Contents

Part III Vernacular contexts of public reason and critique

Part IV Epilogue: a professional dilemma?

Contributors

F. Niyi Akinnaso is Associate Professor in the Department of Anthropology, College of Arts and Sciences, Temple University, Philadelphia. His field of particular interest combines linguistics, education and anthropology, and his research has mainly been concerned with Yoruba society, culture, and history.

Janice Boddy is Associate Professor of Anthropology at the University of Toronto, Canada. She is author of *Wombs and Alien Spirits: Women, Men and the Zar Cult in Northern Sudan* and *Aman: The Story of a Somali Girl – As Told to Virginia Lee Barnes and Janice Boddy* (translated into twelve languages) as well as several articles on culture, possession, and feminism.

Lionel Caplan is Professor of South Asian Anthropology at the School of Oriental and African Studies, London. He is author of *Class and Culture in Urban India: Fundamentalism in a Christian Community* and other publications on Christians in Madras, where he has conducted research since 1974.

Paul Dresch is Lecturer in Social Anthropology at the University of Oxford and Fellow of St John's College. He previously taught at the University of Michigan, Ann Arbor. His particular regional interest is in the Arabic-speaking Middle East, and he is author of *Tribes, Government and History in Yemen*.

Georg Elwert is Professor of Social Anthropology and Sociology and a Director of the Institut für Ethnologie at the Freie Universität Berlin. He has conducted fieldwork in West Africa, especially in Bénin. He is author of *Bauern und Staat in Westafrika*, co-editor of *Aid and Development* (a special issue of *Sociologia Ruralis*, 1988) and numerous papers on literacy, education, nationalism and ethnicity.

Wendy James is Lecturer in Social Anthropology at the University of Oxford and Fellow of St Cross College. She is author of *The Listening Ebony: Moral Knowledge, Religion and Power among the Uduk of Sudan*, various publications on North East Africa and co-editor of *Vernacular Christianity: Essays in the Social Anthropology of Religion presented to Godfrey Lienhardt*.

Roger Just is Senior Lecturer in Anthropology at the University of Melbourne. Trained in classics at Melbourne, he read social anthropology at Oxford and has done field research on Meganisi, Lefkada, Greece and in South Sulawesi, Indonesia. He is author of *Women in Athenian Law and Life* and various articles on Greek kinship, family organization and ethnicity.

Michael Lambek is Professor of Anthropology at the University of Toronto. He is author of *Human Spirits: A Cultural Account of Trance in Mayotte* and *Knowledge and Practice in Mayotte: Local Discourses of Islam, Sorcery, and Spirit Possession*. Current projects include co-editing *The Subject of Memory* and the pursuit of fieldwork in northwest Madagascar.

Robert Paine is Henrietta Harvey Professor at the Memorial University of Newfoundland. His areas of fieldwork have included northern Norway and Israel; his interests include the Saami and the Fourth World, pastoralism, politics and rhetoric. In addition to his publications on the arctic region and on comparative topics he has published several articles on Israel.

Shamsul A.B. is Professor of Social Anthropology at The National University of Malaysia, Bangi, Malaysia and teaches politics and culture. He has done fieldwork in Indonesia, Borneo, Japan and Malaysia. His academic contributions have been published in Japanese, German, French, English and Malay. His monograph *From British to Bumiputera Rule* was nominated, in 1988, for the Harry Benda Prize of the Asian Studies Association, USA.

Aidan Southall has taught at Makerere University, Uganda and Syracuse University, New York; he is recently retired from a Professorship at the University of Wisconsin-Madison and lives in France. He has published widely on urban anthropology and social change, especially in East Africa, but also in Madagascar and China.

Jonathan Spencer is Senior Lecturer in Social Anthropology at the University of Edinburgh. He is the author of *A Sinhala Village in the Time of Trouble*, editor of *Sri Lanka: History and the Roots of Conflict*, and has published a number of articles on politics, nationalism and religion in Sri Lanka.

Pnina Werbner is Senior Lecturer in Social Anthropology at Keele University and Research Administrator of the International Centre for Contemporary Cultural Research at the Universities of Manchester and Keele. Her publications include *The Migration Process: Capital, Gifts and Offerings among British Pakistanis*, and a forthcoming book on the poetics and politics of identity among British Pakistanis. She is director of an ESRC research project on 'South Asian Popular Culture: Gender, Generation and Identity'.

Preface

This book is one of five to have been produced from the Fourth Decennial Conference of the Association of Social Anthropologists of the Commonwealth held at St Catherine's College, Oxford, in July 1993. Sections were organized by Richard Fardon, Wendy James, Daniel Miller and Henrietta Moore, each of whom has edited their proceedings. In addition Wendy James acted as Oxford Co-ordinator and it is principally due to her untiring efforts that the conference took place at all. As Convenor, I take the opportunity of acknowledging our debt to her and of registering gratitude to Priscilla Frost for her organizational assistance and to Jonathan Webber for acting as conference Treasurer.

The Institute of Social and Cultural Anthropology at Oxford gave material as well as moral support. The following bodies are to be thanked for their generous financial assistance: the Wenner–Gren Foundation for Anthropological Research, the British Council, the Oxford University Hulme Trust Fund, the Royal Anthropological Institute and the Association of Social Anthropologists itself.

To suppose anthropological analysis can shift between global and local perspectives may well imply that the two co-exist as broader and narrower horizons or contexts of knowledge. Indeed, the relationship seems familiar from the ethnographic record: in cosmologies that set a transcendent or encompassing realm against the details of everyday life; or in systems of value that aggrandize this feature while trivializing that; or in shifts between what pertains to the general or the particular, the collective or the individual. And if knowledge consists in the awareness of context shift, then such scaling may well seem routine. However, this book does not take scale for granted. It examines certain contexts in which people (including anthropologists) make different orders of knowledge for themselves as a prelude to questioning assumptions about the 'size' of knowledge implied in the contrast between global and local perspectives.

Marilyn Strathern

Foreword

This volume is based on papers presented in the section 'Religious and Cultural Certainties' at the fourth Decennial Conference of the Association of Social Anthropologists of the Commonwealth, held in Oxford in July 1993. One of five main sections, it was designed to form an integral part of the overall theme of the conference, on 'The Uses of Knowledge: Local and Global Relations'. The day's meetings were chaired in turn by Gilbert Lewis from Cambridge and Bawa Yamba from Uppsala. Nancy Lindisfarne from London and Paul Dresch from Oxford acted as discussants. To all these, as well as the paper givers themselves and those who contributed to the discussion from the floor, thanks are due for helping to make a coherent and interesting day's exchanges.

It was felt from an early stage in planning the Decennial that it was high time anthropology considered afresh its professional position *vis-à-vis* the world religions. In choosing to focus on 'certainty' as a topical theme, the intention from the start had been to include some papers on religious fundamentalism. It was also planned to maintain a broad view of the theme, however, and not to limit its scope to 'religion' as such. As the conference plans developed, it became clear that there was nevertheless a wide interest in religious topics and a number of papers on Christianity in particular were grouped into an Associate Section chaired by John Peel.

The possibilities for pursuing 'certainty' across several fields in contemporary culture and politics, which became evident in the formal and informal discussions arising from our section at the conference, led to the slightly extended format of the present volume. Paul Dresch and Robert Paine agreed to write additional papers to strengthen the collection, and as editor I would like to express my special appreciation to them.

In the logistical preparations for the conference, sterling support was offered by my co-convenors, by my colleagues in the Institute of Social and Cultural Anthropology at Oxford, by the administrative staff of ISCA and a team of graduate student helpers, and also by my family and a few non-anthropological friends. The ASA Committee lent an understanding ear and guiding hand at various stages, in what became the largest and most complex occasion in the history of the Association. All this background help on the organizational side made it easier for me to devote some time and thought to the intellectual side of the section represented here, and for this I am very grateful; I would particularly like to thank John Davis and Marilyn Strathern for their encouragement, and for their unflinching confidence both in the importance of the aims of the conference and in the detailed plans they evolved.

Wendy James
Oxford, April 1995

Introduction

Whatever happened to the Enlightenment?[1]

Wendy James

NEW KINDS OF CERTAINTY?

One of my long-standing informants, Martha Nasim Ahmed, was displaced in 1987 by war and by 1993 had trekked with several thousand assorted others 650 miles from home, crossing and recrossing the international border between the Sudan and Ethiopia five times. During this time her people became newly prominent to combatants and humanitarian agencies alike, registering and reregistering their names, tribal group and religion along the way. Martha told me:

> 'When we got to Assosa [the first refugee camp], they asked us, all of us, "Are you Christians?" And we said, in fact I myself said when they asked me, "Yes, I am Christian, I am a child of Jesus and I belong to the church." And then this other person who had no particular link, he was asked after me "Are you a Christian?" and he said yes, he was a Christian. It was right there in [the refugee camp] that he came to believe. "I am a person of Jesus." There he was behind me squatting on the ground, saying "Yes. Because of us fleeing through the bush, coming here as forest-foundlings, my Liver told me I should join the Word to my body".'[2]

Having registered these commitments, as a result of external circumstances as much as of their own volition, it is now much more difficult for 'the Uduk' as an internationally visible community to contemplate a safe return to the Sudan, which since their flight has adopted an increasingly harsh form of Islamic militancy.

Here is a conjunction of the written texts of international bureaucracy, the fear of death, the Word of God, the body and the linked dichotomies of ethnicity, nationality and religious choice drawn together in a peculiarly contemporary way. There was not in any previous historical period the need, if one lived in this relatively open borderland, to specify one's identity along all these dimensions. Rarely has the 'choice' of believing in the God of the Bible (in Uduk, renderable only in the evocative idiom of 'joining the Word to the body') been so harshly required. And yet this is occurring in a world which otherwise appears to be opening up all kinds of new liberal freedoms for the person. In the West, academic and political rhetoric alike emphasizes respect for individuals, toleration of minorities and appreciation of 'multicultural' diversity, even seeking to link the very definition of human rights to a respect for cultural difference. At the same time, across the world, ethnic, cultural and religious identity is being used as an idiom in which to pursue exclusive group interests and to strive for power. An idiom of rights based on 'difference', in the hands of a harsh military regime claiming to represent a specific ethnic or religious identity, can be quite transformed from its benign substance in a liberal democracy.

At the ASA Decennial Conference held in Oxford in 1993, slippery problems of this kind arising from the apparent conjunction of 'global' and 'local' phenomena engaged many of the paper-givers and much of the discussion. In this book we offer a set of studies based on the conference section devoted to 'Religious and Cultural Certainties'. All draw on ethnography illustrating the rise of claims to 'global' knowledge in the contemporary world: knowledge of self, of the nature of society and of God. Some are studies of the debates, contradictions and paradoxes provoked 'on-the-ground' by the spread of new knowledge-claims. All, I believe, illustrate how the generation of specific local certainties, in the plural, is gaining momentum through new trends in world communication, and all provide suggestive clues as to how the new certainties are being shaped by assumptions of difference emanating from world centres.

Paul Dresch contributes a chapter (developed from his role as discussant at the conference) on a new kind of certainty concerning personal and ethnic identity as ancestry-cum-heritage in the USA. This agenda is seemingly very tolerant of diversity and protective of persons and minorities but is entangled with intergroup tension and confrontation (a 'need' for 'identity'), even on the campus – though no-one can say whether the tensions against which it offers protection are in part produced by the new 'liberal' discourse itself. The chapter leads our Part II section on the new certainties, because it pinpoints something at the centre of today's influential political thinking. The older European imperialisms were confronted by nationalist movements, more or less at the time of the civil rights movement in the USA. Those movements sought to correct inequalities of power and to secure rights of citizenship for men and women *regardless* of colour, class, religion, tribe and so on – that is, regardless of what today would be called 'ethnic' or 'cultural' or 'gender' identity ('class' has dropped out). What were sought were equal rights for all the people of India, the African colonies, legally disadvantaged American Blacks etc. as citizens of modern democracies and of the world. But the discourse of the post-imperial period, and the post-civil rights period in the USA, has lost something of its grip on the notion of equal citizenship, while retaining elements of the language of rights. The tendency is now to promote those very categories of personal ethnicity, culture and gender which were classed as irrelevant to citizenship a generation ago and were criticized in those countries where they were used as a basis for legal rights (e.g. South Africa, Switzerland). Diversity of individual identity, in the wealthy developed countries, can now become the very basis upon which claims to rights, privileges and respect are put forward, while the structure of society, with all its political, economic and other inequalities at home and across the world, fades from focus. Principles of diversification are pressed logically further and further by the students in Dresch's ethnography of an American campus, where the response is a burgeoning paraphernalia of procedures for guaranteeing individuals proper representation. We reach the point where everyone seems to be able to claim minority status in him or herself and consequently protection from harassment and the invasion of personal space. An important question underlies this study: how far are these developments linked to what is going on off-campus, to the streets where racial, sexual and other violence is said to be growing? How far does this picture of the American social scene reverberate with worldwide patterns of replicating claims to local authenticity? Again, while the rhetoric of defending human rights has extended to aspects of most states' foreign policy, how far is this rhetoric effective in actually protecting human life? How would it compare with the protection formerly offered by now older-fashioned 'Enlightenment' definitions of citizenship, the democratic state and the rule of law?

One of the intriguing themes permeating papers and discussion across the Decennial Conference was that of the provocation of autonomous local self-knowledge by global interaction and global media. Whether or not it is reasonable to focus on the USA as a prime *provocateur* (as Lionel Caplan does forcefully in his contribution here on fundamentalist missions), what is clear is that in many cases the new certainties are being generated, in part, by conjoining the local pursuit of identity or personal religious knowledge with the permissive global circumstances in which the spread of many such claims is seen as natural. Today, it is relatively easy to see how the former colonial administrations were able to 'divide and rule' by producing new forms of nationality and 'tribe' through the bounding of territories, sub-territories and the specification of group rights within them on a supposedly authentic basis of local custom. It is less easy to understand whether an analogous process is going on now in the way that global commercial and political interests endorse the proliferation of ethno-cultural specificity.

The chapters in this volume are the product of several rounds of consultation before, during and after the Decennial Conference. Most have gone through several drafts and it is our belief that our concerns have converged during this process; the book is now offered as presenting a coherent set of explorations of the way certainties have been shaped in recent history and in the contemporary world. Some movements towards certainty have taken a distinctively religious form, or have used religion as a vehicle; but our concerns have not been limited to 'religious' certainty. The wider range of cultural practice, imagery and representation has also offered fertile material; and foremost are the new defining images of ethnic, cultural and national authenticity as a universal fount of singular self-knowledge and a justification for the oppositional classification of others. Now 'certainty' has not always seemed to us, empirically, to take a very benign character; it is not the equivalent of 'truth' in the mainstream thought of any civilization, though various rhetorics of truth may be deeply implicated in its expressions. In fusing, as it may, emotion and intellect, language and action, the abstractions of ideology and the concreteness of land claims, can certainly can be morally and politically threatening.

The benign optionality of 'identity' and 'culture' in some recent academic writing and a neither-here-nor-thereness about the human variety of the world has, I must admit, caused me worry. There is a sensation at times of our being lost in the market place of lifeways. We can probably go some way with Richard Rorty when he suggests that 'the vocabulary of Enlightenment rationalism, although it was essential to the beginning of liberal democracy, has become an impediment to the preservation and progress of democratic societies' and that a vocabulary 'which revolves around notions of metaphor and self-creation rather than notions of truth, rationality and moral obligation' is better suited to 'our' current situation as educated Western liberals (1989: 44). We can supposedly remake our circumstances and ourselves at will and discard the historically outworn constraints of the scientific and universalist thinking of our past. But anthropology does not have the luxury of focusing mainly on 'our' selves and the history of our own thoughts (at least in so far as they may be recorded in literature); it requires a serious engagement with the specific world circumstances in which humanity and its imagination struggles to live now. The human imagination is not everywhere allowed the same free play; external shaping circumstances may not always be visible but they are still there. The (northern) Sudanese women refugees in Toronto portrayed in Janice Boddy's chapter were embracing 'Nubian' identity in early 1992, of their own volition and in a richly expressive cultural mode; the innocent triggers for this were a display of ancient Nubian archaeology in the Royal Ontario Museum and the occasion of International Women's Day with its invitation to celebrate national culture. But Boddy also sketches in the political circumstances behind the refugees' flight from the Sudan, where they would normally claim to be 'Arabs' yet in Canada wish to dissociate themselves from the current Sudanese regime, classed with reason as 'extremist Arabs' and 'Islamic militants'. (This perception is grounded in part on political facts, such as the support given by the Sudan to Iraq during the Gulf War and its dependence since on Iran for the means to prosecute a brutal war against many of its own people.) The Alur, most of whom are now displaced within neighbouring Uganda after a generation of violence and mayhem in that country worsened by the impact of Sudanese wars, are wryly described by Aidan Southall as gaining their 'culture' today (through a community club in Kampala) at the same time as they are finally losing it (in the older sense). The Baganda of the country's heartland are linked to cosmopolitan definition and global networks even more securely; a Ganda radio operates from Massachusetts and there is a healthy air traffic to the USA in Ganda cultural objects. A widespread 'folklorization' or commodification of culture has drawn together the lesser and the more accessible parts of the world, though not on equal terms, as documented particularly well in the companion ASA Decennial volume edited by Daniel Miller.

One of our professional predicaments is that the language of anthropology has been co-opted and often caricatured by the dominant public discourse of cultural diversity to the extent that we find ourselves almost without the words in which to proceed. Roger Just's contribution is a fine-tuned commentary on this problem and takes a special place here as a thoughtful clarification of some of the themes which run through the whole volume. One does not have to be a Greek to recognize that 'civilization' is more than 'culture', especially in its shallow (post)modern form; nor to ask, now that we have given free rein to the consciousness of the moment, recognizing even Tradition as invented and turning culture into Lifestyle, what terms we have left for discussing those continuities of memory, experience and imagination which we used to compare to the grammar of a language and assume were basic to our subject.

At the same time that local specifications of region and ethnicity and the distinctive marking of culture seem to have become internationally required, the world economy (in concealed fashion? – note Dresch below on the Budweiser advertisements tactically portraying 'great African rulers') penetrates all boundaries, including those of national territory. Some religious crusades seeking out local converts openly follow the new economic patterns of circulation. Lionel Caplan's scenario of mass evangelical rallies in Madras evokes not only visual metaphors of upraised hands and a spread of light; the motif of economic power is a stronger metaphor and it is more than metaphor. Not only do the new certainties *seem* to be able to spread like strong currencies into weak economies: they spread with the actual power of strong currencies. While attractively glossed with natural or divine guarantee, they are powerfully fuelled by resources from the rich countries, bypassing the gatekeepers of national sovereignty and the guardians of community to make their claim on individual persons. Exchanges of 'knowledge' or 'belief' used to be multiple, provisional, partial, set within a context of social relations; it was rare for the tokens of ideological exchange to correspond to the whole of a person's being, a commitment demanded by some of the new merchants of faith. Older forms of faith incorporated or at least gave space to doubt and mystery; now we have a commoditized form which offers guarantees.

In a UN canteen in the Third World I asked for vegetarian food and a total stranger came up, offering the hand of fellowship and beaming, 'So you are *born again*?'

The older pattern was for forms of knowledge and claims to truth to be articulated through a mutually-constituting structure of social relations which could also carry counter-views and contradiction, or at least the dampening effects of apathy. In an earlier article Michael Lambek discussed the 'power of certainty' in the sacred texts of Islam, texts which do not open up dialogue as a basis for knowledge, but command an act of submission to the words themselves (Lambek 1990; see also Gilsenan 1987). Both in that piece and in his contribution here, Lambek subscribes to Roy Rappaport's formulation that certainty is the product of acts of commitment in which the discursive and the non-discursive are conjoined (Rappaport 1979). Yet the religious scholar's kind of certainty in practice permits, even requires for its reflexive self-confirmation, the socially embedded presence of complementary perspectives – a division of intellectual labour. In this sense, it is a socially tolerant truth-claim; those who study hard may compete to acquire certain specialist knowledge, but they remain members of a heterogeneous community life. Jonathan Spencer's analysis of a remarkable debate at the end of the nineteenth century in Sri Lanka, between respective spokesmen for Christianity and Buddhism, focuses on this kind of religious-scholarly certainty, still located within a community but transformed to another level of language: the language of formal reason, between proponents mutually 'tolerated' in the sense that they grant each other an equality of status beyond, or beneath, the claims of religious belief. This is fundamentally the Enlightenment starting point and informs many a real-life situation of heterogeneity in human affairs. But religious truth-claims are now potentially disembedded. They are claiming freedom to seek an absolute form and an asocial world arena.

There are both the technical and institutional means for the easy spread of ideas in the world today. Two of the contributions here focus on such patterns of 'spread'. Pnina Werbner discusses the 'travelling fables' of a Sufi saint, whose miraculous deeds in faraway north-western Pakistan carry intellectual conviction and produce emotional commitment among his followers in Birmingham and Manchester. The fables pass on from person to person; though the carriers are linked by aeroplane and telephone, Sufi wisdom of this kind should not be written down (least of all by anthropologists). Another kind of person-to-person spread co-opts the apparatus of modern educational institutions: Shamsul's chapter describes the 'modernizing' political and educational processes which led a generation of Malaysian students, especially science students, to embrace fundamentalist Islam. The 'pious science student' syndrome provoked discussion at the Decennial Conference (echoing Spencer's as well as Shamsul's contribution). It is paradoxically a worldwide phenomenon, with its own momentum of rationalist methods and proofs co-opted into justification of the dogmatic substance of several world religions. It challenges older tolerated forms of a division of intellectual labour within society.

The disciplinary tradition of anthropology still retains a kind of Enlightenment innocence, assuming that it is possible to speak reasonably of various systems of knowledge and human experience and compare them. Heterogeneity and a certain give and take of internal dialogue are also assumed, by good anthropology, for the social worlds we study. We have unself-consciously, in the past, spoken 'of' others and 'of' their religions and notions of truth. For some good reasons, this innocence is under criticism, but we should beware the dangers of other kinds of naïveté. Anthropologists are faced professionally and personally with the awkward problem of describing, let alone analysing, the new globally ambitious schemes of knowledge which take the right to representation sometimes to absurd and intolerant extremes: where if you are not a Muslim, you should not speak of Islam; and if you are a man, you should not speak of women. We used to assume that it was possible to maintain an academic distance and speak or write about others' lives. Critics have extended the fashionable idea of a natural right to cultural difference, to the point where we find them denying a citizen's, friend's or scholar's right to represent, transcend or transform that difference. The assumption of distance in the academic discourse has been collapsed by those who do not like it; 'speaking of' has been elided into 'speaking for'. A Canadian woman was told in a US college that she had no right to speak about Iran (her married home for several years), while her 7-year-old son did have that right as a half-Iranian. Those who defend this kind of right, accorded unashamedly on the basis of biological inheritance, should be reminded of the treacherous potential of the idea when it becomes locked into social and legal structures. By mid-1994 in Rwanda you could be killed for having a national identity card with one 'ethnicity' rather than another written on it.

The idea of biologically given rights finds a particularly strong (and historically crucial) form in the conjunction of Jewish religious ideology and the land-based politics of the state of Israel: Robert Paine's chapter, written specially as a key contribution to this volume, focuses on one of the most potent forms of new certainty in the world. One of his informants draws on the newest of biological images to explain and justify a claim to possession of the Biblical lands of the occupied West Bank: 'This place is in my genetic code.'

What are such claims doing? They are all arbitrary, invoking singularity and placing themselves beyond discussion. They pull together a surprising variety of things in new ways – a Biblical verse, a travelling fable, a vision of Jesus, the land, the water, the body and the genes. Our chapters focus on how and where such new processes of conjoining are taking place; several ask to what extent the power of public reason, as Jonathan Spencer puts it, following Kant, is still in evidence as a source of containment and critical distancing. Is there any evidence of critique? – if not from the 'irony' of the academy – to adopt Richard Rorty's usage (1989) – or the writers and politicians of the 'mature democracies', is there any critical distancing at a community contextual level on the ground? Surely it is not only we in the enlightened academy who can apprehend context and history behind the new movements to certainty; who from an 'ironic' distance can sense the sharpening inequalities, the drawing of new lines and the momentum in places towards violence?

THE WORLD AS IT WAS, AND AS IT STILL IS, ONLY MORE SO

At the ASA Conference, Talal Asad robustly pointed to the continuing presence of boundaries in the world, the presence of haves and have-nots. Following his (1986) discussion of the place of the 'strong' languages of the world, we could suggest that these languages have become the vehicle of distinctly *modern* forms of the idea that a person can 'possess' knowledge, an image which has become the currency of modern identity. The spread of this image of the personal locus of knowledge has followed in time and to an interesting degree in space the erosion and retreat of those clear nineteenth-century rationalities which underpinned the imperialism of that day. In the chapters offered here are several reminders of the formative events of the late nineteenth century in setting the scene for what has happened since – especially Aidan Southall on the long cycles of displacement in northern Uganda, Lionel Caplan on some very recent developments affecting older-established Christian communities in Madras, and Jonathan Spencer on echoes of the nineteenth century in Sri Lanka. The freedom and progress promised by the 1960s era of independence in the former colonies have scarcely materialized and we wonder today whether that 'independence' is something of an illusion. When I speak of the new currencies of certainty as a modern development, therefore, while recognizing a post-imperial watershed, I place the beginning of the modern era in the late nineteenth century.

It is useful to pause a moment and look back on global/local interactions in the pre-modern eras. Several chapters in this collection (and elsewhere in the ASA Decennial volumes) point to long-term continuities: there have been empires and trade routes, centres of cultural and religious influence and political control, and there have been regions peripheral to these political centres and communication routes. Regions have waxed and waned in their centrality and global significance in these respects, as modern Greek villagers never tire of pointing out to Roger Just. No doubt, inscribed in their practices, their partially coherent knowledges and images, are residues of a heterogenous past. This is because in pre-modern times what could be represented as global remained on a relatively human scale. The Romans gradually indigenized themselves on Hadrian's Wall, recruiting and marrying the locals over 400 years; messages came in person or by letter; most armies had to carry their equipment and walk; battles were conducted face to face. Even the Roman gods were indigenized to some degree; there was no doctrinal debate, as far as we are aware, between the truth-claims of the ancient British spirits and the religion of the imperial centre; a working accommodation was reached between them. Observing or neglecting the shrine of this or that Emperor was a pragmatic matter.

Compare even Christian expansion in the medieval period (here I am following Talal Asad's writings on the monasteries [e.g. 1993]). There was active promulgation of the Christian faith but the sociology of it was very different from the workings of the modern (let alone postmodern!) mission. The whole process was embedded in the give and take of local political economy. The monks were able to build a general claim to Truth among other things through what might be seen today as a sort of cultural compromise – their practice of validating, or invalidating, the practices of particular shrines and established rites of the countryside in their own hinterlands. This model is an evocative one in forming a comparison with the global/local relations considered at the ASA Conference, I think – because it is anchored so firmly in the distinctly physical structures of constraining social and cultural authority which the monasteries represented. Like the modern mission, they had to operate through economic and political means; but unlike their modern descendants they had to live with their neighbours, and this fact mediated the religious challenge. The challenge could become a crusade overseas, but accommodation and the ideological ambivalences of the peace were often maintained at home.

In these earlier periods there was a continuing social logic of connection within which the transmission of religious and cultural knowledge took place, a social logic which could be engaged from either side – though no doubt in different ways. The difference today is that this social matrix of transmission has disappeared, or become invisible, at least to many of the potential recipients; ideas arrive like summer storms, backed up by high-tech communication of which one can have no knowledge. In North East Africa, for example, events are not so much something you can opt for; all you can do is try to opt out of them, though they are largely inescapable. Only from the metropolitan perspective do they have a pattern, do they have a structure, a rationale (if not reason) in the recent politics of the Cold War and now its end.

I have had the experience of camping on the ground, with my family but lost and fairly desperate, as we were driving cross-country through the wooded savannahs of the central Sudan. We had struck what seemed at first to be a very good network of wide new roads in this almost empty region. We were glad of these because the 1930s roads of our map seemed to have vanished; but the new ones weren't on the map either. After choosing one set of right-angle turns after another, we realized none led anywhere except blank forest. The clean new tracks turned out to be a satellite-visible grid being constructed for purposes of oil exploration.

We could no doubt be seen via space in some lab in the USA, as surely as can today's refugee camps in the region, but we ourselves could not see the wood for the trees. The next day we were lucky enough to be sent in the right direction by some distinctly pre-modern looking passers-by. At first seeming to be local nomads, these turned out to be employees of the project. As David Harvey (1989) has so vividly conveyed, space has shrunk and homogenized itself for those who have the technical means to manage it, but this produces an increasing differentiation of knowledge and power as between those dealing with space on one level and those stuck on another. Michael Lambek's island of Mayotte is close geographically to the Islamic Federal Republic of the Comoros; but in practical – and political – terms it is privileged to be closer to distant Paris, partly the result of a conscious political choice to be thus 'globally' connected rather than dominated by Mayotte's immediate stronger neighbours.

There is a rhetoric of global equality and the defence of human rights; but a reality of increasing inequality, a reality increasingly hidden. The images of non-Western alternative authenticities dominate the global-elite networks, while the majority of those supposedly represented are stuck in poverty and war and inaccessible, uncontrolled zones on the map. Many ordinary local road, rail and water networks are working less efficiently today than they did three or four decades ago, especially (but not only) in the Third World. There may be an information explosion on the New York/Tokyo axis, but as a number of colleagues at the Decennial Conference were reporting in despair, there are these days no books in African universities. This may be an extreme illustration but the syndrome is general; and as the technology of communications spirals up in sophistication, the relative privilege of those few who control it grows.

I am therefore comforted to find a call, in Alex Callinicos' *Making History* and *Against Postmodernism* (1987 and 1989), for a return to theories of structure and agency. In our present context of considering the spatial aspects of the uses of knowledge, such a return seems required. Locality and region, distance and space, mean little except with reference to the means of access, transportation, communication and control or military surveillance and threat. Conversely, possibilities of evasion, concealment, invisibility and silence, or the maintenance of resistance in an active sense, depend on quite specific geographical and spatial relations. The technical wizardry of modern communications, whether aircraft, electronic or spy in the sky, has in one sense made the world smaller and more accessible: but accessible to whom?

ANALYSIS FROM THE FIELD: ANTHROPOLOGICAL PERSPECTIVES

In the global/local spectrum, anthropological practice has obviously been situated mainly at the local end, in historical communities which exist in complex internal differentiation and in external interrelation with others on the ground. It has also pursued the Enlightenment ideal of assuming human equality and seeking to tolerate and understand. There is nothing to apologize for here and many advantages which we can press as a discipline: while there is everything to be said today for attempting fieldwork among the global elites, our role has often been usefully to distance ourselves from the visible, the orthodox, the dominant and to contextualize it. Our fieldworking approach has in fact been very important as a complement and corrective to many other perspectives which take as their focus of systematic analysis or holistic contemplation ideology itself: the 'history of Islam', the essence of God, or the theory of reason. We are inclined these days to undervalue our own past sophistication as a discipline; we have not by any means always dealt in those Mickey Mouse notions of bounded society and homogeneous culture we now castigate ourselves with. Our way of seeking a contextual perspective upon what presents itself as knowledge should equip us well to tackle the current emerging world forms of certainty, by looking not only at their core but also at their differential engagement with communities in place.

There always have been claims to religious truth, logical validity, sure knowledge – for example, concerning life, death and illness – and anthropologists, because of our fieldworking practices, have long dealt with these. However, we have not dealt with them in conditions of philosophical purity: we have seen how they co-exist more or less with doubt and ignorance and with alternatives. Moreover, we have had to deal with what seems to constitute propositional knowledge as it emerges *piecemeal* from within heterogeneous social contexts of verbal exchange and contested action, rather than through the considered written statements and single-authored accounts which form the main sources for other disciplines. The coherence of our analyses has not been the coherence of dogma or belief: it has been the coherence of the situated community on the ground within which conversation can take place, and can even be extended, in translation and to outsiders, including one or several anthropologists.[3]

Within the local but differentiated social field we typically study, internally heterogeneous patterns of knowledge are not an exception, even in the domain of religion; they are the rule (consider even Durkheim's *The Elementary Forms of the Religious Life* [1915]). We rarely, however, find ideological clashes; we may expect to find, even in the hierarchical or ranked structures, rather what Foucault has termed *le savoir des gens*, an encompassing residue of wisdoms located within community life which can embrace all kinds of substantive difference and logical ambiguity. That understanding, pragmatic rather than ideological, is illustrated beautifully by Niyi Akinnaso's chapter on the way Yoruba divination can incorporate and judiciously reorient aspects of Islam and Christianity; and by Georg Elwert's contribution (a robust defence of vernacular forms of universal reason) on why it may be rationally modern to become a Muslim. Michael

Lambek's Mayotte islanders do not offer such explicit rationalizations; but in the context of myriad comings and goings in their local spiritual economy and through the alternative personae of spirits, they may physically choke on the Quran. Survival through evasion, disguise, bodily rejection; retreat and switching of allegiance: are there not sound pragmatic wisdoms here?

One advantage of taking the periphery seriously, and pressing on with our fieldwork there, is that it can still illuminate from a critical perspective the interrelations between forms of knowledge and between those who pursue knowledge. It can also reveal that from the periphery, the market-place of 'certainties' on offer is less open than might be represented at 'the centre'. For most people, there are very few real options, once the merchant banks and the arms-dealers have made their choices. In the daily lives of ordinary people there may be very little choice as to whether one wears Bata shoes, joins a fundamentalist church, or joins an ethnically based militia and dies for it. The only certainty is a pragmatic one, that you may have to do it. Because you can't always escape to the hills.

Roger Just's dilemma of placing himself, his nationality, his profession and its language in a study of modern Greece, illuminates our whole enterprise in this volume. There people consider themselves (and are respected by us as) founders of civilization and are still puzzling over the peculiarly undermining aspects of modern social-science speak. The Greeks claim to have a richer vocabulary for most things than do the English but they do not have a word which matches the contemporary Anglo-American 'culture'; as a description of their achievements, its slightly patronizing liberalism could scarcely be acceptable to the people who actually *founded civilization*, long before the English language was born.

NOTES

1 Several contributors to the present volume have helped me with the shape and argument of this introduction; none would endorse it all. I would especially like to thank Paul Dresch and Michael Lambek.
2 This conversation took place in January 1993, at the Karmi transit site for asylum-seekers in Ethiopia. The interview was filmed (though not used) for Orphans of Passage (director: Bruce MacDonald), in Granada TV's *Disappearing World: War*. See James (1988, 1994).
3 We never study one person in the field, or even one group, but a more or less systematically connected set of people or groups (even in a refugee camp), and systematically connected voices, opinions or forms of knowledge. The work of Marilyn Strathern has shown how what can be counted as knowledge of human beings, including self-knowledge, is split and refracted along dimensions of sociality – men as against women, perhaps, but not necessarily (1988); Gilbert Lewis has broken down the holism of a ritual 'system' (1980); Michael Gilsenan (1982) and Nancy Lindisfarne (1991) have traced in different ways the internal heterogeneities of what is sometimes called 'the Islamic world'; John Davis has elucidated the way historical tradition may be fashioned out of experience in

counterpoint form as between younger and older peer groups, or between those in control of the state and those at its mercy (1987, 1989). Jonathan Parry has engaged with the practices of several religious traditions in India, in their interaction with economic production and exchange (e.g. 1985). Richard Werbner has explored the socio-spatial rootedness of religious knowledge in rural areas (1977, 1989) and Jonathan Webber has treated the city of Jerusalem as a myriad religious refractions (1978). David Zeitlyn's work on divination has developed a sophisticated approach to the idea of a social division of intellectual labour (for example 1990). Again and again it is within and against *a relational structure of empirically encountered understandings* that we find our own distinct professional knowledge. The relational structure may be one of stability and complementarity; or cumulative differences may be produced and reproduced in forms of knowledge, as between classes in the Marxist sense, or between the centre and periphery of a modern political economy (see the work of Jean and John Comaroff e.g. 1985, 1991) or Don Donham's analysis of the Ethiopian polity (1986) and his general anthropological analysis of knowledge and political economy (1990). In my view, it is the latter kind of analysis from which we can still take bearings on current global/local relations.

REFERENCES

Asad, T. (1986) 'The concept of cultural translation in British social anthropology', pp. 141–64, in J. Clifford and G.E. Marcus (eds) *Writing Culture: the poetics and politics of ethnography*, Berkeley, CA: University of California Press.
—— (1993) *Genealogies of Religion: discipline and reasons of power in Christianity and Islam*, Baltimore, MD and London: Johns Hopkins University Press.
Callinicos, A. (1987) *Making History*, Cambridge: Polity Press.
—— (1989) *Against Postmodernism: a Marxist critique*, Cambridge: Polity Press.
Comaroff, Jean (1985) *Body of Power, Spirit of Resistance*, Chicago: University of Chicago Press.
—— and John Comaroff (1991) *Of Revelation and Revolution: Christianity, colonialism and consciousness in South Africa*, Chicago: University of Chicago Press.
Davis, J. (1987) *Libyan Politics: tribe and revolution. The Zuwaya and their government*, London: I.B. Tauris.
—— (1989) 'The social relations of the production of history', pp. 104–20, in E. Tonkin, M. McDonald and M. Chapman (eds) *History and Ethnicity*, ASA Monograph 27, London/New York: Routledge.
Donham, D.L. (1986) 'Old Abyssinia and the new Ethiopian empire', pp. 3–48, in D.L. Donham and W. James (eds) *The Southern Marches of Imperial Ethiopia: essays in social anthropology and history*, Cambridge: Cambridge University Press.
—— (1990) *History, Power, Ideology: central issues in Marxism and anthropology*, Cambridge: Cambridge University Press.
Durkheim, E. (1915) *The Elementary Forms of the Religious Life*, London: Allen & Unwin.
Gilsenan, M. (1982) *Recognizing Islam: an anthropologist's introduction*, London: Croom Helm.
——(1987) 'Sacred words', pp. 92–8, in A. al-Shahi (ed.) *The Diversity of the Muslim Community: anthropological essays in memory of Peter Lienhardt*, London: Ithaca Press.
Harvey, D. (1989) *The Condition of Postmodernity: an enquiry into the origins of cultural change*, Oxford: Basil Blackwell.

James, W. (1988) *The Listening Ebony: moral knowledge, religion and power among the Uduk of Sudan*, Oxford: Clarendon Press.
——(1994) 'Civil war and ethnic visibility: the Uduk of the Sudan-Ethiopia border', in K. Fukui and J. Markakis (eds), *Ethnicity and Conflict in the Horn of Africa*, (London/Athens, OH: James Currey/The Ohio University Press).
Lambek, M. (1990) 'Certain knowledge, contestable authority: power and practice on the Islamic periphery', *American Ethnologist*, 17 (1): 23–40.
Lewis, G. (1980) *Day of Shining Red: an essay on understanding ritual*, Cambridge: Cambridge University Press.
Lindisfarne (Tapper), N. (1991) *Bartered Brides: politics, gender and marriage in an Afghan tribal society*, Cambridge: Cambridge University Press.
Parry, J. (1985) '*The Gift*, the Indian Gift and the "Indian gift" ', *Man* 21: 453–73.
Rappaport, R.A. (1979) 'The obvious aspects of ritual', pp. 173–221, in *Ecology, Meaning and Religion*, Richmond, CA: North Atlantic Books.
Rorty, R. (1989) *Contingency, Irony and Solidarity*, Cambridge: Cambridge University Press.
Strathern, M. (1988) *The Gender of the Gift*, Berkeley, CA: University of California Press.
Webber, J. (1978) 'Aspects of language and society in Jerusalem', D.Phil. thesis, University of Oxford.
Werbner, R.P. (ed.) (1977) *Regional Cults*, ASA Monograph 16, London: Academic Press.
——(1989) *Ritual Passage, Sacred Journey: the process and organisation of religious movements*, Manchester/Washington: Manchester University Press/Smithsonian Press.
Zeitlyn, D. (1990) 'Professor Garfinkel visits the soothsayers: ethnomethodology and Mambila divination', *Man* 25: 654–66.

Part I

Displacement and the search for redefinition

'Western Civilization Starts Here.'
'Who are the Nubians?'

Signs welcoming Janice Boddy to the
ancient civilization hall of the Royal
Ontario Museum

1 Managing tradition

'Superstition' and the making of national identity among Sudanese women refugees

Janice Boddy

> What it all comes down to is that we are the sum of our efforts to change who we are. Identity is no museum piece sitting stock-still in a display case, but rather the endlessly astonishing synthesis of the contradictions of everyday life.
>
> (Eduardo Galeano,
> *The Book of Embraces*)

A simple hand-drawn flyer reads:

> **Sudanese Women Community Invite You to See Superstition and Traditional Dancing – Free *****

Mid-page, tendrils of smoke rise from a fire to embrace the disembodied head of a woman – eyes closed, restful; hair, uncovered, fanning out from her head as if shocked. Below the picture:

> **International Women's Day, March 8th at 8:00 pm, Location: Eritrea Restaurant 1278 Bloor St. West** [Toronto]

The flyers are displayed in downtown ethnic restaurants, in cornershop windows beside provincial lottery signs and the prices of milk, in specialist travel agencies that broker services for arrivals from North-East Africa. They are distributed among the women's friends and neighbours: Egyptians, Ethiopians, fellow Sudanese. Any and all, but especially Anglo-Canadians, are encouraged to come.

The evening is a success; the restaurant fills to overflowing. Yet those who attend see more than a demonstration of ethnicity: they witness a drama of political resistance, one that skilfully seeks to strengthen the resolve of disparate Sudani refugees and forge them into a unified 'we', a nation in absentia. And the community thus imagined (Anderson 1991; see Appadurai 1990: 5) consists of a partnership of women and men.

The women's performance that night and the overlapping contexts that engulf it – the homeland versus 'the West', various social interests in Toronto, the horror of Sudan's continuing north–south divide – expose a subtle interweaving of global and local concerns. Indeed, the events I detail and attempt to render intelligible raise questions about this analytical dichotomy, suggesting that, just as importations are interpreted and transformed within a local context, what is claimed to be universal is firmly rooted in specific sites and societies (see Amin 1989). Both the refugees and the Islamist government in Khartoum are using increasingly globalized culture-technologies – written history, ethnography, museums – as means of articulating their positions *vis-à-vis* each other and the world at large, yet in ways that make sense in decidedly localized terms. Toronto, of course, is one of these locales. It resists depiction as an essentialized, monolithic entity – 'the West', both ground and by-product of Orientalist discourse – for in its specificity it is at once more than this and less. The actions, statements, indeed *silences* of the refugees must be viewed in relation to their ambivalently multicultural host as well as to the hostile regime at home.

The events I discuss took place between 1991 and 1992. They condense to a singular moment an unremitting contest for certainty that is also a struggle over cultural probity; it is a dispute over knowledge, over power and social discipline, over the practices that are 'authentically' Sudanese. Enemies are identified, 'customs' endorsed or excluded; yet the lines that are drawn remain malleable, imprecise. For refugees, uncertain of their future abroad, there is and must be room for rapprochement. Caught in a web of opposed certainties suspended between two worlds, seeking a future that rejects the present but both valorizes and meliorates the past, they are forced to rethink themselves. So their argument is not without contradiction and ironies abound.

Because my own involvement in this episode was integral to its development, the following discussion parallels that process to some extent. Here 'at home', in the city where I teach, I realized more than ever how perforated are the barriers that separate the anthropologist's reality and her informants'; how each of us might simultaneously realize and rethink herself in the other's representations; how local and how global we all, perforce, must be.

ZAR

The ceremony staged by the women of the Sudanese refugee community in Toronto on 8 March 1992, in celebration of International Women's Day, was a *zar*, a spirit possession ritual. But it was a *zar* transformed in the context of refugee existence abroad.

Between 1976 and 1977 and again from 1983 to 1984, I studied the cult called *zar* as it was practised in a group of villages situated on the Nile some 200 km north of Khartoum. In Sudan, a *zar* is a healing rite; the term also applies to the condition that it addresses and to the spirits whose capricious appropriation of a human body (i.e. 'spirit possession') is deemed to have caused that illness. Both illness and cult are overwhelmingly the province of women. My findings were later published as *Wombs and Alien Spirits: Women, Men and the Zar Cult in Northern Sudan* (Boddy 1989); I summarize a few of its points below.

From an analytical perspective, a woman's dysphoria, precipitated by untoward or anomalous experience that has challenged the culturally constructed self, is converted into a conventional narrative of spirit ingress and appeasement in the process of undergoing a possession cure. Continuing participation in the cult – attending ceremonies, heeding her spirits' requests – supplies a thread of coherence to her life, persuasively affirming once problematic selfhood by providing direct and dramatic experience of what it is not. Spirits who become manifest during a *zar* are alien beings; though they parallel humanity in having ages, genders, religions and nationalities, they are both ontologically different from humans[1] and culturally foreign to northern Arabic-speaking Muslim Sudanese. Their antics and identities, performed during the patient's and fellow adepts' temporally limited bouts of ritual trance, caricature a range of human possibility other than that deemed normal, natural and moral for the women in whose bodies such behaviours appear. Thus the ritual has collective implications as well as individual ones: it is an elaborate dramatization of foreignness that catalyses group understandings, through which women mutually construct an image-in-relief of northern Sudanese identity and experience. At the same time *zar* implicitly domesticates the foreign, enabling its incorporation into the familiar and everyday.

Women's bodies are icons and repositories of community values and morality, conceived of in highly localized terms;[2] possession both challenges and expresses that embodied knowledge, providing those whom it claims with occasion to distance themselves from themselves, yet also to critique, for themselves and the community at large, domination and oppression by a range of historical and contemporary powers. Issues of power that reflect on daily life – the power of some humans over others, the power of religion, custom, gender – are raised during spirit performances but obliquely, via metaphors contained in particular spirit chants or the spirits' complex self-presentations. For instance, a married Sudanese woman may be seized by a male homosexual Arab *zar* who, now in control of her body, dons a man's long shirt, yet who in performance plays hilariously and unsuccessfully at being a married Sudanese woman dressed in a *towb*, the head-to-foot wrap-around veil that women wear in public. The *zar* provokes the taken-for-granted and assumed, throws open to question everyday practices like wearing the *towb*, or the customary social arrangements that privilege men, even men who act as women. In this way a subtle protest is lodged against the constraints that govern women's lives; in exposing these as mutable, however morally appropriate – in opening a space for uncertainty – such constraints are recontextualized, perhaps limited, though not of course undone. For to an extent this means that women are contesting themselves.

SUDANESE WOMEN AND THE PRESENT REGIME

Until 1991 there were only three Sudanese women living in greater Toronto (a city of some 4 million). But as the Islamist regime that had seized power in Sudan at the end of June 1989[3] enacted ever more coercive legislation, setting curfews, sartorial requirements and 'morality' rules, and limiting women's participation in public life, educational institutions and the like, that number grew to thirty. All sought political asylum. Such women hardly represent the majority of Muslim Sudanese; they are not impoverished, illiterate villagers but women of the urban bourgeoisie, some of the lucky few with resources enough to get out. Four are single women who by 1992 had made their way to Canada on their own.[4] All are educated to standards far beyond the norm for Sudanese women: all have high-school leaving certificates, half have university degrees or professional qualifications. Several are pious Muslims, others not overtly religious, a few are acknowledged secularists; yet all are culturally and emotionally northern Sudanese. Still, whatever their private convictions, these are women who, in the cities where most of them used to reside, would probably wince at the thought of being seen attending a *zar*, or would publicly disavow having done so except in jest. *Zar*, whether by Western or strict Islamic criteria, is to them 'superstition'.

I noted that until 1991 there were only three Sudanese women living in Toronto. But there were some 600 Sudanese men. They all knew one another, met regularly, periodically held musical evenings enabling them to socialize and activate their Sudani roots. Yet the community was decidedly skewed, so few were its womenfolk. Earlier I pointed out that women embody local values. Elsewhere (Boddy 1989), along with observers like Sondra Hale (1985), I have noted that in northern Sudan women are regarded as 'symbols of the homeland'; in the villages especially, they are the moral heart of their communities. It is they who keep the home-fires burning while men emigrate for work; it is they who are responsible for the ceremonies (surrounding weddings, births, circumcisions) and daily acts of hospitality and etiquette that punctuate and weave the social world. These are the *'adat* or customs of *dunya*, earthly life. Men's role is to provide the means to sustain such activity and oversee affairs linked to religious concerns (*din*) having properly to do with Islam – such as funerals, or the slaughter of a ram for the Great Feast. Although 1992's ten-fold boost to the refugee community's cohort of women has by no means redressed its lop-sidedness, their number has now, it seems, achieved a critical mass and their presence has become crucial to the

community's self-definition in the present context. Women are the homeland, and now they are here.

For they cannot be what they are in Sudan of the present day. The
present regime sees women's customary roles, duties, privileges, as
immoral, or religious 'innovation' and is attempting their reform. In
Sudan, for example, women are officially and forcefully discouraged from
wearing the *towb*, typically made of a cool, light fabric and worn atop a
dress, as this is considered too revealing of the hair, forearms and neck
(Gruenbaum 1992: 29).[5] Nor may younger (school-aged) women wear the
tarha, or head scarf. Anthropologist Ellen Gruenbaum, who revisited
Sudan in May 1992, describes the case of a woman who, the previous
October,

> was arrested on the street and taken to a 'public order' court for
> violating the unwritten dress code. Although she was dressed in a
> modestly long skirt, loose mid-length sleeved shirt and the light scarf
> which many women allow to fall to the shoulders, she was found guilty
> of creating public disorder and sentenced to receive lashes and a fine.
> The woman had no way to defend herself since she had violated no
> specific statute. Her father paid the fine and successfully begged the
> judge to suspend the lashing.
>
> (1992: 30)

One month later the head of the Revolutionary Command Council and
Prime Minister of the country, General Omar Al-Bashir, ostensibly
answering public criticism that the behaviour and appearance of Muslim
women had so far failed to conform to Shari'a law, declared that 'all
women in offices, public places, streets, educational institutions, etc., should
wear long loose garments and cover their heads. This Islamic style of dress
is known as "Hijab" and is defined in the Quran' (*Sudanow* 1991b: 6).
To offset the cost to women of acquiring these new clothes, the government undertook to provide them with loans from the 'Shari'a Support
Fund', repayable through payroll deductions (*ibid.*; Gruenbaum 1992: 30).
If by 1 July 1992 they had not complied with 'Islamic dress' codes, women
employees and students risked being fired or expelled from school and
arrested. Pressures to withdraw from participation in the public domain
and adopt properly 'Islamic' gender roles are tangible. In 1992, visiting
Iranian President Rafsanjani, as a gesture of Iran's financial and ideological solidarity with the Sudanese regime, provided 1,000 *chadors* (facial
veils) to be distributed among Sudanese women.

In 1991, in an effort to curb the exorbitant cost of customary marriage
rites,[6] the government began to sponsor group weddings. The project
aimed 'to combat undesirable traditions' as well as 'to create stability
among young people and follow the example of the Prophet Mohammed,
who condemned bachelorhood' (Abdelrahman 1991b: 24). What was
formerly a family matter, involving extended networks of kin, has now

become an affair of the state; thus has a crucial basis of women's power, their mastery of kinship rituals, been eroded.

Beliefs and practices long associated with vernacular Islam are now decried as unacceptable by the National Islamic Front-backed 'Salvation Revolution Government' and regarded as sad evidence of the need to improve educational standards. (This is despite the fact that professionals of all sorts are labelled Western, hence subversive, and are encouraged to leave the country.)[7] Illiterate women's lack of religious awareness is seen to impel them, for example, to visit the graves of holy men in order to alleviate illness, and to engage in practices of the *zar* . Although *zar* has always been a matter of dispute between those who regard themselves as pious and those they consider unschooled – and so, in large part, between women and men – until recently it was tolerated, if reluctantly, by the Sudanese religious establishment. Spirits were too much a part of everyday life – their existence indisputable, banal, based on patently Islamic precepts[8] – for clerics and laymen to oppose the cult successfully.

Between 1983, when Islamic law was enacted in the dying days of Nimeiri's regime, and the 1989 coup d'état that inaugurated rule by the National Islamic Front, *zar* underwent a process of folklorization in Sudan's urban zones. Its subtle transformation from religiously informed cult to less threatening theatrical club is instructive. Hurreiz (1991: 152–4) documents how in 1987 a leading *zar shaikh* (male curer) was instrumental in founding the Association of Zar and Folklore Shaikhs, an officially registered society representing dozens of town cult groups. Once formed, the Association sought affiliation with the National Council for Arts and Letters. This, Hurreiz notes, was granted 'in accordance with article (b) of the council's constitution of 1976: "The promotion of theatrical activities, music and folk arts" ' (*ibid*.: 153). Both the *zar* practitioners in question, two-thirds of whom were male,[9] and the authorities at the National Council clearly considered the associated cult groups to be an artistic dramatic society (*ibid*.).[10] Although patients still behave as patients seeking treatment through the *zar*, the Association's founders

> are evidently . . . seeking respectability in the modern idiom of drama and psychodrama and a leading role in their public relations amongst the intelligentsia is played by an influential committee member who is a prominent Sudanese actress and graduate of the Institute of Music and Drama.
>
> (*ibid*.: 154)

Not only was the *zar* being routinized as official theatre, it was also being removed from the religious domain, its healing practices rationalized, perhaps trivialized, and dissociated from Islam. Yet in seeming to question *zar*'s reality by making it 'for show', the shift effectively disguised the fact that *zar* continues to be an essential religious force in countless women's lives. Moreover, the upshot of such Procrustean constraints was public acknowledgement that *zar* is an authentic part of northern Sudanese 'culture'.

Ironically, the process of 'folklorizing' a cult based on resolutely local understandings of society and human existence was an attempt to mould it to the dimensions and categories by which 'cultures' are contained in the West;[11] forms of culture, as Hannerz (1992) and others have shown, are becoming increasingly globalized even if their contents are not. Despite the move and arrogation of the cult by males that it implies – but more likely in part because of these – *zar* has been banned as unIslamic by the masculinist theocracy in Khartoum. Its public and highly theatrical trance rituals are no longer suffered to take place. Like other such practices, it is now wholly linked with pagan custom. Interestingly, however and with rhetorical sleight of hand, it and other such customs are also being portrayed in the media as inauthentic, non-indigenous; as *recent* acquisitions. A report on the Comprehensive National Strategy Conference held in Khartoum in October 1991, states that the goals of the Islamic government 'include the revival of indigenous Sudanese values and identity, the ensuring of freedoms and liberties and improving the standard of living so that inherited values can be safeguarded'. It continues, with regard to policy orientations:

> the most important of these is that the Sudanese people are one united people and religion constitutes an essential factor in the formation of their culture. The Sudanese people are now striving to achieve the renaissance of their civilization on the basis of their past, present and vision of the future.
>
> (*Sudanow* 1991c: 7)

The regime's invocation of history leads directly to consideration of some instructive peculiarities surrounding my own involvement in the Toronto *zar* event.

HISTORY AND IDENTITY

In 1990 the Royal Ontario Museum (affiliated with the University of Toronto and popularly known as the ROM) staged a sophisticated exhibition entitled 'Into the Heart of Africa', curated by anthropologist Jeanne Cannizzo. Through ironic juxtaposition of texts, photographs and artefacts, Cannizzo sought to expose both the complicity of Canadian missionaries and military personnel in Africa's colonization and the ROM's collusion in this process by collecting through these expatriates African exotica for display. The exhibition was designed to shake up a complacent Caucasian public; it had a rather different and unintended effect. Although Africans and African-Canadians had been part of the consultative process, when the exhibition opened its message fell mainly on deaf ears, its provocative ironies lost in literalist confusion. Members of Toronto's large

Afro-Caribbean community, for whom Africa remains the potent symbol of a golden past, were outraged: Cannizzo was accused of being racist and the ROM came under media fire for glorifying the subjugation of African peoples.

In 1991 the museum was about to open its long-anticipated Nubian and Egyptian galleries and, wishing to allay the mistrust of a highly politicized Afro-Canadian community, curators repeatedly vetted the exhibits with its so-called 'Nubian' contingent. The galleries opened in mid-February 1992 to considerable praise; the Toronto 'Nubians' joined the inaugural ceremonies by staging a 'Nubian' wedding in the museum's central hall, for the public to see. A couple of weeks later the ROM held a reception to thank the 'Nubians' for their help. I was invited to attend.

Now, until that point the penny had not dropped: I had not realized that those whom museum officials referred to as 'Nubian' were in fact northern Arabic-speaking Sudanese. Once this was clear, I was intrigued to find Sudanese themselves acquiescing in the description, in advertising further staged weddings and musical evenings as Nubian events. 'Nubian' is a polysemous term; it has a tangled etymology and a complicated history, some of which I describe below. Popularly, however, the term refers to past farming peoples who lived in villages along the Nile from its confluence in Sudan to Aswan in southern Egypt. In the early 1960s their descendants in the area between Aswan and Wadi Halfa, a town in far northern Sudan, were forced to relocate when Lake Nasser began to flood following construction of the Aswan High Dam. Despite the fact that Nubians straddle the international border, the identity has little currency in Sudan today. Such was not the case in the past.

During the medieval period (the sixth to thirteenth centuries AD) Nubia consisted of three and later two kingdoms in which Christianity[12] was the state religion and, south from Wadi Halfa, matrilineality with matrilocal residence were principles of social organization.[13] After Egypt fell under Muslim control in AD 639, Arab nomads and traders began entering the area: slowly at first, then achieving considerable momentum in the fourteenth century as the Nubian polities fell apart. When, in AD 1317, the King's throne room at Dongola was rededicated as a mosque, the event was marked by inscribing the appropriate Islamic date (16 *Rabi'a* I, 717 AH) on a stone in the building's wall.[14] Within a few hundred years Islam was well established and people had adopted Arab pedigrees, most tracing their descent patrilineally from the Prophet's paternal uncle, Abbas. That development, plus the widespread adoption of Arabic, has prompted historians and anthropologists to regard the contemporary inhabitants of the Upper Nile as *Arabized* Nubians (Hasan 1967, Adams 1984).

In archaeological parlance, Nubia is a place: the main Nile valley south from Aswan; and the region's historical Christian civilizations, along with those of Egyptian dynastic influence whose earliest remains predate the medieval period by more than 2,000 years, are considered Nubian.[15] This

accords with ancient sources that refer to people living south of the first
Nile cataract as Nubae and, starting in late Roman times, as Nobatae
and/or Noba (see Adams 1984: 323–4, 386–7, 419–21). Close kinship
between contemporary Nubian[16] and some of the languages of the Nuba
Hills in Kordofan suggests their common origins and either broad distribution or the shattering of a more concentrated population in the past.[17]
According to Hasan (1967: 8), in Sudanese traditions the word 'al-Nuba'
alludes to previous inhabitants of the southernmost Nubian kingdom,
'Alwa, whom the Funj, a federation of emigrant Arabs and African
converts to Islam that dates from the sixteenth century, came to dominate. Given its breadth and plasticity, the word 'Nubian' has at one time
or another encompassed the range of indigenous peoples in north and
central Sudan.

   To contemporary Sudanese, however, the term is more specific, denoting
those who speak a Nubian dialect or identify with the people of the
Dongola Reach where Nubian is still, if decreasingly, spoken. Yet al-Shahi
(1988: 35) points out that even these Nubians 'have discarded their origin
and . . . now claim Arab ancestry'.

   In their introduction to *Vernacular Christianity* Wendy James and
Douglas Johnson (1988: 7) write:

> The culture of medieval Nubia persists on many levels . . . but the polit-
> ical associations of Christianity rule out for modern Sudanese of the
> central Nile valley any overt recognition of this religion as a historical
> antecedent and cultural source. . . . [For them] Islam is . . . a part of
> their national and personal identity. They might well feel that since
> they are Muslims, the ancient Nubians, who were Christian, cannot have
> been the 'same people' as themselves.[18]

My own findings extend the validity of this distinction: the pyramids and
ruined temples of the ancient Kushitic city of Meröe (*ca.* 700 BC–AD 350),
adjacent to the village where I lived, were attributed by locals to the work
of another, earlier race (*jinis*). Indeed, the government's keeper of this
site was decidedly proud of his slim, patrician nose, narrow lips and light
frame, taken to be visible signs of Arab ancestry. As Adams suggests, in
shifting to Islam, Nubians 'have embraced not only a new destiny but a
new history' (1984: 563). And, one might add, a new 'race'.

   Why then has their ascribed Nubian identity not been rejected as false
by northern Sudanese refugees in Toronto? The answer, I think, is complex
and has as much to do with the refugees' lives in Canada as with the
Islamic regime's efforts to forge a new nationalism through its management of history. First the urban Canadian context. Significantly, the identity is patently African, as opposed to Arab or Middle Eastern. In both
Canada and Sudan race is read as an important determinant of social and
political allegiance. In Sudan, where cultural affinity and religion override
skin-colour as the primary criteria of race, most Muslims, however dark,

claim to be Arabs rather than 'Africans' or 'Blacks' (*az-zurug*) – a term
they reserve for people of the south. But in predominantly white Toronto,
northern Sudanese are inescapably Black. Claiming 'African' identity
valorizes their difference from the majority, while conveniently allying
them with a Afro-Canadian community ever watchful of social institutions
that, despite avowed reform, are often systemically racist nonetheless.
For Africans of the earlier diaspora, who compose the majority of Afro-
Canadians in the city, Nubia represents indigenous African civilization,
an exalted past that predates European hegemony. By being Nubians,
northern Sudanese are Africans *par excellence*.

Today it is probably easier to be African in Toronto than Arab, with
the imagery of terrorism, censorship (given the *fatwa* issued against
Salman Rushdie for his *Satanic Verses*) and intolerance which the latter
identity popularly evokes. I was told that the 1991 Gulf War saw a dramatic
rise in hostility directed against people of Middle Eastern origin; Sudanese
Muslims found themselves targeted since the Islamic regime (which the
refugees, ironically, had fled) had chosen to support Iraq.

Nubians are not widely associated with Islam in the popular Canadian
imagination; to the extent that anything is known of them, they tend to
be linked with Christianity or ancient Egypt. Television documentary
series like Basil Davidson's and Ali Mazrui's have affirmed this; one
programme described Nubians as legendary 'Black Christians' who fought
alongside their white brethren against Muslims during the Crusades. Since
ancient Nubia was matrilineal and had queens and queen mothers as well
as kings, Nubians seem the inverse counterparts of patriarchal Muslims
where women's status is concerned. Orientalist essentialism, however
much critiqued in academe, is alive and well elsewhere; thus, by being
Nubian in Toronto one is less hindered in being one's Muslim, even 'Arab'
self. And given the displacement of ethnic Nubians upon completion of
the Aswan High Dam, the identity has romantic overtones: Nubians are
the innocent uprooted victims of development and modern technology. In
short, Nubianness provides northern Sudanese with a positive African
biography and distances them from their currently problematic homeland,
from ubiquitous reports of famine, civil war and the 'Arab' abuse of human
rights.[19]

Such labile use of the term 'Nubian' is hardly without precedent, for
migrant Arab Sudanese in the latter part of the nineteenth century are
known to have invoked it as an inclusive identity to describe themselves
relative to other ethnic groups (and, perhaps, to an earlier hostile regime).
The explorer Schweinfurth observed, for example, that young Ja'ali men
from villages between Berber and Khartoum who, driven off the land by
heavy taxation, had gone south and joined the private armies of slave and
ivory traders, referred to themselves as Nubians. The retainers included
Shayqiyya and Danaqla from the Central Nile as well as Ja'aliyyin; they
lived in fortified stations and took enslaved women as concubines and

their descendants formed settled 'Nubian' communities in the south. Sudanese soldiers recruited from the periphery into the Turco-Egyptian forces were also often known as 'Nubian' or 'Nubi' and played a part in the colonial conquest of East Africa. There are communities today in Uganda and even Kenya known as 'Nubian' or 'Nubi', of mixed provenance but predominantly Muslim with a tradition of historical links to the Sudan through trading or military networks (Schweinfurth 1969 vol. 1: 50, 239, vol. 2: 420–2; Holt and Daly 1979: 70–1; Johnson 1988, 1989, 1992).

For its part, the Nubian identity of Toronto refugees implicitly contains an oppositional stance to the present Islamic regime, one that makes sense in light of both Canadian preoccupations and those of the regime itself. These have to do with managing and organizing history, finding meaning in the past. Islamic fundamentalists have made astute political use of collapsing global certainties and broad dissatisfaction with the legacy of colonialism to provoke a struggle over Sudan's authentic identity and culture (Gruenbaum 1992: 30). That struggle, we have seen, is concerned with purging Islam of 'inauthentic' popular traditions and enforcing 'suitable' roles and behaviours for women but also with rewriting Sudanese history, 'which was falsified by western historians and scholars' (Abdelrahman 1991a: 14). In addition to 'getting written history right' (*Sudanow* 1991a: 4) – restoring the glory of the Mahdiyya [1881–98], the 'first modern state in Sudan' (*ibid.*) – archaeological excavation and museum display are increasingly pressured to emphasize the Islamic past over earlier epochs.

In Sudan today the British are overtly vilified as enemies, invaders, as never before. The battleground at Um Dibekrat,[20] where the Mahdi's political successor, Khalifa Abdullahi, and his cadre fell to Wingate's forces in 1899, has now become a national monument, restored as 'a symbol of heroism and patriotism that celebrates dedicated nationalism' (*ibid.*); despite mistrust of popular belief, it is also portrayed as a site of miraculous healing (Abdelrahman 1991a: 19) and the Mahdists who died there are spoken of as martyrs for Islam (*Sudanow* 1991a: 4).

Indeed, in the Sudanese media there is a concerted attempt to link the government with the Mahdiyya in the minds of Sudanese, thence to map the 'Salvation Revolution' onto the early Islamic state. The Mahdiyya, in other words, provides the pivotal link between the regime and the most sacred past. The Mahdi saw himself as an avatar, recapitulating the Prophet's role, and patterned his movement on early Islamic history; his principal followers were known as *Ansar*, 'helpers', the term applied to Companions of the Prophet at Medina; his lieutenants were designated as successors to *Ar-Rashidun*, the rightly guided caliphs who successively ruled the young Islamic state after the Prophet's death (Holt and Daly 1979: 87–96). Actions of the Sudanese President Omar al-Bashir are likened to those of the Mahdi and, by implication, those of the Prophet himself. Witness the following report of an interview with the grandson of a noted Ansari:

> Talking about the similarities between the Mahdiyya and the Salvation Revolution, Mr. Bashir al-Hilu said that the Mahdi had dissolved the four religious sects and the Sufi tariqas and returned to the pure sources of Islam Quran and Sunna. The NSR [National Salvation Revolution] has banned all political parties and worked for the unity of the country. The Mahdi freed the country from all political and economic pressures. Al-Bashir has done the same thing, declaring an Islamic state and raised [*sic*] the slogan 'live within your own means'. 'Thus I can say that the salvation revolution is the twin of the Mahdiyya,' he said.
>
> (Abdelrahman 1991a: 18)[21]

It is in terms of the Islamic regime's appeal to sacred history[22] – with its timeless, transcendent quality – by which meaningful pasts are collapsed into the present, that the refugees' adoption of Nubian identity can be taken as political resistance. This becomes clearer when one considers the relationships of each to their respective museums. As Benedict Anderson (1991: 178) rightly observes, 'museums and the museumizing imagination, are both profoundly political'.

The National Museum in Khartoum, noted primarily for its displays of Kushitic statuary, sarcophagi, jewellery and reconstructed temple walls, and an unparalleled collection of church frescoes from the Christian period, was closed for some time after the military-theocracy's coup and has been criticized repeatedly for not exhibiting more artefacts from the Islamic era. The Christian exhibits are especially controversial and subject to closure more often than the rest. Since 1991, the numbers of professional staff in the Sudan Antiquities Service and the Department of Archaeology at the University of Khartoum – whose institutional memory betrays a focus on the pre-Islamic past – have been reduced by over half. A recent (1992) museum display captures the prevailing mood: this was the dedication date-stone from the Nubian throne hall-cum-mosque, which was cut from its matrix in the Dongola palace and brought to the local Islamic centre, Khartoum. It was for a time lodged in the museum's foyer,[23] there foregrounding Islam, indicating the moment that significant time began in Sudan, framing and imaginatively colonizing the 'earlier peoples' whose remains are presented within.[24] Just as non-Islamic nations of the state's rejected past are demonstrably contained, so contemporary non-Muslim Sudanese are expected to adopt the monolithic ideal, to relinquish their 'infidel traditions' in favour of religious 'truth' and sacred history.

Unlike its counterpart in Khartoum, the Royal Ontario Museum's mandate is international: it gathers the world into itself with displays from past and present around the globe. Some of these it defines as 'other', some it defines as 'us'. A sign placed at the entrance to the ancient civilizations hall – containing Mesopotamian, Persian, Greek and Etruscan as well as Nubian and Egyptian exhibits – reads: 'Western Civilization Starts Here'. Contrast with the Sudanese case is clear.

The ROM exhibits themselves are clever spatial evocations of Nile architecture and aesthetics that chronicle the region's human past. The two galleries are seamlessly linked, which, however objectionable to Sudani Islamists,[25] does not affront Occidental sensibilities given the Nile's much interwoven past. On leaving Egypt at Philae (a model) one moves in a coil through Nubian time, from sites of ancient hunters and cultivators, through the remains of dynastic (Egyptianized) Kush, Christian kingdoms and the Funj federation of the early Islamic era. The historically sequenced displays stop in 1821 with Mohammed Ali's invasion of Sudan. No window is devoted to the Ottoman, Mahdist, or colonial periods. Yet interestingly, the historical path rounds back on itself: in the centre of the hall but at the end of the visitor's temporal journey, is a case filled with contemporary Nubian 'folk' artefacts, quotidian household objects from northern Sudan including a *tubug* (flat basketry food cover) in traditional colours of orange, magenta and blue; a clay coffee pot; and a finely crafted *tambour*, a native lyre. Time jumps from 1821 to now, a now that is selective, continuous with 'the past'. One must then cross the room, exiting the historical display, to view three cases exhibiting items of mixed periods from several domains of life; these have a 'developmental' cast, showing both external influences and the continuity of local artistic and technological traditions. But whether sequential or continuous, time throughout is linear: contemporary northern Sudanese have *origins* in antiquity and are legatees of a distinguished pre-Islamic past.

'Who are the Nubians?' reads the signboard beginning the exhibit. It answers, 'Nubia has been inhabited since ancient times by different African peoples, all with strongly local and independent traditions.' Nubians, says the museum, are Africans first; Islam is inessential to their ontology. Muslim Sudanese in Toronto, by acknowledging their Nubianness, subvert the Islamic regime's vision of history and its claim to exclusive truth.

Still, Toronto Nubians are Nubian by virtue of those criteria for organizing people, space and time prevalent in Occidental societies, criteria that constitute them as 'a culture' with diverse antecedents and temporal depth rather than 'a nation' with an omnipresent past. Unlike fundamentalist Sudan, the existence of other cultures within its bounds is crucial to Canada's self-image as a nation. Richard Handler (1988: 6ff.) has suggested that the essence of contemporary nationalism is 'possessive individualism': a nation, like a person, realizes its existence through its possessions and proprietary acts. The refugees are caught between clashing images of nation whose proprietary vectors diverge. Islamic Sudan 'has' a sacred history, contains and denies its connection to the non-sacred past, seeks vehemently to eliminate any 'otherness' in its present. The vector of its ownership is exclusionary, desirous of homogeneity. Canada, however, is a young, secular nation deeply threatened by its powerful neighbour to the south, bereft of even the touchstone of certainty that a civilly sacred past provides. It is a nation-in-becoming, enduringly divided, constitutionally crisis prone,[26] yet perennially anxious to defend its own fledgling 'culture' against incursions from a populous and overly confident USA. And so it realizes its nationhood, imagines itself a community, by tentatively building on its plurality: by 'having' natives, minorities, immigrants, refugees and, through a policy of official multiculturalism, encouraging the self-expression of these 'other', more established cultures in museums and folkloric display. Here conformity is induced through selectively valorized difference. Sudanese in Toronto are under considerable pressure within this context to define an authentic culture for themselves relative to fellow minorities and the national whole, to 'be different' in ways that make local (global?) sense. At the same time they are refugees and, if only to legitimate that fragile status, must cultivate a resistant stance to the source of oppression at home. So they accentuate here what is there denounced. Hence the intricate logic of Nubian weddings – kinship rites that are not specifically Islamic – held in the museum, the public, locally politicized institution that is both formally and substantively global, whose glass-encased evidential knowledge grounds northern Sudanese oppositional identity. Of course, the ROM was undyingly grateful to the 'Nubians' for authenticating its exhibition. Each authorizes and so sustains the other.

ENTER THE ANTHROPOLOGIST

At the ROM's Nubian reception (which interestingly, in deference to Islamic sensibilities, was 'dry') I met several Sudanese women, including one of the longer established members, Nyla, whose parents and husband hailed from a village near to where I had conducted fieldwork. When I told her what I had been doing in Sudan, Nyla revealed that the women planned to hold a *zar* and asked if I would be interested in coming along. We exchanged phone numbers.

A few days later I found myself in a modest Toronto apartment surrounded by a couple of dozen 'Nubian' women and their younger children. On the telephone I had been asked if I had written anything on *zar* – the women, having heard of a book called *Wombs and Alien Spirits*,[27] had found it in the library: until then they had not realized I was its author. I was requested to bring a copy of my book as well as my costume for Luliya Habishiya, the Ethiopian prostitute spirit who tries to pass herself off as a Sudanese bride. This *zar* party was to be a display, held in public in honour of International Women's Day; would I be willing to stand up before the expected audience of non-Sudanese and explain in English what was happening on stage? Now in Nyla's flat we were doing a dress rehearsal: Sudanese women on the floor, circling the drums, 'descending' to the spirits' 'threads' (their chants); anthropologist seated on the sofa, book open on her lap, dispensing advice on the order of the spirits' appearance, refreshing the women's memories of spirits' names, personalities, demands. Once the ice was broken the women's memories revived and chants of spirits I'd never before known were being drummed.

The women had circulated a flyer inviting Torontonians 'to see super-stition and traditional dancing'. So I wondered how publicly to present the *zar* as they would want it presented. Their answers were revealing. Sadiya, a qualified physician, sympathized with my plight; then said, 'You know, I don't think there are many women here who really believe in the spirits but *zar* is a part of our culture.' Howa, a psychology graduate from Ahfad University, told me she thought *zar* illnesses were psychosomatic, linked to the repression women experience in their daily lives; she used innumerable psychoanalytic terms to expand on this: reactive syndrome, compensation mechanism and more. Nyla said she thought women used *zar* to get the things they wanted from men and gave an exegesis of the status deprivation hypothesis – to my professional chagrin. But everyone wanted to know my interpretation of the *zar* . . . did I think it was some-thing good or bad; did I think it *primitive*? I replied that I thought it was good, that in *zar* Sudanese women had something that women in my own society lacked. The room heaved a collective sigh of relief. Someone ventured that *zar* was a source of power for women, it was 'empowering' she said, in English; someone else, that women 'feel strong' during cere-monies, where in everyday life they do not. *Zar* is a positive thing, they agreed, because when a *zar* strikes, as Howa put it, 'men can say nothing'.

Following the *zar* rehearsal, sustained at a level of noise and revelry uncharacteristic of staid Toronto, we drank *abray* (spiced *dura* bread mixed with sugar and water) and ate an elaborate breakfast to which all the women had contributed: the sun had now set, it was Ramadan and most had undertaken the fast. Sudanese men began to arrive with more children in tow. As they would be providing music for the event, they too were meeting to practise.

Nyla said the women had also decided to demonstrate portions of a wedding. Would I announce these too? The wedding they enacted next resembled those I had attended in Sudan but inexactly; it was a 'mixed' ritual, the women explained, a synthesis of local traditions that has become the prevailing wedding form in Khartoum and Omdurman. I was given to understand that on performance night the *zar* would come first, followed by the wedding. I took my notes home and prepared my 'speech'.

On 8 March I arrived at the Eritrea Restaurant at 8pm to find the place deserted. A makeshift plywood stage had been erected on one side of the restaurant, a microphone system hooked up and lace curtains hung in front to frame the show, to mark the space off from 'real life'. I found two of the women downstairs, getting ready. We sat at a table chatting as people began to arrive, gradually, Sudani style. By 9.45 most of the women were there and we were ready to start. The audience was almost exclusively made up of Sudanese men, mainly from the north; there were few Egyptians and Eritreans, even fewer *khawajas* (Westerners). The schedule of events had been refined: Zaineb, designated MC, would first welcome people, then introduce the (all female) cast and, given that this was International Women's Day, enumerate their achievements and qualifications. Next, pre-empting the roster, would come the wedding – 'because it makes sense to do it that way'.

The Nubian wedding was executed with the requisite singing and drumming, all parts played by women, those performing male roles wearing turbans and men's clothes. The sequence ended with the bridal dance where a multicoloured wedding veil (*garmosis*) is placed over the bride's head, the 'groom' removes it and the bride begins her dance of restraint, eyes closed, clasped hands covering her face. Several men in the audience who were taken up by the performance came down to the stage to congratulate the groom and ask the bride for *shabal* – a flick of the hair movement said to confer luck. The wedding ended with the groom leading the bride off stage, singers and 'family' participants following downstairs to change.

Next Zaineb introduced 'Dr Ida', an Egyptian woman who is former Dean of Women at Victoria College, University of Toronto and currently President of the Toronto Arab Centre. Dr Ida gave a dignitary's address to the (largely male) audience in English and Egyptian Arabic concerning Canadians' false assumptions about Arab women. Canadians, she said, do not sufficiently recognize the struggles of Middle Eastern women in their homelands and the hurdles that they have overcome. Canada also oppresses women. In Egypt, despite an 80 per cent female illiteracy rate, women comprise 22.4 per cent of university faculty members. In Canada, the comparable figure is only 18 per cent. Here Middle Eastern women not only have to struggle against sexism, they also, as was evident during the Gulf War, confront racism and Orientalism. So we must celebrate International Women's Day, she concluded, and it is good to celebrate it with some of our Canadian sisters.

By now the restaurant was crowded; all chairs were occupied; be-ribbonned children pressed against the stage. Waiters squeezed through the standing throng bearing trays of soft drinks, 'Turkish' coffee, beer. Fragrance rose from painted clay censers, one stationed (idiomatically) at the restaurant door, the other next to a loudspeaker. Two video-cameras and two racks of bright lights swept the audience, coming to rest on the stage.

Zaineb, in stiletto heels, hair elegantly coiffed beneath a delicate Saudi *towb*, then introduced me as Dr Janice, an anthropology professor who would explain in English about this next display of Sudanese women's customs, the *zar*. I had been duly wrapped in my ('authentically Sudanese') iridescent Shendi *towb* and stationed before the mike. Moments into my account, women began to assemble behind me to drum; I nervously skipped to a sequenced recital of the spirits who were likely to appear. But, I warned, since this was a *zar*, anything could happen. The audience laughed, I left the stage, the drumming began.

The *zar* display opened with the 'patient' greeting the *shaikha* (female curer) and her assistants, followed by laudatory salutations to the Prophet. Next the patient was censed. Then the spirits' chants were drummed society by society, one by one, inviting each to descend in turn. Although *zar* rites in Muslim Sudan regularly invoke first the Darawish *zayran* – the Islamic holy men spirits and their daughters – this spirit society was conspicuously absent from the evening's schedule. Seven[28] chants in all were played, starting with Bashir Dagolak, a Hadendowi nomad *zar* from eastern Sudan, played by Nyla, who demanded cigarettes. Then came Sultan al Habish – the Sultan of Ethiopia – who in one woman, swaggered and strutted and waved his scarf above his head, and in another demanded a ticket in Ontario's Lotto 649, hinting at the present impecuniousness of Ethiopian royals. He was followed by Basha Bey, an Ottoman official who strikes his forearms on the ground. Another chant and the European doctor Hakim Basha appeared, demanding a white lab coat and stethoscope. These provided, 'he' asked for cigarettes and whisky. One hand waving a lit cigarette and cocktail glass, the other planted firmly on his hip, he danced an authoritative, rhythmic march and in deep-voiced English announced, 'Hakim Basha is *very* happy!' Then came a chant welcoming all the *khawaja* or Westerner spirits. This was followed by Nimr al Kindo, a spirit who normally wears a leopard skin over his shoulders, herds cattle and comes from southern Sudan; he is a Nuer, supposed to be somewhat wild, and the woman in whom he appeared made flailing gestures, with open mouth and popping eyes.

Last yet not least came the prostitute Luliya Habishiya (Luliya the Abyssinian), played by Amani, the erstwhile groom. Luliya appeared out of sequence in some ways,[29] but was the high point of the display. She began with a *garmosis* covering her head and feigned performance of the wedding dance earlier enacted in good, or better, faith. She then threw off the *garmosis* and, facing the audience, made animated blowing sounds, loud, indignant. Outstretched arms signalling annoyance, she whined (in Arabic), 'Clothes? Gold? No ring?' and motioned to appropriate parts of her body. The audience collapsed with laughter. Someone offered a cigarette and gold bangles, whereupon she cried, 'No beer?' She was handed an empty glass and told it contained whisky. Her eyes bulged, she grinned and danced with the glass on her head. Following Luliya's antics the spirits were dismissed with the *ma'asalama* (good-bye) chant and the women departed the stage.

But the night's entertainment was not over. Moments later the performers were back with me in tow, to perform traditional women's dances from various parts of Sudan, including the non-Muslim south. Lastly,

Sadiya, a medical doctor currently upgrading her skills by taking courses at the University of Toronto, approached the microphone accompanied by a teenaged girl, half-Sudani, wearing three-quarter-length jeans. Sadiya, dressed in a professional's sheer white *towb*, introduced the girl in English as the daughter of Ustaza Atahiya, a famous Sudanese actress and pioneer in women's broadcasting who has acted in numerous films and plays rendered from works of Sudanese literature, including *The Wedding of Zein* and *He and She*. Ustaza Atahiya has spoken out against the repression of women currently taking place under 'this fascist dictatorship with its imported Iranian Shari'a'. The actress had recently fled the regime and come to Toronto but was ill and could not be present tonight. We honour her, said Sadiya, as a model for all Sudanese women; she is a constant defender of women's rights when women in Sudan are being publicly beaten for 'crimes against Islam', are no longer able to attend the university, are imprisoned and oppressed. Next she presented Ustaza Atahiya's daughter with a cloth which, though folded, looked like a homemade Sudanese flag, and called on the regime to respect women's and minorities' internationally recognized human rights. Importantly, their role-model was described as *Zurug*, a woman from the south. With this the evening drew to a close.

MANAGING TRADITION

> The image, the imaged, the imaginary
> – these are all terms which direct us
> to something critical and new in
> global cultural processes: *the imagina-*
> *tion as a social practice.*
> (Appadurai 1990: 5; original
> emphasis)

> We are the children of Mama, born of the wind,
> As we advance by kind, O Lord, our felicitations!
> They have spread our display, they have lined up our chairs.
> Those who mock us alter consciousness in our midst.
> (An opening chant of a *zar* ceremony)

In the light of earlier points concerning the group's strategic adoption of Nubian identity, let me attempt a few suggestions as to what the evening just described was all about. Though the show was supposed to be fun, it put humour to serious use, to enlighten, affirm and legitimate the community politically. It was a display of 'tradition', of vernacular knowledge now outlawed by the regime, of northern Sudanese women's knowledge and power. It was a performance of women's own 'sacred history': the officially denigrated rituals of a profoundly threatened way of life. But more than this, it sought to create a new and broader national consciousness, one that, in contrast to the regime's, is multicultural, humanistic, neither fundamentally nor monolithically Islamic. By provoking laughter among those 'in the know', the women's antics in the wedding and the *zar* stirred group understandings even as they sought to transform them.

First, it is significant, I think, that the wedding was presented prior to the *zar*, which forms its imaginative counterpoint in northern Sudan.[30] The wedding, whose central figure is the meticulously prepared and self-contained bride, expresses axiomatic values – of purity, restraint, physical integrity, fertility, mutual interdependence – values that define both gender and what it means to be Muslim Arabic-speaking Sudanese. *Zar*, for its part, plays with such values, parodies and ritually defies them through the very bodies that, in daily life, embody them. Yet those who are vehicles of this satire are foreigners and spirits, not members of the community lampooned. To Nile valley 'Arabs' who are the country's privileged social group, *zayran* are alien, members of other (spirit) societies both within Sudan's borders and beyond. The reality of such aliens is thus in a sense 'ethnic'; that of the possessed, projected in relief during spirit performance, is normal, natural, hegemonic.

But in the refugee situation all of this is changed, reconceptualized. In the present historical moment of unstable and emergent identities, *zar* and the Nubian wedding *together* symbolize what is newly realized as ethnic in relation to an encompassing urban order. Where before the two ceremonies countered each other, now they jointly counter both the Canadian context, as expressions of Nubian ethnicity, and the current regime, as political defiance.

Through local women's bodies, *zar* in Sudan communicates resistance to social convention and masculine authority but also to foreign oppression and alien threat. Despite avowed disbelief, it is entirely apt that the refugee community's moral custodians – its women – should reassert their proper role and mobilize the stifled cult to oppose an unjust and severe regime that is at once conceived of as male (but does not embrace all Sudani men) and cast as foreign, alien, non-Sudanese. The women's decision to omit the category of Islamic 'holy men' from the familiar roster of spirits, despite the anthropologist's advice, is signal and, I think, instructive. Exploring this elision entails some consideration of the logic of the *zar*.

Zayran are said to occupy a world ethnographically parallel to that of the human and contiguous with it, though invisible to us corporeal beings most of the time. Spirits are ethereal counterparts of human types and historical personalities, yet, as noted before, all of them are 'others': there exist no *zar* analogues of the spirits' local hosts. Darawish spirit society is comprised of Islamic scholars and saints from Egypt, Iran, the exemplary past, and comes closest to depicting an authoritative, literate, universalist

Islam that is much admired though inaccessible to the unschooled majority. It is a society of model Muslims: devout men and their pious daughters, never their wives, whose behaviours are but approximated by northern
Sudanese. Since male Darawish exaggerate local masculine ideals, even a
pious man might admit to being possessed by one without gravely injur-
ing his reputation. As befitting their lofty station, Darawish *zayran* are the
first to be drummed in possession rites. *Zar* societies deemed least ideal,
hence unlike Arab Muslim Sudanese and regarded by them with ambivalence if not enmity, are summoned last; these are the Africans, 'southern-
ers': Dinka, Nuer, Azande.

In Toronto, however, these values are overturned: here northerners are
also Africans and the once exalted Darawish dangerous aliens, paragons
of a dreaded theocracy. If this is so, there is more; for the logic of *zar*
seems also to have shifted significantly, rotated on its axis in the service
of a novel message. By eliminating the Darawish, rather than including
them but drumming them last, the cult's hierarchy of otherness is not just
reversed but undone. Within Sudan, manifest *zayran* are culturally foreign;
what is neither explicitly nor faithfully performed is 'ourselves'. In
Toronto, on the other hand, the avowed aliens – Islamic authority figures
– are wittingly excluded, their ideality denied. What is dramatically reproduced must thus, in a sense, be 'us': a reformulated nation, conceived in
absentia in a foreign land and, perhaps, affected by it; an inclusive nation
unlike that of the Islamic regime, or even of the pre-exile past. Spirits
portrayed during the *zar* are all part of the make-up and history of modern
Sudan, whether Hadendowa from the eastern desert, Muslim and
Christian Ethiopians from the borderlands, colonizing English, cattle-
keeping Nuer and Dinka – not unlike Nubians in the present and the past.
All are joined in a single polyphyletic whole.

Yet it is the evening in its entirety, not just the dramatized *zar*, that
grounds this observation. That night the refugees embraced as legitimately
Sudanese a wider scope of customs and peoples than would have normally
been the case within the 'Arab' Sudan, through their performance of
dances from the 'African' south and the honours accorded the exemplary
Sudanese woman, a 'Black' actress, Ustaza Atahiya (who, incidentally, had
recently played the role of a *zar* spirit possessing a man in a popular
Sudanese play).[31] Through artful management of the spirit possession
genre the women both distinguished themselves from their oppressors and
sought to forge unity by fostering the audience's recognition of their
mutual context, to 'imagine' a community through theatrical performance
and so realize a greater 'we'. They used a healing cult in an effort to heal
the nation.

Still, in the exile situation *zar* alone was insufficient as a narrative of
resistance and reformulated identity. It needed the contextual ground
of the wedding to 'make sense'. If the 'Nubian' wedding crystallizes specifically Sudanese but not specifically Islamic ideals, *zar* mocks both with

equal flair – in, for one, the person of Luliya Habishiya, the distorted local 'bride'. The women did not refrain from levelling a barb or two at themselves – as brides, medical doctors, consumers of finery – nor did the audience of men emerge unscathed. The hegemony of northern culture – of the refugees' prior position – was playfully and performatively undermined. But whatever the ceremonies' ludic content, together, even in simulation, they are political representations of officially discredited *'adat*, northern Sudanese identity, to refugee northern Sudanese. And jointly they are the province of women as keepers of *'adat*.

Moreover these 'traditions', folklorized at home and now abroad, were presented in a forum that lent wider political legitimacy both to the expatriate performance and to its feminist message. The wedding and the *zar* framed the address by the President of the Toronto Arab Centre, herself a woman, who recognized Sudan not as an African nation but as part of the Middle East, and who applauded Sudanese women's struggle against patriarchal injustice. In so doing, she effectively clarified the evening's political import while opening up its apparent message of identity. Whereas the homogenized wedding is a statement of greater Nubianness and the modified *zar* presents Nubia's African circumstance and colonial past, the invitation to officiate at the evening was issued to a self-identified Arab. Clearly, Sudanese refugees are keen to maximize their options for support and Egypt has openly contested the current regime even while Iran and Iraq have championed it. It is significant, however, that Dr Ida was not marked as a Muslim. And as an Egyptian, she is of course a woman of the Nile, historically from the same two worlds – African, Arab – whence come the Muslim Sudanese.

My presence, too, probably served to validate the dramatized cultural bricolage. The authentication I provided was that of Western secular scholarship, of an academic text that both documents Sudanese traditions currently suffering repression in Sudan and affirms their significance to northern Sudanese social identity. My interpretation of the role of Islam in Sudanese women's lives is at odds with the regime's aspirations. Indeed with my fellow actors I too had donned the proscribed *towb* – though mine, of course, was not a costly *towb* made of sheer imported fabric but instead a 'locally' woven one.

In some respects the evening was a staged collision of certainties, givens, absolutes. Note that when beginning the *zar* women sang greetings to the Prophet: hence, Islam itself was not denied, merely a class of powerful, tyrannical Muslims, avatars of the enemy regime. In Sudan *zar* shows considerable deference to Islam, for no spirits are summoned during Ramadan, no rituals held even for display. The date of the performance, 8 March 1992, fell within the fasting month and still the show went on. In the clash of calendars, International time overrode Islamic, so challenging the disciplines and truth-claims of Islam, insinuating a secular community where religion is a private affair. But more than this, during the evening the certainty that is Islam was made to confront another, equally absolute and transcendental: that of secular humanism 'enshrined' in the International Declaration of Human Rights. Women's absolute rights, especially, of free association, movement, education, have all been eroded in Sudan since 1989; even before that, when, in the early 1980s, fundamentalist Saudi Arabia extended its economic and political grasp. Patriarchal domination and local (Sudanese) male privilege were thus called into question that night by a temporary community of women which was international in fact as well as in name. Recall too the evening's venue, the Eritrea Restaurant, whose overtones of liberation are plain.

An international 'imaginary' (see Appadurai 1990) was being invoked that night but to profoundly nationalist ends. Note that the flyer announcing the event was issued by Sudanese, not 'Nubian' women. Ironically, the women who spoke for Sudanese womanhood were those whose privileged class and cultural position once depended on the oppression of non-Muslim Sudanese women and men; and it is this elite position that has made it possible (even personally necessary) for them to oppose the regime. Yet I dare not think that their broader vision of the country is a cynical one. The group's public identification as 'Nubian' makes sense not only in terms of a politicized, Afrocentric Black community in Toronto and the 'bad press' accorded Arab Sudanese, or of the current regime's historical assertions, but also in terms of a reconceived nation comprised of *Africans*: Nubians and Nuer alike.[32] Theirs is not an image of nationhood where minorities must either adopt the religion and culture of the majority or face elimination but where each distinctive 'culture', each site of local knowledge, Muslim and majority or not, is equivalent to every other within an encompassing whole.

All these humanist, nationalist and feminist messages were presented, fittingly for Sudan, within the framework of International Women's Day when, as with the *zar*, 'men can say nothing'. In that they symbolize, iconically and metonymically, the Muslim community's boundedness, it is apt that northern Sudanese women should be vehicles for an image of openness and change. Sudanese women in Toronto were using the *zar* as women have long done in Sudan, to refashion who they, as Sudanese, are but also who they are not. They were structuring their historical experience, investing it with continuity and moral significance (see Palmié 1993), publicly reworking the import of what everyone – audience and performers alike – already knew. Thus they were attempting to transform an entrenched and exclusionary nationalism that had fuelled their disenchantment and precipitated their flight. If the transformation they sought occurred only in the imagination, it was no less crucial for that. Their invitation to attend an evening of 'superstition and traditional dancing' was a deeply political act.[33]

EPILOGUE

In October 1992, the Royal Ontario Museum mounted a one-day open workshop on Nubia in conjunction with a guided tour of the Nubian and Egyptian galleries. Three 'Nubianists', myself included, gave lectures on Nubian culture and history; my topic was the position of women in the Upper Nile valley, then and now. Several 'Nubians' attended; the women had made 'Nubian' pastries – baclava, sambusa and the like – and 'Nubian' musicians initiated the event. A 'Nubian' man later chastised me for not having pushed my theme of matrilineal survivals and women's political roles far enough.

Towards the end of February 1993, I telephoned one of the women who had participated in the *zar* to ask if the group was intending to repeat its performance on 8 March. 'No,' she replied, 'we have all become too absorbed in our lives in Toronto. But the organization is still there. Now we are very involved in working for human rights in Sudan. And we have been having meetings with people from the south to talk about things, to see if we can get to the root of the problems between us.'

At the end of March 1993 I ran into a former student of mine, a Ugandan woman pursuing graduate studies in another field. She told me that she had several Sudanese friends and one day had asked them to show her 'something Sudanese'. They played her a videotape of our International Women's Day *zar*.

ACKNOWLEDGEMENTS

Research in Sudan was undertaken with grants from the Canada Council and the Social Sciences and Humanities Research Council of Canada; I continue to be grateful for their support. I am deeply indebted to the people of 'Hofriyat', northern Sudan but especially the women and lately to women of the Sudanese refugee community in Toronto. I owe much to Julie Anderson for helping me to remain in contact with Hofriyati during these difficult times and to forge links with the Toronto Sudanese. Thanks to Wendy James, Ronald Wright and Michael Lambek, who read earlier drafts of this chapter, for their thoughtful suggestions, many of which have been incorporated into this version. I alone remain responsible for its contents.

NOTES

1 Spirits are said to be composed of air and fire; humans of water and earth.
2 Space does not permit me to develop this point fully here; it hinges on the association of womanhood with the household and household enclosure (*hosh*) and with internal affairs of the village. Apropos of this and as I briefly discuss (p. 20), the proper conduct of earthly social life – appropriately bearing and socializing children, keeping up kinship networks, performing the ceremonies that orient the course of everyday life (marriages, namings, circumcisions) – is primarily the responsibility of women. An inward orientation for women is, in part, realized and maintained through infibulation and re-infibulation

(following childbirth), the painful shaping of their bodies to society's image, whose moral meaning is reiterated in the disciplines and duties that govern their daily lives and in the metaphors of enclosure and fertility surrounding these. Spirits, who are ethereal beings, take advantage of 'openings' – in the social fabric, in women's bodies – to enter the women as a means of gaining access to earthly delights. See Boddy 1988, 1989.

3 Sudan gained its independence in 1956 with formal dissolution of the Anglo-Egyptian condominium administration (effectively British rule) and its replacement by a parliamentary democracy. The first period of democratic rule was unstable and short-lived, ending in 1958 with a coup led by General Abboud. Escalating popular unrest in the north and resistance to Abboud's heavy-handed Arabization and Islamization policies among non-Muslim peoples of the south succeeded in forcing the government to dissolve in 1964; a tactical alliance of the country's several opposition groups provided transitional administration. When parliamentary elections were held again in 1965, the result was another coalition government. As new elections were being planned in May 1969, the army returned to power in a coup led by Colonel Nimeiri, who subsequently banned all opposition parties. Under Nimeiri's rule troubles between north and south continued despite a 1972 truce in the civil war. Exacerbating the problem, he declared Shari'a law for Sudan in 1983, presumably hoping to forge closer ties with powerful Arab states and appease Islamic militants at home. His regime ended with his own military overthrow in April 1985. After a brief transitional period elections were held in 1986 and again in 1988. On both occasions the results were precarious parliamentary coalitions which failed to achieve peace. The main political parties in Sudan have always been based on sectarian and/or regional interests and parliamentary rule on unsteady pragmatic alliances. In the 1980s these became increasingly reliant on the powerful Muslim Brotherhood, which supported the 1989 coup. Under the current brutal but well-entrenched regime, policies of Islamization continue in the face of southern and increasingly northern, resistance.

4 By March,1993, that number had swelled to almost eighty.

5 Gruenbaum (1992) notes that the majority of urban and rural women have not yet adopted the 'Islamic' dress but that they are afraid of suffering the consequences of non-compliance, described below.

6 See Boddy 1989.

7 One woman ventured that the regime could not last long without this exodus, for the refugees have become a major source of foreign currency, channelled into Sudan in the form of remittances to kin. The pattern – of defending the boundaries of the moral society while selectively admitting external influences and subordinating these to internal reformulation – is intelligibly northern Sudanese.

8 *Zayran* (*zar* spirits) are typically considered to be a class of *jinn*, beings whose existence is verified in the Quran.

9 The *zar* in cities and larger towns differs from the rural *zar* in a number of ways. Salient here is that town cult groups tend to be relatively permanent organizations, each associated with a leader, a *shaikha* (female) or a *shaikh* (male). In the rural areas the cult is less strictly organized and curers are engaged on the basis of kinship with the patient or proximity, though for specific problems women will seek out curers in distant locales whose reputations they know of from friends and kin. In both towns and villages, however, female curers are the majority, which makes the move to form an association of *zar shaikhs*, initiated by a man, particularly interesting.

10 Of course, this aspect of the cult has been emphasized by anthropologists since Leiris (1958), although I am uncertain of the extent to which such discourse

played a role in the *shaikh's* decision. I am grateful to Michael Lambek for raising this issue.

11 Recent extensions of more anthropological culture concepts (e.g. as in cultural studies) notwithstanding.

12 Coptic, mainly, but see Vantini 1981 for consideration of the complexities of this.

13 It is believed that patrilineal succession was the rule further north. Dr N. Millet, curator, ROM, and specialist in Nubian archaeology, personal communication, 1992.

14 See Holt and Daly 1979: 23; Jakobielski 1986; al-Shahi 1988: 34.

15 See Adams 1984; Shinnie 1967; Trigger 1965.

16 There are three Nubian speech groups: Kenuz in the far north, Mahas in the centre and Danagla in the south of this zone. Kenuz and Danagla are mutu-ally intelligible, Mahas is distinct and its speakers obliged to converse in Arabic with the other two (Adams 1984: 48).

17 Adams (1984: 384ff.), however, suggests that the 'Nobatae' mentioned in late Roman texts as inhabiting the west side of the Nile south of Aswan and the 'Noba' of further south described in Axumite texts of the same period, but even earlier by Strabo and Ptolemy, may be different peoples.

18 In 1813 the Swiss explorer Burckhardt learned that:

> According to their own traditions, the present Nubians derive their origin from the Arabian bedouins who invaded the country after the promulga-tion of the Mohammedan creed, the greater part of the Christian inhabi-tants . . . having either fled before them or been killed; a few . . . embraced the religion of the invaders.
>
> (Burckhardt 1819: 133, cited in Adams 1984: 563)

19 See, for example, Benjamin Weiner (1993):

> What do we know about Sudan? That nation has been embroiled in a decade-long civil war pitting the Arab Muslims of the north against the black Sudanese Christians and animists of the south. . . . The fundamental-ists, supported by Iran, appear to be winning the war against the black Sudanese.

20 Holt and Daly (1979: 119) refer to the place as Umm Diwaykarat. It is located in southern Kordofan not far from Aba Island, where the Mahdist revolt began.

21 The Mahdi is seen as having laid the foundations for the great Islamic state; but, just as Abu Bakr succeeded the Prophet's leadership upon his death, it fell to the *khalifa*, Abu Bakr's Sudani personification, to build upon his work. Indeed, today's Mahdist revival has more to do with elevating the image and achievements of the Khalifa than those of the Mahdi himself (see al-Assad 1991: 20–1) and for obvious reasons: a descendant of the Mahdi was head of the government which al-Bashir's coup replaced.

22 For discussion of this issue with regard to Islamic fundamentalism elsewhere, see Caplan 1987 and Zubaida 1987.

23 I am grateful to Julie Anderson, an archaeologist with the ROM's continuing Nubian expedition, for this information given to me following her return from Sudan in early 1993. The stone has since been returned to the Dongola mosque.

24 It is ironic that both the particular ideology of nationalism and the institution through which it is here expressed originate in the disparaged West.

25 This is significant given more recent intensive interconnections as well: Egypt's role in conquering the Sudan in 1821, in helping to overthrow the Mahdists at the end of the nineteenth century, its official role in ruling Sudan with the British until 1956 and the current antagonism that divides the two countries.

26 The events surrounding the Toronto *zar* took place in the midst of one of the worst constitutional crises Canada has undergone. An accord which would have made Quebec a signatory to the present constitution went down to defeat outside Quebec, in part because there was no provision for recognizing aboriginal peoples as founding members of the nation. This prompted endless soul-searching among media and politicians and a series of telecast 'townhall meetings' where notables, politicians and 'average Canadians' debated issues of cultural distinctiveness (for Québecois, aboriginals, ethnic minorities) and the future direction of the country.

27 The book had been shortlisted for the 1990 Governor General's Literary Award in Non-Fiction; this provoked a rant in the Toronto press along the lines of 'What does a book on Sudanese women have to do with Canada?' – through which the Sudanese community became aware of its existence.

28 Seven is a propitious number; in the *zar* cult there are said to be seven spirit societies (though in fact there may be more than this in some parts of Sudan); the patient steps over the sacrificial victim seven times; a major curing ceremony lasts for seven days; and so on.

29 Ethiopian spirits are generally drummed early on in a *zar*; however, female spirits are sometimes classed together as *As-Sittat*, 'the Ladies', and summoned at a later point.

30 See Boddy 1989, especially Chapter 9.

31 My suspicion that she was the actress involved in folklorizing the *zar* has been neither verified nor fully allayed.

32 In subsequent talks, some of the women pointed out that their Africanness was what made them who they are as Muslims and that the regime's denial of its Africanness is what stands in the way of a solution to the civil war.

33 From my own perspective at least, a final irony: it may be that the *zar*'s potential to engender a locally nuanced feminist consciousness (see also Hale 1986: 28–9), which I postulated in my book for women in the village of Hofriyat, can only bear fruit outside Sudan itself and in the hands of those who are sceptics. Whatever the truth of this comment, it vitiates neither the vernacular knowledge that grounds the *zar*, nor the cult's vital role in affirming local values threatened with erosion by forces beyond local control. Moreover, since one member of the 'cast' suggested the women should set up a 'house of spirits' (*bayt ad-dustoor*) in Toronto, it would seem logical also to question the relevance of disbelief.

REFERENCES

Abdelrahman, Halima Mohammed (1991a) 'A History of Heroism; Um Dibekrat: The Memory Revived at Last', *Sudanow* XVI(12): 14–19, December.
—— (1991b) 'Collective Marriage: A Radical Change in Sudanese Society', *Sudanow* XVI(12): 24, December.
Adams, W.Y. (1984) *Nubia: Corridor to Africa*, London: Allen Lane.
Al-Assad, Nagat (1991) 'Lessons from a Glorious Past', *Sudanow* XVI(12): 20–1, December.
Al-Shahi, Ahmed (1988) 'Northern Sudanese Perceptions of the Nubian Christian Legacy', pp. 31–9, in W. James and D.H. Johnson (eds), *Vernacular Christianity: Essays in the Social Anthropology of Religion Presented to Godfrey Lienhardt* (JASO Occasional Papers no. 7), Oxford/ New York: JASO/Lilian Barber Press.
Amin, Samir (1989) *Eurocentrism*, trans. Russell Moore, New York: Monthly Review Press.
Anderson, B. (1991) *Imagined Communities*, London: Verso. 2nd edn.

Appadurai, A. (1990) 'Disjuncture and Difference in the Global Cultural Economy', *Public Culture* 2(2): 1–24.

Boddy, J. (1988) 'Spirits and Selves in Northern Sudan: The Cultural Therapeutics of Possession and Trance', *American Ethnologist* 15(1): 4–27.

—— (1989) *Wombs and Alien Spirits: Women, Men and the Zar Cult in Northern Sudan*, Madison, WI: University of Wisconsin Press.

Burckhardt, J.L. (1819) *Travels in Nubia*, London: John Murray.

Caplan, L. (1987) 'Introduction', pp. 1–24, in L. Caplan (ed.), *Studies in Religious Fundamentalism*, London: Macmillan.

Davidson, B. (1984) *Africa: A Voyage of Discovery*, (video documentary series) John Percival, producer. Mitchell Beasley Television, R.M. Arts and Channel 4.

Galeano, E. (1991) *The Book of Embraces*, trans. C. Belfrage with M. Schafer, New York: W.W. Norton.

Gruenbaum, E. (1992) 'The Islamist State and Sudanese Women', *Middle East Report* 22(6): 29–32.

Hale, S. (1985) 'Women, Work and Islam: Sudanese Women in Crisis', paper presented at the annual meeting of the American Anthropological Association, 3–8 December, Washington, DC.

—— (1986) 'The Wing of the Patriarch', *Middle East Report* 16(1): 25–30.

Handler, R. (1988) *Nationalism and the Politics of Culture in Quebec*, Madison, WI: University of Wisconsin Press.

Hannerz, U. (1992) *Cultural Complexity: Studies in the Social Organization of Meaning*, New York: Columbia University Press.

Hasan, Yusuf Fadl (1967) *The Arabs and the Sudan from the Seventh to the Early Sixteenth Century*, Khartoum: Khartoum University Press.

Holt, P.M. and M.W. Daly (1979) *The History of the Sudan from the Coming of Islam to the Present Day*, London: Weidenfeld and Nicolson.

Hurreiz, Sayyid (1991) '*Zar* as a Ritual Psychodrama: from Cult to Club', pp. 147–55, in I.M. Lewis, Ahmed al-Safi and Sayyid Hurreiz (eds), *Women's Medicine: The Zar-Bori Cult in Africa and Beyond*, Edinburgh: Edinburgh University Press for the International African Institute.

Jakobielski, S. (1986) 'Polish Excavations at Old Dongola, 1978/79–1982', pp. 299–304, in M. Krause (ed.), *Nubische Studien: Tagungsakten der 5te Internationalen Konferenz der International Society for Nubian Studies, Heidelberg, 22–25 September 1982*, Mainz am Rhein: Verlag Philipp von Zabern.

James, W. and D.H. Johnson (1988) 'Introductory Essay: On "Native" Christianity', pp. 1–14, in W. James and D.H. Johnson (eds.), *Vernacular Christianity: Essays in the Social Anthropology of Religion Presented to Godfrey Lienhardt* (JASO Occasional Papers no. 7), Oxford/New York: JASO/Lilian Barber Press.

Johnson, D.H. (1988) 'Sudanese Military Slavery from the 18th to the 20th Century', pp. 142–56, in L. Archer (ed.), *Slavery and other Forms of Unfree Labour*, London: Routledge.

—— (1989) 'The Structure of a Legacy: Military Slavery in Northeast Africa', *Ethnohistory* 36(1): 72–88.

—— (1992) 'Recruitment and Entrapment in Private Slave Armies: the Structure of the Zara'ib in the southern Sudan', *Slavery and Abolition: Journal of Comparative Studies* 13(1): 162–73.

Leiris, M. (1958) *La Possession et ses Aspects Théâtraux chez les Ethiopiens de Gondar*, L'Homme: Cahiers d'ethnologie, de géographie at de linguistique. Paris: Plon.

Mazrui, A. (1986) *The Africans* (video documentary series) BBC TV and Washington: WETA TV. Co-production with Nigerian TV.

Palmié, S. (1993) 'Against Syncretism: Africanizing and Cubanizing Discourses in North American Òrìsà Worship', paper presented at ASA Decennial

Conference, IV, Oxford.

Schweinfurth, G. (1969) [1883] *The Heart of Africa: Three Years' Travels and Adventures in the Unexplored Regions of Central Africa, from 1868 to 1871* (2 vols), trans. E.E. Frewer, London: Sampson Low, Marsten Low and Searle.

Shinnie, P. (1967) *Meroe: A Civilization of the Sudan*, New York: Praeger.

Sudanow (1991a) 'Getting Written History Right', XVI(12): 4, December.

—— (1991b) 'Cover-up', XVI(12): 6, December.

—— (1991c) 'National Strategy Conference: Laying Foundations for the Future', XVI(12): 7, December.

Trigger, B. (1965) *History and Settlement in Lower Nubia*, Publications in Anthropology No. 69, New Haven, CT: Yale University Press.

Vantini, G. (1981) *Christianity in the Sudan*, Bologna, Italy: EMI Press.

Weiner, B. (1993) 'The Crime of Turning a Blind Eye', *Globe and Mail*, Commentary, Toronto, February 12. First published in *Wall Street Journal*.

Zubaida, Sami (1987) 'The Quest for the Islamic State: Islamic Fundamentalism in Egypt and Iran', pp. 25–50, in L. Caplan (ed.), *Studies in Religious Fundamentalism*, London: Macmillan.

2 History and the discourse of underdevelopment among the Alur of Uganda

Aidan Southall

In our endless quest for the other, unrewarding so far in itself but valuable in its by-products, the quarry still escapes, twisting, turning, finally, disconcertingly, backwards into ourselves. At which point, having lost the real other, we turn to trivial pursuits examining ever more minute aspects, ever more intricately excavated and creatively imagined interior structures and processes of our own behaviour wrung out in studying the now departed other.

Old tribes became ethnic groups, having supposedly bounded cultures, which we deludedly studied (I was saved by the Alur). Then they lost their boundaries and became fuzzy sets, perhaps no longer cultures at all but only creolized 'knowledges' (Parkin 1993: 84).

Global knowledge has attained the capacity to feed all people and provide them with satisfying affluence and to equilibrate our numbers harmoniously with the global bounty of nature. But global political economy, through the interlocking global elite which manages the production and distribution of knowledge, has other goals. Full knowledge gives pleasure but such knowledge can be so perverted that sharing it causes more panic than pleasure. Bosnians kill one another because, through intertwined histories, they had chosen God in three different aspects which cannot all be true. We could stop them but that would destabilize the currencies on which the banks depend to channel and manipulate the global network of the production and distribution of knowledge and its power.

The dominant anthropological discourse now takes place within certain recognized but unstated parameters, tacitly omitting others previously accorded great significance. This results in a lop-sided narrative which seems like a Zen acrobat to be walking a tightrope with only one leg.

The 'knowledge' I have studied for forty-five years, emulating at a pale distance Sir Raymond Firth's unmatchable record of seventy years and more, is commonly called Alur, although like most real ethnic names it is not without its obscurities. The knowledge of the Alur used to appear to them full and satisfying but has come to seem globally limited, fragmentary and even destructive. To call this process creolization is a worthy attempt to neutralize and mystify the global relation of inequality. We still, willy-nilly, live this inequality, however hard we try to persuade ourselves that we do not think it.

In the glorious ethnographic present, we used to reconstruct what we thought might once have been the culture and society of the other, disingenuously allowing our readers to slip into the assumption that that was what we really saw. Then we tried to give honest, bare descriptions uncontaminated by theory. But realizing we had deceived ourselves again, we returned to theory, which often became more fascinating than the facts. Perhaps the dialectic returns us to a more dispassionate consideration of the relation between the two.

If you try to study a 'knowledge' this long, you may be bewildered by the numbers of different processes of change which are all going on together. I was myself growing and changing as a person, while anthropology itself kept changing, alongside the more revolutionary changes which engulfed the Alur; not to mention the fact that, on my last visit, I hardly ever met anyone who was alive and known to me on my first visit, apart from young children who were now very old men. In many important ways, the society I visited and the culture I entered in 1992 were not the same as I had visited in 1947. Fortunately, the Alur in 1992 did still identify themselves as Alur in apparently the same way, though recognizing that this identity was not really the same.

With these cautionary provisos, I sketch the trajectory of Alur knowledge as a series of pulsations through an hour-glass. The device is mine, not theirs; intended simply to render concisely vivid the major changes which I see as having occurred. The hour-glass is the traditionally spacious homeland of the Alur, out of which they have been increasingly propelled south-eastwards, by a series of pulsations of intermittent intensity, through a restricted, alien, Bantu corridor, into the yet more alien but infinitely expanding world of the national capital of Uganda (see Figure 2.1).

The first pulsation occurred in the twilight period of European penetration, when the Africans affected had little idea of what was happening to them and most of the Europeans had little idea of the further implications of what they were doing. But in the fanciful imagination of hindsight, African events uncannily prefigure subsequent European action. Thus King Alworung'a of the Okoro Alur and King Ujuru of the Panduru Alur were fighting in a feud, with a stereotypical origin of disputes over dynastic marriages and bridewealth cattle, later exacerbated by the first appearance of firearms in the region. The resulting political and territorial polarization prefigured the coming division into British and Belgian Alurland by the formal demarcation of a new international boundary, between Uganda and the Belgian Congo (Zaire), running west from Lake Albert up to the Nile–Congo watershed.

In local knowledge, flexible boundaries arose historically from the complementary opposition of local groups, while in global knowledge rigid

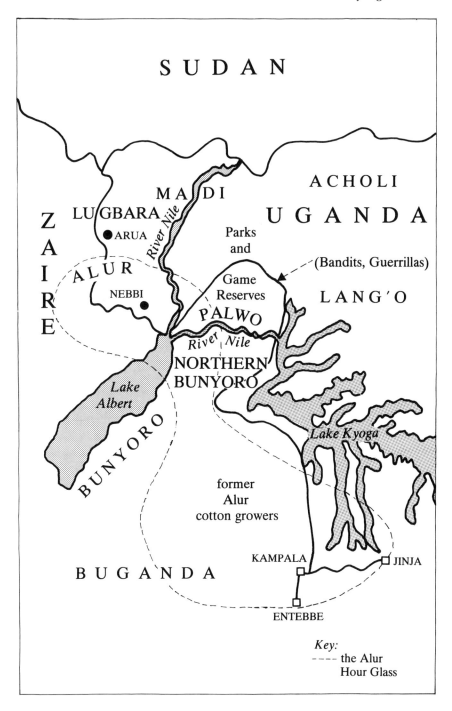

Figure 2.1 Schematic diagram: Alur in Uganda and Zaire

boundaries were fixed by scientific marking of features in the natural land-scape. The Nile itself was transformed from an ecological bond uniting the Alur living on both its banks, into an ethnic administrative boundary dividing them and confining them to the west bank only, with the loss of half their livelihood. Colonial science distorted indigenous history and knowledge and was ratified, over the heads of the Alur, as the triumph of scientifically controlled nature and reason over savage culture.

This episode established part of the contour of the Alur hour-glass, which was completed as the British laid waste northern Bunyoro, with the army of the Baganda, in order to subjugate King Kabarega of Bunyoro. The country was depopulated and, as a consequence, invaded by sleeping sickness, while the royal service of the intercultural pantheon at Mount Gisi was thereby terminated and an epidemic of spirit possession broke out among the Alur. Thus British and Alur created and deployed their practical and esoteric knowledges without either of them linking the two together, or realizing that the one reflected the other. The military action of the British had an impact on the ecology and economy of the Alur in the Nile valley of which the former were unaware. It impoverished them in diet, in income, and in health because of sleeping sickness. It imposed a spatial and ethnic gulf between these two Lwo populations, Alur and Acoli, who might previously have been impossible to distinguish by anything more than a gentle cultural gradient. Such imposed gulfs would be the cause of civil wars over half a century later. It also cleared the way for European missionaries to spread the Christian gospel through Bunyoro to Alurland without the slightest idea that their global religious knowledge was already anticipated by a powerful occult and spiritual knowledge of indigenous and transethnic dimensions, centred upon Mount Gisi in the kingdom which had been laid waste and humiliated.

The second pulsation arose from paired, complementary processes, one of war and the other of peace. In the characteristically colonial trick of 'voluntary compulsion', the First World War involved small numbers of Alur (for they were by then only barely under the yoke of colonial admin-istration) in an unprecedented movement totally outside their known world. Having been exposed to this mind-blowing experience of sudden global knowledge, many of them could not settle down on returning home after the war but decided to go back down country to work for wages or grow cash crops, both of which were forcefully encouraged by the colo-nial administration. The Second World War blew up both these processes to much larger proportions. Recruitment under heavy pressure for the King's African Rifles took much larger numbers of Alur down country to the military training centres around the capital and the distant theatres of war in Ethiopia and Burma. Correspondingly larger numbers were unsettled by this shattering experience (of global knowledge) to the point of inability to settle down again to rural life, so that many of them and numerous others under their influence, returned down country after the war to enter the growing capitalist sector of the colonial economy in one capacity or another. The Alur demonstrated a completely different appreciation of the penetration of global (capitalist) knowledge from that of their Lugbara neighours, by largely refusing to be recruited *en masse* as unskilled labour on the Indian-owned sugar estates in southern Uganda, whereas the Lugbara were recruited in large numbers. The Alur preferred, in more entrepreneurial fashion, to rent land from Ganda landowners in share-cropping arrangements which, exploitative as they were, allowed them much more freedom and profited them more.

Was this difference an expression of the different political regimes of Lugbara and Alur? Both had varieties of segmentary lineage system (Middleton and Tait 1958: 203–29) but Lugbara polities were much smaller than those of the Alur, with no ritually centralizing institution of divine kingship, such as the Alur had achieved on a moderate scale. My fragile hypothesis would be that the Alur kingship brought its people, or was an expression of, a wider level of socio-political consciousness, while the Lugbara were more firmly and locally encapsulated within their small lineage polities. The Indian sugar managers would simply have said that the Lugbara were better workers.

On the spiritual dimension, the death of Alur soldiers far from home, beyond the possibility of proper funerary rites, had led to a distinctive new brand of spirit possession, known as Jok Memba. *Jok* is the Nilotic word for divinity or spirit. The English word 'member' bore witness to the intrusive force of global knowledge, while the outbreak of such an epidemic was still interpreted in local knowledge by the fact that the major spirits of the region (transcending the Nilotic–Bantu linguistic divide) had been wandering out of control ever since their proper service by the kings of Bunyoro was cut off by colonial warfare. The emblem of Jok Memba was a white cotton cloth flag on a tall pole. When I first visited Alurland in the 1940s a very large number of homesteads were flying it. Cotton cloth was, with guns, a principal materialist symbol of the capitalist penetration of global knowledge and Jok Memba's flag one of the first common alien emblems. A tiny piece of white cotton on a stick also came to signal the presence of domestically distilled (illegal) liquor for sale, another intrusive phenomenon of global knowledge pregnant with evil consequences for the future.

Traditional millet beer had been drunk primarily by adult men, as an accompaniment to festivals, rituals and major agricultural operations. The increasing distillation of *waragi*, or 'Nubian gin' (Arabic *arak*),* by village women on the domestic hearth, marked a giant step forward in the monetization of the indigenous economy and an ambiguous step in the emancipation of women, as well as the growing disillusionment with

* *Editor's note*: For a discussion of the spread of things 'Nubian', see Boddy's discussion in Chapter 1 above.

the indigenous economy as such. By 1992 those left behind from migrant work, young and old, male and female, were able to sit around at nine in the morning sipping *waragi* as it dripped warm out of the housewife's still.

The next rude break in the Alur regime of spirit and of political economy was not the coming of independence in 1962 but the explosion of violence and disorder following Idi Amin's coup in 1971. Just as Amin preached 'double production', under which the production of the economy fell by half, so also he preached ethnic integration whereby ethnic hostilities rose to lethal levels never known before. The influence of his deeds was notably more powerful than his words. In this atmosphere, Alur settlers growing cotton on land leased in Buganda escaped as best they could. Buganda, with its 'freehold' land, had been the Mecca for all those who wanted to produce and market cash crops undeveloped in their home areas. The very area in which the Alur had been concentrated in Buganda subsequently became the infamous Luwero Triangle in which mountains of skulls are now displayed to tourists.

Northern Bunyoro, depopulated by the war against Kabarega and the subsequent sleeping sickness, offered the obvious substitute for Buganda to the migrant Alur, once resettlement was permitted. It was much nearer and more convenient, being only just across the Nile from their homeland. Besides, it was ancient Nilotic Lwo territory. It was the home of the great spirits at Mount Gisi, accredited to both the Nilotic Alur and to the Bantu Banyoro. This dovetailed into both the economic and the occult or spiritual needs of the Alur. Depopulated and practically abandoned for over half a century, northern Bunyoro was the cheapest and most easily available fertile land left in Uganda. It lay midway between the Alur homeland and the Buganda areas they had been forced to leave. They settled it in increasingly large numbers, till the Banyoro, who have never recovered economically or spiritually from the defeat of Kabarega and the transfer of a large part of their kingdom to Buganda by the British, no longer regard it as Bunyoro but as an extension of Alurland. In fact, it had been the ancient home of the Nilotic Palwo but an integral part of the greater Bunyoro–Kitara complex. The mothers of Bunyoro kings came from Palwo.

The economic settlement of the Alur had its occult counterpart. The traditional influence of the Alur kings lay not only in their ability to make rain but in their mystical power to control witches. When they rubbed the sacred lily bulb *lenga* on their royal stools the witches came crawling before them with red eyes and as their identity was therefore known to the King, their activities could be kept within reasonable bounds. The sanction was that witches who became a nuisance, attracting multiple accusations, were subjected to the chicken-poison oracle. Those who were repeatedly declared guilty by it were put to death, or at the very least driven into exile, with northern Bunyoro being the most likely reception area.

The colonial government made all witchcraft illegal, without much comprehension of what it was. To make an accusation of witchcraft was now just as criminal as to practise it. The execution of a witch was simply murder and so came to an end, except that in extreme cases a person who had become a notorious focus of witchcraft accusations might still occasionally be put to death in an outburst of consensual rage. In such cases, local police, government chiefs and courts, sharing the same local knowledge system, simply failed to prosecute.

When I arrived in Alurland in the late 1940s, the major complaint against the colonial government was that witches were not being controlled and were multiplying. Forty-five years later the situation had become chronic. Witchcraft accusations had proliferated and without any effective means of resolution, they accumulated permanently into a thick, miasmal network enveloping the whole population. Persons who acquired the reputation of notorious witches were forced to leave home. They would first take refuge with kin, such as a mother's brother, in other settlements where they were less well known, but if their evil reputation continued they would have to leave Alurland altogether and the natural place to go was northern Bunyoro. Despite this safety valve, the Alur homeland became infested with an evil atmosphere of unresolved witchcraft accusations and counter-accusations. Educated Alur say that anyone who achieves success in education or enterprise is an inevitable target of witchcraft. Alur making a living in Kampala are afraid to go home, fearing that they and their children will fall ill and die. For most, this is witchcraft, for the extremely sophisticated it is poisoning, which is equally metaphysical. The matter transcends logic, for the successful person is not only suspected of succeeding through witchcraft; but is in double jeopardy as an object of envy who also becomes the focus of witchcraft attack.

As a result of these processes, the territorial, social, cultural and psychological gulf between those at home, at the top of the hour-glass, struggling painfully with fragmented local knowledge, and those abroad at its expanding base, edging their way into the realm of global knowledge, is increasing. Alur students at the boys' and girls' secondary schools and colleges around Kampala have already lost the ability to read and write in their own mother tongue. Alur society and culture are polarized at either end of the hour-glass. One end holds the impoverished peasantry, with a few brave teachers, symbol managers (such as pastors, catechists, learned men, healers), administrators and entrepreneurs. This is the land of irredeemable Alur culture and speech, for the cultural elite leaves as it is produced. Around the capital are the ambitious and the enterprising, their children educated in English and unwilling to contemplate going home.

One might ask if the gulf provides a kind of protective defence for Alur indigenous culture and local knowledge in the homeland. The answer appears to be that the integrity and vitality of Alur culture and its local knowledge have been too eroded and damaged for this to be the case. Unfortunately, it is precisely those with the greatest knowledge, ability, energy and resources to carry Alur culture forward in positive adjustment to the onslaught of global knowledge who have left their homeland to an increasing extent and say they are afraid to return. Their personal culture is becoming more and more divorced from its indigenous roots, creolized, more and more compromised by the forces of global knowledge within which they have to operate. Yet they have taken specific and unprecedented steps to strengthen and promote Alur culture in Kampala. These efforts must perhaps be seen as a reaction to the gravity of the threat, rather than as an actual strengthening. It is the creation and organization of the Nebbi Community as a formal association in Kampala (see below) which is the principal expression of this. It is thus when their culture is eroded and their local knowledge impotent that Alur ethnicity attains its clearest expression.

Throughout most of the twentieth century, the Alur have pressed for clearer administrative recognition of their ethnic identity, such as was allowed to many peoples of Uganda under the colonial regime who had the advantage of occupying administrative districts which bore their own names. I cannot here explore the dubious or false basis of many of these names. Under the colonial yoke they became an involuntary part of the group heritage and as such efficacious. It was this efficacy which the Uganda Alur were denied, apparently because of the small size of their territory and population, itself a product of the slicing away of over half their numbers and territorial space into the Belgian Congo, by that same process of administrative decision-making which colonial knowledge believed to be based upon sound data and principles of natural science and reason, while the values of human culture and local knowledge thereby violated were rated inferior and initially classified as savage and ephemeral.

In independent Uganda, as in most of Africa, ethnic considerations were officially banned but unofficially ubiquitous. Ethnic associations were strongly frowned upon but every politician relied primarily on ethnic ties for votes and support. By a quirk of history, the efforts of Idi Amin and his successors to reform the administrative system, however corrupt and chaotic their practice, resulted in dividing up the country into a much larger number of districts than had existed in colonial times, which turned out to benefit the Alur. The former West Nile District was cut up into parts awkwardly named South-West Nile, North-West Nile, East-West Nile and so forth. The South-West Nile District was later more appropriately named Nebbi District, after a rocky hill and shrine in the centre of it, near the chief fork in the only major road, at which the District Headquarters began to develop (Nebbi corresponds to the Arabic *nabi*, 'Prophet'). Nebbi District in fact corresponded to the territory of the Uganda Alur, so that they got their own district at last but not with their own name. They were thus able to establish the Nebbi Community, which was quite obviously in practice and intent an ethnic asociation of the Alur, while correctly claiming officially that it was an association with membership open to all.

The Nebbi Community was thus able to organize cultural and recreational events in Kampala to promote general Alur interests and the expression of Alur culture through speech, song, music and dance in a folkloristic sort of way. The most united and enthusiastic expression of Alur culture was thus achieved outside, not inside, the homeland by those who are in the process of losing it.

For very good reason, the Alur feel neglected and forgotten in their own 'nation state'. Most people in south Uganda are vague and misinformed as to who they really are. Through a quarter of a century of political turmoil they have always, through public ignorance, been misassociated with the wrong side and blamed accordingly. Under Obote's first government the Alur were seen as sharing the taint of the Lang'o, as also Lwo, or just generally as 'northerners', regarded by the prosperous Bantu south as trying to get their own back and, in the end, making a mess of it. When Idi Amin came to power, from no-one really knew where but certainly from the north, the Alur were again seen as being in complicity and when, finally, the Acoli, after terrible suffering and discrimination under both Obote and Amin, became the last, irreconcilable guerrillas refusing the peace brought at last by Yoweri Museveni in 1986, the Alur were seen as a kind of Acoli, in the wrong again. The ethnic emphasis in Uganda has now shifted to the south-west but has accomplished little as yet to redress the unjust neglect and deprivation of the Alur. Uganda as a whole is better off but in this discourse of development, local knowledge is drained and diluted, while global knowledge imposes a new deception and dependence, with Structural Adjustment as its latest poisonous flower. The spatiotemporal polarization has its manifestations in all fields: politico-economic, occult-spiritual, cultural and intellectual. It is framed by the developing class polarization of the nation, which combines the covert privileging of one ethnic group over others with differential selectivity within each.

While 'cultural survival' nobly battles to defend the Yanomamo and other small indigenous peoples still stigmatized by them as tribes, and many aesthetically admirable but anthropologically illiterate books and films celebrate and lament the disappearing world of rich and beautiful cultures, we have not incorporated this perspective into our theory very well. We have to consider the kind of cultural survival which may reasonably be expected, or feasibly fought for in an unredeemed and globalizing world, for indigenous peoples of different sizes, structures, strengths and situations; and how anthropology should adjust to this, other than by becoming an antiquarian study of the quaint. It is a very old problem always assuming new dress. We used to mourn helplessly for past massacres and injustices, applying 'urgent anthropology' to record the cultures of small threatened peoples before they were forgotten altogether. But now the problem is reversed, as the progressive loss of creative autonomous cultures threatens ourselves more immediately, not just as 'victims of progress' but as signals of our own decay.

Parkin recently noted with enthusiasm the vigour of the concept of culture, in descriptions not of small-scale remote societies but of fragmentary contexts, peripheries (crossroads of migratory and marketing routes, refugee camps, inner cities, low-income quarters and elite neighbourhoods) which (following Nugent) 'have become the centre for current anthropological study' (Parkin 1993: 82–3). If this be so, it is certainly an exciting development, filling the gap left by the mythical tribe, but it appears to me that if they are the centres of study and even 'the greatest conceptual innovation' (*ibid.*), they are not yet the centres of theory, as applied anthropologists are frequently reminding us. Perhaps the study of creolization (*ibid.*: 84–5) and its further theoretical elaboration may supply the answer.

As with most ethnography, some elements of the Alur situation are distinctive but some are common elsewhere and some have already been reported by others. The witchcraft syndrome is absolutely protean and polythetic, defying any attempt at bounded definition.

Yet certain very profound logics recur again and again. It is very general in southern as well as northern Uganda for people to be deeply suspicious, perhaps paranoid, about success. 'There is no honest tradesperson,' is constantly being said, a view which bears hard on Muslims, who are strongly associated with trade in rural Uganda, especially since Idi Amin tried to redress the balance in their favour. That it corresponds with the capitalist fetishization of money and commodities is undeniable and this is one of the most potent aspects of global knowledge. Of successful farmers people ask, 'How could anyone succeed so much?' It is a case of *hybris*. The distinction between the real and the fetishized is quite clear. It is all right to build a house, however large, as long as you do it yourself with your kin, friends and neighbours. But if you do it with money, a fetishized substance over which no-one has any control, people will believe that you acquired wealth to do it through the power of witchcraft. 'The love of money is the root of all evil' is a favourite proverb, repeated every day. So successful women traders were thought by their *very success* to be killing other people's children. Consequently, when the AIDS pandemic blew up in Uganda, it was all those evil people who succeeded so much under Idi Amin who were thought to be responsible. Amin caused such destitution and desperation that everyone tried to become a trader to survive, so traders could no longer be so despised, although the prejudice remained. AIDS was associated with people who had gone on a 'pilgrimage of greed' (*magendo*, black-market profiteering). Traders always sought negative reciprocity, so they may well have cheated Bahaya on the main trade route from western Uganda into Tanzania. The Haya were reputed to be the most powerful witches (apart from the Zanzibaris), so they were believed to have punished the traders by bewitching them with AIDS, which was thought to serve them right. Any malady popularly linked to sexual excess was naturally associated with the Haya, who had been the only professional prostitutes in Kampala before 1960 (Southall and Gutkind 1957). The Rakai District of Buganda had the highest incidence of AIDS and it shared a common border with Buhaya. The earliest deaths from AIDS in Rakai were of traders in this border area west of Lake Victoria.

There are echoes here of the Tiv concept of talent (*tsav*) and its potentially evil power (Bohannan 1957: 162). In Nyakyusa the most successful traders were reputed to use witchcraft medicine to achieve success and wealth (Wilson 1959: 59). The bitter or dirty money reported by Parker Shipton for the Kenya Luo (1989) and by Sharon Hutchinson for the Sudan (personal communication) is an expression of a similar logic, having something in common with Taussig's devil in Latin America (1980: 94–6). For it is, of course, 'the difference between natural instruments of production and those created by civilization' so heavily belaboured by Marx. In this broad view, where the chief fetishizers are capitalist entrepreneurs rather than fantasized African savages, one of the worst elements in the gulf between the anthropologist and the other is overcome. If culture is better seen as creolization, witchcraft may be better seen like capitalist media magic as fetishism.

I have dealt here, among other things, with the decay of an indigenous system of belief and healing, brought about by the insidious penetration of colonial and global capitalism, fully recognizing that, paradoxically, some African systems of healing (the Yoruba, for example) have survived more strongly, for reasons that have not been properly investigated. These may even be held up by Western psychiatrists as examples of methods more successful than our own in dealing with human problems such as depression, now regarded as an increasingly serious scourge in the West, especially among the young, and cause of an alarmingly rising rate of suicide and attempted suicide, a symptom of the general malaise so constantly written about. But a naive Western admiration for exotic systems of healing forgets that they are all doomed by the spread of information age capitalism within which they can only survive as disembodied New Age curiosities.

Buganda is in many ways the polar opposite of Alur within the state of Uganda. It is the largest, most central and materially well-developed, wealthiest, most educated, best known, most written about and most influential. Here the forces of capitalism have obviously played much longer and more strongly than in Alur. Yet although the Ganda speak, read and write English more than the Alur or any other Ugandan people, their culture, certainly modifed, is much more securely preserved than that of the Alur. They are extremely proud of their ethnicity. Despite and because of their proficiency in English, there are far more published writings, scholarly, literary and popular books, pamphlets and newspapers in their language than in any other in Uganda. Ganda have even been able to disseminate their culture abroad. They have always had influential friends in Britain and have dominated the image of Uganda there, except when it was temporarily poisoned by Amin. There is even a regular Ganda cultural TV programme broadcast in Massachusetts and there is considerable air traffic to North America in Ganda cultural objects, baskets, drums and regalia to authenticate Ganda rituals overseas. A Ganda maidservant in Kampala has even developed an export in herbal powder for lengthening the labia minora. Young Ganda girls who had dropped this custom became nervous when Idi Amin said they must return to traditional culture, so the enterprising maidservant met a felt need, by coaching and demonstrating to university students and then, as her fame spread, generalizing her services to Ganda abroad and becoming an independent businesswoman. It would not be hard to think of other comparable examples, such as the Yoruba in London and New York, by contrast with the peoples of the Nigerian Plateau, who are almost unknown abroad and whose metropolis at home is dominated by other Nigerian peoples.

Is it then the general rule that cultures which are initially largest, strongest and closest to the forces of change survive best and those which are smallest, weakest and most remote do worst? This recalls Marx's suggestion that what India needed was not less capitalism but more. There are clearly different dimensions of cultural survival. It is a very different perspective from the old notion of uncontaminated cultures surviving in remote places.

For the Alur, there is a real question of whether their culture can survive in any significant form. As for Ganda culture, there is no question of its survival, though it is vastly transformed and, at least for anthropologists, some of its finest and most distinguished features have already gone, along with much that was colourful and exotic. For the French, the threat is obviously more distant but very real. Their seeming intransigence during the GATT negotiations was most deeply linked to their well-justified fear of cultural domination by the American global media Leviathan. Here is another strong band of continuity between the supposedly dominant and the dominated cultures, where global is local and local global. The paradox of late capitalism is that free trade and monopoly become equivalent on a global scale, in cultural as in all other products.

REFERENCES AND BIBLIOGRAPHY

Bohannan, P. (1957) *Justice and Judgment among the Tiv*, London: Oxford University Press.

Middleton, J. and Tait, D. (1958) (eds) *Tribes Without Rulers: Studies in African Segmentary Systems*, London: Routledge & Kegan Paul.

Nugent, S. (1988) 'The peripheral situation', *Annual Review of Anthropology* 17: 79–98.

Parkin, D. (1993) 'Nemi in the modern world: return of the exotic?' *Man* 28, 1: 79–99.

Shipton, P. (1989) *Bitter Money: Cultural Economy and some African Meanings of Forbidden Commodities*, Washington, DC: American Ethnological Society Monographs.

Southall, A. (1954a) 'Alur tradition and its historical significance', *Uganda Journal* 18, 2: 137–65.

—— (1954b) 'Belgian and British administration in Alurland', *Zaire* 5: 467–86.

—— (1956) *Alur Society: a Study in Processes and Types of Domination*, Cambridge: Heffer.

—— (1971) 'Spirit possession and mediumship among the Alur', in John Middleton and J.H.M. Beattie (eds.) *Spirit Mediumship and Society in Africa*, London: Routledge & Kegan Paul.

—— (1975) 'General Amin and the coup', *Journal of Modern African Studies* 13, 1: 85–105.

—— (1980) 'Social disorganization in Uganda', *Journal of Modern African Studies* 18, 4: 627–56.

—— (1988) 'The recent political economy of Uganda', in H.B. Hansen and M. Twaddle (eds) *Uganda Now: between Decay and Development*, London: James Currey.

—— (n.d.) 'Alur migrants', pp. 141–60, in A.I. Richards (ed.) *Economic Development and Tribal Change*, Cambridge: Heffer.

—— and Gutkind, P.C.W. (1957) 'Townsmen in the making. Kampala and its suburbs', *East African Studies* 9, Kampala: East African Institute of Social Research.

Taussig, M.T. (1980) *The Devil And Commodity Fetishism in South America*, Chapel Hill, NC: University of North Carolina Press.

Wilson, M. (1959) *Communal Rituals of the Nyakyusa*, London: Oxford University Press for the International African Institute.

Part II
Emerging world forms

'I know I am called to blow the trumpet for the Lord. . . . So I affiliated to the [. . .] whose moorings are in the USA.'

(*Evangelist in Madras to Lionel Caplan*)

3 Race, culture and – what?

Pluralist certainties in the United States

Paul Dresch

The 'new racism' became an issue in America in the mid-1980s. Responses at universities drew public comment. Indeed comment on such matters as curriculum change and speech codes outweighed that on events provoking these and general patterns informing them (e.g. *Economist* 10 Feb. 1990, *Esquire* Nov. 1990, *Los Angeles Times* 12 Feb. 1991). Yet discussing the issues at the colleges themselves is difficult. The rhetoric of 'anti-racism' is such that to question it is to lay oneself open to the charge of being racist; to question such tags as 'diversity' or 'multiculturalism' is to risk being thought an appalling bigot and perhaps to be marginalized in institutions that promote the terms.[1]

A prominent term is 'culture'. The presumption of bounded units has been dropped by anthropologists discussing the wider world. But at home, as it were, such 'cultures' are increasingly part of public imagery, as if foreign and domestic space alike were divided among discrete types of people. Their substance and their number are indeterminate. The term itself, though, is no surprise. Whether in America or Britain, 'culture' has in some respects filled in for 'blood', as ethnicity works discursively much as race once did (Just 1989) – 'I've nothing against them but their *culture*'s different'– and the usage of bar-room bores is currency with those who think themselves progressive: both accept a simple tie between persons and definitions. To examine how such terms are used I shall draw on newspaper clippings from Ann Arbor, Michigan, a college town in the news on these questions in the late 1980s. The inhabitants of the town itself number a little over 100,000. It is dominated by the university. The concordance of interest between university-based and town-based journalism is close.[2]

The terms used by public papers are important collective representations and part of the issue is the conflation of public and collective terms with personal identity. What 'members of the culture' think, in their little groups or individually, is irrelevant to much that happens.[3] The terms of the public world are reproduced in, for instance, student essays. These are littered with phrases such as 'racial heritage', 'ethnic identity' and (symptomatically) 'ethnic race'. Very much in the manner of the public prints, 'culture' is used in association with, for instance, skin-colour and biological descent:

> my mother is Hispanic (containing Incan Indian and Native American . . .). My father is German, English, French-Canadian and Swiss. . . . I often like to call myself the epitamy [sic] of the American Melting Pot. I am ashamed of none of my culture.[4]

The last line follows commonsensically, with a power exegesis could only lose. 'Maintaining your ethnic individualism is important,' 'Everyone's ethnic identity must remain intact,' and there is value in the different ideas of a 'diverse' group. 'Diverse' and 'diversity' intercut with 'culture' equally in accounts by those keen on difference and by those who find it deeply worrying.

DIVERSITY IN CONTEXT

By 1988 'diversity' had been taken up by the University of Michigan administration and was much promoted. The University President, it seems, used the word fifty-five times in thirty-five pages (*Daily* 12 Jan. 1989). More generally, it was central to a rhetoric of vast ambitions:

> We believe the University has a mandate to build a model of a pluralistic, multicultural community for our nation, an environment which . . . draws its intellectual strength from the rich diversities of peoples of different races, cultures, religions.[5]
>
> (*Record* 10 Oct. 1988)

And 16 January 1989 was declared 'Diversity Day'. This was intended to appropriate Martin Luther King Day, the celebration of which had been a demand of Black activists in the previous two years. The following year, 1990, 16 January again became MLK Day but within an official context of 'diversity' not everyone found sympathetic (*Daily* 11, 16 Jan. 1989; 15 Jan. 1990). Between about 1985 and 1990 there occurred a highly charged, highly visible, series of events which turned upon racist insults, very freely made accusations of racism and sexism and expressions of concern about freedom of opinion and of speech.[6] The pattern recurred in many places. Official policy at universities took such uniform shape as to form an orthodoxy.

The atmosphere was hardly eased in the Michigan case by poor relations between the university and the state government, or by chronic money problems ('Regents OK budget with $1.9 million deficit', *Record* 5 Aug. 1985; 'State leaves U-M budget "very tight" ', *News* 28 July 1988). This gave prominence to certain state-level politicians. More importantly, the university exemplified a widening of scale that is common in market systems, shown here by federal funds outweighing, in the end, state support (*Record* 28 Sept. 1992). The University's concerns were less with its immediate hinterland, therefore, than with what administrators referred to as 'peer institutions' and some 36–88 per cent of students were 'from out of state' (*News* 1 July, 3 Nov. 1987).

> Virtually all of the out-of-state students come from powerful schools, very well-funded schools in the richer neighbourhoods. . . .
>   The high schools are in the fancy suburbs of New York, New Jersey, Massachusetts, Pennsylvania.
>
> (*News* 7 June 1987)

Michigan has 'fancy suburbs' of its own. But the number of imported students raised concerns locally. An edge to debate was given by the prox-imity of this leafy academic enclave to Detroit, which exemplified in stark form the idea of a city dying before one's eyes: here were (predominantly Black) schools that were neither well-funded nor powerful, large parts of the middle classes having left the area. The state as a whole seemed scarcely in better shape as long-standing forms of automobile manufac-ture collapsed. Management largely stayed put (often in locations adjacent to Detroit), while production was dispersed to, for instance, Mexico and Texas.

Constraints and ambitions affecting an official response to the changing world were named by officialdom. The number of high-school graduates in Michigan was expected to drop by 19 per cent between 1988 and 1992, for instance, and the university wished to retain its 'market share' (*Record* 12 Dec. 1988). Nationwide, meanwhile, 'By the turn of this century, one third of college-age students will be Black or Hispanic.' And, with busi-ness interests in mind, 'the growing internationalization of America suggests that understanding cultures other than our own is necessary . . . for our very survival as a nation' (*Record* 10 Oct. 1988).[7] Home and abroad were proclaimed similar and the university was uniquely equipped to link them, master as it were of two worlds.

Universities are singular institutions. In the 1980s, as the gap between rich and poor widened and funds to support less wealthy students were cut, they stood out with clarity. At Michigan, at the time in question, 55 per cent of students' parents had an income of between $40,000 and $100,000 and the parental income of 10 per cent was $100,000 and more (*Daily* 15 Mar. 1989). The figures contrast with those for the surrounding state or the country at large (see Table 3.1). The public issues, however, were almost wholly those of 'women and minorities', particularly the latter: the rhetoric of justice had moved from wealth as an issue in itself, to wealth as the substance of group ranking, to group identities being much spoken of and wealth a subject not addressed.[8] It was said by those of socialist leanings (perhaps those threatened by the newer rhetoric) that, as with wider concerns of American society, the rhetoric of race and gender was yet another way not to talk of class. Certainly, the function of universities in defining an expanding middle class (see Bourdieu and

Passeron 1979: Epilogue) encountered the constraints of economic recession. Structural disadvantage became highly visible. Political rhetoric therefore stressed group identities running normal to the axis on which inequality itself was measured. Such identities are conventionally referred to as being or as having cultures.

Table 3.1 Percentage of families in different income brackets, 1989

Income Brackets	U-M students	Michigan	United States
$20,000 per annum	10	24	25
$20,000–40,000	25	31	32
$40,000–60,000	30	24	22
$60,000–100,000	25	16	16
>$100,000	10	5	5

Source: Figures from *Daily* 15 Mar., 18 Sept. 1989 and United States census 1990, tape files 3a and 3c

'Multiculturalism' reproduces in official form demands made against officialdom. Such demands retain the language of general ideology and turn it to new ends whereby, for instance, freedom of expression and prescriptive approval are identified without any sense of paradox: an Office of Minority Affairs 'would assure free cultural expression by promoting positive projections of the cultures, histories and activities of ethnic and racial minority groups' (*Daily* 19 Mar. 1987). The very language of numbers and 'representation', hence legitimacy, sways in new directions: 'To insist that administrators may define what counts as a racist act . . . is itself a racist policy. Such determination can only be made by a body representative of the entire campus, including a preponderance of people of color' (*Daily* 12 Apr. 1988), who at that time comprised about 15 per cent of the student body. Legitimacy within a previous regime was not wholly reducible to numbers either: 'that there are ten times as many Catholics as Jews is rarely seen as a reason for allotting influence in these proportions' (Wolff 1965: 14), let alone counting up all the Protestants, very different among themselves.[9] The proper form was not to count. The moral preponderance claimed in the new style, by contrast, involves an explicit stress on numbers. The categories are specific. That Blacks made up only 7 per cent or so (in 1987 only 5.3 per cent) of Michigan students and 12 per cent of the nation was a matter for public debate. To say 40 per cent or so of students are self-defined as Protestant (as are maybe 60 per cent of the nation) or 30 per cent as Catholic (25 per cent of the nation) would be thought eccentric; to pursue the folk belief that 30 per cent of undergraduates are Jewish (about 3 per cent of the nation) would in local terms be unthinkable. Contradictions between the interests of groups (some marked, some unmarked) determine the language in which problems may be trapped and managed. Between two regimes of public morals lie difficult ambiguities.

'Minorities', for their part, may be rolled together as 'people of color.'[10] But, numbers aside, the categories are not equivalent. A Black student notes, 'Whites often think that I come from some respectable suburb due to how I carry myself (my manner of speaking, for example). They find it hard to believe that I am ... from media-degraded Detroit.' Their assumption seems to be that Black Detroit must be low class. An Hispanic student, on the other hand, suggests, 'Asians were often adopted into the white culture easily because many of them were well off. They easily fit into the higher class lines.'

The relationship between race or ethnicity and class (at least differences in wealth; in local terms 'class' is addressed gingerly) is a perennial interest of American sociology. To address the question empirically is sometimes to take the categories too literally.[11] But the relation haunts political rhetoric. Through much of the 1980s the most interesting figure in national politics was Jesse Jackson, whose two campaigns for the Democratic nomination, reported often in terms of 'race', involved a refreshing bluntness: 'Fifteen percent of our nation is now in poverty. Thirty four million people, 23 million white and 11 million are black and brown. This is beyond race! Don't color poverty black or white or brown.'[12] What is striking about Jackson's rhetoric is how closely sectional identities and economic justice were interwoven. In university politics it was otherwise. Here 'ideology' is best not reduced to analysis of 'real' interests but addressed through considering, for example, rival 'narratives' (Rosaldo 1989: 73, 166). The economic overlap between universities and the surrounding world might be expected, however, to be the locus of more active protest. This overlap was clearly marked. Close to 50 per cent of a nationwide sample of Black students, for instance, were from families with incomes of less than $21,000 per annum (*News* 17 July 1988; only 10 per cent of Michigan students, of all sorts, fell into this income bracket). Black groups were conspicuous among protestors throughout the period. In the case at hand neither the form nor the vigour of protest is imaginable without them. But the terms of concern were broader.

One of the first 'racist incidents' to draw wide attention in the Michigan case was an Asian-American finding 'Die Chinaman, Hostile Americans want your [yellow?] hide' scrawled in his library carrel (late 1985). Two predominantly Jewish fraternities had suffered anti-Semitic graffiti. (This is the only case where group identity is invoked symmetrically; later we have graffiti saying 'Jew haters will pay', 'Long live Israel.') Fliers were slipped under doors, declaring 'open season' on Blacks and announcing 'darkies ... belong hanging from trees'. By April 1989 one finds the generic form: 'Faggots, niggers and spic-lovers – BEWARE!' Explicit protest on behalf of both the insulted and the under-represented centred, for its part, on a United Coalition Against Racism, UCAR. It was proper that the best known of the coalition's (Black) leaders would also write, 'Daily insensitive on rape issue' (*Daily* 6 Oct. 1987). The official response ('diversity') addresses difference of all sorts, as if everyone's problems are of a kind with those of Blacks, on whose political claims many groups in the last three decades have piggy-backed.[13]

PLURALISM

A singular claim (perhaps several more than one) is encompassed in a form of pluralism. Thirty years ago, in a period of economic optimism, Robert Wolff suggested that an important principle of American politics was less 'one man-one vote' than 'every legitimate group its share'.

> Any policy urged by a group in the system must be given respectful attention no matter how bizarre. By the same token, a policy or principle which lacks legitimate representation has no place in the society, no matter how reasonable or right it may be. Consequently the line between acceptable and unacceptable alternatives is very sharp, so that the territory of American politics is like a plateau with steep cliffs on all sides rather than like a pyramid. . . . The most important battle waged by any group in American politics is the struggle to climb onto the plateau.
>
> (Wolff 1965: 45)

This takes groups too much for granted. Pluralist politics will produce identities as much as incorporate identities to hand already. Quite which groups are formed or recognized also begs large questions (and for what purpose; these symmetries are not the whole of life). Yet Wolff is surely right that:

> at any given time the major religious, racial and ethnic groups are viewed as permanent and exhaustive categories into which every American can conveniently be pigeonholed. Individuals who fall outside any major social group – the non-religious, say – are treated as exceptions and relegated in practice to a second-class status. Thus agnostic conscientious objectors are required to serve in the armed forces, while those who claim even the most bizarre religious basis for their refusal are treated with ritual tolerance and excused by the courts.
>
> (*ibid.*: 41)

Wolff's privilege of the dissenting individual is of its time (see also *ibid.*: 37). The principle of selective legitimacy applies more broadly.

There are sets of people, conspicuous enough as sets to be called 'ethnic' were this the Pathan borderland (Barth 1969), whom the rhetoric of race and culture ignores. In this area of Michigan, for instance, certain poor whites were linked with each other by kinship and common geographic origin, distinguished by very noticeable accents and conspicuous for the solidity of their attachment to much that defines an underclass: no field-worker would have missed noting them.[14] One can hardly believe they were in less severe trouble than their Black economic equals. They were never a public issue. Poor Blacks, for their part, were not the subject of sustained attention. Local connections affecting them were aired, as in this piece by a member of the Black Student Union:

> A black student (especially from Detroit) can not call the University to task for its obligations to blacks without . . . making that same pro-test to the Detroit Board of Education. . . . Detroit schools are admin-istered by people who don't lose a minute of sleep worrying about how people graduate without knowing how to read or write. They don't miss a second of *The Cosby Show* worrying about the gross number of black dropouts. . . . You've got to go to the source. . . .
>
> How many blacks here have gone back to their junior highs to show these kids that there are alternatives?
>
> (*Daily* 5 Oct. 1987)

Such pleas for local action disappeared in the global rhetoric like twigs down a waterfall.[15] By far the more powerful imagery was that identifying individuals with categories of national and global scale. Ordinary people were stood at the centre of vast issues.

CATEGORIES AND PERSONS

The politics that drew attention to universities in the 1980s is dubbed by Charles Taylor (1992) 'the politics of recognition'. This is accurate ethno-graphically as well as analytically. The very term recurs throughout claims and counter-claims of the period. What must be recognized is an identity, which its partisans 'celebrate' among themselves and in public settings.[16] The domesticated, official version may include such features as a 'folk-loric dance troupe' directed by a 'senior programs analyst in the Office of the Registrar' ('U celebrates Hispanic Heritage Month', *Record* 8 Sept. 1992). Also, much celebration and protest is soon routinized: a picture of someone screaming fiercely – caption, 'A woman practices saying "no!" ' (*Daily* orientation issue, Summer 1993) – is what one expects. But in an earlier phase celebration released great collective energy. The energy was released against 'the white male', a figure not wholly imaginary but power-fully imagined,[17] and many public events were celebrations of reversed oppression in which everyone (white males included) could join.

The style of presenting and reporting such celebration became predictable. Toni Morrison, the famous Black author, visited:

> Smiling, Morrison, accepted a standing ovation before she began to speak. 'This is going to be good . . . but *long*', warned Morrison, who spoke for two and a half hours. . . . In her low-sung, punctuated

speech, Morrison used 'unspeakable things unspoken' as 'cannon-fodder', pointing her fire at white male cultural literacy. . . . Her idea of 'cannon defending canon' decried the white male measuring rod which has broken literary works that do not bend to fit the white mold of literature.

(Daily 10 Oct. 1988)

The complexities of Morrison's own great fame and enormous sales would not be addressed in a setting such as this.[18] The style is well known and of a sort open to satirists. But, to borrow Claud Cockburn's phrase, reality goes bounding past the satirist like a cheetah past a greyhound.

Audre Lord, a self-identified 'Black, feminist, lesbian, warrior, poet, mother', urged people in the University community last night to use their individual power to further social change in the world. . . . In a strong, lyrical voice, Lorde interspersed readings with strong statements. . . . A cancer survivor, Lorde says her struggle with cancer has empowered her.

('Poet speaks out about women's power', *Daily* 31 Mar. 1989)

The style of reporting owes more to *Reader's Digest* than to *Worker's Daily*. In familiar fashion, the individual speaker is an example to all and each may respond in a community of shared feeling: 'It's that sense of witnessing that has a lot of power' ('Women's studies ignore minority', *Daily* 2 Sept. 1986). The appeal is as much to the educated middle classes as to those in fact dispossessed, sometimes more so. Confusingly to some (e.g. *The Times Higher Education Supplement* 2 Mar. 1990), this asks to be taken seriously.[19]

In a world where no-one feels particularly safe and none can identify readily the source of their fear, the personal and collective merge persuasively. A very long piece from a professor in the linguistics department presents personal misery with embarrassing public candour. Towards the end she explains why she has written the piece now, not earlier. A woman of whom she approved had been denied tenure and, at the same time, 'my program director in linguistics has told me I cannot teach introductory and intermediate syntax next year. . . . That is, I've nothing important left to lose that he has the power to take away from me.' Events thus form a pattern. Of applications for tenure in the preceding year, throughout the university, it seems, half were successful in the cases of both male and female applicants; but 'if we want to see more women on this campus, why aren't we tenuring every single one . . . ? The answer is self-evident.' The public and the personal are indissoluble. 'I have a good self-image . . . yet whenever I talk to the director of my program, no matter what the issue, I get tense and afraid.'[20] The wrongs done particular people merge with the position of social categories in what Hughes (1993) tags a 'culture of complaint'.[21] The particular complainants may be unexpected;

the categories are broad and the fate of large groupings is felt by persons whose positions in the world are various. While experience may be heightened, the categories are flattened, each becoming equal to the others and internally uniform.

A feature of the rhetoric is the collapse of identifying terms from social organization onto individuals: '"Although King was a minority [not 'member of a minority group', note], his dream was to bring unity for everyone", said Ronald Maine, a member of the Black student union' (*Daily* 15 Jan. 1986). The generalized individual of public rhetoric and the real individual with a personal life fit together, as we know, persuasively. Collective identity involves similar ambiguities. Some identities may be grounded in biology (an important feature of women's groups), others in terms that place them as much beyond question. The most prominent of these is culture:

> by definition Asian-Americans are a new culture because we have different experiences from anyone else in the world. . . .
> Walking down the street for me is a completely different experience than what it is for a white American.
>
> (*Daily* 31 Jan. 1986)

Culture naturalizes identity. One can imagine identities formed *ex nihilo*, then filling with distinctive ways of life, as perhaps with colonial 'tribes' in Africa (Ranger 1985) or American immigrants (Herberg 1983): they become, as it were, 'real' to those within and those without. In this case no comparable 'filling' has happened yet.[22] The naturalization is instead rhetorical and moral, the assertion that an identity is more than voluntary association – more, that is, than a 'clique' (see Moffat 1986: 164). The proof is experience. None can argue with another's experience and to question whether the experience of several 'others' is congruent is inadmissible. To doubt, reciprocally, whether one's fellows in a group share one's personal experience raises questions only about oneself.

Some categories are mutually exclusive, others are complementary. Women, for instance, appear in every category but male. The language of competitive disadvantage produces multiple bids. 'Very few institutions exist to celebrate their achievements. . . . It is vitally important to celebrate Black women, who are doubly excluded from society's recognitions and rewards' (*Daily* 18 Jan. 1989). Arithmetic here leads to contradiction: by comparison with women in general, Black women suffer disproportionately; by comparison with Blacks in general, women escape lightly. The addition would be simpler with the claim that 'Gay Black men suffer a double burden of discrimination and are isolated from the Black community . . . ; as a Black gay man I have issues and concerns that are different from a white gay man' (*Daily* 19 Jan. 1989) but the fragmentation of claims here begins to undermine their practical, though not rhetorical, force. (Audre Lorde covered all the bases.)

Neither addition nor subtraction is intended literally. However, the language at issue is in general underpinned by an idea of bounded sets whose overlaps might define sub-sets:

> There is one group of people that, thus far, has not become vocal on this diverse campus. Ironically this group is the most truly diverse group of people found in our society . . .
>
> We are the products of people who have ventured across the racial lines: we are people of multi-racial heritage. . . . We are not celebrated by a special day or week . . .
>
> Because we are scarred, we are compassionate. We can usually relate to all races and ethnic groups with this compassion. We are used to being multi-cultural; it is natural to us.
>
> ('Affirm multiracial heritage', *Daily* 29 Mar. 1989)

The elision of race and culture is almost standard. The elision of group and individual, their presumed concordance of type, deserves noting. The 'multicultural individual' is conceived as part of a group (defined here by its heterogeneity); the group (as such and as yet, invisible) must be recognized by the society at large; and the knot between group and individual is tied by appeal to what is fatal, which is birth. Much has been made and rightly so, of the image of choice in marketing and popular culture (see e.g. Beeman 1986). The denial one has a choice is at least as powerful. Here is an offence to individualist values, where experience may cluster in powerful forms.

A long features piece ('Multiracial Americans strive for clearer sense of who they are', *News* 18 July 1988) suggests how inexorably the categories are reproduced. The bid for legitimation is less to be expected. A person whose father was a Black American soldier and whose mother was Korean, for instance, is quoted as wanting a new category on things like census forms: 'A new classification would provide a group identity for multiracial people. Being able to check a box on a form that acknowledged their varied racial and cultural background would end the feeling of isolation' (*ibid.*). Note again the apposition of racial and cultural. But the idea that one's isolation might be lessened by the layout of official forms is striking. Between the global and the personal nothing intervenes, as though no-one has family, friends or workmates. Someone else, a Spanish-Korean American, reports: 'People of monoracial background say, "Well, you have a choice. You can pick black, white or Hispanic. What's the big deal?" ' but then he feels by making any such choice he is rejecting half his family [*sic*]. To treat people as 'just people' would by these standards be extremely difficult.

Even where the choice of identity is to some degree open there is pressure not to decline a choice and identities are in no doubt to those promoting them. The period 14–26 September 1987 was designated 'Hispanic heritage week'. This coincided with a visit by Jesse Jackson mediating part of the local dispute over 'racism'. Unfortunately an attempt by the Executive Officer of the Coalition of Hispanics for Higher Education to reach the University President on Jackson's coat-tails led Jackson to tell him, 'Get your own agenda.' The Hispanics were thus slighted by the Blacks and seemingly by everyone else:

> As an Hispanic student . . . I find the *Daily*'s failure to recognize the Hispanic event and moreover the Hispanic populous [*sic*] at this University highly offensive. It is my opinion that this is just another blatant example of how Hispanics . . . are being overlooked.
>
> (*Daily* 24 Sept. 1987)

Who are these Hispanics? The writer of this angry letter was later quoted on the problem: 'part of a lack of Hispanic unity is that many Hispanics fail to identify with their ethnic background. "I think a lot of Hispanics don't recognize they're Hispanic," she said' (*Daily* 29 Sept. 1987). A further contributor went on to say, 'I know of Hispanic students who have never met other Hispanics except in class.'[23] This is not surprising if so many are as little obvious as the silent majority. Even where the markers might be thought more obvious, however, there is no guarantee of solidarity: 'Asians', for instance, are not reliably a 'solidary' group. An in-group language of betrayal has long been available in the form of such tags as 'oreo-cookie' and 'banana' (white on the inside, respectively black or yellow on the outside; if an Hispanic equivalent exists, it has not acquired wide currency). The degree to which such language sticks, as it were, varies greatly from case to case; the degree to which it is stuck to one varies more. But the constraints are supposedly comparable for all.[24]

Scale adds further complications. Hispanics apparently made up 8.1 per cent of the US population in 1988 and were concentrated in certain states: 33.9 per cent of them in California, 21.3 per cent in Texas (*News* 7 Sept. 1988). Ann Arbor, it was said, counted Hispanics as only about 3 per cent of its population and the university only 2 per cent. The Co-chair of the Hispanic group there, who had grown up in Laredo ('95 per cent Mexican-American' by one account), was quoted as follows: 'My brother explained to me the need for Hispanics up north and if anybody was going to increase [the number], I should be one of them' (*Daily* 18 Nov. 1987). The university, by contrast, might apologize that it lags behind Berkeley on Asian numbers but Berkeley has more Asians immediately to hand, or that other institutions in Michigan have more Native Americans.

PERSONS IN SPACE

The fact the language of pluralism is delocalized requires more thought than it receives. If one is locally short of some category of people, one can skip the immediate surroundings and look for them elsewhere: so

Michigan, for instance, can turn to neighbouring Illinois ('UM recruits minorities in Chicago', *News* 13 Nov. 1989). Increasing the number of Black students proved difficult at first. Hiring Black faculty, however, received great emphasis. Claims were plausibly made that progress on this front derived from recent policy but a disappointing total 'reflects the competitive market conditions under which faculty of color are recruited'.[25] One must simply spend more. Notoriously, the composition of institutions may then change though the total pool of applicants is no wider than before, and market exchanges are not symmetrical. A Michigan dean, for instance, famously misspoke: 'Our challenge is not to change this University into another kind of institution where minorities would naturally flock in greater numbers. I need not remind you that there are such institutions, including Wayne State University and Howard University.'[26]

A serious row ensued. In contrast, no row ensues from the claim that qualifications are needed 'whether the degrees come from U-M, Michigan State, Wayne State or by mail' (*Record* 25 Jan. 1993). Students from 'the fancy suburbs' are not, one gathers, flocking to Wayne State. Yet the language of group equality treats successful institutions as points of insertion for concerns that are somehow everywhere and nowhere. A 'material' analysis becomes oddly difficult.

A strand of Harvey's (1989) presentation of recent history is that capital's control of space locates labour in particular places. The argument holds when labour is dispersed to capitalists' advantage: the political base once provided by industrial areas is swept away. Harvey accounts admirably for the weakening of class politics. His treatment of more recent concerns is formulaic. The oppressed are as one: 'colonized peoples, blacks and minorities, religious groups, women, the working class' (*ibid.*: 49); 'women, blacks, colonized peoples, minorities of all kinds' (*ibid.*: 104); 'blacks, women, ethnic minorities of all kinds' (*ibid.*: 152); 'racial minorities, colonized peoples, women etc. . . . are relatively empowered to organize in place but disempowered when it comes to organizing over space' (*ibid.*: 303). 'Multiculturalism' presents the opposite view. Only in space does it flourish freely, or rather at 'nodes' that connect more immediately to one another than each to its hinterland.[27] Quite privileged people can speak as (not for) the oppressed and the global can be absorbed in the merely personal.

Activists were aware of the dangers. They returned continually to questions of financial support and of brute numbers. A. Sivanandam was quoted on 'how authorities attempt to turn institutionally based racial conflict into a question of attitudinally based "cultural diversity" ' (*Daily* 19 Nov. 1987).[28] Whatever note was taken of this, it did not much affect the rhetoric. 'Attitudes' are a feature of claims from several sides at the start of the issue. They remain so to the end. Offences illustrate 'institutional racism' (or 'sexism'; the two often go together) but are treated as if they derive from personal wickedness, corresponding to a general tendency for disagreement with any norm to be seen as denoting a 'type' of person. Accusations against teachers and officials, therefore, result not only in silence from the authorities (these have nothing to gain from taking a position) but in personal testimony: 'this is not the so-and-so I have known for so many years' (see e.g. *Daily* 29 Jan. 1988; 6, 11 Jan. 1989). Symmetrically, concerns and accusations are usually prefaced with the compound form, 'As a whatever, I think (or I feel, or I am) . . .'[29]

The personal is a feature of the protests as much as of the official response, forming, one suspects, the common terms in which claims find their wide legitimacy. This is no longer quite the 'new ethnicity' of the 1960s (Glazer and Moynihan 1963, 1975). The latter word itself is rather little used. Indeed 'ethnic' claims are now part of a rhetorical set that also includes at least sexual identities and even identities based on sexual preference, a single language being used of all. There are persons in each of them.

Blacks, to take the most striking case, are rhetorically lost among the others. Whether or not one cares to accept the identity (many might reject the terms), statistically Blacks in America are in awful shape: their death-rate was 38 per cent above that of whites in 1975 and 48 per cent above that of whites ten years later; notoriously, homicide is a major cause of death (the leading cause for young Black males in Michigan), some thirteen times the corresponding white rate; Black babies are twice as likely as white to die in their first year (*News* 14 Apr. 1988) and so on (e.g. *News* 17 July 1987; 15 Jan., 17 July, 23 May 1988). The rhetoric fails to match the case. The formal equality of identities recognized ignores the inequalities both within these sets and between them. The problems of Asians, let us say, are notoriously not those of Blacks; those of college professors are not those of the unemployed, and sex cross-cuts the categories of 'race' and class. But for some people difference of any kind is suspect:

> Due to the recent outbursts of racist incidents being overly publicized . . . I feel that it is imperative that certain masked issues be addressed. . . . I believe the next step to putting an end to racism against Blacks is to integrate Blacks and Whites and make them both . . . *totally equal*. . . .
>
> It disgusts me when I pick up the *Daily* and read "University to Recruit More Minorities." What exactly does this mean? . . .
>
> [T]hese groups do not realize what they will have to give up to achieve equality. But then one must wonder again – is it equality that they really want or is it supremacy?
>
>   ('Will this madness ever stop?' *Daily* 19 Mar. 1987)

The letter contains a quotation (to good to be true, one almost thinks) from Ayn Rand, prophet of the individual will. Group claims and rights take their form in a wider setting.

DIFFERENCE IN A WORLD OF SAMENESS

Egalitarian ideologies, as Dumont long ago suggested, pose problems of how to conceive difference,[30] and around this turn several strands of rhetoric: the slogan 'separate but equal' offends the liberal mind (one knows what it has meant in practice), while equality to the less liberal mind implies uniformity, the flouting of which gives deep offence. Wolff mentions 'the bearded and be-sandalled "beat" ' (1965: 37). The prominence of individual 'misfitting' in the later 1960s (underway, indeed, when Wolff wrote) requires no comment. But the principle adduced for individuals in the face of dominant groups applies as much to 'communities of equals'; as in high-schools, for instance, where 'cliques' seem statistically the norm and morally suspect to all but those within them.[31]

The same applies at the next stage of mass education, that of undergraduate life. This has been written about by Michael Moffat (1986, 1989), who previously worked in India and helped translate Dumont's main ethnographic monograph. Moffat's account of New Jersey undergraduates develops the point that the ideal is of 'natural', 'friendly' manners, whereby the group is unstructured and entirely undifferentiated.[32] Moffat does not use the term but *communitas* comes strongly to mind. Difference, even separation, is thus problematic and privacy is cause for bafflement ('I try to be friendly but ...' – Moffat 1986: 166, 168). The theme recurs in a Michigan features piece on attitudes towards students from the New York area, stereotypically Long Island. A local student

> says he tries to be friendly to out-of-staters but sometimes he doesn't seem to get anywhere. . . . 'It seems, for some reason, that they don't really want to hang out with you that much. . . . So I feel uncomfortable because I'm like, Why can't I get to know you?'
>
> (*Daily* 20 Feb. 1987)

Identities introduced into such a field acquire a distinctive quality, being not only everywhere and nowhere but simultaneously present and absent. The point is neatly illustrated in one of Raymond Chandler's letters, dated January 1950:

> I don't see how you can expect the Jews not to be oversensitive but at the same time I don't see why I should be so unnaturally considerate of this oversensitiveness as never to use the word Jew. . . . It really seems at times that the Jews ask too much of us. They are like a man who insists upon being nameless and without an address and yet insists upon being invited to all the best parties.
>
> (MacShane 1981: 208)

The Jewish-American case is in many respects 'modern', prefiguring more general patterns by often several decades.[33] The same problem faces an identity that has more recently become an explicit part of the American scene: 'What does it mean to be an Arab-American today? I guess it means a number of things. It means keeping alive your cultural identity just as other ethnic groups do. It also means dismantling stereotypes' ('Arab-Americans face prejudice', *Daily* 30 Mar. 1988). Where the identity at issue can rest upon something as little complex as ancestry, the markers recognized as 'cultural' from within may be precisely those 'stereotyped' from without. A student account of life in the dorms quotes a Black student to the effect that whites stereotype Blacks as *inter alia* 'good dancers' and 'passionate'. Some pages later the first speaker's (Black) neighbour is quoted: 'When U of M won the NCAA [basketball] championship, many African Americans danced in the streets; Whites demolished stores and flipped cars. We are a passionate people – we often express ourselves through dance and song.'[34] A distinctive set of silences ensues whereby what is said of a group from inside must not be said from outside, though the imagery (usually vacuous, as here) is shared. Insider terms are notoriously touchy. The very existence of a group may in public be occasion for careful silence. Indeed, much that an ethnographer elsewhere would write about as obviously important (in older ethnographic style, 'Chapter One: The People and the Country') is proscribed.

The idea of a 'majority culture' fails to catch this quality. Moses Mendelsohn's advice to be a Jew at home and a German on the street is inapplicable if the street, as it were, is all there is, which popular sociology (Riesman *et al.* 1950; Whyte 1956; Lasch 1979) has suggested for decades is increasingly the case. The tension between group identity and individualist ideology might once have been handled by hierarchies of context: 'on this view it is necessary to make a certain number of distinctions – between what is public and private, for instance' (Taylor 1992: 62). The idea behind 'bananas' and 'oreo-cookies' is that such distinctions are not the most important. Unless authority is to erase identity, the private inside should properly face outwards.[35] The 'multicultural' idea is similar, although the place of authority is not in fact that of subordinate groups (again authority disappears from view), and in public institutions the 'private' sphere may be claimed to be a liberty conceded, not a right on which collective forms are built.

The implication of this was presented by the *Daily* as dawning with apparent suddenness. The university, not for the first time, tried to impose a general conduct code on students, this time with the aid of 'multiculturalism' and 'diversity'. This was denounced as:

> a unilateral attempt to divide students by confusing the issue of administrative control of life outside the classroom and the problems of racism, sexism and anti-gay bigotry; . . . a cheap power grab designed to cover up institutional racism and the racist views of the University administration.
>
> (*Daily* 11 Jan. 1988)

Or, more vigorously put, 'the vaguest, nastiest, most obnoxious code . . . to date; the loudest "fuck you" . . . in years' (*Daily* 8 Sept. 1988). The interesting feature of the proposal, for the present purpose, was precisely its division of space: one could say more or less what one wished (First Amendment-fashion) in a 'public forum'; in academic centres (classrooms etc.) one should not 'stigmatize' or 'victimize'; in halls of residence the greatest care should be taken not to wound or give offence (*Record* 5 June 1989). The most private of spaces from the students' viewpoint – one marked ideally by rough informality (Moffat 1986) – was that most closely controlled in public terms; the freedom associated with informal friendship was sanctioned in impersonal space frequented by the likes of campus evangelists.

Again authority declined the option of explicit rules. A pamphlet on 'What students should know about discrimination' warned that disciplinary action would follow behaviour that, for instance, 'creates a hostile or demeaning environment'. No test of this was spelled out. On the last page students were told, alarmingly to many, that 'Experience at the University has been people almost never make false complaints.' Various attempts to codify behaviour and speech were struck down by the courts. Though attempts showed perseverance ('faculty briefed on draft 12.2 of student rights statement', *Record* 12 Oct. 1992), the goal was in the end despaired of. As one strategy declined, so others rose: an initiative to have students volunteer support for a code, promotion of sundry classes and symposia, the establishment of 'dialogue groups' and suggestions of compulsory training for such employees as librarians. Much of this might seem less to do with 'ethnicity' than with the management of institutions.[36]

The image of spontaneous protest disrupting, even overturning, a system of control is attractive (quite empowering in itself, e.g. *Daily* 16 Jan. 1989) until one considers how widely shared are the terms and how little upset are those holding power. In the minor case of universities, administrators have been keener on, let us say, 'diversity' than have most students. In the wider world, opposition to such ideas has an almost archaic flavour.[37] Even the idea of separatism, fairly prominent in Black rhetoric, need occasion little inconvenience: 'A cohesive Black community, operating at full capacity would represent a formidable economic entity . . . would white America really want an empowered, ethnocentric Black community, another sector of competition rich in resources?' (*Daily* 24 Jan. 1989). Yet the modern market works through sectors, created as much as exploited by complex (quite impersonal) structures of capital. The marketers are there already. Budweiser beers, for example, run a series of advertisements featuring 'great African rulers', the commissioned paintings for which feature kings and pyramids.[38] A magazine called *Hispanic* (with Linda Ronstadt on the cover) turns up in supermarkets. Advertising takes 'diversity' for granted, with the billboards for products often changing cast, as it were, from one part of a city to the next; as indeed might the front office, then middle management, less easily the shareholders.[39] Fatality and choice are, at this level, one. The divisions proposed as natural feel entirely real.

Social structure (specifically, class structure) may change little as the 'cultural' patina shifts and the fracturing of a 'dominant ideology' is not a wholly convincing claim here. Rather, the dominant ideology and the discourse it validates have themselves mutated. The rapidity of the process has been impressive. The coherence of the new public rhetoric is as great as that of the old, the room for dissent or difference as small.

The prominence of 'lesbian and gay male' identity is the most striking case. Male homosexuality, at least, was surely one of the great taboo unmentionables of American public life (one would sooner have confessed to communism) but the identity has been institutionalized with rather little fuss. Indeed the ritual respect of the general press means any man who prefers sex with other men is 'gay' prescriptively. As Wolff pointed out, the terms change faster than the game:

> There is a very sharp distinction in the public domain between legitimate interests and those which are absolutely beyond the pale. . . . With bewildering speed, an interest can move from 'outside' to 'inside' and its partisans, who have been scorned by the solid and established in the community, become presidential advisers and newspaper columnists.[40]
>
> (Wolff 1965: 43–4)

Recasting the public categories is, by this account, not fundamental; nor is the prominence of the personal new in itself, whether in the lodging of moral claims or in the control of institutions.[41] What is new is a redistribution of personal and public. Homosexuality is exemplary. An area almost prescriptively private (the very model, one might think, of an issue to be approached in terms of individual rights) is a criterion of membership in a public category. The categories are rhetorically equal – gay, Black, Asian, Hispanic, female – much as Wolff describes, though the sum of personal disadvantage within these sets is, in older terms of wealth and power, unequal, even incommensurable. To invoke inequalities in the older mode becomes cause in the new mode for grave offence.

DIFFERENCES ARE ALL THE SAME

'Diversity day' was proclaimed in 1989. Going back to the *Daily* for the time one finds, among the official language, angry imagery and comment to the effect that the (Black) group whose day it was had been dispossessed, their day co-opted. The *Record* deals hesitantly with the claims of groups. Four years later the image of MLK Day in the *Record* (11 Jan. 1993) is very different. The 'MLK Symposium Planning Committee

Events' listed number eleven. Three now include in their titles the term 'dialogue', of which the first is ' "Creating multicultural spaces: student voices." A panel of intergroup dialogue facilitators talk about their experiences working with differences on campus.' Four others deal with Africa (the weight of an issue leaves its trace in numbers). Near the head of the list comes a less expected entry: ' "Executive summary: total quality management and diversity." Wayne Wormley, American Institute for Managing Diversity Inc.'

Quality management has achieved a good deal of space. Unfortunately it is hard to follow merely from press cuttings but some insight might perhaps be given by the last of the *Records* in my collection (7 June 1993). Again, this is a world of few explicit rules, wherein authority, although by no means absent, takes the form of mediation and exhortation that is common in 'an era of resource constraints.'[42] Group identities might prove valuable, if only for self-defence. The older hierarchies of work are proclaimed by those controlling them to be not reliable.

> All of us are living and learning 'in permanent whitewater' and we can choose to be either the battered log that gets jammed against the river's edge ... or the 'go-with-the-flow' log that continues downstream. ...
>
> Individuals with high self-esteem who feel good about themselves ... and who are assertive adjust to change much more easily. ...
>
> Other things to try while developing a positive attitude [include], use prayer and/or meditation [and] read a positive book.[43]

The stress upon the individual is hardly less in the image presented of dialogue-facilitators at work: in dialogue groups students were 'able to learn about themselves as individuals and about other groups'; 'It was really a big challenge to create an environment where people felt confident enough to share themselves' (*Record* 25 Jan. 1993). The language of diversity comes close to that of longer-established 'professional development' (even 'personal development'). There are cases one would hesitate to parse:

> This year's People of Color conference is dedicated to drawing upon people of color from various cultures so that we can continue to strengthen ourselves and emerge as a powerful force in this society. ...
>
> 'Globally Pulling our Cultures Together: Positioning Ourselves to Empower, Impact and Excel' is the conference theme.
>
> (*Record* 15 Feb. 1993)

The language should not mislead one (the local paper can head a social note, 'orthodontist hailed'; there is nothing special here). But the use of 'cultures' occurs in a setting rather different from that underlying American anthropology's concerns, some decades back, with 'cultural relativism'.

Twenty years ago, David Schneider was quoted to the effect that (white) American ethnic groups were 'desocialized': 'the cultural *content* of each ethnic group ... seems to have become very similar to that of others but the emotional significance of attachment to the ethnic group seems to persist' (Glazer and Moynihan 1975: 8). In other words, only the identity and rather arbitrary 'markers' distinguish one such from another (see Barth 1969).[44] Apart from sub-cultures (tattoo-freaks, low-riders, leather-fetishists), there may indeed be 'content' to groups of many sorts, there may indeed be 'culture'. But the site of the term's main use is now the public domain where, whatever one brings to it, the same representations are used by all. Rather than quasi-autonomous units 'misfitting' in some degree the dominant rules, the rules now *establish* differences of which they themselves are not explicitly part. Race and culture are simply 'there'.

An alternative language of social analysis is turned completely inside out. A speaker from the United Automotive Workers union, for instance, derived class society from racism and sexism:

> The white male power structure has shaped a nation that excludes women and minorities. ... The bottom line is who controls the land and its resources and that is the white male. ... Because white males have perpetuated certain myths and economic ideals throughout U.S. history, other groups have been unable to shake off the effects, creating a class system. ...
>
> ('UAW leader shares tips to fight racism, sexism',
> *Record* 13 Mar. 1989)

This view of American history appears in the University of Michigan's official newsletter. Some idea of the world in which the *Record* operates is given by an earlier piece in the same issue, 'Ford funds scholarships for women and minorities', in which we are told Ford has given $5.5 million to various colleges and that the University of Michigan has acquired $200,000 from this: 'Each school must give priority to Ford employees ...; the grants are the result of a 1980 conciliation agreement between Ford and the US Equal Opportunities Commission.' As a sign said on a local factory, 'Ford and UAW – Working Together'. Many are now not working at all, unfortunately, as the car industry undergoes 'restructuring' and jobs are exported elsewhere.[45]

The labour aristocracy that provided an important instance of 'white male power' disappears almost before the rhetoric of race and gender (colour and sex, to be less genteel) can reach it.[46] Clearer oppositions, in these terms or others, might be expected to take practical form as new social patterns solidify: a politics may emerge, commensurate with labour's problems or nowadays with those of the marginally employed. On the other hand, the present way of seeing the world may prove persuasive. The reasons for taking universities seriously are thus compelling, for they provide a model of post-industrial and post-liberal politics where much of the reality politics once addressed has been written out: the bottom sections of the social pyramid are seldom present. If certain new political interests resemble 'Marxism without the economics', here is a setting imposing few constraints.[47]

The passage cited above ('UAW leader shares tips') accords with many people's common sense. One finds students, for example, good-naturedly (and doubtless in good faith) attributing colonialism simply to 'racist attitudes' and all forms of inequality are perceived in a uniform shade of grey: 'To separate issues of racism from issues of sexism, homophobia and classism is ignoring the ways in which all of these are connected and doing a disservice to everyone' (*Daily* 13 Jan. 1989). One could not say this statement is wrong. One cannot, though, go far with the idea of 'classism' before encountering specific problems; nor, one would have thought, can differences among the problems listed be postponed indefinitely.[48] Yet if capitalism is the result of myth and class inequality might succumb to campaigns against prejudice, the personal is also the crux of history. 'Week focuses on Hispanic women' (*Daily* 8 Sept. 1988), for instance, cited a speaker whose father was a cane-cutter and whose mother was a factory-hand in Puerto Rico: 'this week we are celebrating and yes, this week we are challenging ourselves and each other as a strong and noble people to reach great heights'. The commentary then explains that 'this problem extends beyond the millions of Hispanic women and is a personal history for Tirado' (the speaker). Those for whom 'beyond' suggests the opposite direction, from the personal to the fate of millions, are suspected of bad faith.

Very much as in the earlier account of Audre Lorde's speech, personal testimony requires a personal response: 'Look: when we stretch our muscles, it hurts; but (if done correctly) we are not inflicting pain on ourselves, rather we are releasing pain stored in our bodies. The mind works the same way' (*Daily* 13 Jan. 1989). Those of dominant groupings may thus adjust themselves to others. Others may adjust themselves by similar means. A certain stress on individual character is part of any politics: Jesse Jackson included routinely in his speeches lines such as 'Just because you were born in the slum does not mean the slum was born in you', and drew to the polls a great many people who had never voted.[49] In the organized version of diversity, however, the idea floats free of the immediate structures to which originally it responded. At the official 1993 MLK celebrations the opening address was given by 'author Bebe Moore Campbell':

> We must love ourselves back to emotional health first and economic well-being will follow. . . .
> The future of African-American families lies in self-love and self-healing, not in government loans and enterprise zones.
>
> (*Record*, 25 Jan. 1993)

Good news for those who govern America.

WHY WE HAVE CULTURES

Individualism has quirks of its own, not uniformly covered by general literature. But the rhetoric remains such that individual and group are defined with clarity, being placed always in either apposition or opposition.[50] What might have served as mediating terms instead become aligned with the terms opposed. 'Culture' is the main instance. It is this which inserts one in 'dialogue', one culture against another, while accounting for who one is in terms beyond further question.

Explaining the folk sociology of New Jersey undergraduates, Moffat (1986: 169) writes of 'culture' as 'a way of going to another level of analysis' than those of friendship or racial difference: it would avoid the contradiction between the value of undifferentiated *communitas* and the fact we are not all the same. In some circumstances the terms 'race' and 'culture' may indeed be differentiated, 'culture' being more polite. In other circumstances, as we have seen, there is no real distinction made between culture, race and ethnic group. All are items in a rhetoric of pure difference. This is not to say all such terms are identical. Their use may, when context allows, be transparent coding: 'race' by itself will mean simply Blacks;[51] 'minorities' will mean 'Blacks and Hispanics' (people of, say, Chinese ancestry are counted in or out quite whimsically); 'ethnic group' is a term that more readily stands for Italians, Irish, Poles and others whose differences within the category 'white' are confined to very limited situations.[52] Were the categories consistently applied like this and admitted to be incommensurable, the language of pluralism would collapse. Muddle is essential to public language. The muddle is evident in official tables listing data 'by race' where the 'racial' categories are in fact those of affirmative action: Black, Asian, Native American, Hispanic and white. Constructing almost any sentence around 'the XYZ race', inserting the terms on offer, drops one into the world of Sax Rohmer's Fu Manchu books.[53]

Culture has a sense of the personal, yet works to the same pattern: indeed it restores one earlier feature of 'race', that at least 'everybody had one' (Tonkin *et al.* 1989: 15), as well as promising for the moment that all are again of equal worth. But you cannot, rhetorically, be without one. Though compound uses may pair the term with an antidote to misapplication, the term by itself seems to refer to a quality of individuals. It assigns them their identity.[54] We are what we are. You are what you are. What connections we may have are, at bottom, contingent for we are persons of different types.

A certain irony should be found in the fact that culture, in its current sense, was invented as the opposite of race and as a means of denying the idea of racial fate. The outcome is suggested by Stocking's famous papers on the subject (1968): 'race' acquired a biological rationale in the late nineteenth century and a critique was mounted of its formal misfit with the data; to the remnants of biological fact was added (prematurely) a second layer, 'culture', to account for the residue biology left unexplained. The idea of race was left untouched. Common usage recuperates the division, taking the added term as a polite equivalent of the term in place already, much as happened latterly with sex and gender.[55] Moffat, the anthropologist, implies some improvement would be wrought if anthropology were better known: 'Notably missing was the idea that culture can fundamentally determine habitual modes of thought and deeply affect behavior' (1986: 171). In fact that idea, whatever the terms used, is embedded firmly.

Differences in manners, which govern interaction in public space, are assimilated to differences in substance, fundamentally dividing types of people. Local students' discomfort with Long Islanders, touched on earlier (see also *News* 10 Sept. 1987), drew this commonsense comment from a psychology professor: 'I expect that it gets mixed in with Midwestern attitudes to Jewish people, because most of the New Yorkers here – or certainly a large number – are Jewish and they have very different cultures' (*Daily* 20 Feb. 1987). Yet there are Jews in the Mid-West and New Yorkers who are not Jews. It is as well one remembers this, for around the psychologist's suggestion are in fact set rather blunt (rather worrying) assertions of disproportionate wealth, disdain for others and what students call 'obnoxious' behaviour. In this minor case, as much as in that of 'Black culture' versus white, at the point where people interact the issues that in fact divide them become unspeakable.

Paradoxically, the appeal to culture suggests a world where mutual stereotypes would be taken as true, though spoken of only in formal 'dialogue'. Case by case, each culture in isolation, one might echo the Edwardian literati and describe this as 'true inwardness'. As part of a general rhetoric, however, it puts us all on a level again, all different in the same way. And all conveniently separate. The identity comes first. The naturalizing substance follows and thereafter there is no discussion.

> '[Asian-American culture]'s not a mixture of the two and it's not measurably one or the other. It's completely separate. ...'
>   'It is easier to explain what Asian-American culture is not than what it is. Because so few people acknowledge its existence, few people can identify it.'
>
>   (*Daily* 31 Jan. 1986)

And the reduction to absurdity, though no-one must say so:

> 'It's a good opportunity for people who are gay and bisexual to know about their culture and to feel validated', said business school senior Mark Chekal, president of the Lesbian and Gay Business Association.
>   (*Daily* 29 Mar. 1989)

CONCLUSION

Charles Taylor (1992), having removed contemporary concerns to the safer ground of past philosophers (Rousseau, Kant, Hegel), argues that the decline of hierarchical values involved a shift from concepts of unequal honour to those of equal dignity and respect and thus of 'recognition'.[56] The same argument that applies to persons applies, he says, to 'cultures'.

> As a presumption, the claim is that all human cultures that have animated whole societies over some considerable stretch of time have something important to say to all human beings. I have worded it this way to exclude partial cultural milieux within a society, as well as short phases of a major culture.
>
> (1992: 66)

Partial cultural milieux, to follow such terms, are the problem Taylor chose (or was asked) to address. The place of groups constituted by subordination or by inclusion in a market-system is not, one might think, that of pre-colonial India or China. But the author expresses no doubt that the objects of his moral scrutiny exist independently. If the questions are more pressing now it is simply because the objects have intermingled: 'all societies are becoming increasingly multicultural, while at the same time becoming more porous' (*ibid.*: 64).[57]

From an anthropologist's viewpoint the important thing about America, in this connection, is that 'porosity' is *not* the issue. The axis around which so much else turns (Black and white) has been there almost since the start and 'cultures' are now prominent not in the meeting of separate worlds, but in the most integrated of all national economic systems. Only within it, or systems like it, is common sense of the form one finds in the Michigan student newspaper: 'No culture in this multi-cultural society should have power over any other culture' (*Daily* 31 Jan. 1986).

Revisiting Michigan in 1991 one found everything quieter than two and three years before, the *Daily* a shadow of its former self. Local informants dismissed the change unsociologically, as usually informants do: the particular activists had graduated, the administration had bought them off, this or that group had been intimidated.[58] Yet the terms of activists are now partly those of powers they had once opposed, moving readily from the *Daily*, as it were, to the *University Record*. That which was attacked as enforcing a moral norm now extols diversity and brooks no argument.

> "Multiculturalism" is *the* job of the University right now. ...
>
> There needs to be a high degree of encouragement of the development of research and instructional initiatives to promote multiculturalism.
>
> ('Much remains to be done ...', *Record* 25 Jan. 1993)

Among the cultural certainties on offer is the certainty of 'culture' and thus of essential difference among identities spawned by a single rhetoric.

What centre there might be to the whole of which these are parts becomes invisible.

NOTES

1 'What happens if a dean or department chair's definition of "diversity" differs from Duderstadt's [the university president]? . . . "You aren't going to be put in jail," said Assistant to the President, Shirley Clarkson, "but you won't get a positive evaluation" ' (*Michigan Daily* 12 Jan. 1989).

2 The two papers mainly quoted are the *Michigan Daily* (student-run, university-based) and the *Ann Arbor News* (town-based). The *Daily* acquired a certain notoriety, and many faculty members claimed firmly they never read it. Nor should it be taken to represent an homogenized 'public opinion' among students. Most were apathetic. But, like *Time Magazine* in another context, the *Daily* defined quite closely what could and could not be readily expressed. *Record* refers to the Michigan *University Record*, an official self-representation 'for faculty and staff'.

3 The difficulties of pursuing something called 'American culture' are well established (see e.g. Varenne 1986). The more pressing question is what appeals to 'culture' disguise or omit of the functioning of 'ideology' (Keesing 1987): in the present case, rather neatly, 'culture' is itself part of a local ideology, but what people make of collective representations is as variable in Michigan as among the Kwaio.

4 This is from a collection of essays kindly given me by colleagues and acquaintances. Overall they are very like those elicited by Moffat (1986, 1989). I did not elicit any myself. Views differ legitimately, but my own is that the last thing a student beginning anthropology needs is to focus on his or her own experience. The pieces I quote are from 1990.

5 Public pronouncements centred on University Presidents. Harold Shapiro held the job until early 1987, promising many things (e.g. 12 per cent Black enrolment within five years, *Daily* 26 Mar. 1987) and then leaving ('Shapiro takes Princeton job', *News* 28 April 1987). Robben Fleming acted as interim President. During his brief tenure 'diversity' became a prominent term (*Record* 11 Jan. 1988). The job then fell to James Duderstadt. It is he who is quoted here. His freshman room-mate remembered wondering in 1964 where they would all be in twenty-five years' time, to which Duderstadt replied he hoped to be President of a major university (*News* 8 Sept 1988).

6 These events continue. In March 1993 a sociology professor teaching quantitative methods was denounced, and the case showed features of those five years earlier. The time when such things seemed the direct result of pressure from student groups or the media is long past.

   The best known of the books provoked by current changes is probably D'Souza 1991. Much that he says is true (on some points he could have been fiercer), but the worth of his intervention was crippled by his previous history: 'it is not pleasant to see a man who did so much to poison the wells now turning up dressed as the water commissioner' (Menand 1991).

7 'Increasing international dependence is creating powerful forces favoring multiculturalism' ('The Michigan Mandate: a four-year progress report, 1988–1991', Office of the President, University of Michigan, 1992). This is common sense to business people. Yet the link between domestic 'cultures' and foreign 'cultures' is not obvious; and area centres, which promoted such basics as foreign languages, are increasingly subsumed in 'international centres'.

8 Two official reports make the point, providing between them 105 graphs and

tables in official terms of affirmative action, with none at all that mentions income within or between such sets: 'Minority students at the University of Michigan' (Affirmative Action Office, Office of Academic Affairs, 1987); 'The Michigan Mandate: a four-year progress report.' In a vast bureaucracy there are figures of all sorts. Some, however, are more prominent than others, and some are oddly hard to find.

9 Presumably Wolff had in mind Herberg's quirky classic of a decade earlier, where Protestant, Catholic, Jew divided roughly 17:6:1 (Herberg 1983 [1955, 1960]: 46, 211 and *passim*).

10 The advantage of this term to hard-pressed administrators is clear. Why Blacks should accept the term is not clear, though historically it was once applied to them exclusively.

11 Whether people in some group feel collectively hurt because 5 or 50 per cent are officially poor is not itself a statistical question. Statistics are of particular importance in political calculation, however, and, if directed towards a clear end, the language of numbers can be compelling. See the opening paper in Barker and Walters 1989.

   Class is a relation of economic domination which defines groups of people consistently, not simply as individuals at one point or another in their lives. Often one is told there is no such thing. At a guess, we might find the term used in future by people of dominant sets (those where 'ethnic' hardship is implausible) in describing their rise to prominence – perhaps in some attenuated form such as 'symbols of class'.

12 This is from a quite lengthy account in the *Washington Post* of 21 May 1984. The passage quoted is cited in Barker and Walters 1989.

13 In early reports (*Daily* 21 Feb. 1986, 10 April 1986) one finds United Community Against Racism. The title stabilizes in the papers in early 1987. The watering down of Black claims within a pluralist rhetoric was complained of at several points (see e.g. *News* 23 April 1987, 15 Jan. 1989, *Daily* 11 Jan., 13 Jan. 1989).

   The insults and threats that made news ('We're going to fuck your shit up. Bomb threat, bomb threat, bomb threat. I'm going to fuck you up your anus', for instance, cited *Daily* 4 Mar. 1988) were presumably the work of very few students. However, universities socialize or define the middle classes (see Bourdieu and Passeron 1979) and British readers might assume that being middle class of its nature involves polite hypocrisy. In this case it does not.

14 These were locally known as 'Ypsituckians', a term compounded of Kentucky, though their origin was not so limited by state, and 'Ypsilanti', a town adjacent to Ann Arbor. 'Ypsi' was not, to use the native term, 'upscale'. One should bear in mind that towns are administratively autonomous and economic inequality can thus be made to fit closely the geographic categories: the stereotypes become true. On a larger scale the same applies to big cities (Detroit, for one), whose 'suburbs' have a separate tax base.

15 Both UCAR and the university came in fact to promote 'outreach programs' (*Daily* 30 Jan. 1990, *Record* 18 Jan. 1993). There is no cause to doubt anyone's good faith. Nor is economic inequality ignored in the pages of the *Daily* (e.g. 15 Sept. 1989). But the local and the economic alike have the character of marginalia.

16 See e.g. *Daily* 24 Sept. 1987, 15 Jan., 24 Mar. 1988, 27 Jan. 1989. 'Celebration' was a term used freely by activists of many stripes. At the same period, confusingly, 'celebratory' was a term of condemnation used by the left of the aestheticization of politics. An ethnographic treatment would reach further afield to examine, for instance, the likeable American custom of town parades – where in effect people march past themselves to their own applause.

17 'White male' develops features of the earlier WASP, which had clear associations of wealth and power. But as part of an exhaustive set it had also to cover
   proletarians and poor farmers. The new coinage assimilates 'ethnic' whites and
   drops the women – the effect of (largely white) feminism has been large. The
   incommensurability of persons within the set remains.

   An Ypsituckian neighbour (see note 14) had incontinent children, endless
   stray cats around his ramshackle dwelling, numerous relatives in the state peni-
   tentiary or the 'mental facility', and very little prospect of his personal lot
   improving. One would turn from a day of university 'white male' rhetoric to
   him tinkering with his yard-full of broken washing-machines and think, 'Surely
   they don't mean him?'

18 In 1993, between drafts of the present chapter, Morrison received the Nobel
   Prize for Literature.

19 The insecurity of the middle classes has been much written about (e.g. Lasch
   1979: 105–33). The point was put to me that people are in the same position
   as companies on the stock exchange: the slightest sign of weakness and one's
   'symbolic capital' evaporates. Everyone is therefore individually 'positive' with
   others – unless sufficient come together to be 'positive' as a group, building a
   public claim on what was private misery. Another aspect, perhaps, of the 'sharp
   lines' that Wolff (1965) noted.

20 This piece was published in two parts (*Daily* 30 and 31 Mar. 1987). It catches
   an atmosphere of unspecific menace one often heard in conversation but rarely
   saw fixed in print, e.g. a reference to the 'climate of fear that is part of graduate training in economics' (*Daily* 31 Jan. 1989). The detail of personal crisis
   turning upon a course in introductory syntax is of its time and place. So too,
   were there room to quote, would be the author's acceptance of such terms as
   'excellence' around which much unhappiness is ordered.

21 Hughes' intent is polemical and his tirade directed in part at intellectual dishon-
   esty. The spectacle of prosperous academics retailing their supposed oppression is distasteful; but one needs to consider why so many find the claims
   plausible.

22 Again from a student essay: 'although East Asians share a culture of their own,
   there seem to be divisions within'. As, for instance, among Chinese, Japanese,
   Koreans, Vietnamese and Cambodians.

23 The speaker quoted here also used the rhetorical figure noted for persons of
   multiracial heritage above: the Hispanic association deserved consideration
   because 'we have more diversity in our group than others'. Strongly marked
   terms like this are quickly substantialized and appear in unexpected settings:
   by 1992 one finds mention of a 'Diversity Choir' (*Record* 9 Nov. 1992),
   and then of administrative staff sewing a 'Diversity Quilt' (*Record* 1 Feb.
   1993).

24 The supposed comparability of cases produces symptomatic slips: e.g.
   'Complaints by the sufferers of racism (whether anti-Black, anti-Jewish, or anti-
   female) are irrelevant until validated by whites' (*Daily* 1 Mar. 1988). Incidents
   such as white women saying Blacks have tails they wrap up and stuff in their
   pants (*Daily* 3 Nov. 1987) are by contrast not strongly marked.

25 'The Michigan Mandate: a four-year progress report.'

26 The quote continues, 'Our challenge is not to emulate them, but to make what
   is the essential quality of the University of Michigan available to more minorities' (*Daily* 12 Jan. 1988). Howard is an 'historically Black college', and by
   most accounts an extremely good college. Wayne State (near the centre of
   Detroit) gets it from all sides, as we see below.

27 What is localized in the older form Harvey describes so well is now an underclass, excluded from the classical relations of labour and corralled or policed

in specific places. The newer language of (delocalized) pluralism goes on above their heads.

Where space and place are co-terminous matters greatly, not least in the apparatus of federal government. Here Ronald Reagan's Attorney-General, Edwin Meese, had claimed the constitution was colour-blind and set about reversing rules on federal hiring.

28 For Sivanandam's views see e.g. Sivanandam 1985.

29 'I feel very threatened by your rejection of my views on [check one] phallo-centricity/the Mother Goddess/the Treaty of Vienna/Young's modulus of elasticity' (Hughes 1993: 66). Plenty of this goes on. Yet two things need adding: that conventional categories must be invoked, and that one need not belong in a particular category to invoke it. At which point we are dealing with a style of interaction that extends far beyond the question at hand: the want of principle that colours much use of the present language by academics can as soon be found in novels about advertising.

30 The argument has been expanded and reformulated several times but the original version, as in *Homo Hierarchicus* (Dumont 1970), retains its force. India, the Asianists will insist, was never all hierarchy, and 'racial' divides in America have often been more caste-like than Dumont assumes. Nonetheless the connection proposed between 'scientific' racism and democratic ideology fits quite well with American history (see e.g. Fields 1990).

31 Again and again informants come back to high-schools as a model of society. The outsider is struck by how very much contemporary memory resembles the Lynds' accounts of schools in 'Middletown' almost seventy years ago (Lynd and Lynd 1929). At about the time I left Michigan (1989) Sherry Ortner was proposing work on high-schools, which will give us the current state of play.

32 See Moffat 1986, 1989. Something similar occurs with many egalitarian rhetorics, as for instance in tribal Afghanistan where 'smooth' forms of interaction are reckoned inauthentic (Anderson 1982).

33 The literature on American Jewish identity is so vast as to overwhelm one. For a readable general account see e.g. Rosenberg 1985.

34 Again this is from material collected by professional acquaintances. I should like to thank many people who have discussed the topic and tracked down material; but so few wish to be named it seems best to treat all alike. The 1989 riot, by the way, was claimed to have done $84,000 of damage (*News* 7 April).

35 Imagery of a personal inside and outside is prominent, e.g. 'True equality rests on the feelings within that there are no differences, that everyone is the same' (letters page, *Daily* 16 Nov. 1987).

36 Commercial organizations quickly took up the theme. National Public Radio (22 June 1989) broadcast a piece on 'sensitivity training' at Johnson and Johnson. This included the real-life tale of a Black employee wanting to order fried chicken and water melon in the canteen, feeling he couldn't because such food was stereotyped, deciding he would after all, feeling bad about it afterwards … and so on. Once the question is posed, there is no right answer. Employees are meanwhile schooled as good corporate citizens by those employing them.

37 At the height of the transformation Ronald Reagan's Secretary of Education, William Bennett, was greatly exercised about 'multiculturalism'. But large business corporations digested the idea more rapidly. As with rhetoric against 'the white male', there was a feeling of the target being squarely missed.

38 'Great African rulers' only came to my attention in *Black Collegian*, a publication whites scarcely know of unless doing 'research'. Reading matter is highly fragmented. Only advertisers and pollsters, one sometimes feels, know what all the different groups are reading – or for that matter saying.

39 As Harvey suggests (1989), there is every reason to expect such strategies: not only must markets always be created anew, but technologies of batch production allow a single enterprise to subdivide its market by 'consumer preference'. An earlier regime of production had an interest in promoting 'cultural' uniformity.

40 Perhaps surprisingly, Wolff's primary case of a topic becoming suddenly 'respectable' is poverty.

41 In the 1950s and 1960s homosexuals were 'purged' from Michigan, and students suspended were told they might be readmitted after private psychiatric 'cures' (*Daily* 25 Jan. 1988). Students violating a speech and conduct code at Wisconsin in 1989 were 'ordered . . . to undergo mandatory psychiatric and alcoholic counselling' (*Daily* 1 Nov. 1991). *Plus ça change.*

42 'Enhancing quality in an era of resource constraint.' Task force on costs in higher education, University of Michigan, 1990.

43 One can encourage successful change by 'self-talk'. This works because 'the brain believes that what it is told is true'. Breathing is also good. 'As you breathe in, think wonderful things, of quiet, of peace. Breathe out negative thoughts, anxiety, tension' ('We need to become "go-with-the-flow" logs', *Record* 7 June 1993). The piece was so prominent (and the theory of brain function so unexpected) that I telephoned a local informant to ask what it signified. The answer was not very helpful. Ethnography here would depend upon finding 'go-with-the-flow' workers.

44 Rosaldo is informative on essentializing uses of the term. There are no discrete 'cultures' but only 'borderlands' in which plural personalities might form (Rosaldo 1989: 216). The conclusion of the book thus undermines the starting point, the Stanford debate over 'multiculturalism'. Presumably 'culture' can be dissolved by the provisional use of terms such as 'power' and 'history'.

45 In the period under review Ford workers escaped more lightly than most. Ford's operations had already been 'downsized' at the start of the 1980s. In the late 1980s it was General Motors workers whose jobs were threatened, and latterly scheduled to be removed (see e.g. *Ypsilanti Press* 3, 13 June, 4, 10 July 1993).

46 The decline of traditional labour power and of expectations of upward mobility have coincided, since the 1970s, with the rise of political claims based on sex and colour. There has not been an intersection of interest. For a discussion of the loss of effective voting power attendant on widening economic difference, see Edsall 1988 (also Edsall 1984), with which Davis' wider argument (1984) runs largely parallel.

47 The phrase 'Marxism without the economics' has occurred several times in conversation. For an example in print see the *Guardian* 11–12 May 1991. For similar arguments see the *Independent* 8, 14 May 1991. The discussion of American events in both British papers suffers from misplaced emphases. Both, however, express the concern that a politics of difference may displace electoral possibilities of social transformation. The *Guardian* piece quotes a member of George Bush's administration wondering whether it was worth even having a domestic policy.

48 The key phrase occurs in what locally might be called 'positive' and 'negative' contexts. 'UCAR stands against racism, sexism, classism, homophobia, and all forms of oppression' (letters page, *Daily* 20 Nov. 1987). 'It's no longer a movement against racism. It's a movement against racism, classism, sexism, militarism, and heterosexism' ('UCAR, Black groups react to controversial split', *Daily* 20 April 1988).

49 Again the quote is from the *Washington Post* 21 May 1984.

50 Opposition to the rhetoric of group identity took the form of voluntarist appeals to individual responsibility. Shelby Steele's fluent essays on race, for

instance, drew wide attention and fierce denunciation on just these grounds (Steele 1990, Reed 1991).

51 This is not a matter simply of labelling by a dominant group (Tonkin *et al.* 1989). The term 'race' is integral to a good deal of Black rhetoric drawing on such early writers as Du Bois, quite apart from the nationalist tradition of Turner, Garvey and Malcolm X. An essentialist reading of the term is, however, common among other people too (see Fields 1990).

As late as 1982 one finds arguments about the concept of race in American anthropology textbooks turning on differences between 'lumpers' and 'splitters': overall, the concept seemed to be losing currency (Littlefield *et al.* 1982). The timing is curious to one whose first encounter with biological anthropologists, in Britain a decade earlier, was with an already commonsensical view that the concept was meaningless. Presumably behind this lay Harrison *et al.* 1964. For a similar, American, intervention see Livingstone 1962.

52 Yet any group, of whatever colour, can be called 'ethnic'. The categories can be arranged as a series of exclusions and the classification therefore has a good deal about it of hierarchy in Dumont's sense not just of ranking. Black versus white is not formally of a kind with Herberg's 'Protestant, Catholic, Jew', or with Italians versus Irish. In many circumstances, anyone can be 'white' unless they're 'Black'.

53 The official taxonomy seems rather to be fraying. The 1992 *Statistical Abstract of the United States* (Washington: Government Printing Office, 112th edn., p. 18) allows that, 'As of April, Hispanic persons may be of any race.' Good news for Hispanics. When the government printer says Blacks may be of any race the game will at last be over.

54 'Popular culture' does not invite the belief that it is all of anyone's world; the phrase 'public culture' depends for its effect on the premise that it is shared only partially. But the word's associations with something shared by individuals and integral to their status are often its attraction. Consider, for example, the recent popularity of 'culture' in management and business literature, where what is at issue are power relations discussed previously in less invasive terms of contract.

55 A woman carrying the ceremonial mace at a meeting of the University Senate: 'I was terrified I would drop it and be a total disgrace to my gender' (*Record* 8 May 1989). For complete linguistic collapse, however, we can turn to a British newspaper: 'Doctors reject right to choose babies' gender' (*Independent* 30 June 1993), a choice that might apparently 'take place before or after conception'.

56 Taylor's argument, which leaves aside sociology, would lead one to expect a literature of difference and recognition to appear around 1800: what in fact appears is Stendhal. The world in which 'recognition' is so compelling a claim is surely one in which the person is subject always to large-scale organizations: everyone feels oppressed but none knows by whom.

57 There is more than word-play at issue. Discussing the Rushdie furore, Taylor presents liberalism as an 'organic outgrowth' of Christianity, unavoidably at odds with 'mainstream Islam' (Taylor 1992: 62). 'Awkwardness' arises from the presence in our midst of people 'who belong to the culture that calls into question our philosophical boundaries'. But 'Liberalism is also a fighting creed.' Afficionados of John Buchan will remember the opening scenes of *Greenmantle* (1915): 'Islam is a fighting creed, and the Mullah still stands in the pulpit with the Koran in one hand and a drawn sword in the other.' This is scarcely the real shape of the problem.

58 The conspiratorial style of explanation is common and forms a complement to pluralist rules. In the case at hand it was said the *Daily* had run foul not only

of the administration but of Zionist groups who disliked its opinions on Palestine. For the present purpose we need only note that, given the patterns outlined above, one can hardly even ask what happened.

REFERENCES

Newspaper citations are provided in the text, not listed here.

Anderson, J. (1982) 'Social structure and the veil', *Anthropos* 77, 397–420.
Barker, L.J. and R.W. Walters (1989) *Jesse Jackson's 1984 Presidential Campaign: challenge and change in American politics*, Chicago and Urbana, IL: University of Illinois Press.
Barth, F. (ed.) (1969) *Ethnic Groups and Boundaries: the social organization of cultural difference*, Oslo: Universitetsforlaget.
Beeman, W. (1986) 'Freedom to choose: symbols and values in American advertising', pp. 52–65, in H. Varrenne (ed.) *Symbolizing America*, Lincoln, NE: University of Nebraska Press.
Bourdieu, P. and J-C. Passeron (1979) *The Inheritors: French students and their relation to culture* (trans. Richard Nice), Chicago and London: University of Chicago Press.
Davis, M. (1984) 'The political economy of late imperial America', *New Left Review* 143, 6–38.
D'Souza, D. (1991) *Illiberal Education: the politics of race and sex on campus*, New York: Free Press.
Dumont, L. (1970) *Homo Hierarchicus: the caste system and its implications* (trans. Mark Sainsbury), Chicago, IL: University of Chicago Press.
Edsall, T. (1984) *The New Politics of Inequality*, New York: Norton.
——(1988) 'The return of inequality', *Atlantic Monthly*, June: 87–94.
Fields, B.J. (1990) 'Slavery, race and ideology in the United States of America', *New Left Review* 181, 95–118.
Glazer, N. and D.P. Moynihan (eds) (1963; 2nd edn. 1970) *Beyond the Melting Pot*, Cambridge, MA: Harvard University Press.
——(1975) *Ethnicity: Theory and Experience*, Cambridge, MA: Harvard University Press.
Harrison, G. (1964) *Human Biology*, Oxford: Oxford University Press.
Harvey, D. (1989) *The Condition of Postmodernity*, Oxford: Basil Blackwell.
Herberg, W. (1983) (originally 1955 and 1960) *Protestant, Catholic, Jew: an essay in American religious sociology*, Chicago: University of Chicago Press.
Hughes, R. (1993) *Culture of Complaint: the fraying of America*, New York: Oxford University Press.
Just, R. (1989) 'Triumph of the ethnos', pp. 71–88, in E.Tonkin, M. McDonald and M. Chapman (eds) *History and Ethnicity* (ASA Monograph 27), London and New York: Routledge.
Keesing, R. (1987) 'Anthropology as interpretive quest', *Current Anthropology* 28/2, 161–76.
Lasch, C. (1979) *The Culture of Narcissism: American life in an age of diminishing expectations*, New York: Norton.
Littlefield, A., L. Lieberman and L.T. Reynolds (1982) 'Redefining race: the potential demise of a concept in physical anthropology', *Current Anthropology* 23/6, 641–727.
Livingstone, F. (1962) 'On the non-existence of human races', *Current Anthropology* 3/3, 279–81.
Lynd, H.M. and R.S. Lynd (1929) *Middletown: a study in American culture*, New York: Harcourt Brace & Co.

MacShane, F. (1981) *Selected Letters of Raymond Chandler*, London: Jonathan Cape.

Menand, L. (1991) 'Illiberalisms' [review of D'Souza 1991], *New Yorker Magazine*, May 20, 101–7.

Moffat, M. (1986) 'The discourse of the dorm: race, friendship and "culture" among college youth', pp. 159–77, in H. Varrenne (ed.) *Symbolizing America*, Lincoln, NE: University of Nebraska Press.

——(1989) *Coming of Age in New Jersey: college and American culture*, New Brunswick, NJ and London: Rutgers University Press.

Ranger, T.O. (1985) 'The invention of tribalism in Zimbabwe', Gweru (Zimbabwe): Mambo Press (printed version of lecture given at the University of Zimbabwe, August 1985).

Reed, R. (1991) 'Steele Trap' [review of Steele 1991], *The Nation*, 4 March, 274–810.

Riesman, D. with N. Glazer and R. Denney (1950) *The Lonely Crowd: a study of the changing American character*, New Haven, CT: Yale University Press.

Rosaldo, R. (1989) *Culture and Truth: the remaking of social analysis*, Boston, MA: Beacon Press.

Rosenberg, S.E. (1985) *The New Jewish Identity in America*, New York: Hippocrene Books.

Sivanandam, A. (1985) 'RAT [racism awareness training] and the degradation of black struggle', *Race and Class* 26/4, 1–33.

Steele, S. (1990) *The Content of our Character: a new vision of race in America*, New York: St Martin's Press.

Stocking, G. (1968) *Race, Culture and Evolution: essays in the history of anthropology*, New York: Free Press.

Taylor, C. (1992) *Multiculturalism and 'the Politics of Recognition'*, Princeton, NJ: Princeton University Press.

Tonkin, E., M. McDonald and M. Chapman (eds) (1989) *History and Ethnicity* (ASA Monograph 27), London and New York: Routledge.

Varenne, H. (1986) 'Creating America', pp. 15–33, in H. Varenne (ed.) *Symbolizing America*, Lincoln, NE: University of Nebraska Press.

Whyte, W.H. (1956) *The Organization Man*, New York: Simon and Schuster.

Wolff, R. (1965) 'Beyond tolerance', pp. 3–52, in R. Wolff, H. Barrington Moore and H. Marcuse, *A Critique of Pure Tolerance*, Boston, MA: Beacon Press.

4 Certain knowledge
The encounter of global fundamentalism and local Christianity in urban south India

Lionel Caplan

INTRODUCTION[1]

There can be few narratives which convey so starkly the impact of global on local forms of knowledge as those relating the history of Western Christian missions to peoples of the non-Western world. The shape of Christianity in south India today – and more particularly of urban Protestantism, with which I am especially concerned in this chapter[2] – reflects 'indigenous' accommodations to Euro-American theologies and mission strategies in the course of Western colonial and post-colonial domination. Thus a rigid distinction between local and global in this context is difficult to sustain, since what began as an import from the West evolved over many years into an Indian Christian synthesis, a species of *local* religion.[3] But if globalization is not a recent phenomenon, its contemporary character differs perceptibly from that obtaining in the past. In south India, as elsewhere, the most rapidly expanding form of contemporary mission Christianity is fundamentalist Protestantism[4] – a term which, for my present purposes, embraces evangelical and Pentecostal religiosities.[5] Originating mainly in North America, where such forms of Christianity have taken firm root since the Second World War and especially during the past quarter of a century, they are being exported around the globe by US-led and -financed missions and para-church organizations, challenging the religious cultures which had previously evolved under the aegis of the historic churches. This chapter examines the encounter between these two kinds of religiosity.[6]

One way to approach this 'cultural struggle' is to regard it as an opposition between 'faith' and 'certitude'. Towler has recently suggested that faith, which he deems the characteristic cognitive style of 'conventional' Protestantism, implies 'a continuous act of aspiration'. It demands awareness of the 'inherently complex and problematical character of the events and experiences demanding explanation'; doubt is therefore an intrinsic part of faith. By contrast, 'sectarian religion' – and here he would probably include varieties of fundamentalism – is characterized by certitude (Towler 1984). A spate of recent analyses of fundamentalist approaches to religious phenomena similarly identifies as a crucial feature the insistence on privileged access to absolute truth. '[Fundamentalists] are convinced that their purchase on the truth is, like the truth itself, complete and absolute, unqualified by partial understanding or error' (Deiros 1991: 169). Their need to consider scripture inerrant and to 'subscribe to a fixed and rigid creed' renders them, in Ostow's view, 'reluctant to tolerate doubt, uncertainty and ambiguity' (1990: 101; see also Marty and Appleby 1991; Lawrence 1990; Averill 1989).[7]

In Madras city, the capital of Tamil Nadu state in south India and the locus of my study, this new and aggressively promoted form of global Christianity has, during the past two decades, come increasingly to challenge one variety of Protestant religiosity and reinforce another. Indeed, the notion of a solidary corpus of local religious knowledge confronting or encountering an alien cultural flow is much too simplistic for it masks, among other things, a profound discrepancy of religiosities within the Indian Protestant community of Madras. The dominant sector (both lay and ecclesiastical) has for some time been committed to theological liberalism, social 'activism' and a collaborative approach to non-Christian religions – the ingredients of 'faith'. The majority of ordinary Protestants, by contrast, eschew such tendencies, retaining strong beliefs in the centrality of worship and the total veracity of the Bible, alongside attachment to everyday knowledge about misfortune which they share with the non-Christians among whom they live. In this chapter I consider how the fundamentalists encounter these opposed religious proclivities. I first examine the contexts in which their certainties are asserted; second, identify those aspects of fundamentalist belief and behaviour which accord with local knowledges and finally consider how Madras Protestants assess and respond to these new global religiosities.

PROTESTANT MADRAS

Christians in Madras were estimated to number 237,000 in 1981 or just under 7.5 per cent of the city's population.[8] There are reputed to be more churches in Madras than in any other south Asian city (Hedlund 1986). Within the Christian fold Protestants are a minority, comprising perhaps 30–35 per cent of the total, or some 80,000 people. Cities like Madras were never included in the 'comity' arrangements obtaining among Protestant missionaries, whereby each Society focused its efforts on specific areas and refrained from entering the 'territory' of another. As a result the missionaries of numerous organizations were active in the city.[9] Nonetheless, conversions among the resident population of Madras were never very numerous and missionaries frequently complained of the difficulties and frustrations attending their work in this large urban centre.

Protestant numbers only expanded as a result of migration from various

parts of south India by those already professing Christianity. The principal Protestant migrations occurred in response to infrastructural growth
and economic developments in the metropolitan region during the second
and third quarters of the twentieth century and especially following
independence. A minority, who had been able to take full advantage of
educational opportunities in mission schools and colleges, began to fill
some of the senior positions which had previously been monopolized by
Europeans in the large commercial, industrial, educational and administrative organizations of the Raj.

These new Protestant elites also entered the churches which had previously been reserved for Europeans, occupied the pews the latter had
vacated, continued to worship in English and assumed lay control of ecclesiastical structures created with the formation in 1947 of the ecumenical
Protestant Church of South India (CSI).[10] The CSI – which federated
the Presbyterian, Congregational, Methodist and Anglican churches in
south India[11] – is the largest Protestant church in India and contains the
biggest non-Catholic following in Madras, with nearly half the city's
Protestants in its membership. The CSI leadership, as well as the community's Westernized elites, many of whom serve the church in various secular
capacities, have a strong commitment to the social gospel. This is a direct
legacy of the dominant liberal theological emphasis within Euro-American
missionary circles which gained the ascendancy in the early part of the
twentieth century and especially as independence approached. In the
context of contemporary south India the social gospel means a concern
for economic development and the alleviation of hardship. The CSI is
involved in a host of programmes to improve environmental conditions
and better the life-chances of those most in need. These various
welfare schemes are meant to benefit the poor irrespective of religious
affiliation.

One obvious corollary of this kind of intense engagement with the
'world' is that religions other than Christianity, and relationships with
non-Christians, are conceived in a positive light. Protestant leaders of
the CSI and other major denominational churches acknowledge the
'spirituality' in Hinduism and other religions.[12] Among other things,
Protestant leaders of mainline churches like the CSI tend to eschew
the negative attitudes and aggressive evangelism which characterized
the early missionary approach to Indians of other persuasions. This
may be partly to avoid offending the sensitivities of both government
and militant Hindu organizations but it also emerges from an outlook
which seeks to communicate the values of Christianity through example
rather than exhortation. Ecumenical sentiments are frequently heard
from the pulpits of elite congregations and are widely shared by well-to-
do, cosmopolitan Protestants who are regularly engaged in welfare
and development activities as part of their commitment to the social
gospel.

POPULAR RELIGIOSITIES

The vast majority of Protestants – those outside the small power bloc – are indifferent to or at best weakly committed to the social gospel. Norman (1979: 6) has suggested that 'everywhere in the Third World' we find a tendency for sophisticated elites who comprise the church's leadership to 'superimpose the liberal and radical political idealism ... of the developed world upon the diffused religiosity around them' (*ibid.*). For most ordinary Protestants in Madras this 'diffused religiosity' suggests, for one thing, a sharing with non-Christians of popular ideas and practices concerning the causes of and remedies for affliction. In a study of 'intermingling patterns of culture' among Protestant groups in south India conducted in 1953, Diehl found that despite a century and a half of missionary influence Christians still revered a range of (non-Christian) ritual specialists (magicians, soothsayers, 'god-dancers', fortune-tellers, 'persons inspired by the gods', etc.). People 'are apt to show confidence in [these] professionals who offer their services ... at times of unexpected crises'. He concluded that it was 'not so much the person exercising this practice as the conceptual outlook behind it that has a hold on people' (Diehl 1965: 135–6). Twenty years later when I conducted fieldwork in Madras I also found that the majority of non-elites, like the Hindus among whom they live and work, continued to attribute many if not most kinds of everyday misfortune (joblessness, illness, unhappy marriages, disobedient children, examination failures, etc.) to either sorcery (*suniyam*), the capricious acts of evil spirits (*pey*), or other kinds of mystical agents (Caplan 1987b). In the (English) words of an Anglo-Indian: 'When something goes wrong people here in Madras think, "Ah, this one's been conjured, or that one's been pilled" '.

At the same time, the religious proclivities of most Protestants include an attachment to the pietism bequeathed them by the early missionaries, who insisted on the centrality of the Bible and worship in Christian life. Protestant families still identify the observance of Sabbath, daily prayers at home and belief that the Bible is God's literal truth as the core of their religious convictions. The persons who most persistently articulate this view today are the lay preachers, who emerge from the same neighbourhoods and social backgrounds as the majority of Protestants and share their conservative outlooks. While lay preachers are sometimes criticized by clergymen and church leaders for their lack of originality and anti-intellectualism, they express the religious predilections of most church members in the CSI's Tamil congregations, who welcome the Bible-based sermons they preach – calling for simple devotion, warning of the dangers of sin and promising individual salvation.

Both aspects of popular religiosity, however, have been effectively demoted in the course of the twentieth century. The Euro-American missionaries, like their successors in the Indian church hierarchy, by and large refuse(d) to countenance indigenous ideas about misfortune. Thomas (1982) has traced the gradual decline in magical practices and beliefs in England during the seventeenth century. By the era of Protestant expansion throughout the non-Western world these beliefs had all but disappeared from orthodox religion (see Wilson 1973: 71–82), so that the missionaries who arrived in India had been trained in a post-Reformation atmosphere which disparaged thaumaturgical solutions. I was often told by people who had been educated or worked in Christian establishments before independence that the missionaries never spoke about such matters, except to dismiss them as nonsense, or to laugh them away. In the words of one fundamentalist critic, 'The church has many Saduccees – those who deny all that's miraculous and supernatural' (Stanley 1991: 134). In brief, then, Protestants looked in vain to their missionaries and their indigenous clergy for a satisfactory response to their traditional explanations of adversity. Cosmopolitan Protestant elites reinforced ecclesiatical derogation of popular beliefs by dismissing them as the 'superstitions' of simple and uneducated co-religionists.

Further, that aspect of popular religiosity which invoked a simple, conservative approach to Christian belief and practice – the legacy of early missionaries – had by the early part of the twentieth century also been demoted. It was, as I have indicated, overtaken by a theology of liberalism and the social gospel espoused by a confident, modernist and increasingly development-oriented ecclesiastical hierarchy, supported by a rising middle class. The mass of ordinary Christians, denied the authenticity of their own religious outlooks by the dominant segment within the church and community, are precisely those most attracted to and by recent fundamentalist ideologies which have transformed the Christian 'scene' in Madras.

GLOBAL FUNDAMENTALISM

Fundamentalism in Madras cannot be fully understood simply in the context of historical developments within the Indian Christian fold or even the wider political setting of south India. The post-Second World War Protestant mission field has been transformed as the USA's global economic dominance, its anti-Soviet crusade and the rise of the New Right combined to encourage a reawakening of fundamentalist Christianity. To evolutionism and modernism, which had been the bugbears of fundamentalism from the earliest days, was added the threat of communism, the definition of which soon came to include any government intervention in social arrangements, or any hint of political (as well as religious) liberalism (Barr 1977: 109).[13]

This North American world-view has been systematically exported to all parts of the globe as fundamentalists have become increasingly wealthy and influential at home. By 1986 well over half the 38,000 US personnel in Protestant missions overseas – with a total operating budget of over $500 million – were associated with fundamentalist organizations (see Wilson and Siewert 1986). Ammerman suggests that fundamentalists tended to see 'American military and economic might as guarantors of their ability to evangelize the world' (1991: 40). In the 1970s and 1980s numerous USA-based missions and para-church organizations with a conservative fundamentalist outlook established branches in many areas of Asia, including south India, where they created links with local Christian groups and imported their communications skills, refined in domestic contexts, to these new international settings. It was evidence of how, with their commodification, religions in the USA were expanding their markets (Appiah 1991: 344).[14]

In Madras, foreign missions based mainly in the USA provide financial and other forms of support for most of the large and successful fundamentalist congregations. These missions also seek out independent groups which show signs of expansion, to offer them association and assistance. Many of the latter succumb, although a few choose to retain their autonomy. One well-known evangelist with branches in several parts of Tamil Nadu state has been approached on numerous occasions but has so far resisted any 'takeover' attempts. However, many small sectarian groups with ambitions to grow, or evangelists convinced they have been specially chosen by God, frequently seek to attach themselves to such missions. One explained: 'I know I am called to blow the trumpet for the Lord. ... So I affiliated to the ... whose moorings are in the USA.' Some members of elite CSI congregations and the church's lay leadership find such foreign ties threatening: a prominent member of the church acknowledged that '[T]here is a lot of money on and in fundamentalism ... everywhere you look there is some American fundamentalist group offering money to someone to set up something here.' Some missions do not confine themselves to assisting only fundamentalist organizations.[15] They occasionally offer clergy from mainline churches like the CSI the opportunity to undergo specialist training in their theological colleges abroad, or arrange speaking tours in the USA for senior ecclesiastical figures. In these and other ways they seek to influence the 'modernist' churches to adopt a more sympathetic attitude to fundamentalist doctrine and practice.

PROMOTING FUNDAMENTALISM

Foreign evangelists provide models for the many local charismatic figures who claim to have been chosen to do 'God's work'. The preaching skills, modes of self-presentation and performance techniques of the former are known to and emulated by the latter, despite not having access to the same kinds of sophisticated technologies.[16] The most important occasions on which fundamentalist doctrines are promoted are the 'Crusades' –

open meetings extending over several evenings – which are organized by fundamentalist organizations and usually attract many hundreds and even thousands of spectators. Crusades are carefully structured, following patterns developed abroad. 'Big time evangelism', according to Marsden, regards the winning of converts as a science and has developed increasingly sophisticated techniques of persuasion (1987: 242–3).

Crusades feature entertainment by gospel singers, nowadays using modern electronic instruments and complex (usually Japanese-made) sound systems; 'messages' by locally popular personalities; and, to crown the evening, the appearance of the star evangelist, who, in presenting the 'Word of God', might use lighting and microphone techniques borrowed from the latest pop singers. These events are advertised by leaflets distributed at all Madras churches, and on the city's ubiquitous wall posters. When I was most recently in Madras in late 1991–early 1992 there were at least a dozen such Crusades being promoted simultaneously by poster and street banner.[17] Frequently the star attractions are foreigners, who tend to come to Madras in the pleasantly temperate winter months and link up with one or more fundamentalist groups who make the detailed arrangements for the visit.

Most local evangelists operate within a neighbourhood context, visiting homes and preaching to a range of small independent prayer groups. Some establish and lead their own fellowships to which persons from different denominations and sects (or none, for they sometimes attract Hindus) in the vicinity affiliate on an informal basis. I first heard about Sister Rachel's assembly when I was visiting members of a CSI congregation situated in a densely populated part of the city inhabited mainly by small artisans and secure but low-paid employees of industrial and public concerns. My host, a third-generation Christian and regular church-goer, mentioned how several members of his immediate family, though staunch CSI supporters, often attended a nearby assembly run (in their own home) by a couple who welcomed all those who came for help and comfort.

On the two occasions I was present there were perhaps a dozen adults, mainly women (several of whom I recognized as members of the CSI congregation), and as many children in the room. Sister Rachel, a quiet, serious woman, led them in singing and prayers – mainly personal requests for boons – and then offered a lengthy Bible reading and exegesis. Finally, she called for 'testimonies'. The women who stood up to testify spoke not only or even predominantly of their own problems but of those relating to their close kin. They referred to a variety of challenges and difficulties overcome within the family – employment found, examinations passed, surgery undergone without ill-effects, a good marriage arranged, an illness healed and so on. These successes were all attributed to the prayers offered and fasts undergone by Sister Rachel, who, they attested, was being 'used mightily by God'. After the testimonies, when most of the people had left, she invited a few women to meet her individually in another room to discuss their problems. Her husband occasionally takes the service but acknowledges that only his wife has the requisite gifts which give her the 'power' to transform people's lives in the way we heard.

One CSI congregant who was among the women present when I attended the assembly later told me:

> Our pastor is a good man who serves God in his way but he has too many members to worry about so he can't listen to our individual problems. Anyway, he is only the bishop's employee and doesn't have the power of someone like Sister Rachel, who is especially chosen by God to do His work.

Though the activities of such evangelists are restricted to local areas and tiny followings, they tend to emulate (and frequently criticize) the performance styles of the more popular figures. If they achieve extra-neighbourhood reputations, they might be invited to share the platforms of the more famous evangelists, possibly of those from the West. Eventually, they may hope to achieve sufficient fame to attract large audiences on their own. (At that point they would probably begin to preach in English and have a Tamil translator.) The most popular indigenous evangelists are known and travel throughout south India and to other parts of Asia, where the local Tamil communities organize Crusades. Several have now established organizations to handle their business and travel arrangements, reply to the countless letters asking for help and advice, and promote the records and tapes of their songs and sermons, which are broadcast on commercial radio stations beamed to south India.[18] The most successful evangelist in south India has upwards of 100 employees to run his many enterprises, which include, in addition to the above, a 'Prayer Tower' (where, for a fee, daily prayers are offered during the first years of an individual's life); weekly open sessions, where families can meet counsellors to request special prayers and watch videos of the evangelist; a 'degree'-giving Institute of Evangelism; and (still in the planning stages) a medical college.

Like famous fundamentalist preachers in the USA, these local evangelists represent themselves to their publics by means of narratives which draw heavily on the imagery of death/destruction and rebirth (see Ostow 1990: 106). Their autobiographies, which become public knowledge through print and by word of mouth, contrast their lives before and after their transformation from nominal to true Christian, from doubter to believer. They portray themselves, in the period prior to 'conversion', as on the brink of spiritual and/or physical death. They speak and write of bodies 'full of sores and pain', scholastic failure and unemployment, association with unsavoury people, sin-filled lives (smoking, drinking, cinema-going, wearing jewellery, political activity), being on the verge of suicide and, in at least one case, taking poison and being pronounced dead.

The evangelists' first encounter with Jesus is invariably dramatic and assumes a Biblical quality. Luminous hands lift them up to heaven, as in the case of a well-known female preacher, whose biography goes on to report how she:

> heard a voice saying 'My child, my child, my child.' I looked up and the sky opened and I saw a person hanging from a cross. Like Jacob, I met God in a vision. He said 'I have selected you for my work.'

For others, like a popular evangelist who admits to having once been a political activist in the Dravidian movement, the encounter with Jesus is prefigured by a blinding flash of light:

> There was a bright light which blinded my eyes and I felt a hand grasping mine and pulling me upwards into the heavens. I heard a voice saying 'My son, I have forgiven you all your sins.' I knew my conversion was like Paul's the Apostle.

They hear God's voice speaking to them, see His finger pointing to an open Bible, or meet him face to face in a vision. 'I felt the presence of another being in the room. . . . He was the most wonderful person I had ever seen. He told me he was Jesus and we talked for three hours.'[19] The biography of one North American preacher who rose to prominence in the 1940s relates how his conversion came when he was visited by 'an angel bathed in light'. Such books were familiar to several evangelists in Madras and undoubtedly influenced how they chose to represent themselves (see Lindsay 1950; Lanternari 1976: 329). The creation of these local texts and the imagery they promote can therefore be seen as reflecting increasing tendencies towards what Deiros refers to as market-oriented evangelism (1991: 164).

CHARISMATIC FUNDAMENTALISM

These preachers constantly reiterate the messages of fundamentalist Christianity. They inveigh against the 'coldness' of worship in the traditional churches and the absence of 'strong', i.e. evangelistic, sermons. They attack the clergy for their failure to provide spiritual leadership. They blame the ecclesiastical hierarchy for having allowed the 'cancer' of modernism to sweep through south India, into the Christian colleges, schools and churches (see Daniel 1980: 89–90). The social gospel favoured by the church and community leadership is derided for, among other things, neglecting the quest for individual salvation. Protestant theological institutes and the religious intellectuals who dominate them, are especially vilified for teaching their students (the future clergy) that the Bible contains truths but not the Word of God. In contrast, the fundamentalists insist on the total veracity of the Bible and reject the notion of competing interpretations. They promote once again the simple 'Christian virtues': in the words of one, 'the body is a temple of God and must not be defiled by smoking, drinking, adultery or fornication'. In short, the new fundamentalists have revived the message of certainty brought by the early missionaries but subsequently overtaken by the social gospel of 'faith', with its acknowledgement of alternative truths.

Fundamentalist evangelists, therefore, advocate views about the nature of Christianity which readily accord with those of ordinary Protestants in Madras. Even more importantly, the majority of these preachers are in tune with popular beliefs about the aetiology and character of misfortune and, furthermore, offer a means of deliverance from it. This requires a word about the Pentecostal leanings of most such figures. Although the first Pentecostal missionaries came to south India in 1908, soon after the 1906 Los Angeles revival which signalled the birth of the 'tongues' movement, as it is sometimes known, it grew slowly and haphazardly in these early years (see George 1975; Sara 1990).[20] It was only after 1960, with the 'charismatic revival' in the USA – most of the major 'televangelists' in North America are Pentecostals – that its impact was felt around the world; it is now widely recognized as the third largest 'force' in Christendom (Goodman 1988: 52).

The success of Pentecostalism in the non-Western world is often attributed to its reaffirmation of local knowledges about the 'supernatural' causes of affliction. In cultures with strong beliefs about the efficacy of mystical agents, writes Wilson, 'the appeal of any missionary denomination which includes thaumaturgical elements should be precisely these, rather than other features of its teachings, activities or organization' (1973: 121). Similarly, Anderson argues that where possession and ecstasy are culturally normal, 'Pentecostalism is fully normal and healthy' (1979: 15). Even the Fuller Seminary in California, one of the most respected theological institutes in the USA, dominated since its founding after the Second World War by fundamentalists and 'progressive' evangelicals, introduced a new course in the 1980s on 'Signs, Wonders and Church Growth', 'on the assumption that much of church growth around the world was associated with charismatic signs' (Marsden 1987: 292).

Far from rejecting popular theodicies, Pentecostals in Madras are wholly in tune with them. During one visit to a neighbourhood evangelist I was told:

> The most common causes of troubles in people's lives are evil spirits (*pey*) and the work of sorcerers (*suniakaran*). The *pey* possess people [on their own or at the behest of sorcerers] and bring calamities and failures, misunderstandings in the home and especially illnesses. If a sorcerer sends an evil spirit he is probably being paid by someone who is angry [with the victim]. People go on seeing doctors to cure their diseases but they don't get better. You have to get rid of the spirit first and only then the person will improve. Sometimes sorcerers use magical

substances to harm their victims. Once a young woman was brought here and they said she was ready to be married but whenever boys came to see her they ran away. Her relatives couldn't understand it because she was fair and beautiful. So I prayed and asked for God's power and I soon found out that it was the girl's own aunt who was responsible. The woman depended on her niece and didn't want her to get married, so she had paid a sorcerer to put some paste on the girl's face to make her look like like an old hag when boys came to see her.

These kinds of popular belief are shared with Hindus and others outside the Protestant fold. But they are Christianized, by identifying the sources of affliction – evil spirits, sorcerers, etc. – as the servants of Satan. For the first time in the experience of Madras Protestants, then, there is a Christian rationale for and response to such traditionally recognized symptoms of evil in the world. Moreover, these fundamentalists are unanimous in characterizing the lesser deities of non-Christian religions as part of the Satanic pantheon. Just as the early Christians made demons of the gods of Greece and Rome, the Pentecostals relegate Hindu divinities to a similar status (see Russell 1977: 58). While the more popular preachers are somewhat circumspect in expressing such views, because of the growing sensitivity of militant Hindu organizations such as the Rastriya Swayam Sevak Sangh (RSS), neighbourhood evangelists, away from the public glare, continue to offer such unecumenical opinions. (Indeed, Catholics fare little better in the demonology of the average Pentecostal preacher.) Even the CSI's somewhat feeble attempts to 'indigenize' its ritual is seen by some fundamentalists as a concession to Hinduism, a compromise with devil worship. 'There can be no fellowship between light and darkness,' I was told.[21] Such views are especially disapproved of by the orthodox Protestant churches, which continuously seek dialogue and accommodation with Hindu organizations.

Pentecostal evangelists not only acknowledge the reality of evil spirits and other malign agents in the everyday lives of those whom they attempt to persuade but seek to demonstrate their power to overcome these forces. They therefore put the greatest doctrinal stress on the significance of the Holy Spirit in the Christian trinity and identify for special attention its powers or 'gifts' – as set out in Paul's First Letter to the Corinthians (I Cor. XII: 4–11).[22] While all those who receive baptism in the Holy Spirit may obtain one or more of these gifts, only those specially chosen by God – the charismatics – are granted the majority of, if not all, the boons. One Pentecostal leader related how he had come by his charisms:

After I accepted Jesus, God would talk to me, as you and I are talking now. Then I was filled with the power of the Holy Spirit and got the gift of tongues. After that, God began to give me many gifts without my asking: about ten gifts he has given me. The latest is prophecy.

Some claim gifts not on Paul's list, such as the abilities to identify members of an audience who are afflicted in some way, to nullify the effects of sorcery or witchcraft, even to bless and curse in the name of God.

The most important charism is that of healing, for it is on the extent of this power that most charismatics base their claim to be 'used mightily by God' and it is on their ability to heal that their reputations ultimately depend. The most prominent charismatic figure in Madras speaks of being anointed with the Holy Spirit in order to be used 'for the comforting of the sorrowful and for the healing of the sick in body'. The public appearances of the more popular Pentecostal preachers are almost invariably represented as 'divine healing Crusades'. One wall poster, announcing the meetings of a US evangelist, advertised him as the 'World-renowned Outstanding Healing Gift Minister. Millions Receive Healing all over the World. The Blind See, the Deaf Hear and the Lame Walk'.[23] One CSI clergyman, critical of these activities, commented that 'healing has become big business here. At the rate these healers are healing, there shouldn't be one unhealthy person left in Madras.'

One 'Good News' Crusade I attended, which featured an American charismatic well known to local audiences, was held over a period of seven nights on a huge area of beach used for various kinds of public performance. On the evening I was present there was an audience of some 10,000 people, according to the stewards. After several choirs and soloists had sung gospel songs and a brief speech had been made by the head of the organizing committee (which included members of numerous sectarian groups as well as representatives of several independent fundamentalist-leaning fellowships), the star evangelist arrived with a large entourage, several of whom preached to the crowd briefly, with one also reminding them that the evangelist's latest cassettes and pamphlets were available at the stalls situated around the grounds. As it grew dark and the lights came on, he took the stage. As he moved around with a portable microphone, tossing it from one hand to the other, throwing his arms and legs about, his Tamil translator moved with him, duplicating his every gesture. The emphasis throughout the hour-long 'message' was that a miracle was about to occur in everyone's life. 'I am expecting a miracle, a great miracle. You will see proof of the living God tonight.' The Evangelist continuously referred to Jesus' healing miracles and called on those who needed healing to raise their hands (nearly everyone in the vast audience did so). He then proceeded to admonish the evil spirits which brought each illness and commanded them to leave 'in the name of Jesus'.[24] The excitement of such an occasion invariably produces some dramatic results and the evangelist's media team were on hand to record on tape, film and video the 'testimonies' of people who claimed to have been delivered of their particular problems. A group of specially trained assistants was, as usual, also available to counsel those who had, as a consequence of their experience, decided to accept Christ as their personal saviour.

ASSESSING CHARISMATICS

Pentecostals have experienced the fastest recent growth of any Christian group in south India and one report suggests that by 1986 they were the third major 'tradition' in Madras, exceeded only by the Roman Catholic and CSI churches (Hedlund 1986). Nonetheless, Pentecostal and other fundamentalist groups still attract a comparatively small proportion of the Christian population to their ranks. Most people retain their attachments to the institutional churches, because, it is said, they feel bound by sentiment to the churches of their parents, prefer to celebrate their marriages there, wish to have burial rights in their cemeteries, or because it is still considered somewhat disreputable to join a sectarian group outright.

But if most Protestants remain anchored in the historic churches, fundamentalist views and practices have increasingly become part of their religious culture. Most Protestants outside the tiny elite attend many of the large Crusades which take place in Madras each year and in this way become familiar with fundamentalist discourses. Apart from the drama and entertainment value (the music is almost always lively), they appreciate the oratorical skills and 'strong messages' of the evangelists, which speak to and reinforce their own knowledges about both the basic truths of Christianity and the aetiology of affliction. A few members of the historic churches have been persuaded to the extent of taking 'second baptism' and participating fully, if secretly, in the rites of one or other fundamentalist fellowship. Some attach themselves for a time to a sectarian leader in the hope that his or her charismatic intervention will cure an illness, deal with the effects of sorcery, or be instrumental in obtaining a much needed job. Many more attend the regular prayer meetings of neighbourhood evangelists to 'be in the presence' of the Holy Spirit, as well as to hear the 'Word of God' and savour the 'warmth' of worship said to be so lacking in their own churches. Pastors of (non-elite) CSI congregations often complain that after Sunday services in their own churches, 'everyone' goes to the Pentecostals. According to one: 'I can name at least fifty members of my congregation who come for the 7:30am Eucharist service, go home for breakfast and by 10am are at the Pentecostal assembly.'

Even so, they are by no means invariably persuaded by the charismatic claims of the evangelists. The latter are judged, sometimes harshly, by ordinary people who can (and do) withdraw their support at any time. A preacher's large following, his or her thriving organization, or a substantial prayer hall, usually built with donations from individuals who have personally experienced the evangelist's gifts, or with the help of foreign sponsors, are visible evidence of divine and human favour. However, preachers who are deemed to have become too self-seeking, or to have forgotten that they are God's servants and not the other way round, can quickly forfeit the trust of ordinary people. There are several failed charismatics who serve as apt illustrations of how once-popular evangelists can fall short of their ministry and lose their followings. Assessments are also based on the success of the charismatics in granting supplicants' wishes. The evidence for their powers is available for everyone to see and hear, since, as I have noted above, those who have been the beneficiaries of these charisms publicly 'witness' to the gifts of the evangelists. Ordinary people are often accused by the latter of being fickle but, as befits the growing commodification of religion, they 'shop around' for the latest spiritual 'products', sometimes discarding the old. During the intervals between each of my visits to Madras (see note 2), it became clear that some earlier favourites had lost popularity and new stars had arisen.

But it is not only the public which judges them; they assess one another as well. Local charismatics are intensely competitive and their evaluations of one another are rarely generous (though I have never heard a foreign preacher criticized). They frequently attribute stubborn 'symptoms' in their clients to the incompetence of healers who 'treated' the victims of mystical attack before them and underline the near fatal consequences of putting oneself in the hands of a less gifted or, worse still, 'false' healer. They are especially caustic about other charismatics known to have health problems, for this is clear evidence that they are unable to heal themselves, let alone others. I have heard at least one well-known evangelist attacked for continuing to hold down a job since, his critics asserted, 'You can't do God's work part-time.' The lesser figures also accuse the more popular ones of abandoning the 'true gospel' so as to curry favour with a wider public.

This constant sniping among local healers, like the fickleness of the public's loyalty to particular individuals, paradoxically attests to a vigorous, even buoyant charismatic scene in Madras. Thomas' (1982: 771) argument that in seventeenth-century England the 'epistemological demand for certain knowledge' based on demonstration ultimately eroded the status of magical beliefs would not be readily applicable to the south Indian situation I have described. Failure to demonstrate healing power may diminish public confidence in particular preachers, but not in the certainty of local knowledge which these charismatics reinforce.

CONCLUSION

The recent effervescence of fundamentalist forms of Christianity in urban south India represents a striking instance of how international power realignments shape and transform the processes of globalization. Fundamentalist knowledge has been generated within the USA metropolitan setting, promoted abroad through US finance, personnel and technologies and authenticated largely by US dominance. The link between North American power and its global cultural products should seem too obvious to need stating, yet Said has recently felt compelled to draw attention to the considerable 'swathe' the USA now cuts through the rest of the world and the 'almost total absence' in writings by literary theorists, historians and anthropologists of 'any reference to American imperial intervention as a factor affecting the theoretical discussion' (1989: 214). Just as the 'success' of eighteenth- and nineteenth-century Protestant missions outside the West cannot be understood apart from the 'old colonial' contexts in which they took root, any understanding of con-temporary fundamentalist influences must consider the religio-cultural implications of this 'new colonial' situation. To avoid the 'circumstances of global power' is to invite the kinds of critique directed at so much post-modernist writing (Harvey 1980: 117).

The increasing pre-eminence of fundamentalist Christianity in urban south India (as elsewhere) can be read as a reassertion of religious certainty and exclusivity against the established churches' admissions of doubt, accommodation and ecumenism, ingredients of the social gospel which has been ascendant within the Protestant church and missions for the better part of a century. The earlier Protestant missionaries had offered their converts the certainties of denominational paths – albeit competing certainties – and a guarantee that Hinduism was the road to perdition; certainties backed, it should be said, by the power of the colonial state. In time, however, the emerging Protestant middle class rejected denomi-national verities and the church itself, along with the community's elites, turned towards a religion of 'faith'. With independence, such an official Protestant stance enabled the church to survive in an increasingly self-conscious 'Hindu' environment.

The great majority of ordinary Protestants continued to favour a reli-gious culture comprised of two distinctive (and in certain senses conflicting) sets of beliefs and practices. One, the legacy of their early missionaries, stressed a simple, pietistic and Bible-centred approach to Christian life and worship. The other constituted a species of popular knowledge about misfortune through which they (along with the non-Christians amongst whom they lived) understood the world of adversity around them. Both kinds of certainty were effectively denied by the church hierarchy, as by urban Protestant elites. The confidence of most Protestants in the veracity of such knowledge helps to explain, on the one hand, its persistence in the face of marginalization and, on the other, the success of global (especially Pentecostalist) fundamentalism in the past few decades. The ideologies purveyed by the foreign evangelists and their local counterparts accord with and give credence to these local certainties.

The advance of fundamentalist forms of Christianity in south India might therefore be understood both as the certainty of global power located within the metropolitan centre and as a meeting of global and local religious verities. The duality, however, can only be heuristic; for, as we have seen, global knowledge (that of the early missionaries) became part of local Protestantism, while one aspect of popular religiosity (ideas about mystical agency) was incorporated (if instrumentally) in the epistemology of global fundamentalism.

What I remain uncertain about is the different statuses of the certainties encountering one another. Lambek (in Chapter 11 of this volume) suggests we might look to Bakhtin for a useful distinction between the certainty of authoritative discourse that is externally imposed and the certainty of internally persuasive discourse. We can tentatively characterize the discourses of early Euro-American missionaries and contemporary US fundamentalists as *explicit* credos from without, while popular explanations of misfortune would count as *implicit* forms of certainty. But this would be to essentialize these knowledges which are, in practice, constantly reformulated and, as Bakhtin notes, in dialogic interrelationship (1981: 341–2). Moreover, in the urban south Indian context the authoritative discourses of Western religious ideologues have in the past been and continue in the present to become internally persuasive for large sections of the local Protestant community. At that point they are transformed from global to local certainties.

Attention to global–local interchanges raises questions about the view long held in south Asian studies that we can only make sense of 'minority' world religions by situating them primarily in the Hindu context (see Dumont 1970: 205–11). Such an approach attributes little relevance to transnational politico-religious currents; or, as one critic puts it, 'foreign influence is submerged in an all-pervasive Indian sump' (Stirrat 1992: 196). In his own study of Catholicism in Sri Lanka, Stirrat acknowledges the importance of indigenous Sri Lankan forces but insists on the need to take account of 'the wider world of the Catholic Church' (*ibid.*). Making a not dissimilar point, Werbner (in Chapter 6 of this volume) suggests that there are crucial aspects of Sufism which transcend specific cultural environments. Thus an interest in processes of globalization requires us to keep both parts of the equation in our sights. As anthropologists, our focus almost inevitably falls on the 'vernacular' (James and Johnson 1988), on the subaltern communities and localities which respond to (even resist) invasive cultural forces (Hannerz 1992: 35). But 'globalization' is not a monolithic process, with similar outcomes in every instance. The situation I have discussed in this chapter demonstrates aspects of local mediation, homogenization and creolization of cultures but also reveals the inexorable spread of Western religious ideologies. One certain knowledge is that the encounter we are attempting to understand is not an equal one.

NOTES

1 I am indebted to Wendy James for her stimulating pre-conference notes circulated to participants in the Section on 'Religious and Cultural Certainties' at

the ASA Decennial Conference in July 1993 and for subsequent editorial advice. Thanks are also due to Pat Caplan for helpful comments on an earlier draft of this chapter.

2 I have followed developments in Madras for nearly twenty years, conducting fieldwork there in 1974–5, 1981–2 and 1991–2. The most recent visit of approximately four months was made possible by an award from the Nuffield Foundation and a supplementary grant from the British Academy, to whom I express my gratitude.

3 Lambek (in Chapter 11 of this volume) makes the point that the 'local' culture he observed in 1975 was a product of much earlier, mainly Islamic, influences which had reached Mayotte.

4 The notion of 'fundamentalism' has acquired some extremely negative connotations of late and clearly should only be employed as a comparative, analytic term with the utmost caution (see Caplan 1987a). The term does, however, have a respectable ancestry in the context of twentieth-century Protestant history and it is for this reason that I feel justified in using it without constant resort to inverted commas.

5 Although there are some significant theological distinctions among fundamentalists, evangelicals and Pentecostals, there are also important similarities (see Wilcox 1992). Deiros (1991) conflates these terms in his discussion of Latin American fundamentalism, while Anderson argues that Pentecostalism should be regarded as part of the fundamentalist movement (1979: 6).

6 The specific political contexts in which Western religious ideologies are purveyed and understood have been transformed since (and by) India's independence. Whereas until well into the twentieth century Christian missionaries benefited from official protection if not active state support, the post-independence era saw successive governments curtailing missionary numbers and activities. At the same time, Indian Christians have come to regard themselves as a vulnerable minority in a population increasingly jealous of its 'Hindu' character.

7 Shamsul (in Chapter 5 of this volume) suggests a not dissimilar divide among Malaysian university students. On the one side are those associated with the radical *dakwah* revivalist movement, who insist on the certainty of Islamic 'revealed knowledge' and on the other are those who, through commitment to unrevealed (human) knowledge gained from social sciences, tend to affiliate to the moderate wing of *dakwah*.

8 Some two-thirds of Indian Christians reside in the four southern states of Kerala, Andhra Pradesh, Karnataka and Tamil Nadu. They form the largest minority in the latter, with a population in 1981 of approximately 2.8 million or just under 6 per cent of the state's total.

9 The first Protestant mission in south India was a Lutheran station established in the first decade of the eighteenth century in the Danish territory of Tranquebar on the Coromandel coast. The first mission in Madras city was set up in 1726.

10 The CSI was formed in part because the missionaries realized the folly of perpetuating their denominational distinctions in the Indian context. Increasing interdenominational co-operation in the health and education fields and the emerging Indian nationalist movement, further encouraged ecumenical thinking. But its realization was at least as much due to an emerging Indian Christian middle class which could not tolerate rigid denominational barriers in the course of economic and social advancement (see Caplan 1980).

11 Baptists and Lutherans were the only two major Protestant denominations which remained outside the union.

12 As Marsden points out, the suggestion that God reveals himself in non-

Christian religions can have 'profound implications for missionary programs' (1980: 167).

13 In the USA of late the association between fundamentalism and right-wing politics has become explicit (see Wilcox 1992). Deiros, writing about the 'phenomenal' expansion of fundamentalist groups in Latin America, suggests that the link between this growth, the US (Republican) administration's political offensive and support for right-wing regimes is 'forged of ideology, history and world-view, not of conspiracy' (1991: 176–7).

14 Such forms of Christianity have not only been exported outside the West of course. Coleman has studied a Swedish sect which has been heavily influenced by US fundamentalism (1991).

15 Some of the more 'progressive' fundamentalists are ready to engage with and thereby influence modernist churches, which contradicts the general tendency towards separatism among such organizations. Thus Billy Graham has often been attacked by other fundamentalist groups for co-operating with non-fundamentalist churches, as has Jerry Falwall of the 'Moral Majority' for his readiness to make common cause with unbelievers (see Ammerman 1991: 46)

16 Deiros notes how in Latin America local evangelists 'consciously imitate US counterparts' (1991: 164).

17 For the first time in 1992 I noticed one such Crusade being advertised on a huge billboard of the kind which normally only announces a new film. The US evangelist's face appeared between the giant cut-out figures of several Tamil movie stars in Ramboesque poses.

18 Since they cannot broadcast on state radio in India, these evangelists buy time on such stations as Radio Ceylon and Radio Seychelles. There are, as yet, no televangelists in south India.

19 The US evangelist Pat Robertson was said to 'scandalize' Biblicist fundamentalists of the Falwell ('Moral Majority') type because of his reports of conversations with God (Averill 1989: 115).

20 Anderson reports that scores of Pentecostal missionaries went abroad in the early years of the twentieth century convinced that with their facility for 'speaking in tongues' they would have the miraculous ability to preach the gospel in the languages of the natives. He reports widespread disillusion when they discovered that glossolalia meant something quite different (1979: 139).

21 The staid Fuller Seminary in California was 'chagrined' at the advice given by one member of staff to Christians who happened to visit 'pagan' temples on their travels in foreign lands: they would be well advised, he suggested, to 'exorcise their homes from demons' who might have 'attached themselves to persons or luggage' (Marsden 1987: 294).

22 These are prophecy, tongues, healing, faith, interpretation, discernment, wisdom, miracles and knowledge.

23 This excerpt from Matthew XI: 5 is frequently quoted in the advertisements of fundamentalist evangelists. Leaflets promoting the appearance of Morris Cerullo, 'the World Famous International Evangelist', at the Royal Albert Hall in London in 1992, announced his 'Great Miracle Crusade – Salvation – Healing – Miracles' and ended with 'The Blind See, the Deaf Hear, the Lame Walk'.

24 Anderson notes that Pentecostal healing prayers almost always include a commandment to the 'deaf spirit', the 'cancer demon', etc. to come out in the name of Jesus (1979: 95)

110   *Emerging World Forms*

REFERENCES

Ammerman, N.T. (1991) 'North American Protestant fundamentalism', pp. 1–65, in M.E. Marty and R.S. Appleby (eds) *Fundamentalisms Observed*, Chicago: University of Chicago Press.

Anderson, R.M. (1979) *Vision of the Disinherited: the making of American Pentecostalism*, New York: Oxford University Press.

Appiah, K.A. (1991) 'Is the post- in postmodernism the post- in postcolonial?' *Critical Inquiry*, 17: 336–57.

Averill, L.J. (1989) *Religious Right, Religious Wrong: a critique of the fundamentalist phenomenon*, New York: Pilgrim Press.

Bakhtin, M.M. (1981) *The Dialogic Imagination*, M. Holquist (ed.), trans. C. Emerson and M. Holquist, Austin, TX: University of Texas Press.

Barr, J. (1977) *Fundamentalism*, London: SCM Press.

Caplan, L. (1980) 'Class and Christianity in south India: indigenous responses to western denominationalism', *Modern Asian Studies*, 14: 645–71.

——(1987a) 'Introduction', pp. 1–24, in L. Caplan (ed.) *Studies in Religious Fundamentalism*, London: Macmillan.

——(1987b) *Class and Culture in Urban India: fundamentalism in a Christian community*, Oxford: Clarendon Press.

Coleman, S. (1991) 'Faith which conquers the world: Swedish fundamentalism and the globalization of culture', *Ethnos*, 56: 6–18.

Daniel, J. (1980) *Another Daniel*, Madras: The Laymen's Evangelical Fellowship.

Deiros, P.A. (1991) 'Protestant fundamentalism in Latin America', pp. 142–96, in M.E. Marty and R.S. Appleby (eds) *Fundamentalisms Observed*, Chicago: Chicago University Press.

Diehl, C.G. (1965) *Church and Shrine: intermingling patterns of culture in the life of some Christian groups in south India*, Uppsala: Hakan Ohlssons Boktryckeri.

Dumont, L. (1970) *Homo Hierarchicus: the caste system and its implications*, trans. Mark Sainsbury, Chicago: University of Chicago Press.

George, T.C. (1975) 'The growth of Pentecostal churches in south India', MA thesis in Missiology, Fuller Seminary, Pasadena, CA.

Goodman, F.D. (1988) *How about Demons? Possession and exorcism in the modern world*, Bloomington, IN: Indiana University Press.

Hannerz, U. (1992) 'The global ecumene as a network of networks', pp. 34–58, in A. Kuper (ed.) *Conceptualizing Society*, London: Routledge.

Harvey, D. (1980) *The Condition of Postmodernity: an enquiry into the origins of cultural change*, Oxford: Basil Blackwell.

Hedlund, R.E. (1986) 'Church planting in selected Indian cities', unpublished seminar paper, Church Growth Research Centre, Madras.

James, W. and D.H. Johnson (eds) (1988) *Vernacular Christianity: Essays in the Social Anthropology of Religion, Presented to Godfrey Lienhardt* (JASO Occasional Papers no. 7), Oxford and New York: JASO/Lilian Barber Press.

Lanternari, V. (1976) 'Dreams as charismatic significants: their bearing on the rise of new religious movements', pp. 321–35, in A. Bharati (ed.) *The Realm of the Extra-human: ideas and actions*, The Hague: Mouton.

Lawrence, B.B. (1990) *Defenders of God: the fundamentalist revolt against the modern age*, London: I.B. Taurus.

Lindsay, G. (in collaboration with W. Branham) (1950) *William Branham: a man sent from God*, Jeffersonville, IN: William Branham.

Marsden, G. (1980) *Fundamentalism and American Culture: the shaping of twentieth-century evangelicalism 1870–1925*, New York: Oxford University Press.

——(1987) *Reforming Fundamentalism: Fuller Seminary and the new evangelicalism*, Grand Rapids, MI: William B. Eerdmans.

Marty, M.E. and R.S. Appleby (eds) (1991) *Fundamentalisms Observed*, Chicago: University of Chicago Press.

Norman, E. (1979) *Christianity and the World Order*, Oxford: Oxford University Press.

Ostow, M. (1990) 'The fundamentalist phenomenon: a psychological perspective', pp. 99–125, in N. Cohen (ed.) *The Fundamentalist Phenomenon: a view from within: a response from without*, Grand Rapids, MI: William B. Eerdmans.

Russell, J.B. (1977) *The Devil: perceptions of evil from antiquity to primitive Christianity*, Ithaca, NY: Cornell University Press.

Said, E. (1989) 'Representing the colonized: anthropology's interlocutors', *Critical Inquiry*, 15: 205–25.

Sara, K.O. (1990) 'A Critical Evaluation of the Indian Pentecostal Church of God – its origin and development in Kerala', MA thesis, Serampore University.

Stanley, R. (1991) 'Signs and Wonders', *India Church Growth Quarterly*, 13: 133–7.

Stirrat, R.L. (1992) *Power and Religiosity in a Post-Colonial Setting: Sinhala Catholics in contemporary Sri Lanka*, Cambridge: Cambridge University Press.

Thomas, K. (1982) [1971] *Religion and the Decline of Magic*, Harmondsworth: Penguin Books.

Towler, R. (1984) *The Need for Certainty: a sociological study of conventional religion*, London: Routledge and Kegan Paul.

Wilcox, C. (1992) *God's Warriors: the Christian Right in twentieth-century America*, Baltimore, MD: Johns Hopkins University Press.

Wilson, B. (1973) *Magic and the Millennium*, London: Paladin.

Wilson, S. and J. Siewert (eds) (1986) *Mission Handbook: North American Protestant ministries overseas*, Monrovia, CA: Missions Advanced Research and Communication Center.

5 Inventing certainties

The *dakwah* persona in Malaysia

Shamsul A.B.

INTRODUCTION

This chapter is about an Islamic revival movement, popularly known as *dakwah*, at the grassroots in Malaysia. More specifically, it is a narrative and analysis of how one becomes a *dakwah* activist, a much neglected question in the study of Malaysian Islamic revivalism.

The central focus of nearly all the studies of Malaysian *dakwah* has been on the movement as a group or organization, its origin, performance and the impact on contemporary society (Mohamed Abu Bakar 1989; Chandra Muzaffar 1987; Nagata 1984; Zainah Anwar 1987; Hussin Muttalib 1990). With the exception of Zainah (1987), none of these studies has shown any serious interest in the life of the ordinary *dakwah*, the individuals who form the bulk of the collective of tireless and 'faceless' activists of the movement. This chapter hopes to redress the situation.

Although the main focus of this piece is ethnographic in nature, it also addresses itself to a central sociological issue; namely, the continued importance of the traditional role of education, formal and informal, in 'inventing certainties' through competing truth-claims that demand both total as well as diverse response. Seen from Gilsenan's viewpoint, it is a 'struggle over the definition of what is the tradition' (Gilsenan 1982: 15), in this particular case the struggle over defining what is the 'authentic Islamic tradition', a crucial element indeed that has motivated Islamic fundamentalist movements worldwide. The struggle has always been fragmented, because the process of establishing the authentic tradition has in itself created many traditions within, which inevitably come into opposition with one another.

In the Malaysian context, at the grassroots, the struggle seems to be between the 'radical' and the 'moderate' *dakwah*, which my research shows can be traced, to a great extent, to the 'educational conditioning' of the *dakwah* activists; first when they were at secondary school, and later when they were university undergraduates. Why arts students become 'moderates' and science students 'radicals' is examined in this context. The focus on students is intentional because the Malaysian *dakwah* movement was primarily initiated by university students; in the early stage by those study-ing in local universities and later by those studying abroad.

Before proceeding to the main part of this chapter, I first present a brief overview of the Malaysian *dakwah* movement, spanning a period of about twenty-five years since 1969 (for further background see Shamsul 1983, 1989, 1994).

THE PHASES OF THE MALAYSIAN *DAKWAH* MOVEMENT

Religious revivalism in general, in my opinion, has been motivated by a number of reasons. In no particular order of importance, they are as follows: first, as an attempt to overcome the pressures of modernization or to construct a reply to it; second, as a type of anti-imperialist, anti-hegemonical movement; third, as an expression of spiritual renewal generated from within a given religion, such as the move to 're-Islamize knowledge'; fourth, as a counter-movement to rationalization; fifth, as an attempt to resolve how to live in a world of radical doubt; sixth, as an expression of modernity through reformulation of cultural *gestalt*; seventh, as a reinterpretation of traditional symbols and systems of meaning; and, finally, as an attempt to reinvent and reconstruct tradition, thus allowing a redefinition and/or reassertion of ethno-religious identi-ties in a plural society.

Islamic revivalism in Malaysia can be seen as having gone through at least four main phases thus far: namely, 'the reawakening period' (1969–74); 'the foward movement period' (1975–9); 'the mainstream period' (1979–90); and '*dakwah* and industrialized Malaysia' (1991 onwards). I now outline briefly the central features of each of these periods to allow us to observe the shifting contexts through which the *dakwah* movement has meandered in the past two decades.

As most observers contend, the 'reawakening phase' (1969–74) had its origin, arguably, in the aftermath of the Sino-Malay riot in Kuala Lumpur, Malaysia's capital city, on 13 May 1969. This followed an earlier, larger-scale riot in 1945 when religious and millennarian motives were also central to the actions and reactions of Malay-Muslims. The main differ-ence was that the 1945 riot took place chiefly in the rural areas but the 1969 riot was essentially an urban event. All Malay-Muslim university students then resided in Kuala Lumpur, many in the area where the riot took place.

The pivotal event that gave birth to Islamic revivalism in Malaysia occurred in August 1969 on the campus of the University of Malaya, when the National Association of Muslim Students (NAMS) decided to set up a youth organization operating outside the campus, named Angkatan Belia Islam Malaysia (ABIM), or Muslim Youth Movement Malaysia. The proposed body was intended to enable graduates to continue their post-campus *dakwah* activities. By 1971 Malaysia had three other new universities – namely, Universiti Kebangsaan Malaysia (UKM), Universiti Pertanian Malaysia (UPM) and Universiti Sains Malaysia (USM) – which meant there was a sudden expansion of the student population and hence a larger constituency from which to recruit new *dakwah* activists and supporters.

There was another form of 'revivalism' in Malaysian society as a whole as a result of the 1969 racial riot. Between May 1969 and February 1971, Parliament was suspended and the country came under emergency rule. This became a period of serious 'rethinking, reflecting, bargaining and reconcili- ation' at all levels, including the individual level. The pro-Malay Muslim affir- mative New Economic Policy (NEP) was born out of this 'big rethinking' process. The birth of the Islamic revivalist movement in Malaysia must be seen as part and parcel of these wider social developments.

The single most important event that gave the *dakwah* movement, particularly ABIM, its much needed political credentials in the eyes of the Malaysian public took place in December 1974, when thousands of students demonstrated in the streets of Kuala Lumpur to protest against peasant hunger and poverty. The whole event was organized and led by the *dakwah* leaders within the student organization. The year 1974 was also the time when Partai Islam, a long-time Malay opposition group to the government, joined the ruling coalition, thus leaving a political vacuum into which ABIM comfortably slotted itself, not surprisingly with a good deal of support and sympathy from disappointed Partai Islam supporters.

Therefore, it could be said that the *dakwah* movement in the first phase moved very quickly from a position of concern with conscientization to one which found a controlling position in national politics through student activism. This helped to make Malaysia more Islamic-inclined and the movement was now able to address Islamic issues more positively in the wider society.

The second phase (1975–9) was really a 'foward movement' period for the Malaysian *dakwah* movement, for two inter-related reasons. First, the movement had become consolidated and had, after about six years, found its niche in the Malaysian socio-political sphere. Second, the United Malays National Organization (UMNO), the dominant Malay party in the ruling coalition, was still struggling to resolve an unprecedentedly bitter battle amongst its top leaders. This helped to make ABIM (with its progressive approach, not representing Islam in a black–white, evil–good, right–wrong manner and not believing in imposing Islam on non-Muslims) appear a reasonable and credible political opposition.

Until about 1976/7, ABIM and the national Muslim student body, NAMS, were dominated by arts students, with a small number of science students involved, because most of the Malay-Muslim students were in the arts faculties and they ran most of the student organizations. After that period ABIM and the influence of its type of *dakwah* declined, at least in the local campuses. Student unions and NAMS in local universities were taken over by the new *dakwah* student group, dominated this time not by arts but by science students. By then the population of science students had increased dramatically because all the science faculties in Malaysia were operating at full capacity.

The new *dakwah* group was known on campus as the IRC (Islamic Representative Council) and had its origin overseas, established by government-sponsored Malay-Muslim science undergraduates. Because this group was born out of the Malaysian socio-political milieu and was informed mainly by sectarian Islamic groups based in the Middle East and South Asia, its focus was more 'religion for religion's sake' rather than 'religion for society's sake'. On the campuses, there was a clear division between the moderate ABIM and the radical IRC supporters, who both looked down upon each other in a 'holier than thou' attitude.

By then, the government had finally come out with a concrete response to the Islamic challenge. The challenge for the government was not so much to dismantle the *dakwah* movement – it was now too late or almost impossible to do so – but more to co-opt or mainstream it first and then shape it to a form that would serve government interests.

The 'mainstream' phase (1979–90) saw a renewed focus on Islam by the Malaysian government as a result of international and domestic factors. This phenomenon gradually increased throughout the 1980s. It also related to the coming of a new Prime Minister, Dr Mahathir Mohamed, who took up the position in 1981 after an influential period as Acting Prime Minister. In the government's estimation the potential combination of the student-based *dakwah* movement with Partai Islam, which had left the governing coalition and resumed its traditional role as the Malay-Muslim opposition, was politically explosive. Domestically, the government adopted a give-and-take method of partial co-option, whereby it decided to offer its own version of '*dakwah*ism', one that was more moderate, tolerant and suitable to the multi-ethnic society of Malaysia, in which the Muslim and non-Muslim populations are about equal in number. Further, in demonstrating that its Muslim-oriented foreign policy was 'sincere' and not merely for show, the government introduced a series of policies implementing things Islamic. Millions of dollars were spent on various Islamic-oriented causes between 1979 and 1982, such as the establishment of the Southeast Asian Islamic Research Centre based in Malaysia; the introduction of Islamic religious knowledge as a subject in the O-level examination; the official launching of the National *Dakwah* Month and the announcement that the economic system would be remodelled on Islamic lines, beginning with the establishment of bodies such as the Islamic Bank, Islamic Pawnshop, Islamic Insurance and Islamic Economic Foundation.

Many state governments within the Federation of Malaysia began to introduce their own Islamization rules and programmes, mainly in areas of Islamic moral codes of behaviour, such as banning Muslims from drinking alcohol in public. Hence the momentum of the government *dakwah*ism generated by the federal government began to spread not only in urban areas but also to the rural areas, where Islam has been practised for generations, though not in the overt and self-righteous '*dakwah* way'. In short, *dakwah*, the well-known urban phenomenon, had by the end of the 1980s truly 'migrated' to the rural areas, where the wearing of *mini telekung* (a head cover coming down to the chest) by women, for instance, was now a common sight, not through the efforts of any *dakwah* group from the movement itself but through the government's efforts.

In the general public sphere, the impact of the *dakwah* movement and the change it has wrought in the social fabric of Malaysian life is widespread, felt not only by Muslims but also by non-Muslims; namely, Malaysians of Chinese and Indian origin. Consequently, Muslim and non-Muslim (read Malay and non-Malay) relations have become somewhat tense and awkward at times because of the influence of strict behaviour codes practised first by the *dakwah* and later by the Muslim majority (Zainah 1987; Ackerman and Lee 1988). One example that demonstrates how the *dakwah* ethos has permeated every layer of society, both within and outside the Muslim community, and how it has affected everyday forms of social interaction at the grassroots level, concerns the Malay-Muslim dietary rules or food taboos. Many Muslims now will not eat food brought by non-Muslim colleagues to social gatherings, be they at the workplace or at the homes of non-Muslim colleagues. In the past such food, as long as it was not pork, was eaten without fuss. These food taboos have now extended beyond not eating pork to not eating anything cooked by non-Muslims, because they have not 'cleansed' their cooking utensils in the Islamic way. The non-Muslims see this development as representing an increase in Muslim intolerance of non-Malays and non-Muslims.

The *dakwah* movement is here to stay in Malaysia. It has now moved from a peripheral position, when it first appeared in 1969, to a central position in social life. It has also spread from urban to rural areas and extended its influence from the middle class, where its founders were located, to both upper and lower classes. It has become so pluralized ideologically and so widespread in its influence that, phenomenologically, one could virtually choose to be an extremist or moderate *dakwah* and change position as one pleased according to one's situation, the time or one's station in life. In daily interaction, to be *dakwah* could simpy mean just being more religious and strict in one's observance of the Muslim behaviour codes, or it could mean being a committed activist.

Now we turn to the major focus of this chapter, that is, the creation of the *dakwah* persona through a process which could be termed the 'invention of certainties'.

THE *DAKWAH* PERSONA INVENTED

What I present here is an analysis of how six male students from my university, Universiti Kebangsaan Malaysia (UKM), became *dakwah* activists from their high-school days, remained very active during their four undergraduate years on campus and continue to be activists to this day even after having left university. I have known the six students since 1986. I did not attempt to interview female *dakwah* activists after being refused several times on 'religious grounds'.

Allow me to begin with a rather personal note. It is not a coincidence that one of these students is related to me and has just completed his science degree at UKM. As far as I am concerned, he was the catalyst that made me embark on this research project. I have known his mother since my childhood because we belong to the same clan in a matrilineal society of Adat Perpatih, Negeri Sembilan, living and growing up together in a cluster of seven extended family homes. The other five students are from non-matrilineal Malay backgrounds. Three studied arts and the other two science for their undergraduate degrees.

My research on the present subject began not as a formal project. It started as a family counselling exercise, when the mother of my relative and eventual key informant came to see me, very upset and worried, to seek advice and help to 'save' her son from 'masuk jadi *dakwah*' (literally, 'enter to become *dakwah*'). The son was still in high-school at that time, in one of the special junior science colleges created by the government for Malay-Muslims, studying science and wanting to be a medical doctor.

Initially, I took a very casual attitude to this matter, and casual too were the discussions I had with him. They were more like 'big brother talk' sessions. But it became a little more serious after I gained his confidence and he became more frank and open. We then began to talk as if we were equals. I was amazed at the amount of knowledge he had not only about the history of the *dakwah* movement in Malaysia but also about the different groups within it and their orientations. Then I began to feel that he was becoming more and more like a 'key informant' rather than the 'client' of a counsellor.

What made me decide to accept my relative as a key informant and embark on this research was the fact that, at that time, I was teaching some aspects of the topic '*Dakwah* Movement in Malaysia' as part of a course on Malaysian society. By then the literature on *dakwah* had grown much faster than the movement itself but none of it had really explored how these activists, at the individual level, had become *dakwah*, with the exception of the work of Zainah Anwar (1987).

While the discussion sessions proceeded with my informant–relative, who was still at high-school in early 1987, I was not only teaching *dakwah* in Malaysia at the university but also being affected by its intense

activities both in and outside the university. Moreover, since 1983, I continually heard from university bureaucrats, academic staff, general staff and
students who were directly or indirectly associated with the *dakwah* movement, the view that the science students were more *dakwah* than the
arts students. At that time too, in 1987, I had with me an honours' year
arts student, who was a committed *dakwah* activist himself, as a supervisee researching into '*dakwah* and rural leadership in Malaysia'.

The choice of the six students on whom I focus here was made simply
through personal networks. The science students who became my key
informants were introduced by my informant–relative and the arts
students by my honours' year supervisee. After about seven years of
personal relationship with these six key informants, we have become good
friends. It also took me this long to unravel their life stories, the texts and
sub-texts and begin to understand and empathize with their commitment
to *dakwah*. Nonetheless, I would like to emphasize that my research is
not a psychological study of the '*dakwah* mind' but it leans rather towards
the study of the 'social construction of the *dakwah* activist'.

Thus, what I present is not a full biographical study of these six key
informants but a brief summary of my findings. I have also managed to
have indirect contact with thirty more student *dakwah* activists because
each of my key informants runs his own small discussion group or *usrah*.

The six key informants came from large, low-income families residing
in rural Peninsular Malaysia: one is the child of a settler of a government-
funded plantation-like institution, called FELDA; two are children of
single-crop rice growers; and the other three belong to families who are
rubber smallholders. None received Westernized pre-school education but
all received pre-school informal religious instruction, mainly learning how
to dress properly in accordance with Islamic dress codes, to read the Quran
and memorize verses relevant to daily prayers, as well as to practise the
ablution rituals and daily prayers correctly and to fast during Ramadan.

In terms of age, the three arts students are slightly older than the three
science students because they experienced thirteen years of secondary
schooling, spending one extra year at A-level, rather than the twelve years
at school which the science students had before they enrolled at the
university. They were born in either 1969 or 1970, when the *dakwah* movement was beginning. They went to school in the mid-1970s, when the
second phase of the movement had just begun. They joined the university, around 1986 or 1987, when the movement was going through its
third phase, or the mainstream period, during which time the government
managed to separate the moderate *dakwah*, mostly made up of arts
students, from the more radical movement, mostly followed by science
students.

In my opinion, the best way of presenting a combined analysis of these
six biographies is by narrating and analysing the 'educational conditions'
and circumstances which made the students *dakwah* activists; first when

they were at school and later when they were undergraduates. I believe the twelve or thirteen years they spent at school were a critical period, when not only was the state in a position to 'indoctrinate and shape' them, but so too was any other group with dedication and a creative strategy to penetrate the highly controlled and protected school system. The students' four years at university could be considered as the consolidation period.

CARVING THE PATH TO *DAKWAH*

In the comparison which follows, I have simply called the arts students 'the arts key informants' and the science students 'the science key informants', in a discussion of their respective experiences first in school and then in university.

Educational conditions at school

Each of the arts key informants spent thirteen years in school, from the ages of 6 to 18, with the first six years in primary school and the next seven in secondary school. At the end of the fifth year of their secondary education they sat for their O-level examinations; at the end of their seventh, for their A-levels. The three science key informants went through the same six years for their primary school education but spent a year less on their secondary education. After finishing their O-levels, they took A-levels at the end of their sixth year. Thus they spent twelve years in school, from the ages of 6 to 17, a year less than their arts counterparts.

It is important to point out that none of the key informants went through any pre-school education, because it was not available in rural Malaysia in the mid-1970s. This means that they were exposed to *dakwah* much later than the 1990s generation of Malay-Muslim children. At present, pre-school education is available in almost every part of the country and is run mainly by private interests. Many *dakwah* groups have set up their own private kindergartens, charging nominal fees and hence attracting a large number of low-income parents. Besides introducing the basics of reading, writing and arithmetic, like the rest of the non-*dakwah* kindergartens, the *dakwah* groups also introduce lessons on Quran reading and how to make ablutions and conduct prayers. Therefore, many Malay-Muslims children are now exposed to '*dakwah*ization' at a very young age, around 4 or 5 years old.

However, the first serious exposure to *dakwah* for the science key informants was when they were about 12 years old, after entering the junior science colleges (around 1981/2). The arts key informants experienced *dakwah* much later when they were about 15 years old (around 1984/5). At that stage they were preparing for their O-level examinations and attending free tuition classes run by *dakwah* organizations.

The crucial factor to take note of here is the fact that both the 'arts' and 'science' students received a similar education until they sat for the government's national evaluation examination at Grade 5, when they were about 10 years old. A year later, the top students from this examination were selected to enter a dozen or so fully residential junior science colleges located all over the country, to continue their schooling at the secondary level. The rest of the students usually proceeded to the ordinary secondary school and would not be streamed into 'science' and 'arts' until they were about 15 years old.

Let us now focus, first, on the life of the students in the said science colleges, as narrated by the three science key informants, before turning to the arts students.

The science students

The colleges these students attended were similar to the ordinary co-ed secondary schools except that they were often sited in minor rural towns, but they were provided with the best facilities that the government allocated to its residential schools. The students, both female and male, were housed separately in a number of two-storey hostels next to the main school buildings and each floor was supervised by a teacher who had his or her room at the end of the building, separated from the student dormitories by the flight of stairs. The building was designed to allow the teachers to have direct access to and control of the students, and for the students to have direct access to the teachers, at all times.

The life in these colleges was very regimented; they were run almost like military schools. There was a fixed daily schedule from dawn to dusk that students and in-house teachers had to follow strictly, such as the 'lights-on, lights-off' period. Such an approach was adopted by these colleges for the purpose of 'creating a disciplined and effective learning situation'. Students in each year were divided into small discussion groups, with between ten and fifteen in each group. They met frequently, on their own, with respective subject teachers or with the in-house teachers, to go through their academic problems. Inter- and intra-group competition was often very strong because competitions were organized by subject teachers or the school, pitching various groups against one another, to choose the best to represent the school in local or national contests.

It is not surprising that members of these groups often remained very close to one another outside the study context, such as during games or weekend outings. As they stayed for at least five years in these colleges, by the end of that period a level of group solidarity and loyalty developed amongst members of the discussion groups, which was often maintained after they left the college.

It is such groups that the overseas-originating radical *dakwah* movements, such as the IRC, managed to penetrate. Their members, who mostly became graduate science teachers, returned to serve out their contracts with the government and were posted to these colleges in the early 1980s. They were the first batch of *dakwah*-oriented teachers sent to these colleges and as the majority of them were still single, they were often assigned as in-house teachers to the student hostels.

According to the science key informants, these teachers were extremely friendly and dedicated, when compared to the non-*dakwah* ones, who were seen as too discipline-conscious and too distant from the students. They often went out of their way to assist students both in their studies and in dealing with personal problems. From the science key informants' point of view, the most 'innovative' and 'interesting' activity the *dakwah* teachers introduced was to conduct weekly meetings of all work group leaders in the college, taking them in twos or threes (the male teachers taking the male students and the female teachers taking the female ones), during their allowed weekend outings, to attend the monthly *dakwah* teachers' study group meetings at nearby large towns, state capitals or the national capital city itself. The informants agreed that the experience and the exposure to the mature *dakwah* organization were important in shaping their views, acceptance and finally commitment to *dakwah*.

Contrary to the general stereotype, the informants said that at no time were they coerced or 'brainwashed' to join the *dakwah* movement. They remembered the discussion sessions they participated in on their weekend outings were basically 'academic'. These involved much 're-reading and relearning' about Islam and developing new 'non-Arabic' Islamic perspectives (for instance, Pakistani, Indian, Sudanese, Iranian and Indonesian). The informants studied Islamic history, its variety of practices and also the general problems facing contemporary Muslims worldwide. They also learned about the origins and history of the Malaysian *dakwah* movement, its founders and problems. They were told that the particular group they were in was closer to Islamic principles in its theory and practice when compared to ABIM, which was considered to be too moderate and weak.

After about ten months, the students were then given the task of initiating similar discussions within their study groups at the college but organized as a separate activity, known as 'discussions on general knowledge and public affairs'. Initially, the organization of such sessions was facilitated by the in-house *dakwah* teachers, who decided the schedule for such discussions and frequently offered their rooms as a meeting place. According to the informants, it took between eighteen and thirty months before such discussions became systematized, developed into a permanent feature and attracted 'devoted discussants', both males and females, who joined separate-gendered groups. The college administration or the Department of Education did not know about the existence of these groups until a few years later.

Once these initial groups were established, many of the 'devoted discussants' were mobilized by the teachers and leaders to set up separate smaller *kumpulan diskusi*, or discussion groups, with a maximum of five members, recruited from the 'seniors and freshers' of the college. These small groups operated separately from the larger academic ones (which concentrated mainly on academic subjects) and devoted much time to talking about 'general knowledge and public affairs' matters, particularly pertaining to Islam. Their members found it relatively easy to express dissenting opinions or criticisms about the school, the nation, other Muslims and almost anybody they felt like criticizing. For a group of individuals raised in a military-style organization such opportunities were 'mentally liberating', said the key informants. They called these groups '*dakwah* discussion groups'. It was not long before these gatherings took over some of the academic functions of the larger academic study groups set up by the college. The latter continued to exist but were much weakened.

After the informants left their colleges to enrol in the university around 1987/8, they estimated that these '*dakwah* discussion groups' became even more important to many students because they were small, and intragroup relationships were much easier to conduct on a very personal basis. It was also difficult for the school authorities to identify these groups because of their size; they could easily pass as ordinary informal daily gatherings of friends. In fact, many members of these discussion groups applied for and were enrolled in the same local universities, often studying the same subjects. With such groups firmly established at the junior science college level, one could say that the *dakwah* movement had finally 'migrated' from the university to the schools and established itself as a permanent feature there.

The key informants never failed to stress the fact that they always reminded themselves and every member of these *dakwah* discussion groups that they were the select top students of the country, the cleverest of the lot, and one day they would lead the nation. Hence they must prepare themselves seriously for this important mission, guided by Islamic principles. Their second important mission was to 'Islamicize scientific knowledge', because they were the best science 'brains' in the country and moreover had now acquired a good knowledge of Islam, in terms both of theory and practice. They believed that with the rigorous scientific methods they had acquired in their academic studies they would be able to unravel the scientific principles hidden in the Quran. Such a project, they thought, would also enrich their detailed knowledge of the content and interpretation of the Quran, in particular, and Islamic principles in general.

This was the simple but powerful guiding philosophy of these small *dakwah* discussion groups originating from the junior science colleges, and it did not change very much even after the students entered university. The members of these groups had a very focused purpose for their *dakwah* activities and a mission informed, in many fascinating ways, by a particularly non-Islamic, Western, scientific paradigm for their approach to the re-study of the Quran and Islam.

The arts students

The arts students key informants' experience was, in many ways, quite different from that of their science counterparts. First, they were never brought up in such a military lifestyle. Second, they were not exposed to serious *dakwah* activities until they were preparing for their O-levels. Third, they lived amongst ordinary people in the community and led a life not much different from that of those around them. Fourth, they did not participate in small discussion groups, mainly organized by ABIM, until they studied for their A-levels: that is, about two years before they went to university. Fifth, in their re-study of the Quran and Islam they did not develop a focused paradigmatic approach based on their academic studies. Sixth, they spent much time studying and preparing for their examinations, because they did not have such good facilities at school or at home and felt they were 'weak' students. Hence it did not cross their minds to see themselves as a group of clever students and the future leaders of the nation. As a consequence, and seventh, there seemed to be a stronger sense of humility, and openness or willingness to learn and accept others' opinions amongst the arts key informants, unlike the strongly opinionated, rather arrogant, science key informants. Eighth, the arts students were always able to make criticisms about anybody or anything they were unhappy about, either at home, in class, at the coffee shop, at the bus stop or anywhere else for that matter, without having to worry about the negative repercussions which the science students were constantly subjected to at their colleges. Finally, the arts students' ideas about society seemed to be less idealized than those of the science students.

It is therefore understandable that the continuous mingling and interaction between the arts students and the *dakwah* groups with whom they came into contact, and their contact with society in general, allowed these students to develop a more moderate view of things from all angles. They too participated in activities considered religious or *dakwah*, but these were more artistically-inclined – for instance musical or choir groups, such as *marhaban* or *nasyid*, singing lyrics which praise Allah, listing the good principles of Islamic morality and criticizing wayward Muslims. It was not uncommon for many of these students to play soccer and other games for their health and recreation.

Although they attended *usrah* groups set up by the local *dakwah* organizations, especially by ABIM, and were involved in deep discussions about 'Islamic matters', they also participated in the weekly reading group of their village *yassin* (an often-recited verse of the Quran). They attended the open talks organized by the local mosques for the elderly and the young, were often called upon to take part in Muslim burial and follow-up rituals and were requested by the mosque committee to run Quran reading classes for local children. Their 'Islamic life' was not lived in an enclave, as was the case with the science students. It was an 'interactive Islam' which the key arts informants claimed to be practising, not the highly 'incubated Islam' practised by the science students.

To prove their point, these informants reported that during general elections, unlike the science students in the residential junior colleges, they were able to attend and participate in the political forums organized by the different political parties as part of their election campaigns. They also read all kinds of election literature and listened to cassettes and videos, both the 'open' and 'underground' kind, which allowed them to form opinions on wider social issues concerning the community, the region, the state and the country in general.

These students saw corruption and nepotism at first hand. They had the opportunity, too, to make some pocket money by putting up banners or posters, usually for the ruling party, which paid generously for such jobs. The key informants argued that this experience contributed immensely to their political maturity and acceptance of the reality of Malaysian politics. At the same time, the experience also made them realize what a major task they had ahead of them if they were to 'save society from self-destruction' through the application and practice of Islamic principles and moral codes. An element of self-righteousness was there, as the arts key informants presented their case but it was not as intense as when the science key informants narrated their stories.

When these arts students entered university and formed their own *usrah* groups, their approach to Islam was very different from that of their science counterparts. They certainly seemed more 'social, open and moderate' and were more accepting of the complicated nature of societal reality. They never demanded the easy, overnight, structural changes of the Gunder Frank kind imagined by the so-called radical science *dakwah* students. Their religious commitment was not lacking in social consciousness.

The different educational conditions that the arts and science students experienced, especially at the secondary-school level, without doubt became the basis which created the 'polarity' between their respective approaches to Islamic revivalism. Ironically, the government's modernization programme, the New Economic Policy (1971–90) and the creation of the science junior colleges have hastened the '*dakwah*ization' process at the secondary-school level in Malaysia.

Educational conditions on the campus

For analytical purposes I have divided the discussion in this section into three. The first concerns the science students; the second, the arts students; and finally, there is a comparison of the experience of each group.

The science students

All the 'science key informants' were selected to join a special pre-university (equivalent to A-level) programme at my university, Universiti Kebangsaan Malaysia, after achieving very successful O-level examination results. They passed their pre-university examinations within a year and automatically enrolled at the university. There was no such short-cut for my three 'arts key informants'. They had two years of A-level education, sat for their A-level exams and successfully applied and enrolled at UKM.

Using examination results as a measurement, the three science key informants performed very well throughout their studies in school, were selected to join the special junior science colleges (established by the government in the mid-1970s), scored straight As and were invited to join the special one-year pre-university programme established in UKM. The science key informants admitted that their ambition was originally to be medical doctors, but they failed to qualify for medical school, entry to which is very competitive. They finally found themselves in the science faculty at UKM around the mid-1980s. Their academic journey to the university was very smooth indeed. Each received a full sponsorship from the government, from the first year of secondary school in the full residential junior science colleges until the completion of their undergraduate studies.

At the university, the three science key informants were actively involved in the science-faculty based *dakwah*-controlled student organizations, which also controlled the university's student union, mainly through membership of the various sub-committees. But each also established his own 'cell' or discussion group (*usrah*). The members of these *usrah* groups, who are usually juniors from the same faculty but perhaps from different departments, join for morning prayers, for breakfast and sometimes lunch, dinners and discussions at night. *Usrah* groups often become academic discussion groups too.

However, the main focus of the *usrah* groups in the sciences seems to be inward-oriented in the sense that the priority is towards self-education and self-development, first in the religious sphere and second in the academic context. Religion is of primary importance because it is perceived as a necessary safeguard against the 'bad side' of science; namely its 'secular, agnostic and atheistic' origins. It is against such a background that the idea of the 'Islamization of knowledge' propagated by Muslim scholars from the West, such as the late Ismail Faruqi of the USA, was very popular amongst such students but rather simplistically interpreted to 'resurrect the good side of science' as they saw fit. How did they approach this?

For a start, my science key informants argued strongly that all scientific ideas, concepts and even formulae are to be found in the Quran. Thus their role as Islamic scientists is to study the Quran and reveal these scientific concepts and formulae for the public to know, abide by and learn to apply, thus helping the *ummah*, or Muslim community, to solve many scientific and non-scientific 'mysteries of the world'. They think that they are in a position to do this because they have performed very well in all their exams in the field of natural sciences, have learned all the basic scientific theories and methods, and therefore feel competent to use these in their analysis of the Quran in order to unravel hidden scientific concepts and formulae, besides studying the Quran to enhance their own piety.

However, it must also be mentioned that there are *usrah* groups which are made up of individuals not only from the same faculty but also from the same junior science college previously attended, or from those of the same region who share a common dialect. The social bonding within the latter *usrah* groups seems to be even more solid, because the groups continue to operate at full strength even during university vacations when the members are back in their villages.

The organization, discipline and ethos of the *usrah* groups reminds me very much of how a platoon, the smallest unit in the army, is organized, except that a platoon usually has twenty-one members whereas the *usrah* has between eight and ten members: a more compact unit and of a more manageable size. However, my science key informants say that running their *usrah* groups is like looking after a large extended family, because they often have to deal with the members' personal problems too, mainly money and girlfriend problems.

These *usrah* groups perform many different roles, not least a socializing role in an enclave situation. It is also of significance whether or not the groups still operate after their members graduate. If they do, in what spheres of social life do they exist? If they do not, why is this so? At present, I am researching into this aspect of the *dakwah* movement in Malaysia.

The arts students

The three arts key informants are of a different pedigree altogether. On paper, they were never outstanding examination performers and hence are seen by the public as not up to the academic level of the science graduates. This is also the 'national view' and the trend in local universities in Malaysia since the mid-1970s; on paper, the Malay-Muslim science students are much better qualified than those in arts. This 'academic gap' was created in 1971, when the government launched a massive social engineering programme to mass produce Malay-Muslim scientists, as part of the NEP, in order to match the numbers of non-Malay students in the science, medicine and engineering faculties, as well as to facilitate Malaysia's technological leap to the status of a developed, industrialized nation.

The majority of arts students who enrolled in local universities from the early 1980s onwards were virtual 'failures' in this 'McDonaldization' scheme of producing Malay-Muslim scientists. The term 'failures' was used originally by bureaucrats and educationists from the Ministry of Education to label the students and came to be accepted by the Malaysian public. The three arts key informants belong to this 'failure' category. However, they not only performed very well in their undergraduate studies but also excelled in extra-curricular activities, for example in sports and in organizing welfare-oriented programmes for disadvantaged groups, such as the intellectually disabled. They led some of the student union activities for at least a year as members of sports or welfare programme sub-committees.

The three arts key informants, like their counterparts in the sciences, had their own *usrah* groups, all of whose members were arts students, mostly from the same faculties and sometimes from the same departments, to allow religious and academic discussions to take place together. Like some of the science *usrah* groups, a few of the arts groups have managed to draw members from the same region or dialect but rarely from the same high-schools, because, unlike the science students who were concentrated in residential schools, the arts pupils were more dispersed and had previously attended a variety of non-residential schools around Malaysia.

Although the members of the arts *usrah* groups, at least those of my key informants, spent much time re-educating themselves about Islam, they also made time to participate in sports, such as soccer, badminton and athletics and in what they have called 'consciousness-raising activities' to bring them closer to society, such as collecting donations for the disabled, holding book exhibitions in primary and secondary schools and making greeting cards to sell for Muslim festivities. Several members of these *usrah* groups are also members of the university gamelan musical team.

Because I teach in the arts faculty and one of my key informants was my honours' year supervisee, I frequently debate with these students, mostly as a group, about a topic which is very popular with them; namely, the 'Islamization of social science'. Sometimes this debate is carried into my seminar and tutorial classes.

The students argue from the position that all knowledge about *insan*, or human beings as servants of Allah, within which social knowledge should be included, should begin with the explanation provided in the form of 'revealed knowledge' found in the Quran. On this basis, social science could be Islamized overnight. However, in a patronizing manner, they often reassure me that they do recognize the important contribution of the kind of 'non-revealed, Westernized social knowledge' which I have been teaching, because such knowledge helps us to examine in detail the complex plurality of human societies, the methodology of which is not spelled out in the Quran; only its principles are contained therein. (The translated version of a book by the British broadcaster, Merryl Wyn Davies, *Knowing One Another: Shaping an Islamic Anthropology* [1988], is the students' most popular reference on this matter during these debates.)

The arts students appear to display a willingness to adopt a more outward approach towards religion and society, which could be labelled as moderate. A give-and-take attitude seems to dominate the way they interact at both the intellectual and the personal level. Why this should be so was put to me quite succinctly by one of my key informants during one of our routine discussions, but it was in response to my comment that he and his cohorts were too condescending, self-righteous, simplistic and judgemental in their perception of what they call 'non-revealed, human-produced, Western social knowledge'.

This student said, 'The Quran can only reveal to us the basic principles of society and behaviour; we have to figure out the details. We have also to figure out the complexity of practical life like living harmoniously with non-Muslims in Malaysia.' This sums up why the arts informants seem to be more 'open, outward-looking and approachable' towards society as a whole than the science students whom I have talked to. Moreover, this position has also been adopted by those arts students whom I know of who do not belong to any *usrah* or *dakwah* group but who claim to be no less religious than the *dakwah* students. This is a popular position that only arts students are inclined to adopt.

Science versus Arts: some comparisons

The comparison between science and arts students reveals many differences in the way each approaches religion and perceives society, more than other researchers on Malaysian Islam have ever recognized. There exists a polarity between the more 'open' arts student and the relatively 'closed' science students, in other words between the more 'moderate' arts students and the more 'radical' science students.

My impression is that after twelve years of intensive exposure to the pedagogy and content of rational, Western-based knowledge in their school life, students cannot but adopt this Western approach to acquiring social knowledge in general. There is so much direct real-life experience which contributes towards one's accumulation of social knowledge. Twelve years' exposure to a particular type of knowledge and its acquisition system must leave an indelible mark on one's intellect.

It is not unrealisitic, therefore, to suggest that when the arts and science students became *dakwah*, they embraced *dakwah* according to their 'arts' or 'science' paradigms, because these were the only intellectual, academic and systematic methods at their disposal to acquire the '*dakwah* knowledge' before them. I consider that their schooling, and the social context within which the 'arts and science methodologies' became embedded in the mindset of the key informants and the members of their *usrah* groups, has profoundly influenced the way they re-study and revive Islam.

CONCLUSION: INVENTING CERTAINTIES THE *DAKWAH* WAY

It is perhaps useful to ask what effect the streaming of secondary-school students into arts and science had on the university students and their politics in the pre-*dakwah* days of the 1950s and 1960s. In those days, it was the 'socialist movement' that dominated student politics. I wonder whether the science students who joined the university's Socialist Club would have preferred the Stalinist brand of Marxism to the Maoist version of Marxism, with the latter perhaps preferred by the arts students? Who can tell?

However, in relation to the *dakwah* movement, the secondary school experience of the students seems to have a bearing not only on the formation of the various groups within the movement but also on the types of *dakwah* which emerged from it and, in turn, influenced the government's choice.

In a wider context, it is difficult to separate the birth of the Malaysian *dakwah* movement and the aftermath of the racial riot of 1969. In fact the riot is significant as a watershed in Malaysia's post-colonial politics, economy and society, and has parallel ramifications with the more bloody racial clashes in 1946; that is, during the brief interregnum period just after the Japanese surrender, before the British could resume colonial rule after the Second World War. Religious elements, both Islamic and non-Islamic, became the natural refuge for Malays to cope with the intense disorientation and social turmoil besetting their lives.

The May 1969 racial riot, of course, brought about different forms of change in the newly independent, multi-ethnic country. However, once again, in a redefined socio-political scenario, religious elements reappeared to provide refuge for the Malays. In 1946 the social context within which the religious elements appeared was one dictated by the need to survive physically a violent and revengeful attack mainly carried out by the Chinese as a consequence of animosity engendered by the war. In 1969 the social context was quite different. Religious elements reappeared as a result of the need to respond to modernizing pressures and to maintain ethnic boundaries for hegemonic political expedience. The Islamic revivalist movement emerged from this scenario and, once established, began to function within its own logic, albeit not unrelated to the rise of Islamic influence globally.

In its initial stages, the Islamic revivalist or *dakwah* movement was inward-looking and chiefly concerned with re-educating the Muslim self. Its general political position was moderate in orientation and was very much a part of student politics in Malaysia, mainly interested in demanding social and economic justice for the weak – the reason behind the 1974 student riot – in the context of a multi-ethnic society. However, its mission was clearly Islamic in the sense that it emphasized the need for the Muslim-dominated government to return to the teachings of the Quran and to try to look at Islam as a possible panacea for the ills besetting society. This was the main feature of the first phase (1969–74) of Malaysia's *dakwah* movement, one which was unmistakably shaped and led by a group of arts students whose beginnings in student activism originated within the arts faculty-based student organizations. This arts-based tradition of *dakwah* continues until the present.

However, in the second phase (1975–9) the moderate *dakwah* of the arts students lost out to the radical *dakwah* brought back from abroad by Malay-Muslim science graduates whom the government sponsored as part of its policy to increase the number of educated Malays, especially in the scientific and technological field. As part of the same policy, the government also created a number of fully residential and government-supported junior science colleges for Malay-Muslim students who were handpicked at the age of 10 after excellent performances in a national government examination. The radical *dakwah* found its way into these colleges as a result of the patient and dedicated campaigning conducted by the *dakwah* returnees from overseas who were posted as teachers in these colleges – but returnees themselves did not attend these colleges, which were set up after they went abroad. *Dakwah* then migrated from the university level to the secondary schools. In the science colleges it was dominated by the radical group. In the ordinary secondary schools the moderate *dakwah* still held sway, but mainly amongst the arts stream students.

The radical *dakwah*, which had a slow start at the local universities, finally found its way into the campuses through groups of students from the junior science colleges. The influence of radical *dakwah* grew as the science student population in the universities increased. By the end of the 1970s, *dakwah* had a strong grip on national student politics, controlling all the student unions in the country. At the same time, the government had begun to respond seriously to the Islamic challenge. Previously it had been unable to do so because of serious internal leadership crises and because it mistook the *dakwah* movement for mere student politics.

The third phase of the *dakwah* movement (1979–89) was truly dominated by the government's effort to 'mainstream' the *dakwah* groups. It began by embracing a number of Islamic-oriented policies, implementing a few Islamic-oriented programmes, funding a number of local and foreign Islamic organizations, setting up a few Islamic-oriented economic institutions, promulgating a pro-Muslim foreign policy and becoming active in Muslim-bloc politics. It emphasized the need for a moderate approach towards Islam in a multi-ethnic society like Malaysia. This was enough to convince the arts-based moderate *dakwah* groups, such as ABIM, to join the government and thus they provided the bulk of the intellectual ideas and practical programmes of the government's *dakwah* programmes. The whole federal and state government machinery embraced the moderate *dakwah* approach, except for the student unions in the government-funded universities. They remained in the hands of the science-dominated radical *dakwah* which the university authorities failed to dismantle, partly due to the inherently weak university bureaucracies and partly because of the resilience of the *dakwah* groups organizationally.

In the early 1990s, when the government was preparing the nation to move into the next century, guided by the vision that Malaysia should be a developed industrialized nation by the year 2020, the moderate *dakwah* position of emphasizing the moral and spiritual foundation for such a vision was written into an ambitious policy statement. The science faculty-based radical *dakwah* continued to exist, despite the government's big Islamic push supported by the moderate group. That the government's 'mainstream' effort continues can be understood as an attempt to cleanse the *dakwah* movement of its radical component.

This attempt at '*dakwah* cleansing' will continue to fail because, ironically, it is the government itself which indirectly nurtures the survival of such radical *dakwah* elements through its very own junior science colleges all over the country. We have observed how these students became *dakwah* at a very early age through the systematic *tarbiyah* (education) approach which the radical *dakwah* group adopted in recruiting new members at the secondary-school level. The powerful positivistic science paradigms of the West seem to have provided these students with the best analytical tools, for the re-study and reinterpretation of Islam, mostly in a narrow, legalistic way, and for their efforts to unravel the principles of modern science which they strongly believe were already in the Quran but undiscovered.

We have also observed how the arts students continue to propagate moderate *dakwah* and thus dominate the government's efforts to 'Islamize' society in Malaysia. We can also suggest, therefore, that the government's efforts to dismantle radical *dakwah* have been initiated by moderate *dakwah* elements in the government. From another angle, this seems to be a political contest between the arts and the science students. As one of the arts key informant puts it: 'Being clever and brilliant like the science students is not good enough in this country. Being powerful is most important and power is what the arts students have controlled in this country for so long.'

In this sense, what we are observing in Malaysia today, both within and outside the *dakwah* context, is the continuous interaction of global knowledge (be it Western or Islamic) and local knowledge (be it indigenous or an indigenized cultural ethos), which hardly pauses to provide a necessary fixed point of reference for society because it keeps on shifting as historical and other circumstances continue to shape the form and content of that interaction.

At another level, particularly in the specific *dakwah* context, crucial questions that have often been asked are: 'Is Western social knowledge the only source of social knowledge? What is the role of revealed knowledge, such as found in Islam?' It is quite clear that this is not only addressing the problems of East versus West, Western versus non-Western but is also questioning and demonstrating the heuristic nature of social analytical tools such as concepts and categories. More importantly, it also gives us an idea of how at the everyday level 'theorizing' takes place in the context of individual and group interaction mediated through truth-claims, dichotomized perspectives, polarities and counter-positions based on perceived differences in systems of logic and epistemology.

However, it could be argued that the perceived difference is a kind of intellectual illusion, as demonstrated above; whereby the science students, for instance, have re-educated themselves about Islam in a detailed and systematic manner, not by using any method borrowed from famous Islamic Sufis or Ayatollah Khomenei but evidently from the positivistic methods of the natural sciences. In other words, when they re-studied Islam to re-educate themselves about religion they utilized an approach which they have learned well and know best; that is, the Western, rational, positivistic scientific method. As a result of this serious and committed re-study they became *dakwah*. Thus they have become *dakwah* with the assistance of positivistic, scientific analytical tools.

In fact, one could also argue that they have adopted a 'radical *dakwah*' position in their approach to Islam – 'radical' meaning that they have adopted a narrowly legalistic, black–white and conservative position regarding Islam – perhaps because they see 'Islamic knowledge' or 'Islamic theology' in terms of 'rules, formulae, equations, right and wrong answers', which is how they perceive the world they live in too, as 'the way natural science studies have taught them'. This is a classic example of an 'invented certainty' or truth-claim that demands total response. 'Certainties' of this nature are evidently divisive. Perhaps that is why the political agenda of this radical *dakwah* group is revolutionary and confrontational.

The arts students' approach to truth-claims is just the opposite, one which is tolerant of heterogeneity and this is demonstrated clearly in their moderate *dakwah* position. According to the students, the intellectual source of such a position is the 'very ambiguous' nature of social scientific knowledge, or the 'yes and no position' popular amongst social scientists which they have come to adopt as a way of seeing society and the position of Islam.

What they have pointed out is essentially how the principle of scepticism shapes the construction of knowledge based on 'human discourse' or 'the non-revealed, human-produced, Western social knowledge' which they have come to accept, but only as one part of total social knowledge, the other part of which is 'revealed knowledge'. Therefore, one could argue that the moderate *dakwah* students become moderate because they are able to tolerate not only the co-existence of 'revealed' and 'non-revealed' knowledge but also the perceived complementarity between the two. Perhaps in this case 'uncertainties' have become the healing power welding together the unweldable. Therefore the political position of the moderate *dakwah* individual is clearly tolerant of any form of plurality and very consensual in nature.

In conclusion, the Malaysian experience has shown yet again that the time-honoured tradition of formal, if regimented, education plays a crucial role in the shaping of truth-claims and invention of certainties in society in general.

REFERENCES

Ackerman, S.E. and R.L.M. Lee (1988) *Heaven in Transition: non-Muslim religious innovation and ethnic identity in Malaysia*, Honolulu: University of Hawaii Press.

Chandra Muzaffar (1987) *Islamic Resurgence in Malaysia*, Petaling Jaya: Fajar Bakti.

Gilsenan, M. (1982) *Recognizing Islam: an anthropologist's introduction*, London and Sydney: Croom Helm.

Hussin Muttalib (1990) *Islam and Ethnicity in Malay Politics*, Singapore: Oxford University Press.

Mohamed Abu Bakar (1989) *Penghayatan sebuah ideal*, Kuala Lumpur: Dewan Bahasa dan Pustaka.

Nagata, J. (1984) *The Reflowering of Malaysian Islam*, Vancouver: University of British Columbia Press.

Shamsul A.B. (1983) 'A revival in the study of Islam in Malaysia', *Man*, vol. 18, no. 2, June.

——(1989) 'From urban to rural: the "migration" of the Islamic revival phenomenon in Malaysia', *Proceedings of the Congress on Urbanism and Islam*, vol. 4, Tokyo: Institute of Oriental Culture, University of Tokyo.

——(1994) 'Religion and ethnic politics in Malaysia: the significance of the Islamic revivalist movement', in C. Keyes, L. Kendall and H. Hardacre (eds) *Asia's Visions of Authority*, Honolulu: University of Hawaii Press.

Zainah Anwar (1987) *Islamic Revivalism in Malaysia*: dakwah *among the students*, Petaling Jaya: Pelanduk.

6 Powerful knowledge in a global Sufi cult

Reflections on the poetics of travelling theories

Pnina Werbner

INTRODUCTION

For his followers and disciples, the charisma of a Sufi saint is an expression of his extraordinary uniqueness. For them he is, by his very nature, an utterly localized individual. The legends about his life objectify this uniqueness, weaving its circumstantial and specified detail into a complex fabric.

Like his individuality, so too the power of a Sufi saint appears to be an absolutely localized, focused power residing in him rather than in his office (Weber 1948: 247, 249, 296). This is almost by definition what makes him charismatic as against merely authoritative. 'Pure charisma', Weber argued, is 'contrary to all patriarchal domination . . . it is the very opposite of the institutionally permanent' (*ibid*.: 248). Through charismatic appeal, the saint gains absolute control over his followers.

As a focused rather than dispersed sort of power, Sufi charisma might seem also to be the antithesis of the kind of dispersed power which, Foucault has argued, characterizes the modernist episteme: a power grounded in the overwhelming self-evidence of a discourse and its panopticon methods of control through surveillance (Foucault 1977). Against such discipline, charismatic leaders of new social movements promise, however fleetingly, a new-found freedom as they challenge an established social order and its institutionalized modes of social control. In Sufism, however, this promise of freedom has itself been institutionalized as a permanent feature of cultic social organization. The result is a duality: on the one hand, the spiritual power of Sufi saints, like other resistances to power, exposes the nature of institutionalized temporal power (Foucault 1983: 211); on the other, somewhat paradoxically, Sufi charisma is grounded in its own recurrent routinizations, structures of authority and modes of control. Freedom and individual autonomy are, in this sense, an imaginative project, obviated in the displacement of one heteronomy or tyranny by another (see Levinas 1987: 22–3, 37–8, 58).

In the light of these considerations the aim of the present chapter is to explore, first, the allegorical structure of Sufi legends as legitimizing discourses – fables which are global and structurally recurrent while being, simultaneously, local and unique. Here I draw on the critical distinction made by Aristotle in the *Poetics* between the 'fable' or plot, defined as a sequence of morally grounded actions, and the embodiment of the plot in a cast of characters and a tapestry of concrete images. Whereas plots are paradigmatic, their embodiment constitutes a specific, imaginatively conceived, localized appropriation (Ricoeur 1981, Chapter 8; see also Becker 1979: 213). Hence Sufi legendary discourses, I argue, are necessarily marked by a recurrent, 'global' plot and a localized 'here-and-now' narrative. If the plot is fixed, its embodiment is creative and relational (Becker 1979: 215).

Yet the narratives considered here – myths and legends about a living Sufi saint – are not simply charters of legitimation. They are the basis for the eliciting of a host of practical activities through which the saint has built up a vast religious organization, stretching throughout Pakistan and beyond it to Britain, Southern Africa and the Middle East (see Figures 6.1 and 6.2). The centre of the cult is the saint's lodge (*darbar*), set in a little valley a few miles outside the town of Kohat in the North-West Frontier Province, Pakistan.

Hence the second strand in my argument is that the powerful coerciveness of Sufi knowledge, its effect of certainty, stems from its location within a broader universal episteme, in Foucault's sense. The episteme promotes self-discipline through an *experienced* sense of globalized, panoptican surveillance. Sufi structures of control are not, from this perspective, merely the outcome of disciples' personal allegiance to a charismatic individual. Instead, they are grounded in an appeal that has three elements:

1 *A discourse of legitimation*, in Lyotard's sense (1984), constituted by paradigmatic fables inscribed concretely in narratives about a local habitus. These narratives mythologize the saint's supreme spiritual power as exceeding that of any worldly, temporal politician.
2 A *globally* shared secret *theosophy* revealed through mystical experience and supposedly arrived at through practice. In the present chapter it will be seen, however, that in the context of global migration and print capitalism, this esoteric knowledge has come paradoxically to be sought by contemporary Sufi disciples not through mystical experience but through intellectual scholarship.
3 A *technology of knowledge* through which the saint controls access to mystical experience and eternal salvation, on the one hand, and to a global means of panoptic surveillance on the other hand. This technology of knowledge enables Sufi saints to sustain hierarchy, centralized organization and absolute authority over their followers, even beyond the grave.

The chapter traces these three dimensions of Sufi certain knowledge through a focus on a transnational Sufi regional cult founded by a saint

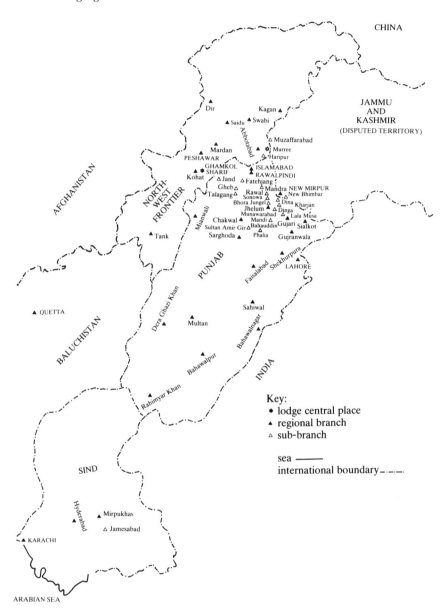

Figure 6.1 The regional cult of Zindapir

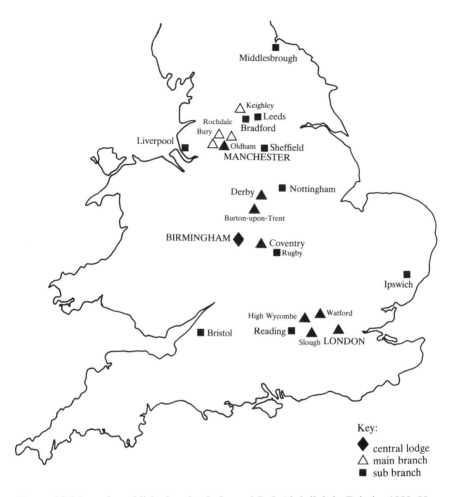

Figure 6.2 Map of established major lodges of Sufi Abdullah in Britain, 1989–90

known throughout Pakistan and Britain as 'Zindapir', the 'living saint'. The account highlights the embeddedness of narratives of legitimacy about this saint in the two other modes of knowledge: abstract, metaphysical speculation and social control.

In recording and analysing these moral narratives I faced an apparently intractable dilemma – how to represent certain religious knowledge from a sceptical standpoint for a *dual* audience: of the saint and his followers who had entrusted me with the mission of re-presenting them to the world as true believers; and for anthropologists-infidels whose interest, I knew, was not in the true reality of belief but in the way that 'thing' called certainty is sustained, imposed or manipulated in the face of opposition, contradiction, change, ambiguity and uncertainty. My non-solution has been to let the narratives about the saint speak, in large measure, for themselves, while focusing on the moral message they contain and the actions they inspire. Whether this version of truth is acceptable to disciples of the saint remains for me at present an open question. The reader may feel free to judge the matter for her/himself.

ON THE POETICS OF TRAVELLING THEORIES

In advance of narrating Zindapir's hagiography, my argument needs to be set in the context of a controversy regarding the relation between (global) 'text' and (local) 'context' in South Asian Islam between scholars arguing that Islam needs always to be analysed in its localized form and others stressing the evident historical spread of orthodox Islam.[1]

In one sense, the debate is not a new one. Barth (1960) and Dumont (1970) both reflected on the historical significance of South Asian Islam's unique hybridity. In a seminal chapter, Geertz (1968), comparing Moroccan and Indonesian Islam, proposed that global religions are necessarily embedded in the taken-for-granteds of local cultural milieus. These arguments take on renewed significance in the light of contemporary deconstructive arguments about meaning and intertextuality. Thus, Edward Said (1983) has argued recently that theories which 'travel' may lose their original radicalism while gaining in critical consciousness.

Recognizing the intertextual dimensions of locally appropriated global religious texts is a critical advance; it highlights the fact that when a world religion encroaches into an already charged social field, both religious practice and scriptural exegesis are likely to be politicized and to lose the taken-for-granted, doxic transparency they once possessed. Instead, they become highly self-conscious, reflexive ideologies. Intertextuality, in other words, relativizes all knowledge.

Two related questions are implied by this reflexivity. First, if global religious knowledge, locally contextualized, is produced within a charged political field, in what sense can it still be said to be commonsensical and embedded unreflectively in a local cultural ethos and world-view, as Geertz proposed? Second, in what respect do travelling theories which change also stay the same?

To address these questions, the present chapter argues for a shift of focus away from sacred texts or pretexts, however variably interpreted, to an exploration of the underlying structures – the moral fables – animating such texts. I propose that the structural logic of these fables, being implicit, is rarely questioned or challenged, even in politicized contexts. Moreover, such fables, rather than being modified in travel, once adopted are a symbolic force reshaping the cultural environments they invade. This is because in most cultures,

> . . . knowledge of plot constraints is unstated background knowledge, like the knowledge of grammar and syntax. It is learned indirectly, first through fairy tales and nursery rhymes (and their equivalent in other cultures) and then from the various media that have access to children.
> (Becker 1979: 217)

Hence, going against the anthropological grain, I propose that Sufi Islam is a global movement which fabulates the *possibility* (if not the actualization) of human perfection. Its shared implicit logic is revealed in the similarities between Sufi legends and modes of organization in widely dispersed localities, separated in time as well as in space.

Since most Sufi mythologies are collected in hagiographies by devoted disciples after a master's death, it is often difficult to show how the different strands of a saint's life, as lived *in practice*, are woven *during his lifetime* into a structured mythic corpus (but see Malik 1990). The present account, based on fieldwork at the saint's lodge in Pakistan and among his several thousand disciples in Britain, considers the way the generation of myths and legends has been an integral dimension of the emergence of Zindapir as a 'living saint' and his foundation of a new Sufi regional cult. Like other living saints, legendary figures in their lifetime, he has revitalized Sufi traditions by appearing to embody in his very life, as observed by his followers, a familiar lore of Sufi tropes.

LEGITIMATION: LIVING LEGENDS

The tapestry of legends, myths and morality tales told by and about Zindapir objectify the saint's divine grace and power through concrete images and remembered encounters. At the same time, the powerful validity of the legends and morality tales springs dialectically from his observed ascetic practices, which embody for his followers fundamental notions about human existence and sources of spiritual authority. This dual basis for legitimized truth – saintly practice and concrete image – makes the legendary corpus about the saint impervious to factual inconsistencies. The 'myths' and 'legends' are conceived of as historically accurate, true, exemplary narratives about an extraordinary individual. If the myths contain self-evident truths which transcend the mundane and are not amenable to quotidian commonsense evaluation, this is because the subject of these tales, the living saint, is an extra-mundane individual, a man outside and above the world rather than in it.

Zindapir: A Living Saint

Hazrat Shah, Zindapir, the 'living saint', born in Jungel Khel in the North-West Frontier of Pakistan, circa 1910, is a man who has achieved saint-hood in his lifetime. This means, in effect, that he is a living legend. His life, as told by him or about him by his disciples, has been the life of a Friend of Allah and as such it is a life motivated and moved teleologi-cally through the guidance of divinely inspired dreams and visions. Every event in the shaikh's (saint's) life has religious significance. The personal joys and crises that motivate the lives of ordinary men – marriage, bereave-ment, birth, love, wealth, happiness – although known to his disciples and often appearing to be (from a Eurocentric perspective) key turning points in his career, are regarded by them as having no causal effect upon his moves and decisions. They are mere coincidences, to be brushed aside and ignored. He has been guided, like all Sufi saints, only by religious imper-atives known to him through visions and dreams (Schimmel 1975; Kakar 1982; Ewing 1990b).

As is customary, the saint's deeds and sayings have been of enormous importance to an inner circle of close disciples. They have repeatedly tried to gather some of the key narratives documenting his life and miracles into a 'book' to be printed and widely circulated, but the saint has always withdrawn his permission at the last moment, offering no explanation. As a man who continuously stresses the infinity of his generosity, abundance and knowledge, it seems likely that he is reluctant to be reified and contained in the finite confines of an object-book. In similar vein he allows no pictures of himself to be circulated, fearing people may 'worship' his circumscribed image. His charisma thus remains personal and immediate, actively flowing from his very presence, and the legends about him are circulated by word of mouth. As a result, many different versions exist of the same key landmarks in his saintly career. His disciples exchange these narratives, citing authorities who were 'there' to prove that the version they know is the correct one, while simultaneously believing and embracing all the different versions which are, in any case, concrete details aside, mere structural variations of each other.

It is, as mentioned, the concreteness of these myths which makes them authoritative. Religious certainty stems from the embeddedness of a para-digmatic, structural logic (in this case of Sufism as world renunciation) in the indexical particularities of place, time and person (Ewing 1990b; Werbner 1989, Chapter 1) and its validation through visible and contin-uing moral achievements (Lambek 1990). Hence a global logic or common sense is valorized through its concrete localization and embodiment in myths and effective demonstrations of power, morality and social-cum-material investments. This emerges clearly in the legends narrating one of the key turning points in the saint's life – his first public *karamat* (miracle). The following is an account told to me at Zindapir's lodge (see Map 1) by two *khalifa* (spiritual deputies, vicegerents), both highly trusted confidants of the saint, who related the legend in English:[2]

The First Karamat

The Eleventh Baluch Regiment had its headquarters in Abbotabad, although the Regiment itself was transferred periodically from place to place. There came a time when the Regiment was stationed in Qazi Bakr in Gujrat and during its stay there Zindapir Sahib used to go outside the Regiment perimeter fence, to pray on the banks of the canal every night. The second in command of the Regiment, Major Iqbal, lived near the base and one night he went home to see his relatives. As he was passing the canal he saw someone, dressed in a white sheet (shawl), praying, and he recognized that man. Returning later that night, he found an order awaiting him from Headquarters, transferring him to Quetta in Baluchistan. Major Iqbal did not want to go to Quetta, so he went to see Zindapir Sahib and asked him to pray, to say *du'a* (supplication) for him, to beseech Allah that he should not be transferred. To his request Zindapir Sahib responded: 'Why do you come to me? I am only a tailor. Don't disturb me and let me get on with my work!' Major Iqbal said: 'If you don't say a *du'a*, I shall tell the whole regiment that you are a *pir* (saint).'

Until this time Zindapir Sahib had kept the fact that he was a saint, and that he did *zikr* ('remembrance' of God) by the canal every night, a secret. Zindapir Sahib said to the Major: 'Don't say a word to anyone. Just collect your luggage from the railway station and come back here.' There was only one train a day from Gujrat to Quetta and Major Iqbal collected his luggage and missed that train. The very same evening he received a telegram from General Headquarters in Rawalpindi, announcing that he had been promoted to Lieutenant-Colonel and cancelling his transfer. Instead of him, the previous Colonel was transferred to Quetta.

It was explained to me that this first miracle took place after Zindapir had taken *bai'at* (an initiation vow of discipleship to a Sufi saint) at Mohra Sharif (a major shrine at Muree) and, it was thought, after Partition in 1948. Baba Qasim, the saint of Mohra, died in 1943. Between 1942 when he took the vow and became Baba Qasim's *khalifa*, and 1948, Zindapir kept the fact that he was a saint a secret and practised in secret. Yet, I was also told, he already had many disciples inside the Regiment, like Sufi Abdullah, the incumbent *khalifa* and saint in Birmingham, England. Indeed, it is public knowledge that Zindapir performed his first *'urs* – the anniversary of a saint's death/mystical reunion with God – in Abbotabad in 1947, since the 1991 *'urs* was advertised as the 44th.

Such inconsistencies of detail are regarded as quite irrelevant, however, by the saint's followers. Equally insignificant, it appears, is his recent (1990) arrangement of a marriage between his grandson and a daughter of the most distinguished Sayyid family in his natal town (see Figure 6.3). Such personal details are not deemed to challenge his public denials of the importance of wealth, village connections, caste or Prophetic lineal descent. Few wonder why Zindapir refuses to discuss his own lineage in detail (he is a Sayyid, coming from a group of lesser distinction in his village; see Figure 6.4). Similarly, the legends about him, like the tale of his first public *karamat*, are accepted by his disciples as self-evident truths, even though there are several alternative versions of most of these central legends.

One of the other versions of his first *karamat* elaborates the bitter competition between the threatened-with-transfer Major and the new proposed Commander of the Regiment (who is ultimately and miraculously sent to Quetta in his place). Another stresses his past profession as a tailor. I heard this version in Rawalpindi from a non-disciple:

> Before he became a *pir*, Zindapir Sahib was a master tailor-contractor working for the British army. One day a Major came to him and ordered a new uniform. When the Major came to collect his uniform he found that Zindapir Sahib had sewn him a Colonel's uniform. The Major complained: 'I asked you to sew me a Major's uniform. This is a Colonel's uniform!' Zindapir merely said: 'Take the uniform.' That very evening the news came from Headquarters that the Major had been promoted to Colonel.

Knowledge and Common Sense

The plots of Sufi legends are predictable and repetitive. At the same time, the co-existence of many versions of legends about the same saint, seen together, may generate surface factual inconsistencies and contradictions. It is, however, the fable that travels and hence it is the impact of this fable that needs to be considered as it encroaches into quite different and distant cultural and economic environments.

An understanding of the authority of 'nomadic' dominant narratives depends, critically, on a recognition that contradictory commonsense beliefs are not inconsistent through and through: *ad hoc*, unmethodical and contradictory explanations are usually deployed in the defence of paradigmatic 'theories', a core of *consistent* propositions which come to be naturalized and taken for granted and are, in being so, also commonsensical. The fan of secondary elaborations at the margins of such commonsense paradigms serves to defend and reproduce their coherence (Evans-Pritchard 1937;

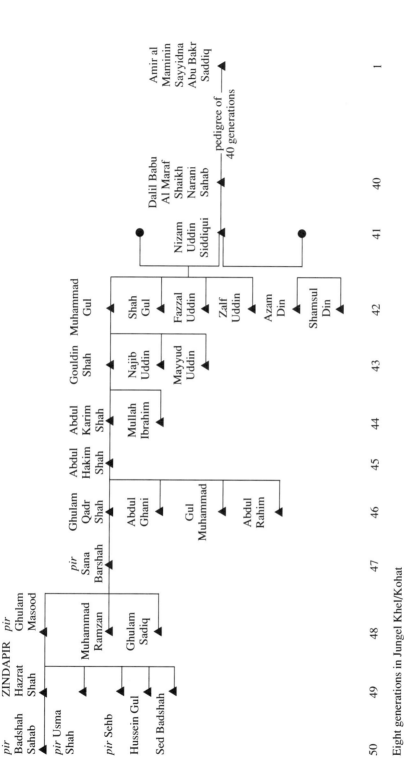

Figure 6.3 Agnatic descent (*shajra nasb*) of Hazrat Shah (indicating main descent groups in Jungel Khel and pedigree line to the Prophet's first Companion, Abu Bakr)

Kuhn 1962; Horton 1970; for a different view on selective reasoning where there is a superabundance of understanding see Werbner 1973; Ewing 1990a; Geertz 1983).

This has practical implications: rather than merely adapting to different environments, a transplanted Sufi fable of perfection generates a powerful symbolic field wherever it encroaches. Like capitalism or modernity, Sufism is a distinct discursive formation which shapes the very habitus it invades, while being authoritatively constituted by its everyday familiars.

In regarding Sufism as a discursive formation, I start from the assumption that discourses are not simply negotiated between equals but are persuasively imposed in any given social context by the socially or culturally powerful. Although Sufi Islam in South Asia is the product of peaceful missionizing, it nevertheless accompanied the Muslim conquest of India (see Gilmartin 1988). Contemporary Sufism draws upon *culturally* recognized sources of power. Such sources may be, as in the case of Zindapir, symbolic and non-verbal ways of bodily self-representation, through which a person marks himself out as an extraordinary, unique individual; an individual who is, simultaneously, an archetypal prototype of a culturally recognized category of similarly unique individuals.

Equally critical is the fact that discourses of legitimation, mythic 'charters', are grounded in valorized social relationships. The relations between Zindapir and his followers are extensions of other socialities. His disciples are not only *pir-bhai* ('saint-brothers'); they are also consociates in other contexts: many serve in the same army or police units, are employed in the same civil service departments, are workers in the same factories (both in Britain and Pakistan), or are neighbours and kinsmen living in the same villages, towns or cities. Continuing contact, migration and pilgrimage link these far-flung members. Equally importantly, members of each branch share relations of sociality and amity which transcend formal occupational relationships. Like Sufi orders in the Ottoman Empire, Zindapir's regional cult has expanded through occupational channels. This means that both saint and disciples have a vested interest in the powerful continuity and legitimacy of saintly charisma.

The moral message of all the different versions of the legend of Zindapir's emergence as a saint is the same: the saint's knowledge transcends place and time and, as such, his authority surpasses that of any powerful warrior or ruler and is global in its reach, penetrating people's inner hearts, the outer limits of the globe and even what is invisible or beyond normal human knowledge. Although the saint's lodge at Ghamkol Sharif is now the centre of his sacred dominion, Zindapir stresses repeatedly that he is merely a guest there, in the house of God. In abandoning his natal home in Jungel Khel and divesting himself of all his prior worldly possessions and even of his name (few know his real name), he has in effect disengaged from any specific place or locality. He protects and nurtures his disciples wherever they are: working in the Gulf, living in

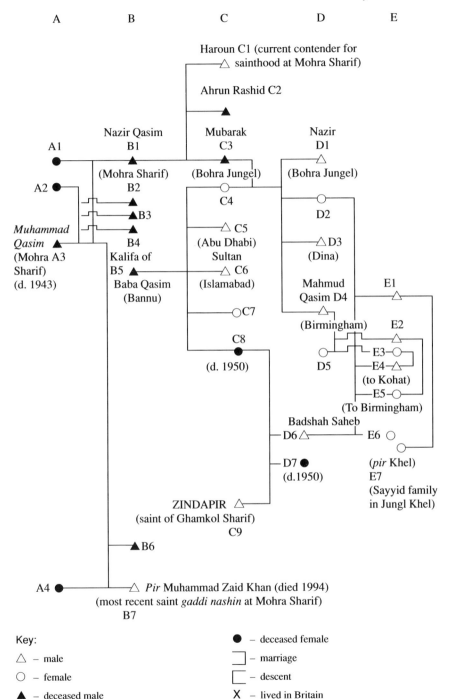

Figure 6.4 Affinal relations of Zindapir and his family

Britain, serving in the Pakistani army. His knowledge is not merely signalled through an ability to foresee the future, to see and control invisible *jinns* and other malignant spirits or know what is in men's hearts wherever they are; it is a concrete manifestation of divine grace, signalled by his power over nature.

The most significant evidence for this power has been the transformation the saint has brought about in the lodge itself, from a deserted wilderness to a place of cultivation. The discovery of water in the lodge is represented as a miraculous gift of God which exemplifies this spiritual power over nature. It was told to me by one of his first disciples and companions, now resident in Coventry and a visitor to the 1989 *'urs* at Ghamkol Sharif. A somewhat similar tale was also told by the shaikh himself in the lodge at Ghamkol Sharif.

The Miraculous Flow of Knowledge

> There was a blind disciple at the lodge and he began to dig a well, just outside the mosque. Some people came by who were searching for oil. They had with them sophisticated seismic instruments. They told the shaikh that according to their instruments there was no water at the excavation site. The shaikh said to them: 'How do you know?' They answered: 'Our instruments show that.' The shaikh asked them: 'Who made the instruments?' They answered: 'They were made by men.' The shaikh said: 'But the water here is shown to me by God.' They dug the well and found an abundant source of water, enough to supply the whole lodge and all its visitors.

A slightly different version was told to me (in English) at the lodge by another early disciple, a man who rose to be a Brigadier and cabinet advisor but has remained a loyal follower of the saint:

> There were eight *jarsa* (hashish) smokers who were digging the well. They dug down to 39 feet and there they struck hard rock. A water diviner was brought along. He declared that there was no water there. But the shaikh said: 'I know there is water there, running from the hill – this way down [pointing]. I know, because I have performed my ablutions in it [in a vision].' So I said: 'We can blast through the rock with dynamite.' Which is what we did. The water below was so abundant that it flowed up to 30 feet. That happened in March 1953 or thereabouts. The shaikh had lived in the cave for six months before the water was discovered.

The Brigadier added that the hashish smokers gave up their habit and became disciples of the shaikh.

The discovery of abundant water gives tangible form to the final phase on the Sufi journey, the achievement of gnosis, *ma'arifa*. The shaikh knew of the presence of water, had bathed in it ritually in his mystical vision, and its actual discovery thus literalizes the flow of divine knowledge and all that emanates from it: water, fertility, abundance, generosity, the concrete objectifications of divine grace.

This is just one of many legends comprising a major legendary corpus about the early life of the saint. Other legends tell of his identification as a saint from childhood, his initiation and instantaneous establishment as a saint by the great saint of Mohra Sharif, his numerous *karamats*, his journey to Mecca where the vision of Ghamkol Sharif, his lodge, is revealed to him at the Prophet's mosque in Medina and many other revelations, miracles and visions which marked his early career. The major turning point in his life was his resignation from the army and the foundation of the lodge at the age of 40. This story, which the saint repeats annually before the culminating supplication of the final day of the *'urs* celebration, is the story of his journey to the wilderness of the valley in which the lodge is located.

The Conquest of the Wilderness

Like most of the key narratives of his life, this one too has many versions, all of them authenticated. Each is a variation on the central mythological episode in the shaikh's achievement of sainthood. The myth is a tale of renunciation, poverty, patience and trust in God (*tawakkul*) before the final achievement of divinely inspired knowledge, blessing and fulfilment (see Schimmel 1975: 117–20; Nicholson 1989: 29). One of the versions, told by a British *khalifa*, recounts:

> Zindapir Sahib left the graveyard at Jungel Khel [his natal village] by foot with his companions. One of his companions had a bag of flour. The shaikh, while walking, felt a burden. He turned back and saw his companion carrying the flour. He asked: 'What is this?' The man said: 'It is flour to make *roti*, bread. It will last two or three days.' The shaikh said: 'And after that, what will we do? Who will feed us then? Throw it away and we shall go in the name of Allah.'

This morality tale implies a *karamat*: Zindapir and the lodge have never lacked food, even though they arrived in the valley empty-handed. The source of food is Allah Himself.

It is said that when the shaikh left his village he took with him only a clay water pot, a jug for performing his ablutions and a praying mat. He sat at a cave entrance where well-known dacoits, resistance fighters against the British, kept their booty. According to one version, the brigands began shooting at him but the bullets did not touch him. Overwhelmed, they approached him, vowed to reform their ways and became his disciples.

Another version, told to me by the Brigadier, who claimed to have been there, tells of a more contemporary kind of journey:

It took us more than three hours, travelling by Vauxhall and jeep, to make our way to the cave. We had to build a road, fill the gullies, as we went along. When we got to the cave there was nothing – no trees, only small bushes. That night I slept on the ground. Someone had brought a rolled-up blanket for the shaikh. We cleared the cave for him. All he had was a Quran. The next day we went off. That was in October 1952.

But it is the myth as told by the shaikh himself annually to his disciples before the final supplication of the *'urs* which is most powerful:

To all the congregation and disciples present. It was not at all my wish to come here. . . . It was only the absolute order of the Prophet (Peace be upon him) that I should proceed to this place. And if this place is now established [*abad*, cultivated], it is due to the express order of the Prophet. *Nafs* [the carnal, vital soul][3] and *Shaytan* [Satan, the devil, the tempter] both said that I should not go here. There was not even enough water for a sparrow (*churiya*). Ajib Khan used to divide his booty in this area. There were not even trees here. The place was barren and arid. Only God was here. At that time the *nafs-shaytan* [devil in the soul/heart] did their best to stop me from coming here. They argued that the people are already my disciples and why should I go there? What is the need to go there? I said to *Shaytan* that I must obey the Prophet. Then I prayed two *rak'at nafl* [optional canonical prayers] and we set out on our journey from the graveyard. And during the whole way to the cave the *Shaytan* was trying his best to betray us, to tell us we should not go ahead. When I reached the cave that was shown to me [in his vision in Medina] I prayed to Allah the Magnificent and the Merciful: 'Oh Allah! I have come only for you here and now I am your guest.' And because of this infinite and absolute faith [*tawakkul*, a key Sufi station on the path] this place is established and fully developed. [Or, in his 1991 sermon: 'With the grace of God, this place is more generous [*sakhi*] than any other.'] I have not asked anyone for subscriptions or donations. . . . Nobody had bowed before Allah on this earth before I came to this place; even sparrows did not live here. When we came here there was water on the other side of the hill. I would like to narrate further that the people of my village came to me and said to me that I should migrate to Bonapir's *zyarat* [shrine] which is on the other side of the hill, where there is . . . plenty of water. I told them that I have come here for the sake of Allah and I don't want to leave for the sake of water.

This is a tale of successful overpowering by the Sufi saint of the devil, wild animals, wild men and the bare wilderness itself. It is the test of absolute faith, the mastery of the *nafs* and its wild, animal-like passions, its desires and temptations. The way to the valley of the cave is thus a concrete embodiment of the battle of the *nafs*. It is the shaikh's *via purga-tiva* (see Schimmel 1975: 4, 98). The fact that the cave is located a mere 2 miles from Zindapir's natal village, on village land, is regarded as irrelevant by his followers and does not either obviate the courage and arduousness of the journey or undermine the validity of the imaginative conception of the valley as a mysterious unknown territory, discovered by the saint following his vision of it in Medina.

The legends are of an ordeal overcome: when the saint arrived in the valley there was no water, no electricity, no roads, no orchards, no gardens, no cattle, no houses, no mosque. Many remember those days and the wilderness as it then was. It has taken almost four decades to build the lodge to its present state of perfection. Virtually all of the labour which went into this building has been voluntary, unpaid. It draws upon cultural premises about religious service and sacrifice. It is these which have enabled the material development of the cult organization, based almost entirely on voluntary donations but conceived of as emanating from the saint's 'generosity' and divine blessing.

The Axis of the World

Once the shaikh arrives at the valley, he never leaves it. From this point onwards the nature of the narrative changes. The first part of the *pir*'s life was that of a traveller, a person seeking divine grace and guided by reve-lations. Once he reaches Ghamkol Sharif, the place where he has built his lodge, he ceases travelling altogether. He leaves his room only to perform the five daily prayers in the mosque or to inspect the preparations for the annual *'urs* festival. Otherwise he goes nowhere, not even to visit his son's house in the lodge itself, or his natal village nearby. His only visible journey is the annual pilgrimage to Mecca. He is a fixed point of stability in a fluctuating universe. People make pilgrimage to come and see him, to consult him about illness, to ask for amulets, medicine and *du'a* (suppli-cations), to seek his advice, to participate in *zikr* meetings, to attend the annual cycle of celebrations. Hence the tales he tells about himself from this point onwards are morality tales of encounters in the lodge or Mecca with the stream of guests, supplicants and pilgrims who visit him both daily and annually and partake of the free sacred food (*langar*) provided at the lodge.

The saint repeatedly makes the point that powerful temporal politicians are forgotten after their death, while the power of God's friends (*auliya*) persists forever. He stresses that although many high-ranking officials and politicians visit him, he treats all who come to him, *badshah* (king) or *garib* (beggar), alike. He asks no-one his or her name. In the morality tales of his encounters with politicians he presents himself as tough and definite: politicians who aspire to acquire some of his powers must confront the fact that they cannot compete with the divine spiritual power he has been endowed with (for similar tales of encounters between Sufis and temporal leaders, see Attar 1990; Schimmel 1975: 347; Geertz 1968: 33–5). And, if his authority is above that of temporal rulers, it also recognizes no temporal political, ethnic or religious boundaries. His tolerance towards members of other religions is stressed in many of the morality tales he tells. By appealing to God rather than merely to the Prophet, he transcends Islam to reach out to all people of faith. In doing so, he underlines his own transcendence, the reach of his dominion. He also asserts the difference between the mystic's knowledge of the inner truth of Islam with its broad, tolerant, universal message and that of the narrow-minded *'ulema*. Hence, interwoven with the tales of encounters with politicians and foreigners are encounters with the *'ulema*, the learned doctors. These prove the *'ulema*'s respect for the saint as a man of true knowledge proven by infinite generosity. Yet although the morality tales illustrate his refusal to recognize distinctions of rank or status, in practice he treats dignitaries and famous scholars with the utmost deference, deviating from his usual routines of fasting and meditation and according them privileged and private access to him (on this Sufi respect for worldly hierarchies, see also Rehman 1979, especially Chapter 4). Just as he denies the importance of these visits and asserts that he asks no-one his name, so too, simultaneously, do the visits prove that he is indeed a great and spiritually powerful friend, *wali*, of Allah.

Zindapir is thus a 'true' saint, a man whose spiritual dominion extends over *'ilm*, the 'external' knowledge of the *'ulema*, and over all forms of temporal power. The legitimacy of this legendary corpus, itself legitimizing the *specific* authenticity of the saint, is grounded in a *general*, abstract, metaphysical, transglobal religious theory, a theosophy of knowledge-power. It is to this I turn next.

METAPHYSICAL KNOWLEDGE: THE JOURNEY OF THE SOUL

There are probably as many versions of Sufi theosophy as there are Sufi mystics, poets, writers and interpreters of Sufi texts and sayings. The theosophy presented to me in detail was that elaborated by Hajji Bashir, the Naqshbandi Manchester *khalifa* (vicegerent) of Zindapir. The *khalifa* relied upon published sources in Urdu (including the letters of Shaikh Ahmad Sirhindi and the writings of Hujwiri) as well as on his discussions with Sufi Abdullah and some of his fellow vicegerents in Birmingham. Our conversations on Sufism took place during innumerable sessions at his home in Manchester and at the lodge in Pakistan. Hajji Bashir is a British Pakistani from Mirpur, now approaching 40, who came to England in his early teens to join his labour migrant father. Leaving school at 16, he worked for many years in a foundry, where he met Sufi Abdullah, the Birmingham saint and *khalifa* of Zindapir, and through him became a disciple and then *khalifa* of the saint in Pakistan. Despite his lack of formal education, what is remarkable about Hajji Bashir's account of Sufi philosophy is its total integration and sheer structural brilliance. For lack of space, I can only hint here at the mystical worlds of spirituality (*ruhaniat*) opened up by his speculations.

In Sufi Bashir's analysis, the different stages in the death and eternal rebirth of the soul are subject to a highly structured cosmology of graded body 'lights' corresponding to ranked ontological spheres, prophetic dominions, colours and domains of experiential knowledge These he has written down meticulously in a book, accompanied by diagrams (for an example of one of the seven diagrams, see Figure 6.5). The theory he outlines is a complex mystical ontological theory, grounded in an ethical transformation of the body. The British *khalifa* of Zindapir, based in Manchester, explained:

> The way to the annihilation/purification of the soul/heart is through *zikr* [the remembrance of God]. In *zikr* you breathe in the word of God, 'Allah', holding your breath as long as possible, then breathe out, saying *hu* ['is']. While holding the breath you hear your own heartbeat and if you perform *zikr* correctly, eventually the heart will take on the chant, Allah, Allah, Allah, so that all the time the heart beats Allah, Allah. At this point the heart will burst through, open up the *arish-e mualla* ['throne of God']. But these are a matter of the *tariqa* ['Sufi order']. Don't write them down.

SECRET KNOWLEDGE AS SOCIAL CONTROL

During the course of my research I was repeatedly told that hidden knowledge in Sufism is arrived at through experience rather than through intellectual scholarship; the way to gnosis is via the heart, through the practice of *zikr* and the love of a shaikh. This Sufi privileging of knowledge as experience over knowledge gained from written sources has apparently been subverted in modern-day Sufism, since esoteric knowledge is paradoxically a more public commodity than the mystical experience it supposedly reflects. This has not, however, undermined the charismatic power of the saint, for the 'real' hidden knowledge believed by his disciples to lead to mystical revelation is of specific technical directives – Quranic verses and *wazifas* (litanies) – which only the saint knows and which are thought to be the sole means of advancing on the Sufi path. The saint's *ijazat*, (permission) is essential before embarking on any form of ritual practice. Without his knowledge and guidance, it is believed, a person may go mad, be 'lost' forever in mystical ecstasy.

Not only Sufi texts, but possible revelation, open up the realms of the religious imagination, legitimizing for Sufi Bashir the saint's absolute authority. Like many aspiring *khalifa* of Zindapir, Sufi Bashir too was

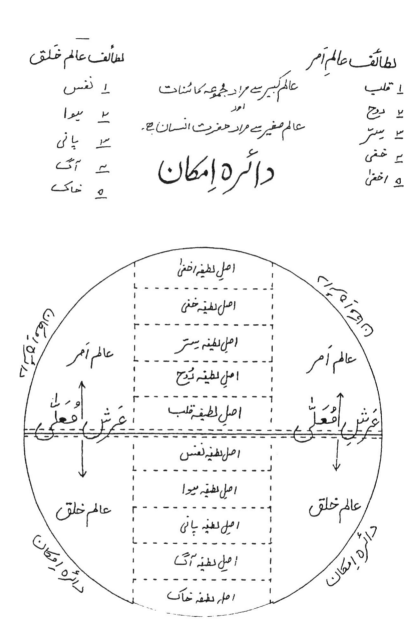

Figure 6.5 The circle of God's realities as represented by Sufi Bashir

determined to reach those realms but the key, he believed, lay with the saint and the saint refused to talk about these matters altogether.

Sitting at the lodge one day with a minor saint, a close affine of Zindapir and a grandson of Baba Qasim of Mohra Sharif, my companion confided in me that he would like to go 'into practice' (i.e. become a saint). I was puzzled: 'But you are a *pir*, the son of a *pir*, the grandson of a *pir* – how is it that you are not in practice?' 'To go into practice,' he told me, 'you need the permission of the *pir*.' 'But,' I wondered, 'there are *martaba*, degrees, stages, on the path. Can you not reach them by doing *zikr*, cleaning your heart and soul?' 'No,' he explained, '*zikr* is not enough. Everyone knows how to do *zikr*, every disciple. To do *'amal* [Sufi practice] you need the permission of the shaikh because in *'amal* you say an extra prayer a prescribed number of times without pause – which means not sleeping, possibly for as long as thirty days. This is why people stand in the water or hang upside down. The shaikh himself has not slept for over forty years. The shaikh prescribes both the ordeal and the *wazifa*.' 'Of course,' he added, 'the saint can transfer all his powers in an instant with his eyes if he chooses to do so.' (To become the recipient of this instantaneous transfer is the dream of all *khalifa*.)

My companion went on to tell me that he would very much like to be a real *pir* because his father's disciples come to him and respect him and he accepts their vows of initiation but he knows he is not a real *pir*, although they don't realize it.

Zindapir, it seems, is reluctant to open up before his disciples and *khalifa* the upper spheres of the world of eternal realities (*'alam-e amr*). He does give *ijazat* (permission) to those close to him to perform *dam*, the blowing of Quranic verses for healing purposes. Each affliction has its *dam* and these he reveals to his close disciples one by one, as favours granted for good conduct.

My assistant in 1991 had been a devoted disciple of the saint for over twenty years and had worked in the lodge as an act of religious service for several years. Did he not wish for promotion on the Sufi path? I asked. He explained that he had, in fact, been promoted several times. The shaikh had given him the power to blow *dam* for snake bites, for pain, for several other things – five *dams* in all. Each *dam* was given separately. Now he can do all of them, any *dam*.

Sufi Bashir explained to me that 'the shaikh never talks about the mystical ideas of Sufism but always gives practical instructions. He keeps saying that you should do the *raza* [pleasure] of God. But how can one do God's will when this [*raza*] is the final stage on the path after you have achieved the annihilation of the *nafs*? The shaikh does not explain what God's *raza* is.'

The authority of the saint over his disciples is immense. No-one makes a move, however trivial, without his permission. The fear of his wrath is deep and anguished. I have seen grown men reduced to utter despair in the face of his anger. They told me they feared that all their good works and devotion over twenty years would be 'wiped out' by the saint in his anger. Zindapir's power is never challenged. First, because his disciples love him deeply. Second, because they believe he knows their deeds and sees into their hearts wherever they are. Third, because he controls the powers of fertility, worldly success, exorcism and healing. Fourth, because on the Day of Judgement, they believe, he will mediate with God to grant them salvation, despite their sins. For those seeking his guidance, moreover, his power lies in his ability to show them the way to divine knowledge.

Yet in literalizing Sufism in magical formula, disciples deny the powerful message of Sufism, even when, as in the case of Sufi Bashir, they know it in theory. One might be tempted to argue that the saint fosters and manipulates this faith in magical formulas and procedures. But this would be to misunderstand his dilemma. As a true mystic, he knows that the granting of litanies and procedures cannot lead a person to the realm of divine realities. Only an absolute act of self-denial, of world renunciation, can do so. Ultimately, then, each individual has to find his or her own path to divine knowledge – this is the paradox of Zindapir's unrevealed secret, a secret which he repeatedly stresses quite openly: 'If you love God, the people (*makhluqat*) will love you. If you believe in God, people will start believing in you. If you remember yourself, then you cannot remember Allah.' The choice between tyranny and heteronomy for Sufi disciples is between two kinds of self-denial, only one of which is real.

CONCLUSION: THE COMMONSENSE STRUCTURE OF ASCETICISM

The weaving and interweaving of morality fables about politicians, strangers, Muslim scholars and afflicted patients by Zindapir all serve to exemplify his transcendence and elevation above ordinary mortals, his domination over nature, temporal power, 'external' religious knowledge and a humanity which recognizes no religious or political boundaries.

Through the morality tales surrounding his encounters with politicians and his rejection of their offers, Zindapir underlines his superior power and *izzat* (status and honour), as objectified in the generosity of the blessed food (the *langar*) distributed freely at the lodge. Yet the fact that these politicians come to him with bribes and offers serves to confirm his high status, while proving simultaneously his renunciation and rejection of worldly power and wealth. Similarly, scholars disdained for their narrow, superficial and divisive knowledge of Islam nevertheless confer legitimacy on the intellectual profundity of the shaikh.

It is because he wishes to tell these tales of exemplary encounter *without* appearing to boast about his fame (thus demeaning his authority by making it dependent on worldly recognition) that the saint weaves different types of tales into a complex tapestry. If he tells of the visit of an important politician, he follows this tale immediately with one about his care for a poor orphan, or his healing of a nameless supplicant. The mythic narrative structure depends on the interweaving of different types of legends and morality tales, which, juxtaposed, deny the potentially subversive messages contained in some of the legends while stressing their moral lessons.

The most important validation of all the legends, myths and morality tales is the saint's extraordinary self-denial. He fasts all year round during the daytime and manifestly has no personal desire for material objects or luxury foods. He is said never to sleep and he prays constantly, day and night. Fasting is not only an important component of his mystical asceticism; it is also seen by his disciples as final proof that the legends about him are all true. He is a man who does not seek money, wealth or secular power, as false saints do. He is God's conduit for food given away in the *langar* but he proves his own disinterestedness, his world renunciation, by eating virtually nothing and especially no luxury foods such as meat, milk, butter or *ghi*. To emphasize this disinterestedness, he forbids the display of collection boxes in the *darbar*. His asceticism remains the cornerstone of his continued and expanding influence for, like the potentially subversive counter-messages contained in the political encounters, the very expansion and development of the lodge also contains a possible subversive counter-message.

Disciples know, of course, that the shaikh has substantial property, several new cars, a large house, money to provide an education for his grandchildren and so forth. But these worldly trappings are regarded as embodiments of God's grace, a divine blessing which proves that 'their' *pir* is endowed with respect and honour unrivalled in the land. Disciples gloss over his accumulation of personal wealth because he has shown that he personally has no interest in the world of consumer items. He proves this by the simplicity of his existence, by his abstinence and bodily self-denial and by his evident generosity and care for his disciples.

The shaikh asks for no money, yet there is always enough. As he told me, so great were the quantities of food and flour brought as offerings (*nazrana*) by the pilgrims to the *'urs* festival that there was enough to supply the *langar* and feed the people for half a year.

The miracle of the lodge and *langar* and the shaikh's generosity, are arguably the miracles of deeply enshrined customs. The shaikh never demands. He has no need to demand, for he trusts in the flow of customary donations, of food and services, provided as *khidmat* (pious service) for the sake of God. His absolute trust is repeatedly rewarded. Before the *'urs* festival volunteers arrive to build and extend the lodge and to help with the preparations. They work tirelessly, day and night, providing their free labour for the sake of a communal project. During the *'urs* convoys of disciples arrive from all over Pakistan, bringing with them sacks of grain and beasts for offering and sacrifice. Cantors arrive to lead the prayers in Arabic. Learned scholars arrive to preach their sermons. Poets arrive to sing their praise songs (*na'ats*) for the Prophet. No-one is summoned; no-one is paid. Entertainment and intellectual content at the *'urs*, like the food of the *langar*, are donated, free of charge. The abundance is created by followers and disciples.

Yet despite their practical knowledge of the effort they themselves have invested and the contributions they have personally made, the disciples continue to regard this abundance as a miracle. In a sense they are right: it is the miracle of selfless custom observed repeatedly (by themselves, as well as by others) in a world where their experience has taught them that selfish interest, political manipulation and greed reign supreme (see Lindholm 1990; Ewing 1991). The fact that this selflessness is inspired by the love of a Sufi saint proves his divine grace. He transforms ordinary selfish human beings (you and me) into people willing to make enormous personal sacrifices, to work day and night without sleep, to dirty their hands doing the most menial and back-breaking tasks, all for no pay, but for the sake of a transcendent cause.

Zindapir's tales and legends, repeated annually in his final speech during the *'urs* festivals and in numerous conversations with and between disciples, all serve to sacralize the voluntary labour and contributions which have gone towards creating the *darbar*. Hence we can argue more generally that the symbolic and organizational unity of Sufi cults springs from the supreme value accorded to world renunciation and otherworldly asceticism in Muslim society. This unity is sustained by myths and legends which link key tropes: the divine predestination of the Sufi saint, his journey, his central lodge, his grave, his generosity, his miraculous deeds, his vast following and his supreme spiritual power.

Seen together, the mythic corpus surrounding such a saint can be analysed processually as depicting his personal transformation as he moves towards the ultimate achievement of gnosis and superior spiritual authority (see Rao 1990). Even in the case of a living saint like Zindapir, where mundane facts are known to many and the less credible details of the legends could (in theory) be checked or challenged, such a challenge never occurs. This is because the beliefs generating the legends also include the secondary elaborations which uphold their validity. Indeed, over time, disciples' tales about their saint's miraculous powers multiply, surrounding the primary legendary corpus set out here with a further set of secondary legends. Their personal dreams and visions of the saint, his encounters with the Prophet or his empowerment of their lives, further enhance his charisma.

This returns us to the question raised at the outset: to what extent is Sufism as a world religion differentially embedded in the commonsense notions of specific cultural environments? I would argue, against Geertz' relativist position (e.g. 1968), that the religious rationality and commonsense values implicit in Sufism *transcend* cultural and geographical boundaries. The underlying logic of the fables constituting this religious imagination is the same logic, whether in Morocco, Iraq, Pakistan or Indonesia. It is based on a single and constant set of equations, starting from the ultimate value of self-denial:

World renunciation (asceticism) = divine love = divine 'hidden' knowledge = the ability to transform the world = the hegemony of spiritual authority over temporal power and authority.

The legends about powerful Sufis from Indonesia and Morocco which Geertz argues exemplify the contrastive localism of Islam tell, in essence, the same processual narrative: (1) initiation through a physical and mental ordeal overcome; (2) the achievement of innate and instantaneous divine knowledge; (3) the triumphant encounter with temporal authority. The same legends can be found in Attar's 'Memorial of Saints' (1990), which records the lives of the early saints of Baghdad. What differs are merely the ecological and historical details: a flowing river and exemplary centre in Indonesia; desert sands and a fortress town in Morocco; the Baluch Regiment, an anti-colonial brigand's valley and corrupt politicians in Pakistan. A single paradigmatic common sense upholds this legendary corpus, while its concrete details – regiments, rivers and desert sands – embody this common sense and suffuse it with axiomatic authority. But the symbolic structure underlying this common sense is as unitary as it is inexorable.

The very uniqueness of the saint, proved in practice by his extreme asceticism, demands that his choices and actions, as embodied symbolically in the primary mythic corpus, be seen as transparently selfless and sincere. Above all, disciples insist that the humdrum, human, familiar motivations and aspirations which dominate the lives of ordinary mortals are quite irrelevant to an understanding of their saint's life. Usual yardsticks of judgement are suspended in favour of a world of teleologically inspired acts of supreme courage, selflessness and faith.

ACKNOWLEDGEMENTS

The research on which this chapter is based was conducted during 1989–91 with the support of a grant from the ESRC UK and a Leverhulme Trust fellowship. I wish to thank both bodies for their generous support. Earlier versions of the chapter were presented at the Pakistan Workshop at the University of Manchester's Satterthwaite cottages and benefited from comments by Francis Robinson and Peter Parkes. I would also like to thank Wendy James for her editorial suggestions.

NOTES

1 The controversy arose in response to the publication of three volumes of anthropological essays which documented the widely varying practices and

beliefs of South Asian Muslims in different parts of the sub-continent (Ahmad 1976, 1978, 1981).

In a critical review, the historian Francis Robinson has argued that local accommodations (such as between Hinduism and Islam) need to be set against an increasing worldwide Islamicization trend. Robinson stresses the role of elite Muslim holy men and legal experts, as well as of print capitalism and other modernist trends, in propagating the spread of a more orthodox, legally based, Islamic knowledge (Robinson 1983, 1986). In counter-response Gail Minault and Veena Das, evoking interpretive and discursive approaches respectively, have stressed the centrality of local textual interpretations, discourses and power structures in the appropriation of sacred Islamic texts (Minault 1984; Das 1984). Lindholm, reviewing the debate, goes beyond this view to argue that Islamic knowledge and practice in South Asia need to be considered apart from sacred texts, in the context of 'oppositional relations', as a (local) 'struggle for identity within a framework of often opposing interests' (1986: 72).

2 The tale was told by both of them together, and my account is constructed on the basis of my notes. All the morality tales told by Zindapir were in Urdu and were translated orally into English at key intervals. I was not allowed to tape these tales or to take notes in the saint's presence, and had to recapitulate his narratives directly after our lengthy meetings. However, he told the same tales, almost verbatim, again and again. The final supplication made by the saint was recorded on tape for two years running and translated in full into English. Most legends about him were told in English by disciples, a few were told in Urdu, often in casual conversations recorded by me later in notes and reconstructed here. There also exists an 'official' typewritten account in English of some of the legends.

3 The *nafs*, the vital, desirous soul, is contrasted with the *ruh* ('wind'), the eternal soul, which was created at the beginning of time and survives individual death. The relation between *nafs* and *ruh* is a complex one, a central focus of Sufi mystical practice.

REFERENCES

Ahmad, Imtiaz (ed.) (1976) *Family, Kinship and Marriage among Muslims in India*, New Delhi: Manohar.
—— (1978) [1973] *Caste and Stratification among Muslims in India*, New Delhi: Manohar.
—— (1981) *Ritual and Religion among Muslims in India*, New Delhi: Manohar.
Attar, Farid al-Din. (1990) [1966] *Muslim Saints and Mystics: Episodes from Memorial of the Saints*, trans. A.J. Arberry, London: Arkana.
Barth, F. (1960) 'The system of social stratification in Swat, North Pakistan', pp. 113–46, in E.R. Leach (ed.) *Aspects of Caste in South India, Ceylon and North-West Pakistan*, Cambridge: Cambridge University Press.
Becker, A.L. (1979) 'Text-building, epistemology and aesthetics in Javanese shadow theatre', pp. 211–43, in A.L. Becker and A.A. Yengoyen (eds) *The Imagination of Reality*, Norwood: Ablex Publishing.
Das, V. (1984) 'For a folk-theology and theological anthropology of Islam', *Contributions to Indian Sociology* (n.s.) 18, 2: 293–9.
Dumont, L. (1970) *Homo Hierarchicus: the Caste System and its Implications*, Chicago: University of Chicago Press.
Evans-Pritchard, E.E. (1937) *Witchcraft, Oracles and Magic among the Azande*, Oxford: Clarendon Press.

Ewing, K.P. (1990a) 'The illusion of wholeness: culture, self and the experience of inconsistency', *Ethos* 18(3): 251–78.

——(1990b) 'The dream of spiritual initiation and the organization of self representations among Pakistani Sufis', *American Ethnologist* 17, 1: 56–74.

——(1991) 'Can psychoanalytic theories explain the Pakistani woman?' *Ethos* 19: 131–60.

Foucault, M. (1977) *Discipline and Punish: the Birth of the Prison*, London: Penguin.

——(1983) 'The subject as power', pp. 208–26, in H. Dreyfus and P. Rabinow (eds) *Beyond Structuralism and Hermeneutics*, Chicago: University of Chicago Press.

Geertz, C. (1968) *Islam Observed*, New Haven, CT: Yale University Press.

——(1983) 'Common sense as a cultural system', pp. 73–93, in *Local Knowledge*, New York: Basic Books.

Gilmartin, D. (1988) *Empire and Islam*, Berkeley, CA: University of California Press.

Horton, R. (1970) [1967] 'African traditional thought and Western science', in B.R. Wilson (ed.) *Rationality*, Oxford: Blackwell Publications.

Kakar, Sudhir (1982) *Shamans, Mystics and Doctors*, Chicago: University of Chicago Press.

Kuhn, T.S. (1962) *The Structure of Scientific Revolutions*, Chicago: University of Chicago Press.

Lambek, M. (1990) 'Certain knowledge, contestable authority: power and practice on the Islamic periphery', *American Ethnologist* 17, 1: 23–40.

Levinas, E. (1987) *Collected Philosophical Papers*, trans. A. Lingis, Dordrecht: Martinus Nijhoff Publishers

Lindholm, C. (1986) 'Caste and Islam and the problem of deviant systems: a critique of recent theory', *Contributions to Indian Sociology* (n.s.) 20, 1: 61–73.

——(1990) 'Validating domination among egalitarian individuals: Swat, North Western Pakistan and the USA', pp. 26–37, in P. Werbner (ed.) 1990.

Lyotard, J.-F. (1984) [1979] *The Postmodern Condition: A Report on Knowledge*, trans. G. Bennington and B. Massumi, Manchester: Manchester University Press.

Malik, Jamal (1990) 'The luminous Nurani: charisma and political mobilization among the Barelwis of Pakistan', pp. 38–50, in P. Werbner (ed.) 1990.

Minault, G. (1984) 'Some reflections on Islamic revivalism versus assimilation among Muslims in India', *Contributions to Indian Sociology* (n.s.) 18, 2: 299–303.

Nicholson, R.A. (1989) [1914] *The Mystics of Islam*, London: Arkana.

Rao, A. (1990) 'Reflection on self and person in a pastoral community in Kashmir', pp. 11–25, in P. Werbner (ed.) 1990.

Rehman, Hafeez ur. (1979) 'The shrine and langar of Golra Sharif', MA thesis, Department of Anthropology, Quaid-i-Azam University, Islamabad.

Ricoeur, P. (1981) *Hermeneutics and the Human Sciences*, ed. and trans. J.B. Thompson, Cambridge: Cambridge University Press.

Robinson, F. (1983) 'Islam and Muslim society in South Asia', *Contributions to Indian Sociology* (n.s.) 17: 185–203.

——(1986) 'Islam and Muslim Society in South Asia: a reply to Das and Minault', *Contributions to Indian Sociology* (n.s.) 20, 1: 97–104.

Said, E.W. (1983) 'Travelling theory', in Said *The World, the Text and the Critic*, London: Vintage.

Schimmel, A. (1975) *Mystical Dimensions of Islam*, Chapel Hill, NC: University of North Carolina Press.

Weber, M. (1948) *From Max Weber: Essays in Sociology*, London: Routledge and Kegan Paul.

Werbner, P. (1990) 'Person, myth and society in South Asian Islam', *Social Analysis*, Special Issue 28, University of Adelaide.

Werbner, R. (1973) 'The superabundance of understanding: Kalanga rhetoric and domestic divination', *American Anthropologist* 75: 1414–40.

—— (1989) *Ritual Passage, Sacred Journey: the Process and Organization of Religious Movement*, Manchester/Washington, DC: Manchester University Press/Smithsonian Institution Press.

7 Topophilia, Zionism and 'certainty'
Making a place out of the space that became Israel again

Robert Paine

Israel, 1983: We stand on a Samarian hillside: a group, mainly American-Jewish visitors to Israel, on a half-day guided walking expedition. Our guide is from a *yeshiva* (an Orthodox Jewish educational establishment) in Judea. What I see laid out in the landscape before me is, to my left and along a stony elevation, an Israeli settlement of white cement bungalows with red-tiled roofs; and in a fold of the valley in front of me, a sprawling Palestinian village with its mosque.

I turn to listen to our guide.

The landscape he 'sees' apparently contains neither the settlement nor the village: what he is telling us to 'see' is the site where Jeremiah was born and where the Maccabees – just across the valley before us – fought and defeated a Roman legion. In directing our eyes to these sites, he refers us to 'over there, by that heap of boulders' and 'beyond those gnarled trees'; neither village nor settlement are used as orientation points.[1]

This episode imprinted firmly on my mind the power of topophilia (Tuan 1974) as a medium of the imagination implanting certainty and its pregnant relevance to Israel and the Zionist enterprise.[2] In this chapter, I hope to suggest something of the diversity of the material and how it might be usefully structured so as to address some of the 'layers' of Jewish experience, in our times, in the landscapes of Palestine and Israel. Some of the layers appear mutually unreconcilable.

CERTAINTY AND PLACE

Before engaging the ethnography, it is necessary to think about the making of certainty, the making of place, and, especially, the role of each in the making of the other. I will then try to show how different generations of Jews in Palestine/Israel (with differences between them concerning Zionist ideology and practice: Paine 1989, 1992) make different certainty–place equations.

Certainty[3] exists in an uncertain world.[4] Thus, in what follows, I write it as 'certainty'. *Place* is also constructed, of course. It brings space and time together. Space itself is a neutral grid on which cultural difference will be inscribed; sociologically, it has, as it were, yet to become. '[E]very-thing that happens must happen somewhere' (Basso 1988: 110). Past events in the service of the present are mapped onto the landscape; and landscapes themselves, ' "detached" from their fixed spatial moorings' become 'eminently portable possessions ... tools for the imagination' (*ibid.*: 102). And as a portable possession, time (no longer chronometric) entwines memory and experience in cultural patterns of different valen-cies – some more memory-activated, others more experience-oriented (the difference will be addressed empirically as we proceed). As place confines experience and memory, so, together, they embue place (see Richardson 1984: 65). Hence the cultural 'truth' in the tautology: 'A landscape belongs to those who belong to it'; and as a landscape 'gains in intelligibility', for those constructing it, 'it gains in visibility – it becomes the 'practical grammar of the arrangement of [their] working space' (Melöy 1988: 400, 389, 390). So in a world full of working spaces – even as there is little 'certainty' – people work to make and maintain a place of their own; and there are two crucial points about that. First, place always 'contains or implies a theory ... of what [it] is produced from, against, in spite of and in relation to' (Appadurai 1993: 6; see Gupta and Ferguson 1992: 11): hence the '*vis-à-vis*' structure of the sections of this chapter that follow. Second, through the constructions given to 'certainty' and place, people manifest, often quite emphatically, much of their self-identity and, at the same time, advertise it to those outside. Indeed, a symbolic geography may develop whereby features in a landscape 'become symbolic of cultural standards and become meaningful in a deeply personal sense' (Bruner 1984: 4). Pocock (1975: 275) speaks even of 'a kind of moral geodesy'.[5] I hope this emerges, as well, from the sections of this piece.

Returning now to the opening episode: one sees the force in Leach's observation that first there are stories to tell, then there are places to hang them on – rather than it being the other way around (1984: 358): this leads to 'the visibility of certain things and not others' (Tuan 1984: 9). Such has been a marked characteristic with Jews/Israelis in Palestine/Israel over the last hundred years – and not just in their relations with Palestinian Arabs but also between themselves. Different, sometimes mutually anti-thetical, symbolic and moral landscapes have been constructed as alle-gories of their respective ideological positions.

Accordingly, much in the descriptions that follow is about:

- moving in as coming home to place
- moving in as coming into someone else's place
- no longer moving in but being born 'in place' (Tuan 1984).

As a Zionist enterprise, the concern is with the transformation of the natural environment – of uncertain and disputed borders – into a national place. For some, this primarily means political territory; for others, it means the sanctification and Judaization of space as well.

What of a 'Zionist' notion of 'certainty'? Is there one? Though this is hazardous ground for a generalization, it might help initially to make a tentative one. First, I think there is much to the statement that 'Jews freely incorporate history into their biographies'; but among Zionists, in the place of 'Jewish' fatalism over their history there is the belief that 'we are now fulfilling our national memory'. That was said to me by a religious person; but here is a secular version and the connection of 'certainty' to place is unmistakable: 'The demographic map [of Judea and Samaria] will be truer to that of the time of the ancient kings of Israel – the Highlands will have a substantial Jewish population again.' So Zionist 'fulfilment', which Zionist 'certainty' is all about, arises from 'doing', not just being.[6] It is an expression of will – that defies history where necessary – of the kind associated with the Masada story (and by extension the Holocaust): 'Never again.' For some, this will has an eschatologic force and *that*, too, has everything to do with place. In sum, Zionists (of whatever stripe) live not by what can or might happen but by what *must* now happen – and will.

One final observation about the sense of 'certainty' in the Zionist context. It appears to be at its most compelling in periods of crisis – of abnormality as opposed to normality; with normality there is likely a fading of 'certainty'. At least this is an hypothesis to have in mind.

THE 'CERTAINTY' OF PLACE FOR THE ZIONIST *VIS-À-VIS* THE DIASPORA

Palestine 1882: The place was desolate: there was not a house or even a booth or a hut, not a tree or a man in sight – thorns and thistles were all that grew upon the land round about us. . . . A fresh breeze wafted down from the Judean hills, good, healthy and restoring the soul. . . . I began to recall the prophetic stories connected with this place. I thought of Samson, the heroic warrior who had battled the Philistines, smiting them with the jawbone he held in his hand. I remembered the blood my forefathers had spilled here: perhaps I had spread my cloak upon their very graves. I felt a powerful love for the place, the love of a son who, after being banished from his father's home, returns there once more – *but his father is no longer there*. Tears fell from my eyes and my heart and soul, too, poured themselves out within me. This place was my home and the place where I would find my peace. And my cradle, too, the cradle of my childhood. . . . So we passed the night, under the stars. . . . At daybreak . . . we set about measuring out the site of the village.

(The diary of Z.D. Levontin, translated and cited by
Schweid 1985: 137–9; emphasis added)

In fact, Levontin's 'certainty' deserted him. Within eighteen months this pioneer had returned to the Diaspora that proved to be his 'home' after all (Elon 1981: 101–2). One insight into this sequence of emotional embrace and disenchantment may be found in the musings of an American Jewish writer on a visit a hundred years later:

> When you are exiled from your land ... you begin, like a pornographer, to think about it in symbols. You articulate your love for your land, in its absence and in the process transform it into something else. We Jews had 2,000 years in which to become expert pornographers with a highly symbol-wrought, intellectualized yearning for this land – totally devoid of any memories or images of what it really looks like. And when Jews came to settle here in this century, they saw the land through these symbols. ... As for what it really looked like, they tried to transform it into the kinds of landscape they left in Europe.
>
> (cited in Shehadeh 1982: 86; see Halkin 1977: 146)

But the 'pioneering' generations of Zionists succeeded in planting a 'homeland' in Palestine. In this effort, much rested with the kibbutz collective with its religion of labour. A member of Kibbutz Degania, the first to be founded, in 1910, recalls:

> [It] ... was a kind of communal 'honeymoon'. We used to go out in the morning to plough while it was dark. ... Here we were on the banks of the Jordan. ... We felt we had become farmers, workers of the soil – our homeland's soil. When dusk fell, we used to return.
>
> After a day of hard and grinding labor, we would sit in a circle, begin with romantic songs, pour out all our heart and then go over to Hassidic tunes, which bring all of us to our feet dancing and perspiring without an end.
>
> (cited in Bowes 1989: 23)

The life was not one of reflection but of action (Katriel and Shenhar 1990), in which each day ended in a ritual of triumph and solidarity. However, the reference to Hassidic tunes could mislead: the life of these kibbutzniks, devoted to the landscape of their making, was also marked by ritual demolition of (Diaspora) Jewishness, as understood by these Hebrew-minded rather than Jewish-minded pioneers whose children were to be Israelis.[7]

Half a century later, testimonies of kibbutzniks in the wake of the Six-Day War of 1967, published in *The Seventh Day* (Near 1971), indicate some of the changing currents, over time, of 'certainty' and place. Matitiyahu is the father of Amitai (aged 25) and Elisha (aged 38); the two sons were born in Palestine but Matitiyahu came, with his father, in the 1930s:

> *Matitiyahu*: My complete identification with the land of Israel isn't accidental or fortuitous. I came to the country completely broken up,

shattered, without any feeling for what I had known in my childhood. I was searching for an identity. I had no deep roots anywhere. When I came to Palestine, I felt I had been born anew. From that moment I began to live.

(pp. 211–12)

Amitai: There's been a lot of talk about territorial expansion and someone even called the war the 'Land of Israel Campaign'. I have a feeling that we've lost something terribly precious. We've lost our little country. My first reaction during a trip through the West Bank just after the war was, 'Fellows, we've got to get back to Galilee as quick as we can and show ourselves that our country – I mean the country we had before the war – is good and beautiful' ... My feeling for the country doesn't derive from the knowledge that it's the Promised Land. There's nothing equivocal about it. I was born here. And this is the difference between me and Dad. Dad came back to the country. I didn't come back, I was born here.

(p. 210)

Both father and son are far from the pornographer's 'love ... in absence'. The pornographer has only memory – a memory detached from experience – but these kibbutzniks, both generations of them, live amidst their experience of Palestine/Israel as homeland – to which are attached (interpretive) memories.

Yet there is a difference between father and son: it is that between 'being born here' (the son) and 'being reborn here' (the father). The issue is not one of exact dates and places of birth – a person could well be born in Palestine and still undergo, experientially, rebirth. Rather, the notion of 'rebirth' (in the present context) provides a person with 'certainty' of place through relating memory to day-by-day experience.[8] It directs our analysis to the phenomenon of taking (re-)possession of the landscape.

First, there had to be knowledge of the landscape – *yedi'at haaretz*: 'to know the country'.[9] Then reconceptualization: 'the need to turn the *geographia sacra* of the Diaspora into tangible reality, to make Eretz Israel [the religious denotation for the land of Israel] a natural, not only a spiritual homeland' (Benvenisti 1986: 20). Finally, possession of the country through physical experience – here the 'knowing' is as the Biblical 'And Adam knew Eve, his wife.'

When you hike in the desert you actively possess its wadis and rocky promontories. The circuitous mountain roads skirting dense pine forests become Jewish when you drive along them. Sighting gazelles, identifying wild plants, excavating archaeological sites are all symbolic acts of possession.

(Benvenisti 1986: 23)

It is a process of becoming 'in place' (Tuan 1984), of constructing not so much a 'symbolic geography' (Pocock 1975)[10] as a moral geography through a 'return to nature' *geist*. Benvenisti (1986: 32) himself was born in Palestine, in the 1930s, and speaking of his own growing up he claims: 'My vantage point was indigenous.' But his autobiography shows how this was not a given vantage point (by the physical fact of birth *in situ*); on the contrary, he was energetic and assiduous in the exercises and rituals of (re-)possessing the landscape.

Throughout the early years of the Zionist enterprise and for decades after the 1948 declaration of statehood, the Exile – the *galut* – in mind was the European. This old-new (Theodor Herzl) state of Israel was Ashkenazi (the Jew of north and north-eastern European descent) in concept and political substance. But by the 1970s it was so in defiance of demography; and with the gradual falling away of political allegiance from the Ashkenazi hegemony of Labour Zionism (culminating in the 1977 change of government from Labour to Likud), the 'second Israel' of the Mizrahim (Jews of Middle Eastern and North African descent) was heard politically and – our concern here – culturally.[11] In particular, an alternative to the charter canon of Ashkenazi memory of the *galut* appeared.

An important example is the shrine to Baba Sali, a Moroccan-born *zaddik*, Jewish holy man or saint, who immigrated to Israel in 1964 (Weingrod 1993). The shrine 'revives memories of Morocco . . . evokes images of what Morocco is imagined to have been like' (pp. 375–6). Along with 'the people, faces, smells and foods, singing and dance, the language,' the shrine *returns* 'one back to another time and place' (p. 375). This signifies a 'deep break . . . with the Zionist ideological system,' for '[a]t the core of its ideology was the belief that coming to Palestine–Israel meant leaving the past behind ("we have come to the land to build and to become rebuilt by it")' (p. 376). The shrine to Baba Sali means that 'it is now possible and, indeed, legitimate, for the *galut* to be literally transported to Israel and openly displayed there' (p. 377).[12] And a non-Ashkenazi *galut* at that!

The Weingrod essay shows us how the Diaspora is always an element in Jewish-Israeli construction of place; and how – in this late or post-revolutionary phase of Zionism – negotiation between people and place is possible.[13] This of itself points to an illuminating difference between place and territory: the non-territoriality of place, in certain contexts, allows for its multiplicity (without division) within a territory. This factor can have direct bearing on people's experience of well-being and its 'certainty'.

THE 'CERTAINTY' OF PLACE FOR THE ZIONIST *VIS-À-VIS* THE ARAB

and when you have built your houses and settled here . . . tens of them will come mounted on horses in the dead of night . . . plundering and murdering.

Bedouin! Such was the warning his guide and interpreter (a Jew from Jerusalem) gave Levontin in 1882 (Schweid 1985: 138). A century later in one of the militarily secure West Bank urban estates, Menachem Ausbacher, a one-time religious political-activist, muses:

> Now, the circumstances are ... we are sitting on our land according to our tradition. Do I have the right to give back my land, which does not belong to me – it belongs to God according to our tradition. He created the circumstances so that I could now liberate the land. But the question remains: the Arab population? That's a question to which I don't have a straight, easy-to-understand answer.

In this section, I look not at the need to build up a 'certainty' of place against memories of the *galut* but the striving for Zionist 'certainty' *vis-à-vis* the Arabs of Palestine. One can be easily led to a portraiture of Israeli Jewish single-minded dogmatism on this point, and that is to be found (and I will give examples), but even among those settled in the West Bank there is a range of ideological positions and, for some, their 'certainty' does not exclude a sense of problem.

Jewish settlers on the West Bank are prone to speaking of 'the Arabs' (never, or seldom, 'the Palestinians') as 'our tenants' on the land. But this can be said in different ways:

> The first Zionist ... [was] God. It was the Land of Israel that God chose as his seat ... and it was the responsibility of the Jewish people to live in the land that God had given to them. . . . And if there are now Arabs in that land, then they took it from the Jewish people! And they know it. . . . To compromise on our own home, a home that belongs not only to us but also to God is abnormal.
>
> (Rabbi Levinger in Reich 1984: 15–16)

> This was really the cradle of the Jewish people. I don't think I have the right to displace anyone who is living anywhere. But if no-one is living there and if I have my roots there, of course I have a right to be there.
>
> (Rabbi Riskin in Wallach and Wallach 1989: 198)

Rabbi Levinger lives (since 1968) in the middle of the Arab town of Hebron;[14] he is a *sabra* (a native born Jewish Israeli). Rabbi Riskin, in 1981, helped re-establish, from Mandate days, the Jewish settlement in Efrat; he is from New York. Riskin offers a gentle and pragmatic (open to compromise) update on the founding Zionist slogan, 'A land without people for a people without a land'. Levinger offers no compromise. I found their respective views voiced among secular Israelis, too.

Kiryat Arba is a post-1967 Jewish township built on the edge of Hebron.[15] Most of its inhabitants are religious fundamentalists (see pp. 171–80 below)); among the secular families are the Haetznis, Elyakim and

Zippora. Zippora, a sculptor, was born in Palestine where her people had lived for several generations. She remembers going to Hebron as a young girl with her grandmother to visit the tomb of Abraham: 'then, Jews were only allowed as far as the seventh step [outside the mosque] leading up to the Tomb. I wasn't afraid. But now, Jews are afraid. What's happened to this nation?'

When the cease-fire between the Israeli and Arab armies was declared in November 1947, Zippora was one of those who did *not* dance in the streets, for 'we had lost the real [Biblical] Land of Israel.' Then after the victory of 1967,

> when we Jews returned to the Land again, there was the shock of all the talk about giving it back 'for peace'. My husband said that must not be allowed to happen: 'too many Jews have died for this place'. He began working with Rabbi Levinger, already in 1968, on plans for the Jewish re-settlement of Hebron.'

Zippora declares: 'We own this land. We're not bringing Israel into Hebron: Israel *is* Hebron!'

Elyakim Haetzni came to Palestine from Germany in 1938 as a boy of 12. He had lived in several places in Israel before moving his law practice and his family to Kiryat Arba in 1972,[16] but '[t]his place is in my genetic code. It was my genetic code that cried out to live in this place' (Reich 1984: 22). Time and again in our conversations he returns to the issue: 'If Tel Aviv, why not Kiryat Arba?' and to what he sees as the 'hypocrisy' of the 'peaceniks' who live in Tel Aviv or even Jaffa and yet condemn the making of a Jewish place alongside Hebron (or even within it).

Akiva Skidell[17] of Kibbutz Kfar Blum, north of the Sea of Galilee (the Kinneret), would 'answer' Haetzni thus:

> Morally, it is no more wrong to build Kiryat Arba next door to Hebron than it was to build Tel-Aviv next door to Jaffa, *except that the conditions have changed*. It's not the historic claim that justifies what we do, though it is part of our motivation. But motivation and justification are two different things. The justification then was that we needed a home, we were being persecuted and had no place else to go. As long as that justification existed, there was nothing wrong about buying land in Palestine and trying to do as little harm as possible. . . Today, we don't *have* to go to Hebron to find more places for Jews to settle.[18]

But for Haetzni, the historical claim is the justification. And the claim itself is remarkable. Unique. 'Of all the ancient peoples – the Etruscans, for example – only the Jews are not in a museum.' If only for this reason, he can live nowhere else. Indeed, he would stay in Hebron (Kiryat Arba) under Arab rule rather than 'retreat' to behind the Green Line[19] of a mutilated Israel. After all, 'This country was *not* empty when the Zionists came. Zionism is *not* predicated on Arab assent.'

Claude Kadosh was born in Algeria and came to Israel by way of France in 1980. At first, his Zionism seemed to me to have a different temper to Haeztni's. Driving with him along some of the Judean byways, he delights in seeing new *Arab* houses and newly sown *Arab* vineyards wrested from the desert:

> Look! These people must believe in the future. I take pride as an Israeli, all this is happening because of *our* guidance and *our peace*. It's the old story of a strong and concerned central government and the settling of nomadic people.

Nevertheless, he says, 'The Arabs want *me* to live somewhere else.' Haetzni says much the same. Even so, when we met at Kiryat Arba, Kadosh, an economist, was directing a development programme for which, he says, he has Arab as well as Jewish backers – just as Haetzni's legal practice has local Arab clients.

> Kadosh the Zionist is also a dreamer. Or, a dreamer, he becomes a Zionist?
> My dream is about this country. . . . And we deliver our message to the world. . . . I'm not talking about borders: I don't put borders in my dreams. My Zionism is not a geographic question. And I don't have to negotiate my dreams. I live by them.

This, too, sounds like Haetzni. By way of 'dream' (a secular substitution for 'miracle'?) they encompass 'certainty'? At any rate, I think Kadosh speaks for both of them when he says of his dream: 'It's not just a right, it's necessity. I've been "educated" by one hundred generations of victims: I'm not accepting that either for myself or for my children.'

And the dream is outside time, though both men wish to see time on their side:

> You ask, 'When will peace come?' You can't scare us with time: we have a history of thousands of years.
>
> (Haetzni)

> When will peace come? I don't know. But what if it takes generations? We are here until the end of time.
>
> (Kadosh)

Contradictions, often ironic, are likely in such situations – indeed, they seem inherent. In closing this section, let me draw attention to the following two items.

Item 1. As mentioned, (re-)possession of the land or *yedi'at haaretz* is predicated on 'knowledge' of the land and that not uncommonly has invited Zionist imagining through Arab imagery. Among 'the first settlers who came to Palestine' (Kimmerling 1983: 184–9), it was not uncommon to view the Arabs as relatives: 'Semitic relatives who greatly resembled "our forefathers".' Kimmerling goes so far as to say: '[i]t followed that if the Jews were returning to the land of the forefathers and wished to renew their ancient culture, they should selectively imitate the customs of the Arabs.' But then, the same settlers might also view the Arabs as native, and natives are not expected to acquiesce in the loss of their land: thus, it was reluctantly acknowledged, only by force could Zionism achieve its aims.

This tangled relationship of Jew to Palestinian Arab, as viewed by some Zionists, has a life beyond that of 'the first settlers'. Thus Benvenisti's first-hand testimony: 'Arab villages and customs are a backdrop, part of the scenery . . . a living testimony to the life of our forefathers' (1986: 24). Amos Oz knows well of what Benvenisti speaks and he extends the imagery to the landscape:

> And then I study the elusive cunning of the Biblical charm of this land-scape: and isn't all of this charm Arab, through and through? The lodge and the cucumber garden, the watchman's hut and the cisterns, the shade of the fig tree and the pale silver of the olive, the grape arbors and the flocks of sheep – these picturesque slopes that bewitched from afar the early Zionists.
>
> (1983: 121)

But then Oz says something few others say:

> These ancient Biblical charms are like the Promised Land unto Moses: For Thou shalt see the land from afar off but thou shalt not go thither. . . . For if you should enter, the Biblical charm will fade like a dream. The penetration will not be one of harmony but of occupation and capitulation and destruction. Where shall we turn our ancient Biblical longings if Samaria is filled with prefab villas?
>
> (p. 122)

Aesthetically, then, Oz leaves 'Arab' and its Biblical charm in *its* place so that it can continue to inhabit the mind as a part of his place, even though – or rather, because – he hasn't occupied it physically. More importantly, it is also a move of considerable political significance for (as the term goes) 'practical Zionism'.

Item 2. By 1983, the Likud government would speak of the 'Green Line' much as Labour cabinet ministers used to refer to Palestinians – 'what Green Line?' Occasionally, though, the issue was brought to light in ways indicative of persisting behind-the-scenes struggles. In 1986, for instance, rows reached the public over the appearance of an official map *with* the Green Line drawn; and over 'the leftist tilt in description of post-1967 settlements' in the new edition of the prestigious *Israel Atlas*. The description had been written by the chief editor who, at the time, was also the head of the Hebrew University's Department of Geography. Distribution of the atlas was temporarily frozen while the offending page was removed and a substitute inserted (*Jerusalem Post*, International Edition, 25 October 1986).

THE 'CERTAINTY' OF PLACE *VIS-À-VIS* ZIONISTS' DIFFERENCES OVER ITS OCCUPANCY[20]

Victory in the Six-Day War put the question: has the State of Israel as a Jewish state 'repossessed' the holy Jewish sites of historical Eretz Israel in Judea and Samaria?[21] Overlaid with implications for Zionist notions of 'certainty' and place, the question still rages. Far from there being a straight secular versus religious division, secular and religious Zionists are found together on both sides of the issue. This is not to say that the secular and the religious embrace common cause for the same reasons. For the religious, the imperatives, either for the repossession of the sites or their relinquishment, have everything to do with (their divergent readings of) Judaism. Between the secular, on the other hand, the opposing imperatives are Jewish history and universal ethics. Finally, all parties to this issue also view the sites as space, as territory, and draw conclusions, on that basis, in the name of the national interest.

Something of this cross-cutting pattern together with the sense (particularly in evidence among 'Greater Israel' supporters) of cultural specificity is expressed in the following:

> It is frustrating that 'historically' and 'geographically' is translated in the Western press as 'for religious reasons'. I am not religious and yet I love my country – Eretz Israel. . . .[22]
>
> When we refer to the Bible, we have in mind a bestseller that happens to contain a tremendous documentation relating to our history. . . . This may be at the origin of a deep misunderstanding: in the eyes of Western Culture, the Bible has a purely religious significance.
>
> (Ne'eman 1982: 19)

Yuval Ne'eman had a high public profile;[23] still more significant, though, is that at a time when 'Greater Israel' (annexation of the West Bank and Gaza) nationalism is widely perceived as religiously inspired – indeed, as *being* a religious phenomenon – Ne'eman is joined by a good many other 'seculars' in the top echelon of the movement. Not personally religious, they still recognize the influence of religion in setting and achieving national goals (Bauer 1985: 101). Thus Elyakim Haetzni, for example, works closely with Rabbi Levinger. Conversely, it is Haetzni who delivers the most scathing rebuke to a leading religious 'dove' for whom the Greater Israel brand of nationalism is offensive to the morality of the Torah:

> So Professor Simon is prepared to give up parts of Eretz Israel in return for peace, eh? 'Even though it pains him' [Simon 1982]! But who does

not have 'pain' in life? We should expect 'pain' if we have ideals. But 'pain' from compromising ideals is *not* a noble pain and no account should be taken of it – it's absurd, contemptible.

However, it is especially in the exchanges between religious protagonists themselves that the subtler insights about place and 'certainty' are revealed. Notable opponents of the Gush Emunim (Bloc of the Faithful) come from a group calling itself Oz veShalom: 'Strength through Peace'. There are two levels of argument; I look at them in turn. The first is about the morality of Judaism in the world of *realpolitik*. In a 'war' of Biblical citation, the Gush Emunim discharges, like so many thunderbolts, such verses as:

Every place whereon the sole of your foot shall tread shall be yours.
(Deuteronomy XI: 24)

And ye shall drive out the inhabitants of the land, and dwell therein.
(Numbers XXXIII: 53)

. . . and when the Lord thy God shall deliver them up before thee and thou shalt smite them; then thou shalt utterly destroy them; thou shall make no covenant with them, nor show mercy unto them.
(Deuteronomy VII: 2)

Cymbals as symbols! Oz veShalom 'replies' with such verses as:

Ye therefore shall keep My statutes and Mine ordinances . . . that the land not vomit you out also, when ye defile it, as it vomited the nation that was before you.
(Leviticus XVIII: 26, 28)

. . . justice shalt thou follow, that thou mayest live, and inherit the land which the Lord thy God giveth thee.
(Deuteronomy XVI: 20)

So ye shall not pollute the land; and no expiation can be made for the land for the blood that is shed therein but by the blood of him that shed it.
(Numbers XXXV: 33)[24]

Of the exegetical debate that follows and the contradictions it brings forth (the adversaries are Rabbis and Biblical scholars for the most part), I can only give here a bare-bones account.[25] But it will demonstrate, among other points, how notions of 'certainty' have moral correlates.

In essence, Oz veShalom's horrified opposition[26] to Gush Emunim rests on the following. The 'Israel' of Judaism has three components: People, Land and Torah (*Am Yisrael, Eretz Yisrael, Torat Yisrael*); Gush Emunim's singular focus on the Land runs contrary to Torah teaching and, accordingly, prejudices the spiritual and moral statuses of the Jewish people.

Oz veShalom places the moral injunctions of the Torah above the matter of political control and occupancy of the Land for '[t]he Promise was not of a continued possession of The Land but of a possession conditioned by observance' (Davies 1982: 101). So too, the 'chosenness' of the Jews entails 'closeness to God rather than ascendancy over other peoples' (Elizur 1978b: 89). Emphasis is placed upon the responsibilities rather than the rights of being the Chosen. The importance of human life is held as a universal precept; thus 'though, under Jewish law [*Halakhah*], it is forbidden to give back even the smallest parcel of the Land of Israel, if there is any question of life and death ... then it is surely permitted to hand back areas of the Land of Israel and arrive at territorial compromise' (cited in Oz veShalom *Bulletin* no. 1, March 1982).[27]

In the contrary view, however:

> All activities designed to transfer ownership of parts of Eretz Israel from the hands of the gentiles to those of the Jews, come within the definition of the Divine commandment to conquer the Land of Israel, outweighing all the commandments of the Torah.
>
> (cited in Aviner 1978: 115)[28]

A way out of this contradiction of values, writes Simon (1983), is to distinguish clearly between 'our religious right to the land ... and the legal-political right' (p. 23). The Torah makes clear that the religious right can by no means be identified with actual occupancy (see Leviticus XVIII: 26).

Here, then, the argument is about occupancy, not possession (unlike the emphasis in secular circles where, as we saw, possession itself has to be demonstrated through occupancy). Simon recognizes that occupancy and settlement of Judea and Samaria is, of itself, a *mitzvah* – a pious deed; but at this time it would amount to one which is fulfilled 'by means of transgression' (against the non-Jewish Palestinian population) and that 'cannot be called a *mitzvah*' (Simon 1983: 24). In the opposing view, however, the wresting of Eretz Israel from Gentile control 'readily falls under the category of *mitzvot* requiring martyrdom' (Ariel 1978: 151), as with the Talmudic injunction about 'obligatory war'. There is, then, a 'contradiction' within the domain of 'our religious right' itself.

It was against this background that Dov Berkovitz interested me. I first heard him speak (in 1983) at a debate with Oz veShalom people, in the seminary in Jerusalem where he was teaching Jewish Studies to students from the Diaspora (principally the United States). Afterwards, I was surprised to learn that he lived in the Gush Emunim settlement of Shiloh. With the Gush, yet (I surmised) not fully of the Gush? An Orthodox Jew and the son of an eminent figure in Jewish philosophy, he had left the United States to find his place and sense of 'certainty' in 'Shiloh' where Joshua had erected the tabernacle. I sought him out, in Jerusalem and Shiloh. I noted in my journal:

In our conversations, he structures his remarks around what he calls the two principles of Zionist settlement: 1. nothing built is to be relinquished,[29] and 2. no Arab is to be expelled from his land. He recognizes the two are in enduring conflict. . . .

He has thought much about his own position and has decided it is more important to fulfill the first principle [no settlement shall be surrendered] rather than surrender to implacable Arabs: 'the Arabs have refused discourse . . . they have refused to recognize the deep importance of Judea and Samaria to Jewish consciousness.' . . .

For the present and the foreseeable future, he lives in Shiloh and commutes into Jerusalem to teach. . . .

For many Israelis, Berkovitz says, the significance of the 1967 'conquest' of Judea and Samaria has moved from being a matter of 'political legitimation' to one of 'experiential realization' and 'visionary history'. Thus he feels that Professor Simon [see above] underrates the critical place Eretz Israel has in Jewish consciousness:[30] 'Geography has a soul, if you give Judea and Samaria back to the Arabs it is the same as surrendering part of the soul of the Jewish people.'

Even in this moderate supporter of the Gush Emunim, then, there are indications of a movement or a slide from the historical 'Shiloh' as place, to 'creating facts' on the ground, and Shiloh the Gush Emunim settlement,[31] and a preparedness for unremitting use of physical force in their support.[32] Much of the explanation is to be found at the second level of argument. It is about messianic fulfilment.[33] In the Gush Emunim view, the overwhelming victory of 1967 was a 'miracle' and then, from the very edge of disaster, the 1973 victory was proof that the eschatological era of redemption had begun:

> Why did the war of Gog and Magog come? . . . After the establishment of the Kingdom of Israel the war can have only one significance: the purification, refining and cleansing of the congregation of Israel'.
>
> (Tal 1986: 320–1, citing a sermon of the influential
> Rabbi Yehudah Amital)[34]

'Possession' quickly acquired dual meaning:

> the devotional settler on recently conquered land is possessed by his messianic zeal, while his zeal transforms the conquest into redemption and temporary borders into eternal horizons, thus realizing the notion of *eretz nachalah*, of possessing the Holy Land by inheritance.
>
> (Tal 1986: 328)

The epistemological implications are radical: notably an 'exegetical reformulation' of time and space and a reconceptualization of the relation between symbol and substance (*ibid.*) – hence a revolutionary or revealed construction of place and 'certainty'.

Time and space are brought together through proclaiming *as of now* the messianic future[35] and political sovereignty over Palestine. Thus life veers towards the pole of Benjamin's (1973) 'instantaneous' and Alter's 'ultimacy' (1973); or in Tal's words: 'History is now understood as time and space reborn – hence, as metahistory' (1986: 331). Similarly, space is reconceptualized as 'sanctified localities and neighbourhoods', so that 'the sanctification of place becomes a practical, political, not simply a theological, necessity' (*ibid.*: 321).

> It is in this process of Judaization of space,[36] that the Gush Emunim have turned symbols into substance, thereby allowing them to take on a very real and sacralized presence. A particular stone, the [Western/Wailing] Wall, the Tombs of the Patriarchs and historical places no longer serve as symbols but have become for Gush Emunim the sanctified reality itself.
>
> (Tal 1979: 12)

Thus 'the mystique of the redemption has become tangible, concrete and actual' (Tal 1986: 320), and Israel not just a Homeland but also and primarily, the Land of Destiny (Schweid 1985 *passim*).

And 'certainty'? It is moved onto a metaphysical plane in which the cosmic and the concrete reflect each other and nurture each other – and where the fulfilment of person and nation happen in the imagery of each other.[37]

Such is the place that is Israel, for some. Any withdrawal from the conquered territories would, in this view, constitute a hindrance to the process of redemption (Ariel 1978: 139). But the majority of Orthodox Jewry within the present State of Israel find in the Torah (tempered with interpretations inherited from rabbinical Judaism of the Diaspora) another Israel – and it is from this tradition that Oz veShalom speaks.

The experience of living, de-territorialized, in the Diaspora brought about a transcendental notion of place – of 'celestial Jerusalem' *even* as the terrestial city was retained in the memory of the past and the 'memory' of the future. So ' "The Land" was not space but place,' and the Torah 'a portable Land' or 'a map without territory' (Davies 1982: 123, 121, 131). This means 'A Jew . . . can continue in his faith outside The Land but not outside the Torah', and that, argues Davies (p. 122), 'is the essence of Judaism'.

There is here a mode of abstraction quite different to that of Gush Emunim, even diametrically opposed. In contrast to the 'self-certainty' (Aviad 1983: 31) of the Gush Emunim within 'an all-inclusive totality [and] a feeling of absolute certainty . . . of divine justification' (Tal 1986: 329),[38] Oz veShalom searches for the fulfilment of 'certainty' in the face of disturbing historical realities. Time and space are historical entities as well as metahistorical; and the Arabs of Palestine, as 'sojourners' in Eretz Israel, as Abraham once was in Canaan (Genesis

XXIII: 4), have historical rights. Note is taken that even the Torah is in-
definite (to say the least) on the boundaries of Eretz Israel (Elizur 1978a
passim; and Tal 1986: 324–5). But nor is it the changing boundary that is
holy, only 'The Land' as place.

THE 'CERTAINTY' OF PLACE *VIS-À-VIS* DIZENGOFF STREET

Throughout the 1980s government and private agencies conducted ambitious advertising campaigns to lure Jews to Judea and Samaria from
anywhere in the world, on the basis of quality of living with bargain
purchases or mortgages on villas, even within daily commuting distance
of such urban centres as Tel Aviv. Here I try to draw out some of the
implications by way of three distinctive scenarios from the early 1980s.[39]

Scenario 1. Ya'akov Fitelson, the Mayor of Ariel[40]

> Ya'akov Fitelson, a computer scientist by training, reached Israel in
> 1972 from Soviet Lithuania. We are in his small office and he opens
> with a geopolitical lecture, standing in front of a wallmap of Israel with
> pointer in hand. There is a portrait of Jabotinsky on the opposite wall,
> one of [Menachem] Begin in his secretary's office but none that I could
> see of [David] Ben-Gurion.
>   'All things in Israel begin in Tel Aviv,' Ya'akov tells us, 'and that city
> is only half an hour away by road; Jerusalem and Netanya are the same
> distance. The Mediterranean and the Jordan Valley are both 35 kilo-
> metres away. The Patriarch's Highway [north–south] and the Trans-
> Samarian Highway [east–west] intersect here.'
>   The message is clear: Ariel is at the centre and a key location from
> any point of view: defence, commuting, commerce.
>   Ya'akov came to Israel because of the 'Jewish problem',[41] and that,
> he says, won't be solved until most of the Jews of the world are living
> in Israel. However, he has disdain for what he calls the 'assimilated
> Jew in Israel' and he is not talking religiously: it is the crass hedonism
> and materialism of Tel Aviv's Dizengoff Street he has in mind.
> 'Assimilation' to the 'decadence of Europe, the vulgarity of North
> America!'
>   Ya'akov is also critical of the pioneering legacy of the older *sabra*;
> 'They were the vanguard but things change – reasons for coming here
> change, factors regarding the settling of Israel change. . . .'
>   As Ya'akov sees it (without a trace of irony) Jewish settlement in
> Samaria is not going to be land-based but will maintain itself on High
> Tech. industries. Arab 'tenants' will continue on the land but the 'sover-
> eign' rights to the land return to the Jews. This we hear pretty much
> wherever we go on the West Bank.

Ya'akov concludes: 'I analyse my position here, a Jew in Samaria, as the owner and the stronger. I have always known that I am the owner historically. I will do what I can for the Arabs without hurting my own people. I prefer *to live* as an imperialist, if you like, than *death* as a pacifist. Our children are free here.' We have heard this before, too.

Scenario 2. Dina Shalit at Ariel (1983) and 'Leah' at Homesh (1985)

Dina works for the Ariel town council, publicity department, her husband for the national organization of the Herut [parent party of the Likud]. They were born in Montreal. They visited Israel several times before making the decision – just last year – to immigrate. They have three young children and the family lives in a small temporary pre-fabricated bungalow – while they await their turn for a new house. Her husband's work takes him into either Jerusalem or Tel Aviv, by his own car, most days of the week.

Dina says that before she came it never occurred to her to ask about Arab–Jewish relations in Samaria and she has never doubted, not for a moment, that the region will be 'incorporated' into Israel. She says they have 'relations' with 'the Arabs' – for instance, they go to the same shop in the nearby Arab village on the Sabbath when their shop is closed; she also says their children play with the Arab children.[42]

The most important reason for their coming to live in Israel was the fear of 'assimilation' should the family remain in Canada: Dina (though secular) is determined that her children grow up as Jews. And the choice of Ariel? This sprang from her desire to 'do something' for Israel and that, she says, is not possible in Tel Aviv. Only in a place like Ariel.[43]

With Rachel Kimor, an Israeli colleague, I visit Homesh, in Samaria not far from Schechem. Rachel has a friend there – 'Leah' (as I will call her):

Leah and her husband, both *sabras*, used to travel a lot in Samaria before they decided to move there from Ramat Gan (a Tel Aviv suburb). She tells us, 'Every time we came out here we felt we belonged. I felt this would be a truer home for here I felt connected to my roots . . . everything I had learned at school [in history].'

But unlike Ya'akov of Ariel, Leah is not disdainful of life in the 'big city', it is simply that 'there we only lived our daily lives.' They had an apartment and a shop in Tel Aviv, they have kept both. The husband still works at the shop, perhaps staying in the apartment two nights a week. Leah is a teacher at the settlement school; living where they are, she is able to tell her schoolchildren Biblical stories of the 'here it all began' kind [Katriel 1993].

Today, though, the fields around her are not worked by Jews; but, she says, looking at how the Arabs around her live close to the land, as did her forefathers, brings her closer, not to the Arabs but to those forefathers. She has Arab neighbours and she shops at a local Arab store but she doesn't speak Arabic and Arab history has no place in the school curriculum.

Thus far in this account, Leah's life resonates with Dina Shalit's of Ariel. However, compared with the upfront and unshy 'certainty' of people at Ariel, our conversations with Leah, sometimes in English and sometimes between Rachel and Leah in Hebrew, soon suggested an altogether more circumspect culture of 'certainty'. It wasn't that Leah had less 'certainty' than Dina, and the 'certainty' had much the same foundation – but its expression (its confession, one might say) was cautious almost to the point of reluctance. Dina was a new immigrant; Leah a *sabra*. I think that had much to do with the difference, in several ways, and some of this became clearer while listening to Rachel as the two of us drove back to Jerusalem.

First, the matter of my presence. Whereas Dina was talking with (a) a fellow-Jew and Israeli resident – my wife – and (b) a fellow-Canadian – myself – Leah told Rachel:

she was uncomfortable about your presence. She didn't understand at all what you were doing ... why you were asking questions. She made sure with me that this was not going to be published in the newspapers. She didn't want to be recorded.

Independent of my presence, though, there was the difference regarding ideology, which is quite often a difference between the new arrival and the native-born. Dina Shalit was not shy of the word 'Zionist'; Leah was. Rachel explains:

it's not only the alienation [in Israeli society as a whole] that stems from modernization, it's also the alienation of the secular part of Israeli society from the ideals of Zionism ... they became cynical about the ideals. [Leah] is sensitive about this negative connotation ... about being too pompous about Zionism ... she doesn't want to sound ridiculous. She doesn't want to be labelled an idealist. She knows there's always the possible accusation that people like her come [to the West Bank] for material reasons and then build up their ideology – so it's phony. She doesn't want to sound phony.

Following on from that, Rachel wonders whether I haven't been asking the wrong question:

If people out here [Samaria] take it as an axiom that this is also the Land of Israel, then the question you're asking isn't, to their mind, the right one. You're asking, 'Why here? But for them it is, 'Why not here? This is the same place as anywhere else – why do you have a special question about it?' They are fighting the notion that there are parts of

Israel they are not expected, or even allowed, to settle. And in her own way, Leah is expressing that when she says 'I like being here, I'm comfortable here: that's why I'm here.'

I think my approach was unfortunate respecting Leah, but Dina Shalit, on the other hand, anticipated it and was not in the least fazed – indeed, she invited us back and it was she who had arranged the meeting with the Mayor.

By all accounts, Dina Shalit and Leah, in the historical quality they both associated with life in Samaria and their sense of being involved in the building of their nation, are, by now, a small minority among the thousands of secular Israelis living in Judea and Samaria. Already in 1983, another Ariel settler told me:

> I'll be happy when it is only a question of money [that brings Jews to the West Bank] for then there'll be no ideological problem left! [For as it is now] people out here may find themselves, each day, having to justify, to themselves as well as to others, why they are living where they are.

And Meron Benvenisti (putting aside the finer discriminations) remarked to me 'Today the only "Covenant" inducing settlers beyond the 1967 lines is a clause in their real estate contract with developers.' Ensconced in their 'dream homes in Samaria' (in the advertisements' phrase), one-time Tel Avivers or Clevelanders (from the USA) enjoy their 'wonderful views over the hills of Samaria' and no longer 'see' the Maccabees.

Scenario 3. Israel Harel, a leading Gush Emunim ideologue

The Gush Emunim in Judea and Samaria, while they do 'see' the Maccabees, also incline to seeing themselves surrounded not just by enemies of the Jews but by Jewish enemies. There is bitterness and political venom towards 'European-minded Israelis', 'peaceniks', 'Hellenists' and even 'my friends in Tel Aviv'. Much as Labour Zionists disdained the Jewry of the Diaspora, Greater Israelites – they see themselves as *the* Jewish nationalists – voice disdain of the Green Liners. Alibis for this view are cited triumphantly. For instance, I was told that an acclaimed Israeli writer, Naomi Frankel, recently dropped her leftish friends to come and live in Kiryat Arba: 'I'd lost my creativeness but when I came to Kiryat Arba I got my wings again,' she was reported as saying.[44]

Says Israel Harel,[45] in conversation with Amos Oz, '[t]he future of Judea and Samaria is an existential problem for the Jewish people'; it leads to the 'major barricade that divides Jews from Israelis':

> The Jews are those who want to live . . . in accordance with the Bible. The Israelis pay lipservice, maybe, to the heritage but in essence they aspire to be a completely new people here, a satellite of Western

culture. For many of those Israelis the Land of Israel is no more than a 'biographical accident'. As it happens they make a decent living here but if they were offered a better job somewhere else, abroad, they'd simply pack up and move. Eretz Yisrael means very little to them.

(Oz 1983: 109, 115)[46]

In their 'certainty', the Gush Emunim feel themselves to be the vanguard of the Jewish cause; and I think they are *fortified* in their 'certainty' by having 'Israelis' as the apostates from the Jewish cause. 'The Gush call us "traitors",' says an Oz veShalom member. It is 'the Gush' who have held the high national profile, for they are 'doing' (especially true in the decade following the Yom Kippur War). Perhaps few among the Israeli public know of Oz veShalom.

WHAT IS A ZIONIST PLACE?

At the (secularist) minimum, Zionism is the return to territoriality of a de-territorialized people. Hence our attention to place. However, place is more than territoriality; encoded in it are behaviour and ideology. What, then, is a Zionist place? Is there such a category? Are there places in Israel that are more Zionist than others? Kibbutz Degania? Ariel? Baba Sali's shrine (Netivoth)? The tomb of the Patriarchs (Hebron)? Kiryat Arba? Homesh? Shiloh? These places (to mention just the very few that are featured in this chapter) suggest there is no one answer.[47] In fact – and this is the burden of these closing remarks – both Judaism and Zionism struggle with ambiguities, at times running to contradictions and ambivalences, respecting the land/The Land.

Some of this has already been noted. For instance, Berkovitz's two principles: nothing built is to be relinquished and no Arab is to be expelled from his land (p. 173 above). Not only are they in enduring conflict but they are joined by a third: Jews must be allowed to settle wherever they will. By first principles, there shall be no *Judenrein* injunction. Thus no boundaries: these belong to a 'European' [read Gentile] view of history; Jewish place, in this rendering, heeds not the constraints of political space.[48] Then there is the imagery of the 'forefathers' (p. 177–8 above). In the (necessary) romance of landscape, they were often the Arabs of Palestine – the very people that Zionism dispossesses. Edward Said (1992: 88) does not let the irony pass unnoticed: 'Zionism aimed to create a society that could never be anything but "native" ... at the same time that it determined not to come to terms with the very natives it was replacing. . . .'[49]

But there is a deeper tension. Behind much of the material we have been handling, I think there is the question – with some very different answers – as to whether The Land is subject or object.

The phrase 'a land flowing with milk and honey' occurs again and again in Biblical literature and as 'a metaphor of fertility [it] is well grounded in ancient historic reality' (Sarna 1986: 46–7). More than that though, I think it is suggestive as a metaphysical metaphor: the Land that is God's and given in trust – on pain of 'keep[ing] My statutes and Mine ordinances' – to the Chosen. This is most vividly expressed in Deuteronomy XI: 10–12:

> For the land whither thou goest in to possess it, is not as the land of Egypt, from whence ye came out, where thou didst sow thy seed and didst water it with thy foot [i.e. laboriously with a foot-operated waterwheel]. . . .; but the land, whither ye go over to possess it, is a land of hills and valleys and drinketh water as the rain of heaven cometh down; a land which the LORD thy God careth for; the eyes of the Lord are always upon it.

In short: unlike the riverine lands (and empires) on its either side, where the land is the object of irrigation, Eretz Israel is the subject of 'the rain of heaven.'[50] What I am suggesting is, first, that 'the rain of heaven' is a (divine) gift. Second, in its God-given perfection the Land possesses the spirit of the Jewish people. It is in this sense that I read Simon (1983: 16): 'The sanctity of the land was intended to serve as a basis for the sanctity of the host.' But should they – the Israelites and the Canaanites before them – 'defile' the Land, they will be thrown out (Leviticus XVIII: 28).

It is in this sense, too, that I understand the panegyric of Abraham Isaac Kook (1865–1935) claimed by the Gush Emunim as their spiritual progenitor:[51]

> In the Holy Land [Eretz Israel] man's imagination is lucid and clear, clean and pure, capable of receiving the revelations of the Divine Truth and of expressing in life the sublime meaning of the ideal of the sovereignty of holiness.
>
> (as translated and cited in Avinieri 1981: 190)

How then can it be treated as object? But the Gush Emunim's disturbance of the equal weights accorded to *Am Yisrael*, *Eretz Yisrael*, *Torat Yisrael* (see p. 171–2 above) introduces just such a Jewish eschatology of possession. On the basis of such texts as Leviticus XXVI: 32–3 and 42–3, the conclusion is:

> Israel and the Land of Israel belong to one another; when united, both flourish and are blessed. The converse is true when Land and people are separated.
>
> (Elizur 1978b: 97)

> In non-Jewish hands, even though they [the lands of Eretz Israel] are inhabited, they are still deemed to be in a state of desolation.
>
> (Neriah 1978: 83)

Characteristically, the Gush Emunim appropriates a distinctive *telos*: its settlements are 'inheritances' with the unmistakable Covenantal/ Redemptive reference – the enterprise is not simply one of secular 'pioneering'. Such manipulation of the cosmography and eschatology of Judaism leads to profoundly disturbing public declarations.

Secular Zionism, too, has, from its beginning, been embraced by contra-diction (with ambivalence) respecting its relationship with the land. On the one hand, there is the land as subject with the Zionist as its natural/native tenant: 'Zionist-Socialism talked about "a new covenant" with the land and nature to replace the old covenant with the God of Israel ... "the land and only the land will be the holy of holies for the Hebrew soul"' (Don-Yehiya and Liebman 1981: 129, 123). On the other hand, the land became the object of their possession: 'We shall redeem you until you are entirely ours' (cited in *ibid*.: 124). Palestine has to be improved: 'Its beauty can only be brought out by those who love it and will devote their lives to healing its wounds' (Haim Weizmann, cited in Said 1992: 85). It had 'to be made useful' (adds Said p. 85) and made com-parable to other landscapes: with artesian wells, and 'made to bloom'.[52]

But there has been a constant problem arising from each of the two sides of Labour Zionist philosophy towards the land. In the case of the 'new covenant' with the land and nature, the 'Tolstoyan' figure of pioneering Zionism, Aharon David Gordon (1856–1922), put it like this:

> the Jews who live here do not yet understand the land they are living in, they are remote from it, they are still distinct from it. . . . Only when you begin to look for something, that something that no Jew can find anywhere else ... only then will you be competent to do something of vital importance for Palestine.
>
> (cited in Buber 1985: 160)

This is a problem of experiential unfulfilment. But on the other side, there is the dilemma posed by achievement: what when Israelis come to feel that the country *is* remade and now has its place alongside others? Does one still call oneself a Zionist? Does one dare (Leah of Homesh)? A place truly possessed, comments Tuan (1984: 4), 'fades from the forefront of consciousness'; it is taken for granted.[53]

Out of such a situation there tends to emerge an astounding cultural and political naïveté:

> *1993*: 'This is the West Bank? I didn't know that ...' (an immigrant from Miami who came to Ariel to check out the real estate bargains).[54]

> *1991*: 'It's like living in the country. The air is fresh, the children run free.'[55]

With the first whiffs of danger, the naïveté may be extended still further:

> *1991*: 'What did I do to deserve a rock thrown at me?'

1991: 'How can anybody be an obstacle to peace who is trying to build a home, raise a family and wants nothing more than to live in peace with their neighbours?'[56]

But Dina Shalit, a Zionist worker in the Territories,[57] is duly sceptical of current developments:

1993: 'I don't have any experience which tells me to trust. I don't think it is reasonable to say "Trust and see what happens." I need time to learn to do that and I don't believe I am being given that time.'[58]

Now to conclude.

The intention of this chapter has not been to bring the reader *à jour* with current events but rather to provide some of the multiple contexts in which events occur. The world hears a great deal about the Arab–Jewish conflict over space; what I have tried to bring to the fore are chords of intra-Jewish/Zionist discord over place. Experience and memory enter into the construction of place but, equally, an ideology of place influences the making of experience and memory. The ideological component that I have recognized in the Zionist case is that of 'certainty'. It is an imperative precisely because of the haunting degree of *uncertainty* in their world of *realpolitik*. Significantly, I think, Israeli scholars have remarked on 'the morbid Jewish fear of the reversibility of territorial process' and on the tendency even within 'mainstream Zionism to evaluate its own territorial advent as tentative and fragile' (Rabinowitz 1992: 81; see Kimmerling 1983).[59]

In these circumstances, 'certainty' is likely to be a matter of defiance, at its best and of irredentism at its most dangerous. Zionism was achieved on the ground through the planting of settlements (see Katriel and Shenhar 1990). Failure – the loss of a settlement – summons the worst fears: 'If we fail [to hold a settlement], our retreat will continue to the desert' (Y. Tabenkin cited in Kimmerling 1983: 85). That was in 1920, when a new Zionist settlement in northern Galilee had to be abandoned under Arab attack. In 1982 the evacuation, as part of the Camp David Accord, of Yamit, an Israeli settlement beyond Gaza, pitted Jewish soldiers against Jewish settlers and 'Jewish presence was seen to be reversible' (Kimmerling 1983: 180). What kind of precedent will Yamit prove to be? Many Israelis are wondering.[60]

ACKNOWLEDGEMENTS

Without persons providing entries for the ethnographer's field journal, little indeed would be achieved and I thank all those who were good enough to talk and explain – many of whom are named in the article. Special thanks to Rachel Kimor and my wife, Lisa Gilad, for the field trips together. I am also grateful to Wendy James, Ron Schwartz, Alex Weingrod and Lisa, for careful readings of my penultimate draft.

NOTES

1 As with all unreferenced citations in this chapter, I am quoting here from my field journal (1983–5).

2 Actually, the episode should not be painted as 'modern'; rather, it springs out of the earlier exilic condition when 'the sages, instead of interpreting the Scriptures by looking at the land, describe the land by reading the scripture' (Schweid 1985: 40). What *is* new is that the same process continues today even as Israelis (some of them) hike through Judea and Samaria, Bible in hand.

3 Without an entry in the *International Encylopaedia of the Social Sciences* (Macmillan 1968).

4 One way of erasing, metaphysically, this element is through hermetically sealing one's chosen world in a religious hermeneutic; and this, too, belongs to the story of Israel and Zionism (the *haredim* or Ultra-Orthodox), but I do not treat it in this chapter.

5 Amos Oz, the Israeli writer, knows about this moving around in time and space to find the right place. Sardonically, he writes of the Israeli scene (1989: 214):

> It is always fascinating to see how people set out on a journey through space when, in fact, they want to journey through time – or the opposite. They travel through time when they really ache for other places. A person who wants to return to Biblical times or to some sort of pre-Biblical Orientalism ups and crosses the Green Line [between Israel and the West Bank]. . . . A person who wants to return to the days of his youth ups and goes to a 'pioneering outpost' in the Sinai. Someone else, nostalgic for his parents' home in the Jewish shtetl of Eastern Europe, ups and tries to re-create the Kingdom of David and Solomon from the year 1,000 BCE Not to mention someone who longs to live in America and creates around him, by mistake, something not unlike the Jewish Warsaw of fifty years ago, convinced that it is an America.

6 Judaism itself is a religion of 'doing' (in contrast to Christianity's emphasis on faith): 'The litmus test in Judaism is "what *mitzvot* [moral deeds] did you perform today?" ' And Israeli scholars point to how this was true even of Jewry (despised by the run of secular Zionists) during the millennia of Exile (Dov Berkovits, personal communication 1983). Conversely, the present-day successors of that Jewry, the so-called 'Ultra-Orthodox', regard the 'doing' of the Zionists as a sacrilege (Paine 1992).

7 Some Jews had always lived in Palestine and at the time of the arrival of the Zionist pioneers: 'Most . . . lived in the "four holy cities", Hebron, Safed, Tiberias and Jerusalem . . . partly supported by charities, partly engaged in small business and in a few crafts . . . fanatically orthodox, they were suspicious of all change and above all of political Zionism.' The incoming Zionists, in their turn, were aghast at what they saw. They were reminded 'of the ghettoes of Eastern Europe from which they had escaped' (Elon 1981: 90–1).

  Of Zionist writers concerned with the cultural mould in the making of the Zionist place, one notes Asher Ginsberg/Ahad Ha'am (1856–1927) and especially Aharon David Gordon (1856–1922), the publicist (and practitioner on a kibbutz for a while) of the idea of a 'religion of labour' (Avinieri 1981).

8 For an analysis of the problems of succession between Zionist generations, especially in the early years, see Paine 1993a.

9 '*Yedi'at haaretz* features in the school curriculum and in army instruction courses as a course in its own right, incorporating geography, geology, history, ethnology, botany' (Benvenisti 1986: 19).

10 Though that too was of great importance: Paine 1993b.

11 This 'second Israel' also includes the Sephardim of northern Mediterranean and Balkan descent but the contrast with the historiography and political iconography of the Ashkenazim is (for Israelis themselves) at its strongest *vis-à-vis* the Mizrahim.

12 Weingrod (1993) notes: 'The architect took care to represent Morocco within a recognizable Israeli container' (p. 379). . . . 'The message is Morocco – but Morocco now set in Israel!' (p. 382).

13 Cohen (1983: 123–4), on the other hand, sees the process as one of 'demod-ernization' and symbolic 'diasporization' leading to the diminution of Israel as 'the holy Land and universal center' and its becoming 'just another state, though governed by Jews'. Ben-Ari and Bilu (forthcoming), in their turn, see that interpretation as instancing 'the distress [of] many Ashkenazi intellectuals' (p. 18). For them, what is really happening is 'the "Israelization" of the Jewish diaspora' (*ibid.*).

14 Hebron is steeped in Biblical history: Abraham – the father of both Ishmael and Isaac – came to Hebron and pitched his tent there; David reigned seven and a half years in Hebron before he took Jerusalem and made it his capital. In the Cave of Machpelah are the tombs of Abraham, Isaac and Jacob and their wives: Sarah, Rebecca and Leah. The Arabic name of the town is Khalil al Rahman (Friend of Allah the Merciful). The Haram al Ibrahimi Mosque was built, centuries ago, over the venerated Tomb of the Patriarchs; today, both Muslims and Jews worship there – separately.

15 There have been Jews in Hebron through the millennia – though not between 1936 and 1967 (two massacres: in 1929 and 1936). For documentation of the current political relationship between Hebron and Kiryat Arba, see Romann 1985.

   Kiryat Arba, or the Town of the Four, is actually another name for Hebron and Hebrew tradition has it that the Cave of Machpelah is also the burial site of Adam and Eve (Oz veShalom *Bulletin* no. 3, 1983: 9) – hence the allusion in the name to the *four* (conjugal pairs).

16 On the day of the massacre of the Israeli atheletes in Munich, Zippora says.

17 Akiva was born in Poland, lived in New York, came to Palestine in 1947. His wife was from Toronto. (He died in the winter of 1993–4.)

18 Amos Oz (1983: 148) succinctly summarizes:

   Justification in terms of the Arabs who dwell in this land is the justness [*sic*] of the drowning man who clings to the only plank he can. . . . And that is the moral difference between the 'Judaization' of Jaffa and Ramla and the 'Judaization' of the West Bank.

19 Marking the armistice lines of 1949.

20 A bibliographic note relevant to the topics of this section is in order. For schol-arly accounts of the place of 'the Land' in Judaism from Biblical times to the present, see Davies 1982 and the essays in Hoffman 1986 – especially Uriel Tal's. On notions of 'Homeland' and 'Land of Destiny' in the Jewish and Zionist traditions, see Schweid 1985, and for a cross-cultural essay see Akenson 1991; on the Gush Emunim, see Lustick 1988, Newman 1985 and especially Aran 1991; and on the debate waging between religious Zionists, pro- and contra-Gush Emunim, see the essays in Tomaschoff 1978 and Landau 1983.

21 In Samaria, places such as Eilon Moreh outside Shechem (Nablus) and Schechem itself, Beit-El and Shiloh. Each contributes to the Biblical story of the making of a place for the Israelites in the land of the Canaanites. They mark Abraham's, Jacob's and Joseph's journeys across that landscape and the places where God (or a divine agent) spoke to them and where tabernacles were built and the Ark rested; the progress of Joshua's conquest of Canaan;

and the delivery of harsh Divine Judgement too, against the backsliding of the Israelites – viz. the destruction of Shiloh and the removal of the Ark by the Philistines. (E.g. Genesis XII.6, XXVIII.19, XXXII.28, XXXV.16; Judges XXI.19; 1 Samuel III.3; Jeremiah VII.12–14, XXVI.6.)

During the 1970s, religious Zionists of the Greater Israel movement (Gush Emunim) established settlements at each of these places (that is, before the Likud came to power). For a history of the settlement drive of the period, see Harris 1980.

22 The narrator also says: 'I used to hike all over it prior to 1948 and managed not to forget it during nineteen years in which I could not even visit my maternal family's homes in the Old City [Jerusalem] and in Hebron' (Ne'eman 1982: 19): in other words, he took part, as had Benvenisti, in the rituals of *yedi'at haaretz* (p. 165 above). In his autobiography, Benvenisti (1986) ruefully acknowledges that such 'obsessive search for rootedness' (p. 20) led 'inexorably to chauvinism and xenophobia' (p. 45).

23 A distinguished academic, commonly described in the media as 'Israel's leading physicist', he then entered politics as an advocate of 'Greater Israel'. With the founding of Tehiyah, the party closely (though unofficially) associated with the religiously motivated group of West Bank settlers (the Gush Emunim), Ne'eman was elected its leader. In the Likud coalition of 1982 he was Minister of Science and Technology.

24 All Biblical citations are from *The Pentateuch and Haftorahs*, ed. J.H. Hertz (second edn., 5742–1981).

25 Much of the debate is conducted in respect of a handful of key concepts prominent among which are: *Lo Tehonnem*, prohibiting transactions with Gentiles, particularly respecting the Land; *Pikuah Nefesh* that the protection of life, of Jew or Gentile, has priority over all else; and *Milhemet Mitzvah*, the injunction of 'obligatory war'. Biblical exegesis always being open to contending interpretations, today's protagonists seek to bolster their respective interpretations through accreditation to the great medieval Jewish sages such as Rashi (Solomon ben Isaac), Rambam (Maimonides) and Ramban (Nahmanides); these references are omitted from the present account.

26 Outspoken on this matter but far from alone, Professor Uriel Tal (1986) sees the Gush Emunim as commanding the people of Israel 'to be holy – but not necessarily to be moral or humane according to ordinary criteria' (p. 327); and again: they teach that "Jews'" ethics are bound by a unique and exclusive relationship to God, totally different from universal ethics' (p. 338). The contrast with the moral temper of Oz veShalom may be gauged from such statements as:

> There is a clearcut message ... not to use our suffering as a pretext for causing suffering to others, not to view the Zionist revolution as an exchange of roles between the ruler and the ruled.
>
> (Uriel Simon)

> For me, the meaning of Zionism is to believe that there is a third option, to be neither victim nor victimizer. But if, God forbid, it turns out that the choice really is between those two awful alternatives, then I would opt for the role of victim.
>
> (Avi Ravitsky)

At the time, Simon was Professor of Bible at Bar-Ilan University and Ravitsky was Professor of Jewish Philosophy at the Hebrew University: their statements appeared in Oz veShalom *Bulletin* no. 6, p. 17 (1985) and no. 2, p. 9 (1982), respectively. The late Uriel Tal was Professor of Contemporary Jewish History at Tel Aviv University.

27 The speaker was, at the time, the Sephardi Chief Rabbi of Israel (not a member of Oz veShalom); the Ashkenazi Chief Rabbi held with the Gush Emunim position.

28 Here it is the founding figure of the Gush Emunim, the late Rabbi Zvi Yehudah Kook, who is cited.

29 A formulation long in currency. One probable source is Menachem Ussishkin, an influential Zionist intellectual in Palestine between the two world wars.

30 I believe this is far from being the case. Meron Benvenisti (Director of the West Bank Data project) told me: 'The West Bank is kept well "out of mind", as far as possible, by the majority of Israelis and so it is relegated to the "back pages" [of the newspapers].'

31 In defiance not only of the indigenous population but, if it comes to such a pass, of the Israeli state as well.

32 But there are still other voices in the Gush Emunim camp: Menachem Ausbacher (see p. 167 above), for example. Caught in a reflexive mood in 1985, he said: 'But no-one can [or should?] live in a purely cosmic world without having one's eyes open to other questions too – what of the command [see note 25] to protect human life, Jew or Gentile?'

33 Sight should not be lost of the likelihood (especially strong in the context of messianism) that the protagonists, in this work of making a 'Jewish state' out of the State of Israel, are like theatre players conscious of earlier 'scripts': the Exodus; the 'generation in the desert'; the conquest of Canaan; the destruction of the Second Temple (in CE 70) and the 'last stand' at Masada or the flight into exile.

34 As Rabbi Waldman, a close associate of Rabbi Levinger, said to me: 'We did not initiate the freeing of Eretz Israel, it was brought upon us and we afterwards saw it as an act of God: He wishes us to build.'

35 One notes with Yuval (1978: 107) 'the proximity of the Advent to the times of those expecting it, a fact which speaks for itself'; and it is upon this 'fact' that much of the 'certainty' of the Gush Emunim rests.

36 Judaization in the political sense. Theologically, the sacralization of specific places is suspect, more like Christian than Judaic practice (Werblovsky 1970: 201); for Simon, it is 'fetishism' (Oz veShalom *Bulletin* no. 6, 1985: 17).

37 Regarding the latter point, much the same could be said of the secular Zionist 'pioneers' of an earlier era who were making a homeland, and it is among them that one first sees the use of the landscape to evoke a sense of belonging (interpreted by some as 'paganism': Don-Yehiya and Liebman 1981: 123). Shehadeh (1982: 86), a non-Jewish Palestinian observer, has this comment on Gush Emunim 'sanctification' and 'objectification' of the landscape:

> Perhaps second- and third-generation Israeli farmers have lost the pornographer's symbolism [see p. 164 above] but the Gush Emunim people who are spilling on to the West Bank have renewed it – ranting and raving over every stick and stone in a land they never knew.

38 Simon (1983: 23) comments, 'Clinging to the dangerous delusion that God will be on our side, unconditionally, by virtue of our Covenant with Him, may lead us to sin.'

39 For a detailed account of Israeli West Bank settlement, see Aronson 1987; and for a survey of Israel's settlement policies, Benvenisti 1984.

40 The settlement of Ariel is sprawled over a 'vacant' (they said) hillside in central Samaria – in fact 3,500 dunams 'of mostly cultivated lands' were expropriated (Aronson 1987: 109). It is to become a 'city' of 150,000 people in 25,000 housing units. It was first settled 'unofficially' in the last years of the Labour government when Moshe Dayan was Minister of Defence: a group of volunteers

formed a *garin* – literally 'a seed' out of which will grow, in this case, a settlement – taking it in turns to camp out on what became the town site. Then, in
1978, during the Camp David talks, 'when every day that we did nothing
was a day lost', the Likud government gave Ariel the big push – thirty-five
families. By 1983, when my wife and I made two field visits, there were 350
families and 'by the end of next year there'll be three times as many and by
1985 we'll be 1700 families'.

41 He was active in an underground Zionist cell in the Soviet Union; later organized street demonstrations and a hunger strike and became a *refusenik*: he
was allowed to leave in 1972.

42 It should be kept in mind that the account is pre-Intifada.

43 Avruch (1981) considers at length the different combinations of factors engaged
in the immigration of American Jews to Israel; see especially, 'Motivations for
Aliya' (pp. 90ff.). See also Rapport 1993.

44 It is perhaps worth noting that both Haetzni and Kadosh once identified themselves with the political left. Kadosh said that when he came to Israel he was
in sympathy with the Peace Now movement.

45 At the time, Chairman of the Council of Jewish settlements in Judea, Samaria
and Gaza; editor of *Nekuda*, the Gush Emunim newspaper; and a West Bank
settlement resident.

46 Elyakin Haetzni, 'secular' but a 'Jew', would agree with every word. For Amos
Oz's response, see Oz 1983: 135ff.

   Not surprisingly, the 'Israeli'–'Jew' divide surfaces frequently in testimonies
of Jewish Israelis living in New York (Shokeid 1988): 'I am an Israeli; I don't
perceive of myself as Jewish. It is only by chance that I was born to Jewish
parents' (p. 41); another declares, 'I have a blindspot two thousand years wide'
(p. 41): that is, his Jewishness was lost throughout the period of the Diaspora.
Another who describes himself as 'anti-orthodox' says, 'there is no longer
anything which connects the Israeli and the Jew (p. 130); still another: 'I am
an Israeli, I cannot become a Jew!' (p. 132). The notion of the chance of birth
was also expressed by Claude Kadosh, only in his case it was the other way
around: 'It is only an accident that I wasn't born here' – i.e. in Israel instead
of Algeria.

47 But there is a pressing need for research. Rabinowitz (1992) calls attention to
the processes by which selected spaces are 'actively transformed by agents
of Zionism' (p. 67). He is particularly concerned with the problematics of
Arab–Jewish urban neighbourhoods (the presence of Arabs in some parts
of Israel may be 'abhorrent' to Jews, while in other parts of the country the
Arab presence seems 'to go unnoticed' (p. 68); studies such as those of Torstrick
(1993) in Akko/Akka (Acre), Rabinowitz (1992) in Natzerat Illit (Upper
Nazareth) and Romann and Weingrod (1991) in Jerusalem have opened the
research.

48 'The frontier is where Jews live, not where there is a line on the map' – Golda
Meir in 1972 (cited in Aronson 1987: 14).

49 At the same time, Said recognizes the Jews, from his point of view, as 'the
most morally complex of all opponents' (p. 119).

50 See Buber 1985: 39ff.; Schweid 1987: 537.

51 He was the father of Zvi Yehudah Kook, to whose *yeshiva* many of the leading
members of the first generation of Gush Emunim went.

52 This was wholly in accord with the secular 'Western mind', Gentile and Jew
alike, at the time of the Balfour Declaration (1917): Palestine was 'a place to
be possessed *anew* and reconstructed' (Said 1992: 9; original emphasis).

53 But it would be misleading to suppose that this condition has an exact and
linear chronology. For example, Amitai, the kibbutznik, probably felt, in 1967,

that his Israel was truly possessed and safe (p. 165 above). Of him it could be said, 'Zionism was right. Fine. But it was an answer to someone else's question' (Schweid 1973: 118). Care should be exercised, too, over the extent to which it is a collective state of mind at any one time – viz. Amitai's father.

54 *Guardian*, weekly edition, 19 September 1993. As per the same report, Ariel now (1993) has 12,000–13,000 residents; an industrial park with an annual production of $400 million (Ya'akov Fitelson is the park's director) – yet 60 per cent of the workforce still commute to the other side of the Green Line.

55 A US immigrant from Cleveland (*Cleveland Jewish News*, 13 December 1991).

56 Both citations from *Cleveland Jewish News*, 13 December 1991.

57 And currently (1994) executive director of a settlers' lobbying and fund-raising group.

58 *Guardian*, weekly edition, 19 September 1993.

59 Frequently I would hear the argument, 'If [we surrender] Hebron, then [the Arabs will want] Tel-Aviv.' See Oz 1989: 229 for a rebuttal.

60 As I complete this writing, the massacre at the Tomb of the Patriarchs in Hebron happens. The gunman was a member of Kach, the party formed by the late Rabbi Meir Kahane. To the best of my knowledge, no person in this chapter belonged to Kach. In Kiryat Arba in 1983, Elyakim Haetzni admitted to trouble with a Kahane element: 'But what can we do? We can't stop them from coming to live in this township even though we detest people of this kind – people of the ultra-right.' On Kahane and Kahanism, see Cromer 1988 and Ravitzky 1985; and see Paine 1995 on the Hebron massacre.

REFERENCES

Akenson, D.H. (1991) *God's Peoples: Covenant and Land in South Africa, Israel and Ulster*, Montreal and Kingston: McGill-Queen's University Press.

Alter, R. (1973) 'The Masada complex', *Commentary* 56 (19–24).

Appadurai, A. (1993) 'The production of locality', paper presented at the IV Decennial Conference of the Association of Social Anthropologists (xerox).

Aran, G. (1991) 'Jewish Zionist fundamentalism: the bloc of faithful in Israel (Gush Emunim)', pp. 265–344, in M.E. Marty and R.S. Appleby (eds) *Fundamentalisms Observed*, Chicago: University of Chicago Press.

Ariel (Shtiglitz), Y. (1978) 'Return of the regained territories – the halakhic aspect', pp. 127–55, in A. Tomaschoff (ed.) *Whose Homeland (Contemporary Thinking in Israel*, no. 4), Jerusalem: Department for Torah Education and Culture in the Diaspora, WZO.

Aronson, G. (1987) *Creating Facts: Israel, Palestinians and the West Bank*, Washington, DC: Institute for Palestine Studies.

Aviad, J. (1983) 'Religious Zionism today', pp. 25–31, in Y. Landau (ed.) *Religious Zionism: Challenges and Choices*, Jerusalem: Oz veShalom.

Aviner, S. (1978) 'Messianic realism', pp. 109–17, in A. Tomaschoff (ed.) *Whose Homeland (Contemporary Thinking In Israel*, no. 4), Jerusalem: Department for Torah Education and Culture in the Diaspora, WZO.

Avinieri, S. (1981) *The Making of Modern Zionism: The Intellectual Origins of the Jewish State*, New York: Basic Books.

Avruch, K. (1981) *American Immigrants in Israel: Social Identities and Change*, Chicago: University of Chicago Press.

Basso, K.H. (1988) ' "Speaking with names": Language and landscape among the Western Apache', *Cultural Anthropology* 3: 2 (99–130).

Bauer, J. (1985) 'A new approach to religious–secular relationships?', pp. 91–110, in D. Newman (ed.) *The Impact of Gush Emunim: Politics and Settlement in the West Bank*, London: Croom Helm.

Ben-Ari, E. and Bilu, Y. 'Introduction' to their forthcoming edited volume 'Grasping Land: Space and Place in Contemporary Israeli Discourse and Experience' (xerox).

Benjamin, W. (1973) *Illuminations*, London: Fontana.

Benvenisti, M. (1984) *The West Bank Data Project: A Survey of Israel's Policies*, Washington, DC: American Enterprise Institute for Studies in Foreign Policy.

—— (1986) *Conflicts and Contradictions*, New York: Villard Books.

Bowes, A.M. (1989) *Kibbutz Goshen: An Israeli Commune*, Prospect Heights, IL: Waveland Press.

Bruner, E.M. (1984) 'Introduction: the opening up of anthropology', pp. 1–18, in E.M. Bruner (ed.) *Text, Play, and Story: The Construction and Reconstruction of Self and Society*, Washington, DC: American Ethnological Society.

Buber, M. (1985) [1952] *On Zion: The History of an Idea*, Edinburgh: T & T Clark Ltd.

Cohen, E. (1983) 'Ethnicity and legitimation in contemporary Israel', *Jerusalem Quarterly* 28 (111–24).

Cromer, G. (1988) 'The debate about Kahanism in Israeli society, 1948–1988', Occasional Paper no. 3 of the Harry Frank Guggenheim Foundation.

Davies, W.D. (1982) *The Territorial Dimension of Judaism*, Berkeley, CA: University of California Press.

Don-Yehiya, E. and Liebman, C.S. (1981) 'The symbol system of Zionist-Socialism: an aspect of Israeli civil society', *Modern Judaism* 1 (121–48).

Elizur, Y. (1978a) 'The borders of Eretz Israel in tradition', pp. 42–53, in A. Tomaschoff (ed.) *Whose Homeland (Contemporary Thinking in Israel*, no. 4) Jerusalem: Department for Torah Education and Culture in the Diaspora, WZO.

—— (1978b) 'Eretz Israel – the Biblical concept', pp. 85–97, in A.Tomaschoff (ed.) *Whose Homeland (Contemporary Thinking in Israel*, no. 4) Jerusalem: Department for Torah Education and Culture in the Diaspora, WZO.

Elon, A. (1981) *The Israelis: Founders and Sons*, Jerusalem: Adam Publishers.

Gupta, A. and Ferguson, J. (1992) 'Beyond "culture": space, identity and the politics of difference', *Cultural Anthropology* 7: 1 (6–23).

Halkin, H. (1977) *Letters to an American Jewish Friend: A Zionist's Polemic*, Philadelphia: Jewish Publication Society of America.

Harris, W.W. (1980) *Taking Root: Israeli Settlement in the West Bank, the Golan and Gaza-Sinal, 1967–1980*, Chichester: Research Studies Press, John Wiley & Sons.

Hoffman, L.A. (ed.) (1986) *The Land of Israel: Jewish Perspectives*, Notre Dame, IN: Notre Dame University Press.

Katriel, T. (1993) 'The politics of representation in Israeli pioneer museums', paper presented at the American Anthropological Association annual meeting (xerox).

—— and Shenhar, A. (1990) 'Tower and stockade: dialogic narration in Israeli settlement ethos', *Quarterly Journal of Speech* 76: 4 (359–80).

Kimmerling, B. (1983) *Zionism and Territory: The Socio-Territorial Dimensions of Zionist Politics*, Berkeley, CA: Institute of International Studies.

Landau, Y. (ed.) (1983) *Religious Zionism: Challenges and Choices*, Jerusalem: Oz veShalom.

Leach, E.R. (1984) 'Further thoughts on the realm of folly', pp. 356–64, in E.M. Bruner (ed.) *Text, Play and Story: The Construction and Reconstruction of Self and Society*, Washington, DC: American Ethnological Society.

Lustick, I. (1988) *For the Land and the Lord: Jewish Fundamentalism in Israel*, New York: Council on Foreign Relations.
Melöy, J. (1988) 'The two landscapes of northern Norway', *Inquiry* 31 (387–401).
Near, H. (ed.) (1971) *The Seventh Day: Soldiers' Talk about the Six-Day War*, Harmondsworth: Penguin Books.
Ne'eman, Y. (1982) 'The settling of Eretz-Israel' (typescript).
Neriah, M.Z. (1978) 'Jewish sovereignty and the halakhah', pp. 78–84, in A. Tomaschoff (ed.) *Whose Homeland (Contemporary Thinking in Israel*, no. 4), Jerusalem: Department for Torah Education and Culture in the Diaspora, WZO.
Newman, D. (ed.) (1985) *The Impact of Gush Emunim: Politics and Settlement in the West Bank*, London: Croom Helm.
Oz, A. (1983) *In the Land of Israel*, London: Fontana Books.
—— (1989) *The Slopes of Lebanon*, San Diego, CA: Harcourt Brace Jovanovich.
Oz veShalom (1982–6) English *Bulletins* nos 1–8, Jerusalem: Oz veShalom.
Paine, R. (1989) 'Israel: Jewish identity and competition over "tradition" ', pp. 121–35, in E. Tonkin, M. McDonald and M. Chapman (eds) *History and Ethnicity*, (ASA Monograph 27), London: Routledge.
—— (1992) 'Jewish ontologies of time and political legitimation in Israel', pp. 150–70, in H.J. Rutz (ed.) *The Politics of Time*, (AES Monograph 4), Washington, DC: American Anthropological Association.
—— (1993a) 'Israel: The making of self in the "pioneering" of the nation', in O. Löfgren and U. Hannerz (eds) 'Defining the National', *Ethnos* 1993: 3–4 (220–40).
——(1993b) 'Masada: A history of a memory', *History and Anthropology* 6: 4 (371–400).
—— (1995) 'Behind the Hebron massacre', *Anthropology Today* 11: 1 (8–15).
Pocock, D.F. (1975) 'North and south in the book of Genesis', in J.H.M. Beattie and R.G. Lienhardt (eds) *Studies in Social Anthropology: Essays in Memory of E.E. Evans-Pritchard*, Oxford: Clarendon Press.
Rabinowitz, D. (1992) 'An acre is an acre is an acre? Differentiated attitudes to social space and territory on the Jewish–Arab urban frontier in Israel', *Urban Anthropology* 21: 1 (67–87).
Rapport, N. (1993) 'Anglo-Saxons in Israel: an exploration of the global eclecticism of immigrant identity', paper presented at the IV Decennial Conference of the Association of Social Anthropologists (xerox).
Ravitsky, A. (1985) *The Phenomenon of Kahanism: Consciousness and Political Reality*, Jerusalem: The Institute of Contemporary Jewry.
Reich, W. (1984) *Stranger in My House: Jews and Arabs in the West Bank*, New York: Holt, Rinehart and Winston.
Richardson, M. (1984) 'Place and culture: a final note', pp. 63–7, in M. Richardson (ed.) *Place: Experience and Symbol* (vol. 24, *Geoscience and Man*), Baton Rouge, LA: Louisiana State University.
Romann, M. (1985) *Jewish Kiryat Arba versus Arab Hebron*, Jerusalem: West Bank Data Base Project.
—— and Weingrod, A. (1991) *Living Together Separately: Arabs and Jews in Contemporary Jerusalem,* Princeton, NJ: Princeton University Press.
Said, E.W. (1992) [1979] *The Question of Palestine*, New York: Vintage Books.
Sarna, N.M. (1986) *Exploring Exodus: The Heritage of Biblical Israel*, New York: Schocken Books.
Schweid, E. (1973) *Israel at the Crossroads*, Philadelphia: Jewish Publication Society of America.
—— (1985) *The Land of Israel: National Home or Land of Destiny*, London: Associated University Presses.
—— (1987) 'Land of Israel', pp. 535–41, in A.A. Cohen and P. MendesFlohi (eds) *Contemporary Jewish Religious Thought*, New York: Charles Scribner's Sons.

Shehadeh, R. (1982) *The Third Way: A Journal of Life in the West Bank*, London: Quartet Books.

Shokeid, M. (1988) *Children of Circumstances: Israeli Immigrants in New York*, Ithaca, NY: Cornell University Press.

Simon, U. (1982) 'The cry of religious conscience', Oz veShalom *Bulletin* no. 1, Jerusalem: Oz veShalom.

——(1983) 'Religion, morality and politics', pp. 16–24, in Y. Landau (ed.) *Religious Zionism: Challenges and Choices*, Jerusalem: Oz veShalom.

Tal, U. (1979) 'The nationalism of the Gush Emunim in historical perspective', *Forum* 36 (11–14), Jerusalem: World Zionist Organization.

——(1986) 'Contemporary hermeneutics and self-views on the relationship between state and land', pp. 316–38, in L.A. Hoffman (ed.) *The Land of Israel: Jewish Perspectives*, Notre Dame, IN: Notre Dame University Press.

Tomaschoff, A. (ed.) (1978) *Whose Homeland (Contemporary Thinking in Israel*, no. 4), Jerusalem: Department for Torah Education and Culture in the Diaspora, WZO.

Torstrick, R. (1993) 'Raising and rupturing boundaries: the politics of identity in Acre, Israel', doctoral dissertation, Washington University, Saint Louis, MO.

Tuan, Y.-F. (1974) *Topophilia. A Study of Environmental Perception, Attitudes and Values*, Englewood Cliffs, NJ: Prentice-Hall.

——(1984) 'In place, out of place', pp. 3–10, in M. Richardson (ed.) *Place: Experience and Symbol* (vol. 24, *Geoscience and Man*), Baton Rouge, LA: Louisiana State University.

Wallach, J. and J. (1989) *Still Small Voices*, San Diego, CA: Harcourt Brace Jovanovich.

Weingrod, A. (1993) 'Changing Israeli landscapes: buildings and the uses of the past', *Cultural Anthropology* 8: 3 (370–87).

Werblovsky, Z. (1970) 'Discussion', pp. 201–2, in M.H. Tannenbaum and R.J. Zwi Werblovsky (eds) *The Jerusalem Colloquium on Religion, Peoplehood, Nation and Land*, Jerusalem: Truman Research Institute.

Yuval, Y.Y. (1978) 'Religious-Zionist messianism: prospects and perils', pp. 98–108, in A. Tomaschoff (ed.) *Whose Homeland (Contemporary thinking in Israel*, no. 4), Jerusalem: Department for Torah Education and Culture in the Diaspora, WZO.

Part III

Vernacular contexts of public reason and critique

The diviner divines:
The Christian consults the Bible
The Muslim, the Quran.
The literate writes;
And the *àghòrò* priest requests white clothing,
So he may be equipped to visit [worship] *Orósùn.*

(New lines recited to Niyi Akinnaso by a
Yoruba diviner)

8 The politics of tolerance
Buddhists and Christians, truth and error in Sri Lanka

Jonathan Spencer

INTRODUCTION*

This chapter is about changing sources of authority within Theravada Buddhism in Sri Lanka.[1] The main empirical evidence is drawn from the encounter between Sri Lankan Buddhists and Christian missionaries in the nineteenth century, especially from one particular moment in that encounter: the public debate between Buddhists and Christians held at the town of Panadura, just south of Colombo, in 1873. From this, I argue that a much narrower idea of religious authority, based in the texts of the Pali canon, emerged among Buddhist reformers in the nineteenth century. The Panadura debate demonstrates this emergence quite clearly but we need to be wary of attributing too much causal force to one example.

The chapter has three parts. The first section sketches the history of public argument and religious 'tolerance' in Sri Lanka, contrasting it with the Eurocentric assumptions of politicians and political philosophers. The second describes the debate. The third uses the aftermath of the debate to discuss the tales we tell ourselves about colonialism; Buddhism in Sri Lanka was transformed during the colonial period but this is not quite the same as saying that Buddhism was transformed *by* colonialists. The history I recount, in however abbreviated a form, is altogether more subtle than that and requires us to rethink our Manichaean division of the world into 'Westerners' or 'Euro-Americans' and 'Orientals' or 'Others'.

Kant's essay 'What is enlightenment?' provides a strikingly clear account of the liberal virtues of criticism in the public sphere. Kant posits 'enlightenment' as the condition which succeeds 'immaturity', and 'immaturity' is defined as 'the inability to use understanding without the guidance of another' (Kant 1991: 54). The precondition for enlightenment is 'freedom to make *public use* of reason in all matters' (*ibid.*: 55). Kant proceeds to delineate what he means by the 'public use' of reason, counterposing it to the occasional sociological necessity for obedience in what he describes

---

* This chapter is for Charles Hallisey, with thanks.

as private actions – the necessity for a soldier or civil servant, for example, to obey orders without question. A clergyman, to take one of Kant's more complex examples, is obliged to teach what his church treats as dogma because his relationship with his congregation is essentially domestic or private. But the same clergyman should be allowed to argue with all the freedom he needs in his capacity as a scholar addressing the reading public. Religion is allowed a central place in Kant's argument 'because religious immaturity is the most pernicious and dishonourable variety of all' (*ibid.*: 59).

Much of Kant's short essay is taken up with the relationship between 'civil freedom' and 'intellectual freedom', but its progressive thrust is unmistakable. Enlightenment is virtually inevitable for any collectivity simply allowed the freedom 'to think for themselves' (*ibid.*: 55).[2] Kant's assumptions about the virtues of scepticism are almost a commonplace of liberal political philosophy. Bernard Williams, for example, explicitly makes the connection between scepticism and tolerance in a recent review of Rawls' *Political Liberalism*:

> Religious tolerance has both encouraged and been helped by religious scepticism; sensible people, faced with the clash of fanaticisms, can reasonably wonder whether any of these positions can be known to be true – whether indeed they may not all be untrue – and their enthusiasm for any of them declines.
>
> (Williams 1993: 7)

Similar assumptions about the relationship of argument and religion surfaced in the liberal reactions to the Salman Rushdie affair. Here, though, 'tolerance' often becomes treated as an essential property of particular traditions or particular collectivities. As a government minister put it, in a statement entitled 'Being British': 'There is ... plenty of room for diversity, precisely because our traditions are those of tolerance' (John Patten in Asad 1990: 459).

Kant's essay was first published in 1784 but traditions of public scepticism and debate were already well established in Sri Lanka. Seventy-two years before Kant's essay, the King of Kandy summoned a Catholic and a Calvinist to his palace to debate their religious differences. Confronted with a knotty difficulty in his argument against idolatry, the Calvinist started to lose the audience's support. (Our source, it should be pointed out, is not entirely neutral.)

> The heretic had no answer to give and became the butt of the jokes of the bystanders, each of whom expressed his opinion; and the King called him a fool devoid of reason who did not understand the books he read and contumaciously persisted in his errors. Put to shame ... [he] seized the catechism ... and began to read therefrom.
>
> (do Rego? in Boudens 1957: 192)

In 1719 the King was entertained by a four-way debate between a Catholic, a Calvinist, a Muslim and a Buddhist. And the great *bhikkhu* (Buddhist monk) Välivita Saranamkara, a key figure in the Kandyan Buddhist revival of the mid-eighteenth century, is said to have owed his initial support to his success in debate against a Hindu at the court (Malalgoda 1976: 60 n. 45).

My point here is not the obvious one of counterposing an indigenous 'tolerance' and openness to debate to the intolerance and closure of the Europeans,[3] although Patten's official complacency about 'our traditions' almost demands a response of this sort. At the least, though, we have to concede that the very idea of public debate was not the invention of eighteenth-century Europeans. For example, models for the calm exchange of argument on religious topics were well established in classical Sinhala literature (Dharmadasa 1992: 95), while debates between religious virtuosi have a long history in South Asia.[4] What is at issue was not so much the possibility of religious critique, as its context, purpose and effects; Buddhist leaders could certainly be more robust with critics when provoked. In 1745, for example, the King arrested and expelled the Catholics for writing an anti-Buddhist polemic called *Matara Pratyaksaya* (Boudens 1957: 197–200; Malalgoda 1976: 35). Mostly, though, such tactics were a luxury that was not available to the Buddhists, as parts of the country were under European domination from the early sixteenth to the mid-twentieth centuries and the events I am describing took place more than half a century after the British conquered the last indigenous kingdom in Kandy. How did Buddhists react to the criticisms of the missionaries who came in the wake of the British in the nineteenth century? Before we answer this question we must first clarify what might have been at stake to Buddhists in such a religious confrontation.

'INDIFFERENCE' AS AN INSTITUTIONAL COMPLEX

One kind of contrast between nineteenth-century Buddhists and Christians is highlighted by Malalgoda. Buddhists did not necessarily see Buddhism and Christianity as opposed to one another in terms of 'truth' and 'error' (1976: 206). One strong reading of his account of the Buddhist–Christian encounter in the nineteenth century is that this was an encounter in which some Buddhists *learned* to think of themselves as belonging to an exclusive religion and learned to treat the ideas and practices of followers of other religions as inherently antipathetic to their own ideas and practices. In short, intolerance was an outcome of religious dispute – and especially of public scepticism. A slightly weaker interpretation of the encounter would treat it as a moment in which Buddhists learned to reinterpret Christianity as rather more than another kind of 'supernaturalism' which, like Vaisnavite Hinduism, could easily co-exist with Buddhism. Or we could combine both interpretations and argue that issues of exclusivity, which had concerned the religious elite in the past –

for example, in the long antagonistic relationship with Saivism – became 'democratized' down in the course of the colonial era.[5]

But religious exclusivity is even now not a universal feature of life for Sri Lankan Buddhists. One day during my fieldwork in the early 1980s a friend and I decided to take a shortcut from the village in which I worked to a nearby village where we had both been invited to attend a wedding. The shortcut in question passed by a local Sufi shrine and then made a terrifying descent down a near vertical slope to the village on the plain below. As we passed the mosque, my friend (a Buddhist) casually gave a coin to a child to put in the mosque's collection box. This is their area, my friend said, so we might as well get some help from their god.

This continuing indifference to religious boundaries at the level of practical religion has been widely reported from all over South Asia, although opinion is divided over how easily we can interpret this as evidence of straightforward 'tolerance' (see note 3). While there has been a great deal of pressure on Buddhists, Hindus, Christians and Muslims to keep to their own religious institutions in the twentieth century, this pressure has been far from uniformly successful. To take one celebrated example, members of all Sri Lanka's religions visit the famous shrine at Kataragama in the south of the island (Obeyesekere 1978, 1981). In a more personal case, Gombrich and Obeyesekere tell the story of a woman, brought up a Buddhist, who became possessed by the Hindu goddess Kali and sought exorcism at a Roman Catholic shrine before ending up a member of a Pentecostal group, where she speaks in tongues (1988: 56–7). And the late President Premadasa made a public virtue of private religious necessity by turning his somewhat eclectic religious practice – although a Buddhist, he too was reputedly deeply attached to the goddess Kali – into a national symbol of multiculturalism.

According to Gombrich, to 'be a Buddhist' in the Theravada tradition is simply to be someone who takes what are known as the Three Refuges (*tisarana*) and the Five Precepts (*pan sil*) (1971: 64–5).[6] This involves the recitation of a short Pali formula. The Three Refuges themselves are the Buddha, his *dhamma* or teaching and the *sangha*, the body of monks (*bhikkhu*) whose role it is to preserve and transmit the *dhamma* and to observe the exemplary life of the renouncer as the Buddha himself had done. The Precepts are the avoidance of taking life, stealing, lying, sexual misconduct and intoxication. Anyone who recites the Pali formula thereby announces that she will observe these Precepts and that she 'takes refuge' in Buddha, *dhamma* and *sangha*. The point here is that in 'being a Buddhist' there is no single essential point of belief or conduct, nor is there any injunction on religious exclusivity. Instead there is a loose triangular frame of reference with reverence for the founder, his teaching and his living representatives as points of orientation. Buddhism has its sources of authority but, as represented in the Three Refuges, these are inherently *plural*, and different Buddhists seeking to justify different practices can appeal variously to the teaching or the monks, or direct to the authority of the Buddha himself, according to circumstances and predilection.[7]

Not surprisingly, this agreeably open attitude appalled the muscular Christians who arrived from Britain in the first half of the nineteenth century.[8] The early missionaries found that Buddhist monks often offered them shelter, food and a place to preach, although the laity greeted their efforts with little enthusiasm. Both reactions were puzzling. In 1827 a missionary was told by a *bhikkhu* 'that the English people worshipped Jesus Christ and that the Singhalese people worshipped Buddha, that they were both good religions'; it was only when the same missionary took to leafleting the temple with tracts condemning the 'sin and folly of image worship' that the monks started to turn against him (Selkirk in Malalgoda 1976: 223). The evangelical explanation for what one observer called Buddhist 'latitudinarian liberality to every other faith' (Tennent in Scott 1992: 357) was 'apathy'. Indifference to religious boundaries was read as indifference to religion. According to the Wesleyan Robert Spence Hardy, 'The carelessness and indifference of the people among whom the [Buddhist] system is professed are the most powerful means of its conservation.' And: 'It is almost impossible to move them, even to wrath' (Hardy in Malalgoda 1976: 212). It was, however, always worth a try.

And so the missionaries came to concentrate on moving the Buddhists to wrath. I want to focus here on the particular form this took in the 1850s and 1860s and on the efforts of the Wesleyans in particular. In 1849 one of them, Daniel Gogerly, published a work in Sinhala entitled *Kristiyani Prajñapti* (The Evidences and Doctrines of the Christian Religion). The work was reprinted several times and in 1861 gained a new introduction, 'Proofs that Buddhism is Not a True Religion'. According to Malalgoda:

> This was, on the whole, a new approach to Buddhism: an approach characterized by appeals to 'evidences' and 'proofs', to reason rather than to emotion. The underlying assumption of this new approach ... was the superiority of Christianity over other religions on the intellectual plane, on account of the soundness of its own principles and the unsoundness of the principles of other religions.
>
> (Malalgoda 1976: 217)

This general trend was even more evident in the title of a work published (in English in 1861 and in Sinhala in 1865) by Gogerly's colleague Hardy, *The Sacred Books of the Buddhists compared with History and Modern Science* (*ibid.*: 222).

These works duly elicited the desired response, if not quite the desired outcome, from the Buddhists. The Panadura debate was the most spectacular manifestation of this and is the subject of the next section of this chapter. First, though, I want to re-emphasize two points about the

Christian challenge. One is the complacent appeal to science and reason as inevitable supporters of Christianity, an appeal which with hindsight we may find hard to credit in the decade which saw the publication of Darwin's *Origin of the Species*. The other is the absolute *certainty* about the outcome of any public argument with the Buddhists, a certainty which was a precondition for the missionaries' readiness to present their case in the public sphere in the first place. Hardy prefaced his 1866 volume *The Legends and Theories of the Buddhists, compared with History and Science* with a brief mention of the signs of a Buddhist fightback against the Christian attacks:

> I have formed bright anticipation as to the future. There can be be no doubt as to the result of the contest now carried on; for although it may be prolonged and severe, it must end in the total discomfiture of those who have arisen against the Lord and his Christ and in the renunciation of the atheist creed that now mars the happiness and stays the enlightenment, of so many of the dwellers in Lanka.
>
> (Hardy in Malalgoda 1976: 213)

THE DEBATE

The Buddhists fought back on precisely the ground established by the missionary attacks and employed precisely the same tactics. In 1862 the first Buddhist printing presses (one of them, ironically, the previous property of the Church Missionary Society – CMS) started publishing responses to the Wesleyans' critiques. (Hardy's exultant comment follows his description of the new flood of Buddhist publications off these presses [*ibid.*].) In 1864 *bhikkhus* at Baddegama accepted a challenge to public debate from Anglican missionaries; this was followed by further debates in different parts of the island. The first two such 'debates' in fact involved the exchange of written responses to the other side's challenges. The first debate proper occurred in 1866. The Panadura debate of 26 and 28 August 1873 was the third and most celebrated of the series (*ibid.*: 224–5). There were three speakers: David de Silva (a Wesleyan) and F.S. Sirimanne (from the CMS) for the Christians and a *bhikkhu* called Mohottivatte (or Migettuvatte) Gunananda for the Buddhists. All the speakers were Sinhala: the terms of the debate may have been set by Europeans but it was conducted in Sinhala by leading representatives of the emerging Sinhala intelligentsia. The debate itself was (rather extraordinarily) about the Buddhist doctrine of *anatta* or 'non-self'.[9] It was held in a bungalow before a crowd of five or six thousand. Each speaker had an hour in the morning and an hour in the evening and the whole debate took two days. De Silva spoke for the first hour and Gunananda concluded the debate.

Gunananda (1823–90) was an extremely important figure in the Buddhist revival of the second half of the nineteenth century.[10] He was

from the south of the island, where he was educated by Christian missionaries, before succeeding to the incumbency of the temple founded by his
uncle in Kotahena, Colombo, in 1858. In 1862 he founded an organization with the revealing name of 'Society for the Propagation of Buddhism'
which acquired a Sinhala printing press and started to produce responses
to the work of Gogerly and others. The editor of the published version
of the debate described him as 'a well-made man of apparently forty-five
or fifty years of age, rather short, very intellectual looking, with eyes
expressive of great distrust and a smile which may either mean profound
satisfaction or supreme contempt' (Capper n.d.: 34). His oratorical style
was unusual. He differed from his contemporary *bhikkhu*s in eschewing
the formal preaching style of speaking from a seated position with a
fan in front of the face; instead he spoke vigorously from a standing position, in a style Malalgoda suggests may have been explicitly modelled on
evangelical Christian preachers (1976: 226).[11]

The contrast between the two chief speakers is immediately apparent
in the way in which they started their opening speeches. De Silva opened
the proceedings by explaining the circumstances behind the debate. In
June he had preached in his chapel at Panadura on the Buddhist idea of
the 'soul'. Gunananda had objected to this preaching. (How he got access
to de Silva's sermon is not clear.) With these circumstances explained, de
Silva launched into the substance of his speech:

> He stated that Buddhism taught that man had no soul and that the
> identical man received not the reward of his good or bad actions.
>
> According to Buddhism, the *satta*, sentient beings, are constituted
> in the five *khandhas*, namely *rupakkhandha*, the organised body,
> *wedanakkhandha*, the sensations, *sannakkhandha*, the perceptions,
> *sankharakkhanda*, the reasoning powers and *winnanakkhandha*, con-
> sciousness. In proof of this he quoted the following from Samyuttanikaya,
> a section of Buddha's sermons and from the Sutrapitaka.
> *Panchime bhikkhave khande desissami. . . .* [12]
> Priests, I will declare the five Khandhas and the five Upadanak-
> khandas; hear it, Priests, what are the five Khandas? Priests, the body,
> whether past, future or present, whether intrinsic or foreign, whether
> gross or minute, base or excellent, remote or near, this is called
> Rupakkhandha, the material form.
>
> (Capper n.d.: 40)

And so he continued for the rest of his hour. The bulk of his speech
consisted of long Pali passages followed by translations, with little attempt
at further exegesis. Towards the end of the speech he briefly introduced
Christian ideas about the soul, supported by a few verses from the New
Testament, before concluding with a direct assault on what he saw as the
abhorrent moral implications of the Buddhist doctrine and a warning
about his opponent's likely rhetorical strategy:

In order to mislead the ignorant, the opposite party might introduce metaphors but in a logical argument metaphors are of no weight and the metaphors when introduced would, he was sure, be found to prove nothing. The identical wrong-doer, according to Buddhists, never suffered for his misdeeds. They denied the existence of an *Atma* (soul) and both these doctrines only shewed that no religion ever held out greater inducements to the unrighteous than Buddhism did.

(*ibid.*: 54)

Gunananda's reply was in marked contrast to de Silva's opening speech; where his opponent had been dry and scholarly, his style was lively and polemical:

He said that much penetration was not needed to form a correct opinion of the Rev. Mr. Silva's lecture to which they had all listened. It was a very desultory and rambling speech, which he was certain nobody understood. In his exposition of the Pali extracts, made from Buddha's discourses, he was not more successful, because he completely failed to convey to those present the correct meaning in intelligible language. A *very few* of his audience, however, doubtless perceived that the main argument of the lecture was to show that because at a human being's death here, his *Pancaskhandha* is completely destroyed, therefore the being who was produced from it in another world was a wholly different being. This was not so.

(*ibid.*: 55; original emphasis)

Gunananda was shrewdly exploiting an obvious sociolinguistic opportunity. Apart from the 200 or so *bhikkhus* who had come in his support, there was virtually no-one in the audience with any knowledge of Pali at all. In rubbishing de Silva's competence in Pali he was implicitly drawing on the crowd's acceptance of one of the *bhikkhu*'s central roles; this was to act as guardian and expositor of the Buddha's teachings, which were themselves preserved in the canonical Pali texts:

And now it behooved him to explain this important doctrine of *Pancaskhandha*, in the explaining of which the Rev. gentleman, owing to his superficial knowledge of Pali, had made such mistakes.

In doing so, he would take good care not to use language that seemed like Latin or Greek to the multitude; and he left to his learned coadjutators [*sic*; i.e. presumably his fellow *bhikkhus*] to judge of the correctness of his interpretation of these doctrines. The great Buddha's last discourse, in which man's nature was explained, was not one that could be comprehended by everybody and much less by a clergyman of Mr. Silva's linguistic attainments.

(*ibid.*: 56)

Gunananda's point that the Buddha's words 'could not be comprehended by everybody' also drew on the generally accepted hierarchy in expecta-tions about access to the teaching, in which it might be taken for granted that the laity required the *bhikkhu*s to explain and elucidate on their behalf.

Some of the contrast between the two speakers could be explained sim-ply in terms of personality. The difference was evident to all and discussed by the editor of the published version. De Silva was described as 'a fluent and learned speaker' who 'forgot that the powers of comprehension in his audience were limited' (*ibid.*: 36). Gunananda in contrast:

> adapts himself to the capabilities of his audience and uses the plainest language that the proper treatment of his subject will allow; [he] winds up a very effective speech, rendered the more attractive by motions made with consummate skill, with a brilliant peroration to which the 'great unwashed' listen with deep attention, and the accents of which ring in their ears for some minutes after delivery.
>
> (*ibid.*: 37).

If we look at what the two men said, as well as how they said it, the contrast goes beyond their ability to deal with the demotic. In due course, Gunananda did introduce passages of Pali into his speech, although never as densely and remorselessly as de Silva. Yet when he did, he relied less on simply providing a direct translation but, as in the manner of modern *bana* (formal preaching), he instead tended to paraphrase or use the Pali as a point of departure for some more immediate rendition of the same point. For example, in his second speech on the evening of the 26th, he quoted a long Pali extract which he followed with this exposition:

> As the meaning of the death and regeneration of a being was, in the extract, sought to be conveyed by a familiar illustration, he would give them a free translation, of its meaning and he had no doubt that his auditory would then be able to better comprehend this difficult doctrine. As the newly plucked talipot leaf, when put in the sun, loses its green colour by degrees and assumes a whiteness, so at his death the sentient being gradually loses the use of his physical senses, such as those of seeing and hearing, owing to the pains of death.
>
> (*ibid.*: 86)

Gunananda's freer approach to the Pali sources, like de Silva's warnings about his opponent's likely recourse to figurative language, point to a fundamental difference between the parties. De Silva's speech was based on a series of important assumptions. These were that an assessment of Buddhism had to be an assessment of Buddhist 'doctrine', in which the teachings on the contingency of the self were central; that Buddhist doctrine was to be found in the canonical Pali texts; and that these texts, if translated, could self-evidently 'speak for themselves'. I shall argue later that one consequence of the religious disputes of the late nineteenth century was that assumptions like de Silva's – assumptions derived from a Protestant Christian model of religious authority – did become widely accepted by Buddhist reformers. But even someone like Gunananda, who was undoubtedly affected by Christian ideas and Christian practices, still continued to draw on the plural sources of authority in the institutional structure of Theravada Buddhism in his oratory. The laity did not simply confront the Buddha's words as the sole source of religious certainty. They relied on his religious descendants, the *sangha*, to preserve *and interpret* these teachings on their behalf. So where de Silva presented them with indigestible translations of abstract arguments from the canon, Gunananda employed Pali passages as sources of authority but tended to use them as points of departure for his freer and more vivid interpretations. What divided the sides was their different expectations about the relationship between the laity and the Word.[13]

A second difference concerned what was or was not considered 'central' to Buddhism. Although the Buddhist doctrine of *anatta* (non-self) attracted missionary attention from the start, it is quite unlikely that it played anything like the central role assigned to it by missionaries in the everyday religiosity of lay Buddhists. De Silva's response to the doctrine continues a vein of hostility found in the earliest European descriptions of Buddhism. Joinville's 1803 report in *Asiatick Researches* uses Buddhist denials of the 'immortality of the soul' as evidence for its antiquity:

> The religion of BOUDHOU ... was in many respects monstrous and unformed. An uncreated world, and mortal souls, are ideas to be held only in an infant state of society and as society advances such ideas must vanish. *A fortiori*, they cannot be established in opposition to a religion already prevailing in a country, the fundamental articles of which are the creation of the world and the immortality of the soul.
>
> (Joinville in Scott 1992: 347)

De Silva's hostility is to what he seemed to see as a challenge to very basic nineteenth-century assumptions about personhood: the difference between humans and animals and the idea that each individual is responsible for his or her actions which will be the subject of divine judgement after death:

> Was it all to be expected that a man who believes his end to be similar to that of a dog, or a frog, would care what actions he committed? Is not the greatest inducement held out to the murderer, the thief and the voluptuary to carry on their unlawful pursuits? What mattered it to them how evil their actions were? They would not be punished in a future life; some other beings would be; but how did that in any way affect them?
>
> (Capper n.d.: 53)

The irony is that, while de Silva's fears are true, to the extent that the teaching does appear to challenge important European assumptions about persons as stable legal and moral agents (Spencer n.d.), recent ethnographic evidence suggests that the teaching is of limited practical import to 'ordinary Buddhists' who continue to talk and act as if they are the possessors of stable, enduring 'selves' (Gombrich 1971: 71–3; Spiro 1982: 85). But this assault on what was taken to be a central doctrine of Buddhism is homologous to the concentration on the Word as the final source of authority. Again we are looking at Buddhism as interpreted through the lens of Protestant Christian assumptions which place greatest value on items of 'belief' and seek authority for these central beliefs in moments of unmediated confrontation with the Word.

Interestingly though, the Panadura debate is not, on the whole, remembered for the views expressed on this, its ostensible subject-matter. It is usually remembered as simply a debate about the relative virtues of Buddhism and Christianity.[14] There is some justification for this, not least because much of Gunananda's response was taken up with his own detailed criticisms of Christianity. (Both sides in the debate showed an impressive command of their opponents' textual traditions.) As the debate developed, more and more of each speech was taken up with rebuttals of points made in earlier speeches and the subject-matter broadened from the exposition of the central points of Buddhist doctrine, to considerations of Buddhist cosmology, the authenticity of the Pali canon and the personality of the Buddha himself.

De Silva's dry performance on the first day of the debate worried his fellow Christians 'and several gave vent to their opinions in rather forcible language at the apparent success of the Buddhists on the first day' (Capper n.d.: 37). At half-time, therefore, the Christians were forced to introduce their substitute, F.S. Sirimanne, a catechist for the Church Missionary Society and a less scholarly but more belligerent speaker than de Silva. He also broadened the attack, for the first time going beyond the 'doctrines' of the Pali canon and criticizing the Buddha himself. In the final section of his speech he focused briefly on the structure of religious authority contained in the Three Refuges. How, he asked, can one take refuge in 'books', or in a man – the Buddha – 'said to have attained the state of annihilation', or in a body of men, the *sangha*, divided by its own internal disputes (*ibid.*: 111–12)? The question was ignored by Gunananda in his first reply that morning and not developed by de Silva when he delivered the closing speech for the Christians on the afternoon of the second day. Gunananda did present his refutation of Sirimanne's attack on the Three Refuges in his own closing speech (*ibid.*: 158–9) but the entire discussion of Buddhism in the broader institutional sense implied in the Refuges takes up less than four pages out of more than 100 pages of the edited debate.

Instead both sides concentrated on the quality of the other's 'scriptures'.

There was no attempt, for example, to weigh up the relative merits of the ethical actions of actual practising Buddhists and Christians (although the Buddhist presses in the 1880s took to publishing choice scandals involving Christian clergymen, culled from Western freethinking publications [Wickremeratne 1969: 142]). Similarly the Christians held back from a central theme in earlier Christian attacks, the 'idolatry' of Buddhist practices. Underneath the increasingly tetchy exchanges of the two days of debate, and despite Gunananda's use of the accepted authority of the *bhikkhu* for rhetorical effect, an unexpected consensus began to emerge: that different 'religions' like Buddhism and Christianity were indeed based on different 'doctrines' which were to be found in their 'scriptures', and that each religion's claims to merit were based on the coherence and veracity – or absence of 'error' – of its doctrines.

De Silva returned to the fray on the afternoon of the second day. His chief innovation in his final address was an attack on Buddhist cosmology, in which he was aided by a globe that he used as a prop in his argument. Gunananda responded by quoting a recently published English critique of Newton (Capper n.d: 153n.) and the editor adds a helpful note that 'Some of the Buddhist priests are thoroughly versed in the works of modern scientists' (*ibid.*: 155n.). In his closing speech Gunananda claimed science (of a sort) and rationality for Buddhism:

> Such was Christianity! It was full of irrational and unreasonable notions.
>
>   But as for Buddhism, the most eminent had in all ages given their testimony in favour of it. The great doctors of the science of medicine, of the efficacy of which there can be only one opinion, the originators of ethics, the propounders of that important and wonderful science, astrology, by which even the date of the death of a man could be accurately foretold, not to mention details and the names of learned men, always invoked the name of Buddha and extolled the praises of him and of his religion, in every one of their works.
>
> (*ibid.*: 165–6)

And he finished with a reminder of Buddhism's commitment to peace and tolerance, before concluding that 'he had, he hoped, to the complete satisfaction of his auditory, proved the truth of Buddhism and the falsity of Christianity' (*ibid.*: 166). The crowd broke out in shouts of 'Sadhu' as he concluded and continued to shout until he rose again and motioned for them to be quiet.

AFTER THE DEBATE

The general view was that Gunananda 'being the most graceful speaker and adapting himself to the popular mind, carried the multitude with him', although the same source reports 'that some of the Christians did not feel satisfied with the result' (*ibid.* [Preface by J. Capper]: xi). In 1879 the

Bishop of Colombo dismissed the debate as 'an ill-judged but insignificant "public controversy" '. The debate was deemed altogether more significant by the Buddhists. The English version of the proceedings was republished in America and attracted the attention of the Theosophists, Blavatsky and Olcott. As a result of the contacts thus established, they came to Ceylon in 1880 and helped the Buddhists consolidate the organizational side of their fightback against the missionaries.[15] Like the Greeks described by Just (in Chapter 12 of this volume), Sri Lankan Buddhists enjoyed the peculiar pleasures of 'their' heritage being appropriated as part of a more 'universal' heritage and the arrival of the Theosophists put the seal on a transnational intellectual relationship between Sri Lankan and European critics of Christianity, some of whose work was translated and published by the Buddhists from the 1860s onwards (Malalgoda 1976: 229). The celebrity of Buddhism spread far and wide in nineteenth-century Britain (Almond 1988), while the global conjuncture spread even further, as the Theosophists were also involved with Hindu reformers in India with their own quite different agendas. In Sri Lanka the Buddhists were able to use the Theosophists' support for their own immediate purposes, without making any lasting commitment to Blavatsky's own brand of transcultural mysticism.

Relationships with Christians were not, on the whole, improved by the debate. In 1883 a procession from Gunananda's temple in Kotahena was attacked by a Catholic mob and one Buddhist was killed. The Catholics claimed provocation as a defence for their actions and the authorities were unable to pin the responsibility for the disturbances on them (Stirrat 1992: 19–20; Wickremeratne 1969: 149).[16] The Kotahena riot was the first of a series of violent clashes between different religious communities over symbolic control of public urban spaces (Rogers 1987: 589–91).[17] At the same time enthusiasts for the different religions continued to attack their opponents in print, although there was no repeat of the Panadura exchange on the same scale. There is little evidence that the public airing of scepticism in any way increased religious tolerance.

The debate itself is still remembered in Sri Lanka. The English text has been reprinted several times and the debate has considerable resonance in nationalist histories of the colonial period. In the 1990s, militant cultural nationalists belonging to a group called Jatika Chintanaya made frequent reference to the debate, and on my last visit to Sri Lanka in 1992 there was talk of restaging the debate, this time between a spokesman for Jatika Chintanaya and a left-wing enthusiast for peaceful, multi-cultural approaches to the ethnic problem. Jatika Chintanaya is a student-based Sinhala Buddhist social movement, strongest in the science faculty of the University of Colombo and highly reminiscent of the Malaysian *dakwah* movement analysed by Shamsul (in Chapter 5 of this volume). Their opposition to 'multiculturalism' was based on the argument that this was an alien 'Western' (or 'Judaeo-Hellenic') concept, to be opposed along with all the other baggage of Western 'rationalism'. A full understanding of this most recent shift apparently *away* from the authority of Western 'rational' styles of argument (although within the context of a continuing enthusiasm for open public debate) requires a much larger investigation into what we could call the political economy of tolerance. Two points need to be registered here: first, public debate in South Asia long predates the appearance of 'Western rationalism'; and second (again), an enthusiasm for debate is as often a mark of intolerance as of tolerance.

COLONIALISM AND BUDDHIST MODERNITY

This is only one of many possible ways in which we can link the arguments of the 1870s with the political conflicts of modern Sri Lanka and, lacking the space to describe any of these connections in the detail they deserve, all I can do in conclusion is trace out some possible links between religious argument in the past and understandings of Buddhism in the present. In doing so, it is important to reiterate my opening historical caution. It is by no means clear how much of the change in Buddhism in the nineteenth century was a direct product of missionary influence. However we assess this, there is no doubt that the debate itself was of limited causal importance. Its interest to us is as a symptom of a more complex process of religious change going on around it.

On the face of it, we would seem to be looking at an exemplary case of the emergence of what Geertz (1968) has called 'scripturalism' (see Collins 1990: 115 n. 51) – a kind of religious response to modernity based on a putative return to sources of textual authority. And this move would also seem to be an exemplary case of the creation of colonial hegemony, not least in the way in which cultural opposition is forced to work within an agenda set by those to which it is opposed – in this case the Christian missionaries' understanding of different exclusive religions, defined by 'doctrines', whose essences are to be located in the originary Word of the scriptures.

This interpretation is certainly close to the consensus in modern histories of Sri Lankan Buddhism, in which the reformist style of Buddhism, which at once opposed and emulated the model of nineteenth-century missionary Christianity, has been categorized as 'Protestant Buddhism' (Obeyesekere 1970; Gombrich and Obeyesekere 1988). So it is that modern ethnographers are told – by Sri Lankan Buddhists – that 'true Buddhism' is a 'philosophy' not a 'religion' (Gombrich 1971: 62–4), or that the religious practices of 'village Buddhism' are no part of 'true Buddhism' (Southwold 1982, 1983). In these cases, 'Buddhism' is being used to refer to a set of teachings or arguments located in the Pali canon and the originary authority of the canon is asserted over the 'later' excrescences of contemporary religious practice. Gradually the technology of print has allowed for a much wider dissemination of the canonical texts in Sri Lanka, although often through the roundabout route of European editions prepared by European Orientalists before being reimported back into Sri Lanka and sometimes translated from English into Sinhala (Gombrich 1988: 195).

So, although the long-term historical impact of the Protestant missionaries was negligible in terms of conversions,[18] it might be argued that their impact was subtler but possibly more profound in transforming the dominant style of Buddhism in Sri Lanka. There are two important caveats to this interpretation. One is comparative – very similar changes occurred elsewhere without such visible prompting from the missionaries. The other is empirical – while there is plenty of evidence of 'Protestant Buddh*ism*' in modern Sri Lanka, actual 'Protestant Buddh*ists*' are somewhat thinner on the ground. The most striking comparative case is Thailand where, as Hallisey points out, a very similar process of Buddhist reform took place, including what he calls 'canonical fundamentalism' but which 'seemed only coincident with the arrival of Westerners' (Hallisey forthcoming). Intellectual traffic didn't only run from West to East: the great reforming Thai monarch Mongkut, who had himself established the first Thai printing press, helped provide capital for the first Buddhist Sinhala printing presses in the 1860s (Malalgoda 1976: 219 n. 83). The Thai case, like the whole history of Islamic 'scripturalism', suggests we might be better employed looking for common cultural predicaments, rooted in broad patterns of socio-economic change, to explain apparently common styles of religious response (see Gilsenan 1982: 13–15). Mongkut's press, like Gunananda's mission schooling and the dislocation brought about in the process of incorporation into the world economic order, are the features we need to concentrate on in understanding these predicaments and responses. What was distinctive about the missionary case at Panadura was not the appeal to textual authority in itself (an appeal with a long history in South Asia) but the expectation that the audience could assess the case on the basis of an unmediated relationship with the texts. This may not have been possible then, but the spread of education and print media in the twentieth century has made it much more possible now.

It is important that we avoid the kind of ironic flattery hidden in those post-Orientalist criticisms which attribute an absolute transformative power to colonizers, leaving the colonized passive recipients of other people's authority, and which invoke a secondary academic flattery in presuming that the motive force in all these changes is something called 'discourse' (which is usually to be found secreted in libraries). What seems like an ironic outcome of the Panadura debate – a Buddhist victory on the day but at the cost of long-run 'Protestantization' – may be better interpreted not as the imposition of a 'Western' scheme on passive Orientals but instead as a moment of elective affinity, albeit within a wider structure of cultural and political inequality. That is the force of Gombrich and Obeyesekere's Weberian interpretation of changes in Buddhism.

'Protestant Buddhism' is more rationalized and less magical and appeals to a stratum of Buddhists, living not as peasants in a peasant society but as aspirant members of the colonial and post-colonial bourgeoisie in a rational, capitalist society (Gombrich and Obeyesekere 1988: 207–12). The flaw in this interpretation has already been indicated: the difficulty in locating more than a handful of thorough-going full-fledged 'Protestant Buddhists'. (And as one Sri Lankan colleague recently complained to me, 'The trouble with this society is it is insufficiently rationalized.') The people we encounter in Gombrich and Obeyesekere's magisterial survey of religious change in Sri Lanka somehow manage to combine apparent attachment to the rationalized virtues of Buddhist modernism with frequent recourse to gods and demons and – among the contemporary Colombo middle class – guru-figures like Sai Baba. In other words, the Buddhism which emerged in settings like the Panadura debate in the nineteenth century did not *replace* other practices and ideas which we might like to think of as 'Buddhist' but took its place alongside them as one more possible religious orientation, based on a much more narrow understanding of the sources of religious authority.

The 'scriptural' interpretation of Buddhism has had its most sweeping effect amongst academic students of Buddhism. In the textual study of Buddhism, the Pali canon has been identified with 'original' and therefore 'pure', Theravada Buddhism, to the systematic exclusion of evidence, from archaeology and the vernacular literatures of the Theravada countries, which might broaden our understanding of the many possible Buddhisms there have been in Buddhist history (Hallisey forthcoming; Collins 1990; Schopen 1991).[19] Ethnographic studies of Buddhism have served to render this identification problematic, even as they reproduce its assumptions. Both Gombrich in Sri Lanka (1971) and Spiro in Burma (1982) assess their ethnographic evidence of the diverse practices and words of modern Buddhists against a normative model of Buddhism derived from the canon. Even Southwold's (1983) bracingly iconoclastic approach, which rejects the authority of the canon altogether, is nevertheless framed within the terms of a choice between 'true' Buddhism and 'false' Buddhism, a choice which has its roots in the nineteenth-century confrontation of which the Panadura debate was one particular moment. One possible conclusion is that anthropologists interested in other people's certainties might profitably start by investigating the genealogies of our own certainties about what it is we are studying.

NOTES

1 For valuable comments and suggestions I am grateful to my co-panellists at the ASA Conference, colleagues at the Centre for South Asian Studies in Edinburgh, Wendy James, Janet Carsten, Nick Tapp, David Gellner, John Rogers and especially Charles Stewart and Charles Hallisey. Specialists will recognize my considerable debt to the work of distinguished predecessors,

especially Kitsiri Malalgoda, whose sociological history of Sri Lankan Buddhism (Malalgoda 1976) remains the essential point of departure for all work in this area. The bare bones of the argument were developed in response to a paper on religious criticism in Islam, (now published as Asad 1993) presented by Talal Asad in Heidelberg in 1991, who also drew my attention to Kant's essay.

2 Kant can be seen as a direct ancestor of Habermas' work on the transformation of the 'public sphere' (Habermas 1989), as well as more recent arguments about the 'reflexivity' of modern institutions (Giddens 1991). The most interesting attempt to analyse the public sphere in colonial South Asia occurs in Freitag's study of colonial Banaras (Freitag 1989: 14–17, 177–96).

3 See my comments on Nandy's (1990) attempt to present just such an argument for pre-modern India (Spencer 1992: 277–8); for a review of the evidence for pre-colonial religious antagonism elsewhere in South Asia see Bayly (1985). Many of the South Asian examples of 'tolerance' can as easily be read as examples of would-be hierarchical incorporation. (I am grateful to David Gellner for this point.)

4 The classic in the literary genre is the *Questions of King Milinda*; it is especially interesting that the translation and dissemination of this work (as both Dharmadasa and Malalgoda point out) was a priority of both eighteenth- and nineteenth-century revivalists, including Mohottivatte Gunananda, the Buddhist speaker in the Panadura debate (Malalgoda 1976: 228; Dharmadasa 1992: 95 n. 26). The most obvious difference between Panadura and earlier pre-colonial religious debates is in the setting: those earlier debates we know most about were staged in front of the King, whereas the audience in Panadura was in some sense 'the people'.

5 I am grateful to John Rogers and Charles Hallisey for suggesting these interpretive possibilities.

6 Others might argue that self-consciously 'being a Buddhist' is itself a departure from earlier practice (see Tambiah 1992: 58–60).

7 This triad may adequately express what it means to 'be a Buddhist' in the long historical run but an understanding of the *history* of Buddhism would need to contextualize these relations in terms of another opposition, that between King (or 'state' or 'ruler') and *sangha* (or body of monks) (see Tambiah 1976).

8 The following summary of missionary activity in the years before the Panadura debate is heavily dependent on Malalgoda's account (1976: 191–205).

9 A note on sources for the debate. News of the proceedings was published each day in English in the *Times of Ceylon* and its editor, John Capper, published the complete text of the speeches, translated into an English version approved by all the participants. This was subsequently published in the USA with an introduction by James Peebles, an American sympathetic to Buddhism, and it was this version which attracted the attention of Madame Blavatsky and Colonel Olcott of the Theosophists (see p. 207). This version was republished in 1953, in a later period of intense religious revivalism and again in 1990 to mark the centenary of Gunananda's death. I have worked from the 1990 edition (Abhayasundara 1990), which includes a preface by President Premadasa and, because the only available copy of the 1990 edition was incomplete, an undated copy from the University of Colombo library which shares the same pagination, which would seem to be that of the 1953 edition. For simplicity's sake I shall cite this as 'Capper n.d.'. It is not entirely clear from the texts I have used which footnotes are the work of Peebles and which the work of Capper. The debate was also given considerable space in the Sinhala press.

10 For more details on Gunananda's life and work see Dharmadasa (1992: 97–9) and Malalgoda (1976: 220–1).

11 The 1990 edition of the debate has an impressive collection of photographs of statues erected in Gunananda's memory from the 1950s onwards, in all of which he is depicted standing and speaking with an open book in one hand and the forefinger of the other raised.

12 I have omitted the rest of this paragraph, which is in Pali, the classical language of the Theravada canon. The next paragraph appears to be a direct translation.

13 Another difference in assumptions about the unmediated power of the Word can be seen in de Silva's opening warning that 'in a logical argument metaphors are of no weight' and Gunananda's eventual response that 'Symbols and figures were the methods of speech in the Buddha's time' (Capper n.d.: 131).

14 Malalgoda (1976: 225–6), for example, does not discuss the fact that the debate was called to discuss Buddhist ideas on the self and this feature is not mentioned in any of the various forewords and prefaces to the most recent publication of the text of the debate (Abhayasundara 1990).

15 The fascinating story of the relationship between the Buddhists of Sri Lanka and the Theosophists is too long to explore here. For more detail see Malalgoda (1976: 242–5) and Wickremeratne (1969).

16 The history of the relationship between Catholics, whose presence dates back to the period of Portuguese rule, and Buddhists is too long and complex to enter into here (see Stirrat 1984; 1992).

17 The Christians involved in these disturbances were members of the relatively large Catholic community, not the Protestants whose evangelists had provoked the debate. The 'religious' or 'communal' disturbances of this period should really be analysed along with other conflicts within the colonized population, such as the disputes over caste precedence within the Sinhala population described by Roberts (1982).

18 The overwhelming majority of Sri Lanka's modern Christians are Catholics, who were themselves the subject of attacks from Dutch and British missionaries in the later colonial period; the Protestant sects so prominent in public debate in the mid-nineteenth century are now (as then) tiny. Since the 1970s there has been an increase in evangelical Christianity but that, as they say, is another story (see Caplan, Chapter 4 of this volume).

19 Charles Hallisey (personal communication) has suggested that it may be that *all* religions are based on multiple forms of authority; it's just that outsiders look to the most accessible clues to their nature and these are as often as not likely to be texts. Thus the familiarity of *both* sides in the debate with the other's 'scriptures'.

REFERENCES

Abhayasundara, P. (ed.) (1990) *Controversy at Panadura or Panadura Vadaya*, Colombo: State Printing Corporation.

Almond, P.C. (1988) *The British Discovery of Buddhism*, Cambridge: Cambridge University Press.

Asad, T. (1990) 'Multiculturalism and British identity in the wake of the Rushdie affair', *Politics and Society* 18, 4: 455–80.

—— (1993) 'The limits of religious criticism in the Middle East: notes on Islamic public argument', pp. 200–36, in T. Asad *Genealogies of Power: Discipline and Reasons of Power in Christianity and Islam*, Baltimore, MD: Johns Hopkins University Press.

Bayly, C. (1985) 'The prehistory of "communalism"? Religious conflict in India, 1700–1860', *Modern Asian Studies* 19, 2: 177–203.

Boudens, R. (1957) *The Catholic Church in Ceylon under Dutch Rule*, Biblioteca Missionales 10, Rome: Catholic Book Agency.

Capper, J. (ed.) (n.d.) *Buddhism and Christianity: Being an Oral Debate held at Panadura between the Rev. Migettuwatte Gunananda, a Buddhist Priest and the Rev. David de Silva, a Wesleyan Clergyman*, introduction and annotations by J.M. Peebles, Colombo: Mahabodhi Press.

Collins, S. (1990) 'On the very idea of the Pali canon', *Journal of the Pali Text Society* 15: 89–126.

Dharmadasa, K.N.O. (1992) *Language, Religion and Ethnic Assertiveness: The Growth of Sinhalese Nationalism in Sri Lanka*, Ann Arbor, MI: University of Michigan Press.

Freitag, S. (1989) *Collective Action and Community: Public Arenas and the Emergence of Communalism in North India*, Berkeley and Los Angeles, CA: University of California Press.

Geertz, C. (1968) *Islam Observed: Religious Development in Morocco and Indonesia*, New Haven, CT: Yale University Press.

Giddens, A. (1991) *Modernity and Self-Identity: Self and Society in the Late Modern Age*, Cambridge: Polity.

Gilsenan, M. (1982) *Recognizing Islam: An Anthropologist's Introduction*, London: Croom Helm.

Gombrich, R. (1971) *Precept and Practice: Traditional Buddhism in the Rural Highlands of Ceylon*, Oxford: Clarendon Press.

—— (1988) *Theravada Buddhism: A Social History from Ancient Benares to Modern Colombo*, London: Routledge.

—— and Obeyesekere, G. (1988) *Buddhism Transformed: Religious Change in Sri Lanka*, Princeton, NJ: Princeton University Press.

Habermas, J. (1989) *The Structural Transformation of the Public Sphere: An Inquiry into a Category of Bourgeois Society*, trans. T. Burger and F. Lawrence, Cambridge, MA: MIT Press.

Hallisey, C. (forthcoming) 'Roads taken and not taken in the study of Theravada Buddhism', in D. Lopez (ed.) *Keepers of the Dhamma*.

Kant, I. (1991) 'An answer to the question: "What is enlightenment?" ' pp. 54–60, in H. Reiss (ed.) *Kant: Political Writings*, trans. H. Nisbet, Cambridge: Cambridge University Press.

Malalgoda, K. (1976) *Buddhism in Sinhalese Society 1750–1900: A Study of Religious Revival and Change*, Berkeley and Los Angeles, CA: University of California Press.

Nandy, A. (1990) 'The politics of secularism and the recovery of religious tolerance' pp. 69–93, in V. Das (ed.) *Mirrors of Violence: Communities, Riots and Survivors in South Asia*, Delhi: Oxford University Press.

Obeyesekere, G. (1970) 'Religious symbolism and political change in Ceylon', *Modern Ceylon Studies* 1: 43–63.

—— (1978) 'The firewalkers of Kataragama: the rise of *bhakti* religiosity in Buddhist Sri Lanka', *Journal of Asian Studies* 37, 3: 457–76.

—— (1981) *Medusa's Hair: An Essay on Personal Symbols and Religious Experience*, Chicago: University of Chicago Press.

Roberts, M. (1982) *Caste Conflict and Elite Formation: The Rise of a Karava Elite in Sri Lanka*, 1500–1931, Cambridge: Cambridge University Press.

Rogers, J. (1987) 'Social mobility, popular ideology and collective violence in modern Sri Lanka', *Journal of Asian Studies* 46, 3: 583–602.

Schopen, G. (1991) 'Archaeology and Protestant presuppositions in the study of Indian Buddhism', *History of Religions* 31: 1–23.

Scott, D. (1992) 'Conversion and demonism: colonial Christian discourse and religion in Sri Lanka', *Comparative Studies in Society and History* 34, 2: 331–65.

Southwold, M. (1982) 'True Buddhism and village Buddhism in Sri Lanka', pp. 137–52, in J. Davis (ed.) *Religious Organization and Religious Experience*, ASA Monograph 21, London: Academic Press.
—— (1983) *Buddhism in Life: The Anthropological Study of Religion and the Sinhalese Practice of Buddhism*, Manchester: Manchester University Press.
Spencer, J. (1992) 'Problems in the comparative analysis of communal violence', *Contributions to Indian Sociology* (n.s.) 26, 2: 261–79.
—— n.d. 'Fatima's story: a case from Sri Lanka', unpublished ms.
Spiro, M. (1982) *Buddhism and Society: A Great Tradition and its Burmese Vicissitudes* (2nd edn.), Berkeley and Los Angeles, CA: University of California Press.
Stirrat, R. (1984) 'The riots and the Roman Catholic church in historical perspective', pp, 196–213, in J. Manor (ed.) *Sri Lanka in Change and Crisis*, London: Croom Helm.
—— (1992) *Power and Religiosity in a Post-Colonial Setting: Sinhala Catholics in Contemporary Sri Lanka*, Cambridge: Cambridge University Press.
Tambiah, S.J. (1976) *World Conqueror, World Renouncer*, Cambridge: Cambridge University Press.
—— (1992) *Buddhism Betrayed? Religion, Politics and Violence in Sri Lanka*, Chicago: University of Chicago Press.
Wickremeratne, L.A. (1969) 'Religion, nationalism and social change in Ceylon, 1865–1885', *Journal of the Royal Asiatic Society* 123–50.
Williams, B. (1993) 'A fair state' (review of J. Rawls' *Political Liberalism*) *London Review of Books* 15, 9: 7–8.

Changing certainties and the move to a 'global' religion

Medical knowledge and Islamization among Anii (Baseda) in the Republic of Bénin

Georg Elwert

EMPIRICAL EVIDENCE VERSUS DEDUCTION

That in 'tribal society' certainties were produced by 'closed systems' in the form of dogmatism, was a conception which since the 1960s flooded the social sciences (Popper 1962). But there were some pockets of resistance in social anthropology, arguing that rationalism and scepticism exist in tribal societies as much in parallel to dogmatism as they do in London (Douglas 1973). Unfortunately the debate came to a halt. Only a few studies tried to find out empirically how certainties are created. The plausibility of beliefs and our routines of dealing with them stem from daily life.[1] We have knowledge about certainties but this knowledge is practical and only rarely verbalized, because it is uncommon to thematize it. Once someone asks you about that, the easiest way of getting rid of the embarrassment is by pointing to 'tradition'. (This applies not only to people near the Equator; ask administrators in Europe about the 'why' of some odd rules of bureaucracy and they will say 'because it always has been done like this'.)[2] How, then, are certainties created and maintained?

My premise is that the way we come to certainties is the product of universal procedures: empirical knowledge[3] and deductive logic.[4] The demonstration of this argument with reference to empirical data will obviously run counter to radical relativist assumptions. The way these two procedures interact varies considerably, however, from one socio-cultural context to another and even within a given local context. Arguments about the universal character of deductive logic and empirical knowledge are not new. Nor do they reveal what we can assume to be natural correlates. What is lacking in anthropological research is a discussion of such socio-culturally placed conflicts between deduction and the empirical. Starting from a seeming conflict of the empirical and logical, I will proceed to examine a radical revision of some certainties by Islamization among the Anii, the unexpected return of a civic ritual and the competing claims to authority behind a new belief about AIDS.

Before discussing this case material illustrating friction between empirical evidence and logical deduction, I will indicate the universality of

reasoning and the cultural specificity of logic-empirical linkages by referring first to a most absurd-looking example – the old Anii women's theory
of the common cold – and then to a very widespread phenomenon, the
self-induced conversion of Anii to a global religion, to Islam. If we want
to explain conversion in a social setting, where 'syncretism' would seem
to offer an easy option, we have to trace precise motives – here related
to normative values rather than to cognition – in order to avoid such
almost unfalsifiable explanations as 'modernization'.[5]

The Anii[6] live in the most northern part of the semi-deciduous rain
forest in the West African republic of Bénin, just on the border with Togo.
They support themselves from swidden[7] agriculture and from what can be
gathered and hunted (though less so today) in the bush. In precolonial
times they made money by selling food to caravans (and were occasionally sold themselves as slaves by their raiding neighbours: 'Dɛndi',
'Wasangari', 'Danxomɛ'). Later money was and still is mainly brought in
by migrant labour. In the past they did not form an 'ethnic group', they
were just a linguistic community of people sharing some social features
with the dispersed western Nago (Yoruba) groups living close to them,
all sharing a history of mutual feuding. Now that state resources have
become an interesting target, however, they are becoming an ethnic group.
Indeed the people of Bassila, a small town community, where my studies
were based, conceived of themselves as an ethnic group. They were
formerly quite heterogenous refugees from different regions, now united
in a defence community by a common civic ritual.

Such processes of group formation are relevant to our subject. But
since 'beliefs' and 'certainties' are an important argument in the self-
presentation of all these community-forming processes, we should first try
to understand, from an example outside this realm of an emerging new
community, what makes a certainty. The case has to be outside that sphere,
since any explanation about 'religious' certainty which dwells upon this
very sphere of the emerging self-image, without considering any wider
validity, risks being circular. So the first persons we should listen to are
the old women who hardly conceive of themselves as Muslims and who
do not feel a part of the Anii ethnic movement.

I asked Anii people in the village of Salmanga,[8] 'Which illnesses have
become more frequent and which more rare?' Venereal diseases and some
infectious diseases had been on the increase. But children's diseases had
been reduced – thanks to a German vaccination programme. 'And,' some
women added, 'the common cold is now more rare.' 'Why?' I asked. 'That
is obvious, because of the new well!' As I still could not understand,
I was referred to the old women – the authority in health matters. 'The
common cold is caused by drinking the fresh rainwater from the ponds,
that clear water from the first rainfall which flows onto the old brown
pondwater. But water from the well, the one they have recently built,
does not cause colds.' ('They' are the European volunteers and the African

health workers, who help to build, through advice and credit, wells in the region and who train Anii in basic health education.)

This and similar reasonings look very odd to the European and African health workers. In order to explain this emic theory of the common cold and similar ones for other illnesses they draw upon culturalist explanations[9] and point to the foundation as 'religion' as if this would exempt us from attempting any further understanding. I will, however, show, against culturalist interpretation, that Anii reasoning even in this extreme case is based upon empirical evidence plus deduction.

The old women's theory of the common cold is strongly empirical! In the days of the first rains, when the rainy season starts, the temperature drops, the huts get wet; thus coughs, sneezes and related symptoms occur or increase. The temporal correlation between the first days of the rainy season and the occurrence of the cold is valid and strongly supports the assumption that the illness comes from drinking the kind of water plentiful at this time. This observation of temporal coincidence or sequence is linked to a more general explanatory model for illnesses. Illness may be hereditary, may be due to injury – rather rare cases – or is caused by wrong nutrition. The danger comes from what you consume. There is ample evidence for this, including the practice of poisoning. Since this aetiology looks empirically valid, there is no doubt that the cold has to be caused by something taken in through the mouth. The only nutrition which is specific for this period and thus can be the reason for the illness, is the clear 'new water'. So there are two arguments which build this aetiology: one rather empirical (the observation of a temporal correlation) and the other rather deductive (illness comes from what you take in).

So far the old women's theory of the cold makes sense. They can infer from the two arguments that first, there is the general rule, that illness is caused by wrong nutrition; and second, there is a correlation in time. But why do they say it now happens less often? In order to explain this, we may use the two concepts of distinct and diffuse empirical evidence. Empirical evidence is distinct, if a correlation[10] or a connection of reason and effect is immediately clear and understandable. Evidence is diffuse, if dispersion, uneven distribution or small quantative differences hinder an immediately evident attribution of cause and effect or veil the perception of a correlation.

When we human beings – be it in Africa or in Europe – are unable to discriminate within the empirical effectively, we infer, we draw upon logical deduction.[11] When reality looks foggy, we use guesswork, or deduction. With diffuse evidence, the prejudice or the plausible inference from similar experiences gains superiority. If we have to estimate the speed of cars, we overestimate it consistently for sports cars. Speed on roads estimated by eyesight is as diffuse a reality as the frequency of colds recalled by memory. If it is secured knowledge (plausible according to several instances) that a certain source of water is the origin of the cold, then the expectation of a change is so strong that it channels the perception. This is not otherwise in our culture. The lay person's belief in the efficiency of drugs against illnesses, for example, is in many cases based upon diffuse evidence and is thus guided by strong hopes (for instance in the placebo effect) and authoritative publicity more than by personal selective experience.

Another case of diffuse evidence can be seen in the reasons for diarrhoea. In spite of massive propaganda from the health education team, only eight out of twenty-eight persons interviewed believed that dirty water might be the main reason for diarrhoea. If one often drinks cloudy water and only seldom gets diarrhoea, this explanation seems rather implausible. Eleven of the twenty-eight persons interviewed, rather, seized the occasion to teach the interviewer that foods forbidden by the elders – sweets and stock cubes especially – cause weak health and therefore also diarrhoea.[12] I was thus drawn into another field of knowledge. Old women especially insisted that sauces should have a bitter taste and that ingredients of unknown origin, like sweets and industrially produced stock cubes (Cube d'or®, Maggi®), should be avoided. They referred to unnamed experiences with badly digested food, symptoms of undernourishment and of poisoning. This body of knowledge may be quite well based. Some of the 'traditional' sauces, of which I collected the recipes, were rich in vegetable proteins. So the evidence for arguing that diarrhoea is caused by infected water is far too diffuse to believe. Whereas the evidence that stock cubes and imported sweets cause illness and that some traditional sauces are good for health, is strongly validated in the eyes of the old women I spoke to.

A contrasting case are the theories about the origin of the guinea-worm, a parasite transmitted through drinking water. The old theory blamed heredity. Wherever the worm occurred, the whole hamlet was infected. (In a hamlet people are related through patrilineal kinship and they get their water from the same pool.) In the 1980s wells were drilled and thus clean water was available at a short distance from the houses. The guinea-worm almost vanished – this constituted distinct empirical evidence and was recognized as such. Without propaganda from the health education team, people switched to another theory about the guinea-worm. Now, of thirty-six people interviewed, only six believed in heredity as the cause of the illness, whereas sixteen argued that parasites were transmitted through water or food.[13]

Obviously knowledge changes. The shifts discussed above follow unmistakably the same principles which in Western society too guide the selection of knowledge. There is no 'pre-logical mentality', no different use of the brain. On the one hand, there is the logical model which has to fulfil the conditions of internal consistency and of consistency with other experiences. On the other hand, there is empirical evidence, which may, if it is distinct, jump over any barrier of perception pre-structured by prejudice. These two elements of knowledge-construction do not necessarily produce a consistent system! In those fields of knowledge which have a high relevance, we try to harmonize them. And only pronounced empirical evidence can win over logical deduction; wherever evidence seems diffuse, we operate by deduction (which again may draw upon validated empirical evidence from other fields).

EXPERIENCE IS SOCIAL EXPERIENCE

That experience is cast into socially organized forms is demonstrated by the 'new appearance' of three illnesses in this region: hernias, hypertension and the 'split head disease'. There is no reason to assume that hernias and hypertension did not occur earlier among this population.[14] But the authority of modern medical diagnosis created its perception. 'It is only since the German whites [i.e. medical doctors] came here, that we have these illnesses,' I was told.[15] Of course, now that there is a hospital with chirurgical surgery many people are told that what beforehand they considered as a 'weakness' or tummy ache is hypertension or a hernia. This perception is also based upon a deduction. The experience that some persons are especially strong in prognosis makes them an authority competent in this given field. Medical doctors are proud of diagnosis as their main intellectual tool. It is, however, as I was able to observe in Bassila and by contrast to what they believe to be convincing, not diagnosis as such but prognosis which creates their authority. It is the prognosis that a specific medicament, treatment or surgical intervention will meet the case which creates their authority and then indirectly gives authority to 'medical diagnosis'. An established authority can, with the help of plausible arguments, make a kind of 'knowledge' acceptable, though the connection of reason and effect remains nontransparent.

Authoritative knowledge diffusion, which in our society is most prominently (but not exclusively) linked to the instituted process we call science, is highly ambivalent. The new illness 'split head' (*ewɔlílà* in Yoruba) is a telling example.[16] Headache, absent-mindedness and indisposition are its symptoms. Earlier, people paid no attention to these. Then schoolteachers emphasized absentmindedness but were not really heard. Now there are the new (travelling) specialists from Togo who produce as a diagnosis the foreboding of severe danger to the lives of those affected, due to their bewitchment. These specialists, who call themselves 'traditional healers' but operate as modern entrepreneurs, make a fortune out of their frightened patients.[17] This commercial form of witchcraft protection is linked to empirical evidence and logic. There is the evidence of the symptoms, as well as the (indirect) evidence of authority, and their generalization leads to the probability of a valid diagnosis. The only difference from 'scientific medicine' is that the path of knowledge leading to this diagnosis is arbitrary and not itself accessible to tests of empirical evidence and logical deduction.[18]

The experience behind social practice and cultural belief is always social experience. This truism, which is however sometimes forgotten, has been the basis of classical phenomenological sociology and anthropology since Alfred Schütz, Peter Berger and Thomas Luckmann.[19] It is revived now by radical constructivism[20] as the idea that every perception is (only?) socially constructed. In some of its formulations, however, radical constructivism loses sight of the point that these constructed perceptions are repeatedly (though not continuously) tested against something called 'reality'. Not all constructions of how reality looks, survive. A construction's success depends not only upon pre-established social plausibility. Yet even before the 'construction' of philosophy, humankind was conscious that tests of some kind against reality should have a recognized status (and possibly even be provoked and organized). Thus empirical argumentation about 'reality' is an inextricable but never isolated, part of all human reasoning (and not a specificity of 'Western' culture as 'postmodern' neo-conservatives claim).

With this in mind, we can now reformulate what 'certainty' could mean in an anthropological context. First, certainties are created by an interlacing of empirical and deductive arguments, which imply the inference of axiomatics and the (re)definition of conceptual limits.[21] In other words: no certainty is purely empirical or logical. Second, the evocation of both types of reasoning is conditioned by structures of relevance and thus by interests, hopes and fears. This implies that experience is also social, in so far as it is the outcome of organized processes of perception.

The processes of understanding we now have dealt with are characterized by their reference to a wider world not accessible to eyesight and personal experience. The medicaments used against hypertension come from Europe; the know-how for surgery against hernias comes from there as well. The schoolteacher complaining about absentmindedness comes from the faraway capital; some of the dangerous witches causing the 'split head' are unknown strangers and the healers import knowledge from another country. Authority gains weight when one has to cope with a distant world. But this authority has also to create its credentials as local experience.

OLD KNOWLEDGE DEVALUED: THE PASSAGE FROM THE *UKONO* TO A 'MODERN' RELIGION

Certainties lost?

Some old people told me of ideas and practices linked to norms in respect of game and trees, which are now falling into oblivion and disrespect. It was not clear whether they had always doubted the validity of this knowledge;

but they quoted younger people who considered the old food prescriptions as inferior to 'the new ways of doing things' (translated into French as *modernisme*) and disregarded some food, fishing and hunting taboos as 'un-Islamic'. These old taboos had a profound ecological impact; they hindered the owners of a territory from going after specific fish or game which lived there. The owners could allow others to hunt or to fish but they were not allowed to eat this meat themselves. They could not cut trees along the rivers or in the forests considered to be the home of these animals, which were for them representations of spirits of nature (*ukono*). Thus no animal was under absolute protection but had its socially protected niche. Game and fish were important elements of the diet. It was due to these restrictions, as we can now see retrospectively, that a balance between hunting and natural reproduction was maintained.

Today in the forests around Bassila at least five vertebrates that were formerly present have vanished.[22] The forest which protected this small rural town is now entirely cut down. Only one Anii, a university-trained forester,[23] calls this an ecological destruction and links the cutting of formerly protected forests to the noticeably lowered groundwater level. But under Islam – to which Bassila switched within two generations – forests cannot be sacred; even this 'ecological traditionalist' accepts Islam as a way to modernity and as the best solution for himself and his people.

What, then, makes Islam so attractive? The old understandings did not fall to a frontal attack. There were – as far as we know – no irritating doubts in those fields of knowledge which had been central in the structures of relevance. There was above all a quest for a new normative frame of reference with an interregional legal impact. Of course, the reasons for Islamization had been several. To say this should be a banality, because a social transformation fulfilling just one function for its protagonists exists only in fiction (including fictitious history). In reality there are bundles of motives which bring together coalitions of actors.

'Those who do not pray': traditional 'religion'

To understand these actors we have to look at those former practices which had to be given up after Islam termed them 'religious' practices, and competing (heathen/'kafir') ones. Previously there was no word for 'religion'. Now it is implicit in the difference between the Muslims (*ginə ma*) and the adherents of traditional religion, who call themselves *gilɛndri*[24] = those who do not pray.

Research with the *gilɛndri* was not easy. First I found only three overtly practising adherents of *ukono*; they were called 'charlatans' and 'féticheuse/féticheurs' in the denigrating jargon of colonial French, meaning fortune-tellers and pagan priests. I witnessed something that first they did not admit: that people came to them to consult the *ukono* (spirit of a natural force) to whom they were an *ukonoyar* (literally, owner of the spirit).[25] Practitioners and customers agreed that for them there was no praying, just asking and seeing (the hidden) through the words of the *ukono*.

Formerly, there were several female and male seers who consulted their *ukono* by ('shamanistic') trance. They were specialists in the opaque and diffuse but they were consulted only in crises. Then they attributed misfortune to violation of taboos and they tried to get compensatory offerings for their *ukono*. These offerings – the immolation of a goat, dog or chicken – were plausible since they were accounted for in terms of the valid social experience of violating or respecting the norms of reciprocity. If no gift demonstrated respect to the spirit, why should it[26] do 'its work' of protection?

These practices are shaped by 'moral knowledge',[27] 'an assorted repertoire of rites, which ... does not form an explicit ideology' (James 1988: 2). In the Anii case there was no centralization of knowledge. Some formative elements still recur, however, with whatever *ukono*: the *ukono* speaks through the mouth of the *ukonoyar* but only the consulting client, not the *ukonoyar*, retains the words. The *ukono* may speak Anii, Nago, Kotokoli or another language according to its assumed origin. Someone (an individual!) brought the spirit – often in the form of a stone – to this place and from that time on a son and then sons of sons, continue the practice of offering and – eventually – praise singing; but there is no praying.

That the *ukono* speaks a foreign tongue is not surprising in this multilingual environment. It was my questions about this fact which caused astonishment. 'Somewhere else you can find that an *ukono* speaks Anii,' I was told.[28] Some of the *ukono* stem from places with an almost entirely different religious practice, where spirit possession of the adepts and not of the priest is characteristic. There the priest is a powerful figure.[29] Obviously the exchange of 'religious' knowledge (as well as agricultural knowledge etc.) with neighbouring and faraway communities was (and is) part of this social system. There was, however, an adaptation process, which conformed these new spririts to the local 'morality'. They could not ask for more services than was standard. Thus: no prayers, no corvée of neophytes and no gifts for the profit of the 'owner' of the spirit. The import of the *ukono* was a process which simultanously stripped them of their original ritual embedding.

The seers, male and female *ukonoyar*, were rather marginal to the society. One had not to trust the plurality of *ikono*, just the *ukono* one had opted for, but if s/he deceive, this would justify a switch to another one. Power was associated with a different realm, with secular rituals of bargaining, attribution of prestige and (perhaps) mobilization for defence. The *ukono* was only consulted on the margins of daily life, 'if the country is in difficulty, if someone is ill or before hunting'.[30] The oracle[31] produced knowledge about hidden reasons for misfortune: reciprocity with the *ukono* was violated, a gift was needed for compensation. The credibility of the oracle was based on the – diffuse – experience of success after such offerings and on the social plausibility of economic reciprocity as a frame of reference. In social life too, economic relations to persons outside the family[32] were governed by reciprocity.

A civic ritual

Most important was a *civic ritual*, a ritual outside the realm of the *ukono*, the annual ritual at the garbage hill (*mpǝlǝma*). The village was cleared and dust and garbage brushed to this hill. Then women and men celebrated with songs and beer those who harvested more yams than the others. The beer was offered by the proud producers. The elders assembled on top of the hill, where the representatives of the old established landowning lineages took their seat at one side; the representative of the latecomer lineages sat opposite them. This man was called *guya*, translated as *le roi* by French colonial authorities, though he resembled rather a people's tribune. A drummer stood in between the *guya* and the establishment. The *guya* then uttered statements which defined or reconfirmed norms and set prices for staple food. The established elders then mumbled a 'yes' or a 'no'. The drummer judged whether there was a majority approving or refuting and drummed only in the positive case. Then, and only then, the statements became law. The establishment had the right to veto but not the right to speak. The *guya* could formulate but not legislate! Thus they had to bargain with each other. Most sentences were in fact a reinvigoration of the old normative values. And some were the intricate product of previous informal negotiations between both sides. To manage heterogeneity is an essential craft of this ritual.[33]

In a form similar to this prototype, ritually organized social cohesion prevailed in the whole region of Anii-speakers and the Nago (western Yoruba) communities living among them. They shared this garbage hill ritual, but never had political unity beyond the sight of their hills. French colonization then changed the economy profoundly through the restoration of peace in a region of constant brigandism and slave-raiding. After the first decade of this French peace new trade routes were opened (less important than the former cola-caravans) and a labour force migrated to the Gold Coast Colony.

Islamization

At this time there emerged a quest by young males to abolish the old redistributive ritual. Some asked Catholic and Protestant missionaries for permission to be initiated into their new religion. But these enlightened Christians insisted that ancestral customs and authority structures, as long as they were not connected to the *ukono*,[34] should be respected. It seems that these churchmen were influenced by the anthropological turn in missionary studies. But they did not notice that the redistributive effect – the distribution of large amounts of sorghum beer and of meat – was very unpopular with young males, who dreamed of selling their surplus on their own account. Islam, however, proved in some places an effective means of getting rid of this ritual. The 'official' argument was that a ritual implying the consumption of alcohol was obviously heathen. At other places, like Bassila, Islamization meant that the ritual was 'de-alcoholized' by stripping it of its redistributive elements: no praise songs, no feasting with meat and beer.

Before Islamization the internal money economy (created by income from the sale of food to caravans) was mostly absorbed by the production and consumption of sorghum beer, which gave some female beer-brewers a very strong economic position. Conviviality was organized by beer bars. Islamization was a powerful means for some male persons to withdraw from this social obligation and to keep their money. It is not surprising that until the 1970s there were no women actively propagating Islam. Islam's anti-alcoholic impetus ruined their business.

That Islam won over the town of Bassila in the two generations between 1908 and the 1960s was due not only to the quest of young men for economic freedom (freedom from redistributive duties). The official arguments, however – 'For Islam [meaning – for the Muslim] there is paradise' and 'In Islam thou shalt not covet thy neighbour's wife'[35] – were obviously not really convincing, since even some of my old informants, who had been protagonists of the movement in its early years, expressed doubts about the reality of paradise and admitted that adultery was already forbidden by the old customs.

The protagonists of the Islamization movement were entrepreneurial young men who acknowledged that the new religion was closer to the centres where decisions were made. Islam offers an interregional, even an international identity; it opens ways of communication along the new routes of trade and labour migration. Before, people were attracted to the region because it was a place to escape the slave-raiding powers in the east (Wasangari), west (Tshamba), north (Dɛndi) and south (Fon); it was a 'borderland'. The maintenance of boundaries through civic rituals and through a transformation of religious rituals was a means of defence. After the French brought peace, the nearby commercial centre of the Islamic Dɛndi, Djougou, was no longer an enemy but a centre of attraction. It was a holy man from Djougou who was first invited to stay in Bassila for teaching. The boundary against Djougou was destroyed in favour of regional integration. Many young men migrated. Some did it consciously as Muslims, others discovered the capacity of Islam to recreate a moral community,[36] which otherwise was bound to the localized ritual of *mpələma*.

Now that food could be imported at low prices, agriculture lost relevance to a degree which created fears among French adminstrators.[37] In the eyes of the locals, who were much less autarky-oriented than the

French administration was, food security depended less upon local conditions than upon access to other regions. This also had the consequence that environmental feedback loops, which were protected by the old hunting taboos, lost relevance in favour of interregional trade and work opportunities. To give up these taboos as un-Islamic created no apparent danger, but just an additional hunting (and income) opportunity.

Insofar as Islam relates to the outside world of market and political relations, Islam was understood as a 'global' religion. But insofar as it was their choice and as this move implied (unadmittedly) selections and adaptations, this new practice was no less local than the old one.

Islamization implies in one respect a new systemic concept of religion, which is revolutionary: it is impossible to be affiliated to several systems of belief and practice. Such a multiple affiliation was a strength of the old situation; it eased the growth and transformation process of culture which we may call syncretism or accretion.[38] Only when multiple affiliation is no longer possible, does the idea of a 'conversion', which we associate so intimately with religion, enter the semantic field. The introduction of an 'either–or structure' is an important means of achieving the self-stabilization of a system of religious practice. It defines clear alternatives, where a change is sought and raises the threshold for change by forcing any other system into a direct and open competition. The Anii Muslims do not deny the efficiency of one or the other *ukono* and its seer's qualities. Most of them hope that prayer will prove to be as efficient as co-operation with the 'spirit'. The few who also 'worship' the *ukono* occasionally do so with a bad conscience. That means they recognize that Islam is a religion which (ideally) imposes an either/or code of belonging[39] (a code which had its own attractiveness, as we have seen for example with the beer-related rituals!).

The new Islamic identity – for a period combined with a quasi-religious belief in socialism – was a powerful lever in abolishing old forms of redistribution, to create new forms of political and economic organization. And as a side effect it brushed away, with some peasants, an almost areligious scepticism and . . . some old certainties.

THE RETURN OF THE OLD CIVIC RITUAL

In Bassila the garbage hill ritual continued after Islamization with the solemn statements by the *guya*, the nodding elder statesmen and the drummer, but the negotiations of power moved slowly from the annual garbage hill meeting to the weekly chatter of 'faithful' men every Friday around prayer-hours in front of the mosque. The cleavage between owners of gathering and hunting rights and those who had to ask for a share, had lost significance. That some new cleavages – old versus young, migrants versus residents – were not represented in any mediation process would prove consequential.

National policy decreed in 1975 that any symbol of 'royalty' should be given up. Some young men with a personal history of migration, socialist activists rather than Islamic ones (though faithful too), interpreted this 'anti-feudal' policy in the sense that the ritual at *mpələma* had to be ended. The *guya* followed without protest and no-one else complained either, because the ritual was not only stripped of its redistributive function but had since also lost its social integration capacity.

In the same year, however, the same young men (who were also in opposition to the landowners) created a new organization which they considered to be something entirely different. They brought together locals and migrants at an 'Assemblée générale des resortissants de Bassila'.[40] Their initiative, necessary for the improvement of public services and the general economic situation, was discussed and money was collected for the creation of community investments. Since then there has been an 'AG' (Assemblée Générale) every year. Those who make a gift are praised, which creates a strong pressure towards financial contribution by the well-off. The spending of the sums collected and the management of the collective investments are analysed in detail and form the subject of remarkably frank and critical debate. The 'AG' discusses misfortune and collective hopes (including the creation of the above-mentioned modern medical centre) and debates the performance of local power-holders. Of course, cleavages between old and young, migrants and locals persist, but they are brought to some compromise. At other places in Bénin, where people tried to copy this successful self-improvement organization, this frank debate proved difficult to copy. In Bassila, however, this structure of control has made, up to now, financial mismanagement impossible. Prominent among the critical voices, the self-installed informal 'audits', was the grandson (son's son) of the important *guya* who led the debates bringing Islamization to Bassila.

This illustrates the return of an abolished structure. The 'AG' manages the local diversity of interests and options. It maintains social cohesion through a ritual exaction of contradiction. And last but not least, it attributes prestige to free-giving donors and conscientious office-holders. The civic ritual of *mpələma* has in a sense returned. This was not a conscious process. In 1989 a meeting of some civic leaders acknowledged my hypothesis about the structural identity of *mpələma* and 'AG' but added: 'In 1975 we would not have admitted this. We were fighting the old!' The basis for this resurrection was social experience. There was an experience that outspoken contradictions must not necessarily be disruptive, that conciliation was possible, that some social control increases personal realms of action. Thus dissatisfaction with a new form of the blockading of options and leaving contradictions unresolved could find an outlet in the creation of a new political structure, which was – and is – socially plausible. There is an unconscious deduction and generalization from an older experience, and there is the present experience which stabilizes the new social structure by a kind of 'normative knowledge'.[41]

COMPETING AUTHORITIES

Some old women still stick to their type of discourse which puts empirical evidence into the foreground. Young males, however, represent, as they say, the 'modern' discourse, characterized by reference to authority. In the same year as the old women of Salmanga explained to me their theory of the common cold, I met a young man from the nearby Dengou, a village which had recently got a well. He was nevertheless fetching water from a muddy creek. My travelling companion, who knew about the well, asked him why he did not take water from it. 'This well is not inaugurated,' was the answer. 'Why should a well need an inauguration? As long as there is water, you need nothing else', was our rejoinder. He answered with perfect logic:

> We were told by the European volunteer that water from a well is better than water from the creek. It is better for health. If it is said to be better for health, obviously someone has to put some drug into the water for the health. This has not yet been done. That's what I mean by not inaugurated and therefore I do not yet use it.[42]

The progress of science neither adds nor reduces the functioning of the logical and the empirical but it gives more weight to authority.

Authorities are not stable by nature; they may compete or may devalue themselves. The current Bénin government's promises about economic recovery for example, proved not to be very convincing. For some young people, this increased the credibility of alternative explanations of economic policy as a conjuration from international imperialism, namely its supposed head the International Monetary Fund (IMF).[43] This shift of authority in a youth sub-culture has a dramatic impact on AIDS policy. It makes a dangerous rumour sound plausible: it is said that AIDS (SIDA in French) does not really exist. 'The imperialists want us to lose joy with sex and are envious of the many children African men produce; they impose condoms in order to reduce our number,' said a pupil quoting a political discourse he had heard in the capital. The initiates to this counter-culture of scepticism against official propaganda recognize each other by the riddle 'What do the letters s.i.d.a. mean in French?' – 'Symptoms invented to destroy the Africans!' (*symptomes inventés pour détruire les Africains*). Diffuse knowledge offers an excellent battleground for competing authorities.

SOME GENERALIZATIONS

Modernization cannot be properly conceived as a unilinear process[44] and it is especially not a unilinear process towards rationalization. I have severe doubts as to whether the role of logic, and especially empiricism in daily life, increases with modernization. It rather seems to me that

228   *Public Reason and Critique*

reliance on authorities develops a bigger role. Such a reliance upon authorities may be called a rationalization only insofar as these authorities constitute institutions meant to select knowledge according to a true/false code
(and not, for example, according to its use for power); and insofar as the
selection process is itself open to logical and empirical control.[45] More
precisely, the effect of reliance upon these institutions (in emic terms of
Western culture called 'science') rather should be named 'scientification
of daily life' (*Verwissenschaftlichung des Alltags*) but this 'scientification'
says nothing about the individual actors' recourse to elements of science.
An increasing reliance upon authorities may lead as well to other
phenomena than 'scientification'.

That an apparently non-rational belief is a consequence of trust in an
authoritative belief system may be a good guess in Western society. Among
the Anii, however, a better working hypothesis might be to look for empirical and logical foundations of certainties. To restrict oneself to a detailed
description of a belief while simultanously conjuring 'Culture', implying
incomparability of different social experiences, can never be a good surro-
gate for explanation.

At the beginning of this chapter I drew attention to some apparently
irrational Anii claims to certainty which others might use as illustration
for arguments in favour of culturalist essentialism. I have tried to show
that even these beliefs are based upon universal forms of the operation of
'rationality',[46] namely empirical evidence and logical deduction. The ways
of reasoning and their pitfalls, rather, are probably universal. The inference of authority and the ways of clearing the path from diffuse to distinct
evidence are, however, specific to a given local cultural milieu. The appearance of new certainties may be linked to experience as much as to the
emergence of new authorities, and to the adoption of new normative
frames as much as to the solving of problems in the field of knowledge.

ACNOWLEDGEMENTS

My thanks go to Gomon Yacoubou dit Saharabar and Gomina Maazou for their
help in fieldwork; and to Karola Elwert-Kretschmer for reading several drafts and
for collaboration in the field in 1974, 1977 and 1990/1. I owe many helpful critical comments to Susanne Brandstädter, Ayşe Çağlar, Wilhelm Theodor Elwert,
Veit Erlmann, Wendy James, Gomina Maazou, Lazare Sèhouèto, Emmanuel
Terray and Lucette Valensi. I have to thank especially many women and men of
Bassila, Salmanga, Penessoulou, Yaari, Mboroko and Manigri for long conversations during my too short stays in 1972, 1974, 1977, 1980, 1984, 1986, 1988, 1990
and 1991.

NOTES

1 The human being as a reasoning creature is conscious of the fact that there
   are few certainties. Uncertainties prevail. As an acting being, a person
   dichotomizes the world into certainties and uncertainties. Practical action starts

from certainties; uncertainties are the object of a special strategy of action: recognition. This chapter does not, of course, argue against Karl Popper's advocacy of an open society but it criticizes his mystification of 'primitive society' (see Spinner 1978).

2 Relating social and cultural practice only to 'tradition' provokes an 'archivist's approach' without rules for the retrieval process, which to my mind is implied in radical relativism.

3 The central role of empirical evidence for knowledge in African cultures was shown by Robin Horton (1967).

4 That the role of logic deduction was for long underestimated, was underlined by Sylvia Scribner (1977: 483–500).

5 For the theory of conversion, see the study of Michelle Gilbert (1988); and for the differentiation of a multiplicity of motives, see John Peel (1977).

6 The Anii were called 'Wɛnji' or 'Wanji' by others except those of the biggest agglomeration, who called themselves 'Basəda', from which derives the French name of the town Bassila. In order to forge out of a linguistic community an ethnic group, 'Basəda' and 'Wɛnji' intellectuals (in the '*souscommission linguistique Anii*', 1977) called their common language (formerly 'Gisəda' or Windji), as well as the people, 'Anii'. The central cultural feature, which some people highlight, has been the annual ritual around the holy garbage hill (*mpələma*). This ritual, however, is shared by the Anii and the Yoruba-speaking people living close to them or between them. Others point to the skilfully cultivated protective forests around the villages and Bassila, consisting of high trees and thorny shrubs, which is also a common element to people in the region with different languages. So some of the Nago (those of Kikele) go along with the Anii in their ethnicity construction.

My fieldwork there started in 1972 with linguistic research (see Georg Elwert 1994). Most data for this paper were gathered in 1977 and 1990 (see Georg Elwert and Karola Elwert-Kretschmer 1991: 28–33, 116–27).

Transcription of Anii and Yoruba concepts and loan-words which entered Anii follows the Alphabet 'Africa' of the International African Institute in the version implemented in Bénin.

7 'To swither' (past tense: swidden) or 'to burnbait' are the precise English verbs for 'slash-and-burn-agriculture'.

8 See Elwert in Elwert and Elwert-Kretschmer 1991: 116. (Salmanga, not Mboroko, as stated erroneously.)

9 This line of explanation creates a specific demand for anthropology, to which part of the profession reacts sensitively, because it creates jobs and consultancies and flatters our professional self-esteem.

10 See Richard Shweder (1977: 637-48) on likelihood.

11 The strength of logical deduction was convincingly shown by Christian Morgenstern's hero Palmström (1920: 27) in what is now a standard quotation from the poem 'The impossible fact':

'Weil, so schloß er messerscharf,   'For, he reasons pointedly,
Nicht sein kann, was nicht sein darf.'   that which must not, can not be.'

'Palmström ... was run over by a car at a bend. .... "How was ... this accident possible?" ... He consulted the statute books and realized soon that cars were not allowed to drive there.
   And he came to the conclusion
   his mishap was an illusion,
   for, he reasons pointedly,
   that which must not, can not be.'
          (The last four lines translated by Max Knight 1961: 35)

12 See Elwert and Elwert-Kretschmer (1991: 124).

13 *Ibid.* 125.

14 African as well as German doctors told me that hernias occur in conjunction with heavy physical work. They pointed out that hypertension also occurs among old peasants and hunters and is not confined to people with a 'modern' style of life.

15 Together with the German doctors came Africans of equal qualification. But it was the arrival of the white doctors (*bayofo-logotoro*) which was perceived as the signal designating a new period.

16 The 'epidemia' of 'split-head' (*tête fendue*) came recently into the region from Togo. In fact it is a 'business' spread by entrepreneurs producing the diagnosis and selling the remedies. It was first accepted among the Nago-Yoruba living close to or mixed with the Anii and until today has only had a marginal impact on the Anii – maybe because of the Anii language, which these healers from Togo do not master.

17 See Simshäuser and Fourn 1990.

18 See Paulin Hountondji 1967 on the difference between science and pre-scientific reasoning. He puts accessibility to empirical and logical testing into the foreground of a theory of science by contrast with lore.

   Modern – industrial – medicine may not, however, be a good paradigm of science. In 'modern' medicine it is sometimes debatable, whether the route by which someone came to their (marketable) knowledge is accessible to inspection and criticism.

19 See Alfred Schütz 1962, Peter Berger and Thomas Luckmann 1967 and as the first and for long the most important author to introduce phenomenology into anthropology, Wilhelm Mühlmann 1966.

20 For radical constructivism in this field, see Karin Knorr-Cetina 1988 and P. Wright & A. Treacher's reader (1984).

   Constructivism is a powerful paradigm in those social fields where diffuse realities can be interpreted flexibly. A generalization from this field, however, seems problematic to me. The evolutionary success of some types of institutional order is also related to material conditions, e.g. in the field of technologies of violence and of food production. Not every aspect of reality is best descibed as merely a socially constructed one.

21 Here I will concentrate on the empirical and the logical. For axiomatic thinking as a universal process, see Sybil Wolfram (1973: 357–74), on conceptual differentiation as a means to harmonize pronounced evidence with a logically consistent model, see David Bloor (1976: 123–30). For a universalist Piagetian position, see Wolfgang Edelstein (1984: 403–39). For a useful overview and a rather relativist comment on the authors mentioned in this note and in notes 4 and 10, see Traugott Schöfthaler and Dietrich Goldschmidt 1984. A noteworthy further development, which blends Fleck and Durkheim, would include Mary Douglas 1986.

22 Most notably catfish, leopard and elephant.

23 Gomina Maazou.

24 Here I quote in the dialect of Penessoulou.

25 In Penessoulou the *ukonyar* is called *ukonoyɛr*. I also heard *ukonoyari* and *ukonoyɛri*. The consultation of the spirit as oracle is called *mbɔlɔ* (pl. *abɔlɔ*).

26 The word 'its' is used as neutral form, since Anii-language has no gender but classes. No *ukono* is in the class of human beings (a-/ba- or u-/ba-); most are in the classes for trees, soil or animals, the u-/i-class.

27 See for this concept also Wendy James 1988: 7, 340.

28 The *ukonoyɛri* of Yaari, 12 November 1977. He went on: 'In Manigri there is an *ukono* that speaks Anii'.

29 The name of the *ukono* of Bakabaka in Bassila *buruku* rather relates to the Fon (*nana buluku*), then to the Kotokoli, whose language he speaks. *Cakpana* of Yaari also from Kotokoli may be assimilated to the *shankpana* of the eastern Yoruba.

30 7 December 1977, Bassila *ukonyar*.

31 In order to produce the oracle the *ukonyar* rhythmically rings an iron bell until quaking shows that he/she is in trance. Then he/she speaks with an altered – high-pitched – voice, the voice of the *ukono*. After waking up from trance the *ukonyar* will not remember these words but may interpret what the client remembers of it.

32 *Gafala* (plural, *bufala*) in the social sense (physical sense: house) of a patri- lineal economic unity inclusive of spouses.

33 See Lambek, Chapter 11 of this volume, for the concept of managing hetero- geneity and for various forms it may take.

34 Here I am quoting interviews from Manigri and Kikele, where the Nago synomym for *ukono* is *orisha*.

35 Heard several times as standing quotations even from the *ukono*-worshipping old Amadou of Penessoulou (8 December 1977).

36 For some people, especially among migrants, the art of writing was an attrac- tion.

37 See Yves Person 1956: 40.

38 For the definition of culture as syncretism see Ayşe Çağlar 1991. For the concept of accretion following Alfred Kroeber, see Richard Rottenburg 1991.

39 The attraction of this either/or code does not imply that everyone respects it. But the importance of this new notion of conversion is reflected in a parallel earlier situation. At the beginning of socialism in Bénin in the early 1970s, there was a charismatic regional politician, a fervent Marxist, Abdoulaye Issa. He recognized that Marxism should deny any (para-)religious character (though he admitted it to the actual initiates) and should not demand the giving up of Islamic practice, a demand which might result in direct competition for converts. For a period this quasi-religious belief in socialism went in parallel with Islam as a force in the creation of new forms of redistribution.

40 General assembly of people from Bassila.

41 This is an allusion to Wendy James' concept of moral knowledge (1988: 340).

42 That there are different approaches within the same society should not be seen as a transitional phenomenon. New experiences, diverging interests and constant adaptation processes make for continous heterogeneity. See Monique Nuijten 1992 and Long and Long 1992.

43 The IMF 'ordered' Bénin to practise structural adjustment with respect to its economy by reducing the state's budget deficit. This meant fewer sinecure type jobs in the civil service, lower salaries etc.

44 Modernization might be conceived of as the combination of expansive commu- nication systems with an expanding commodity economy, leading to the self- acceleration of transformation processes. With such a formal non-normative definition we may imagine a plurality of paths within modernization, including those which proceed through warlordism, nationalism and genocide and other phenomena usually relegated to the remnant category of pre-modernity.

45 See Niklas Luhmann 1984 on the differentiation of the true/false-code from power.

46 I add quotation marks to 'rationality', since it covers several concepts (see Artur Bogner 1989 for the ambiguities of this term in Max Weber, Norbert Elias and the Frankfurt School). These multiple meanings create attraction for a term but also a characteristic vagueness, which provokes scepticism, as to whether there can be any reality behind the word that appears as concept.

One of the meanings of 'rationality' is that of a conscious and optimizable relation of means and goal. That signifies, in this sense, that not every use of a means, which strives for an identifiable goal, is rational. This relation should not be random, it should be reproduceable and there should be an understanding that this relation might eventually be improved. In this sense there can exist several 'rationalities' in parallel and not every behaviour must be rational. The reproductive attribute of rational behaviour in this sense links (but is not identical) with the combination of logical deduction and empirical evidence, which this chapter discusses.

REFERENCES

Berger, P. and Luckmann, T. (1967) *The Social Construction of Reality*, Harmondsworth: Penguin

Bloor, D. (1976) *Knowledge and Social Imagery*, London: Routledge and Kegan Paul.

Bogner, A. (1989) *Zivilisation und Rationalisierung*, Opladen: Westdeutscher Verlag.

Çağlar, A. (1991) 'The prison house of culture in the study of Turks in Germany', *Sozialanthropologisches Arbeitspapier* no. 31, Berlin: Verlag das arabische Buch.

Douglas, M. (1986) *How Institutions Think*, Syracuse, NY: Syracuse University Press.

—— (1988) [1973] *Natural Symbols: Explorations in Cosmology*, London: Random House UK.

Edelstein, W. (1984) 'Entwicklung, kulturelle Zwänge und die Problematik des Fortschritts', pp. 403–39, in T. Schöfthaler & D. Goldschmidt (eds) *Soziale Struktur und Vernunft*, Frankfurt: Suhrkamp.

Elwert, G. (1994) 'Petit dictionaire Anii – Français – Version Préliminaire', *Sozialanthropologisches Arbeitspapier* no. 62, Berlin: Verlag das arabische Buch.

—— and Elwert-Kretschmer, K. (1991) *Mit den Augen der Beniner – Eine andere Evaluation von 25 Jahren DED in Benin*, Berlin: Deutscher Entwicklungsdienst.

Gilbert, M. (1988) 'The sudden death of a millionaire: conversion and consensus in a Ghanaian kingdom', *Africa* 58: 291–314.

Horton, R. (1967) 'African traditional thought and Western science', *Africa* 37, 1–2. Reprinted in R. Horton *Patterns of Thought in Africa and the West*, Cambridge: Cambridge University Press, 1993.

Hountondji, P. (1967) *Sur la 'philosophie africaine'*, Paris: Maspéro. [*African Philosophy – myth and reality*, London: Hutchinson, 1983.]

Ibrahima, Idrissou and Mehl, R. (1990) *Etude sur l'état nutritionnel des enfants de moins de 5 ans dans la Souspréfecture de Bassila, République de Bénin*, Bassila: Service de Santé et Service des Volontaires Allemands.

James, W. (1988) *The Listening Ebony: Moral Knowledge, Religion and Power among the Uduk of Sudan*, Oxford: Clarendon Press.

Knorr-Cetina, K. (1988) 'Das Labor als Ort der "Verdichtung" der Gesellschaft', *Zeitschrift für Soziologie* 14: 85–101.

Long, N. and Long, A. (eds) (1992) *Battlefields of Knowledge*, London: Routledge.

Luhmann, N. (1984) 'The differentiation of advances in knowledge: the genesis of science', pp. 103–48, in N. Stehr and V. Meja (eds) *Society and Knowledge*, London: Transaction Books.

Morgenstern, C. (1920) [1910] *Palmström* (37th edn.), Berlin: Cassirer.

——(1961) *The Gallow Songs*, trans. M. Knight, Berkeley, CA: University of California Press.

Mühlmann, W. E. (1966) 'Umrisse und Probleme einer Kulturanthropologie', pp.

15–49 in W.E. Mühlmann, E. Wilhelm and E.W. Müller (eds) *Kulturanthropologie*, Cologne: Luchterhand.
Nuijten, M. (1992) 'Local organization as organizing practices', pp. 189–207, in N. Long and A. Long (eds) *Battlefields of Knowledge*, London: Routledge.
Peel, J.D.Y. (1977) 'Conversion and tradition in two African societies: Ijebu and Buganda', *Past and Present* 77: 108–41.
Person, Y. (1956) 'Notes sur les Baseda (Bassila – Cercle de Djougou)', *Etudes dahoméennnes* XV: 35–68.
Popper, K. (1962) *The Open Society and its Enemies*, London: Hutchinson.
Rottenburg, R. (1991) *Ndemwareng: Wirtschaft und Gesellschaft in den Morobergen*, Munich: Trickster-Verlag.
Schöfthaler, T. and Goldschmidt, D. (eds) (1984) *Soziale Struktur und Vernunft*, Frankfurt/Main: Suhrkamp.
Schütz, A. (1962) *Collected Papers*, vol. 1: *The problem of social reality*, The Hague: Nijhoff.
Scribner, S. (1977) 'Modes of thinking and ways of speaking', in P.N. Johnson-Laird and P.C. Wason (eds) *Thinking*, Cambridge: Cambridge University Press.
Shweder, R. (1977) 'Likeness and likelihood in everyday thought: magical thinking in judgements about personality', *Current Anthropology* 18: 637–48.
Simshäuser, U. and Fourn, E. (1990) 'Avec le secouriste c'est la sécurité – Über Sinn und Unsinn von Dorfgemeinschaftshelfern – Beobachtungen aus Bénin', *Sozialanthropologisches Arbeitspapier* no. 29, Berlin: Verlag das arabische Buch.
Spinner, H. (1978) *Popper und die Politik*, Berlin: Dietz.
Wolfram, S. (1973) 'Basic differences of thought', in R. Horton and R. Finnegan (eds) *Modes of Thought*, London: Faber and Faber.
Wright, P. and Treacher A. (eds) (1984) *The problem of medical knowledge: Examining the social construction of medicine*, Edinburgh: Edinburgh University Press.

MAIN INFORMANTS FOR THE SUBJECTS OF THIS CHAPTER:

Bassila

Papa Alley, male	(since 1972)
Gomina Maazou, male	(since 1974)
'Maasuyar', male	(since 1974)
Gomon Yacoubou, male	(since 1974)
Kalam Karim, male	(since 1974)
'Afusetu Bukari' (*ukonyar*), female	(1977)

Yaari

'The' *ukonyɛr*, male (1977)

Penessoulou

Amadou 'the' *ukonyɛr*, male (1977)

Salmanga

'*basumpərə*' (anonymous), females (1990)

10 Bourdieu and the diviner
Knowledge and symbolic power in Yoruba divination

F. Niyi Akinnaso

THE CREATION AND CONTROL OF KNOWLEDGE

As Sir Edmund Leach once complained about the field of anthropology in general, the anthropology of knowledge has succeeded in collecting many 'butterflies', whose comparative analyses have hardly gone beyond the development of typologies, such as 'local' (indigenous) versus 'global' (exogenous) knowledge; 'traditional' (native, primitive) versus 'civilized' (imported, modern) knowledge; 'secular' (practical) versus 'ritual' (specialized) knowledge, etc. While such dichotomies may have been useful as a preliminary grid to classification, they now appear to have fossilized into distinctive categories which, it is believed, could be readily identified. One major consequence of this dichotomization is the difficulty it poses for analysing certain forms of knowledge that are, in essence, neither local nor global, neither old nor new, neither practical nor specialized but both and all at the same time. Yet until such forms are critically analysed, the anthropology of knowledge will remain deficient in accounting for the generative capacity of knowledge producers and the processes of change, especially in those diverse areas of experience characterized by the beliefs, rituals and practices commonly labelled as religion.

It is not the case, of course, that some efforts have not been made in this direction (see, for example, Hannerz 1987). However, the dominant paradigms employed so far in generative studies of knowledge – namely, 'syncretism' and 'creolization' – do not appear to be adequate. Syncretism takes as its starting point the clash or interplay between two or more distinct forms of religious symbolism without explaining the dynamics of the interaction, thus excluding the importance of human agency in the creation of religious knowledge. Like the structural-functionalist model within which it was embedded, syncretism recognized change without being able to explain it.

Although the creolization model takes human agency into account, it does have its own shortcomings. For one thing, the model seems to suggest a one-off blending of forms that were previously finite and separate, thus failing to account for established forms of hybridity characteristic, for example, of the composite nature of early Greek religion (Hooker 1976; Bryant 1986) and of the inherently incorporative nature of Yoruba cultural forms, particularly verbal art and popular culture (Akinnaso 1980; Barber 1991; Barber and Waterman 1993). The Greek case is particularly instructive on hybridity:

> Greek religion has a much older and more complex pedigree, retaining diverse elements from a number of different sources. The Mycenaean legacy was itself an amalgam, composed of Indo-European features which had been fused with the practices and beliefs of the pre-Greek populations and subsequently modified under the strong cultural influence of the Minoans and their Near Eastern contacts. Later migratory peoples, including the invaders who destroyed the palaces, introduced additional novel elements. . . . Innumerable deities and spirits of diverse cultural origins thus co-existed in a loose-fitting composite polytheism, the complexity of which was further extended by a variety of regional and local differences in cultic practice.
>
> (Bryant 1986: 271–2)

Second, by focusing on secular knowledge, the model has failed to account for the creative potentials of ritual specialists, the custodians of specialized knowledge, especially in non-literate societies (see Akinnaso 1992), who routinely create new knowledge as they reproduce the old. This neglect may well be due to the reification of the ritual domain by anthropologists, who for so long have presented specialized knowledge as resistant to change, in part because of its association with fixed rituals or ritual practices. It has been argued that change, if it happens at all in this domain, often comes in the form of variability of interpretation, rather than alterations in the formal properties of ritual-based knowledge systems (Robertson-Smith 1889; Radcliffe-Brown 1952; Boas 1955; Abimbola 1976; Bloch 1986; Gajek 1990; Harrison 1992).

The goal of this chapter is to demonstrate how traditional Yoruba specialists create and control knowledge by analysing one type of specialized knowledge, namely divination, and demonstrating how incremental change is accommodated into this form of knowledge, while the canon is being reproduced and retooled to suit the situation at hand.

Specifically, I examine the sources of this knowledge; the 'official' language in which it is encoded; how the diviner uses the knowledge to appropriate power to himself; the relations between divinatory knowledge and social structure; and how the diviner's relatively structured and apparently fixed body of knowledge is adapted to the changing world around him. I argue that divination is a system of knowledge that is at once basic and derivative, fixed and generative, highly structured but also eclectic.

DIVINATION AS KNOWLEDGE AND AS A WAY OF KNOWING

Divination is universally acknowledged as a type of specialized knowledge, one that encompasses, or at least underlies, a people's religion, epistemology, philosophy, myth, history and cognitive system (Durkheim and Mauss 1967; Bascom 1969, 1980; Turner 1974; Abimbola 1976, 1977; Loewe and Blacker 1981; Werbner 1989; Peel 1990; Peek 1991a, 1991b; Abbink 1993). No wonder, then, that Durkheim and Mauss, nearly a century ago, saw in divination the rudiments of a people's system of classification:

> a divinatory rite is generally not isolated; it is part of an organized whole. The science of the diviners, therefore, does not form isolated groups of things but binds these groups to each other. At the basis of a system of divination there is thus, at least implicitly, a system of classification.
>
> (1967 [1903]: 77)

Divination is also a way of knowing (see, in particular, Peek 1991b; Abbink 1993), one that is associated with a specialized ritual which uses extraordinary powers of communication to reveal occult realities. Such occult revelations serve to reassure members of a society just where they stand in relation to one another, in relation to the society as a whole and in relation to the cosmological order which includes, at one end, the plants and beings of the wild and, at the other end, the ancestors and the gods. The success and persistence of divination rituals, like other specialized rituals, depend largely on this reassurance (see Leach 1968; Bloch 1986; Werbner 1989; Harrison 1992).

Whether it is viewed as product or process, divination is also a way of seeking truth and certainty, particularly cultural certainties, as well as authenticity: what people can identify with as their own, in a world that is constantly changing. Throughout the ages, ritual specialists, notably diviners, seers, spirit-mediums and priests, have functioned as custodians of particular certainties, seeking the 'relevance' of such certainties to the lives of individuals, groups and whole societies (see Abbink [1993] for an application of the 'relevance' theory proposed by Sperber and Wilson [1986] to divination). This custodial function is, indeed, central to Yoruba conceptions of a diviner: he is *babaláwo* (*bàbá aláwo* or *bàbá* [*tí*] *ó ní awo*; literally, father who has [keeps] secrets, 'custodian of secret knowledge'). This may well explain why a diviner's knowledge, like other types of specialized knowledge, is envisioned variously as property, wealth, power and authority (see Murphy 1980; Barth 1990; Akinnaso 1992; Harrison 1992; Hoskins 1993) and why access to divinatory knowledge is often regulated, sometimes even blocked, by professional groups, secret societies and the like, which control the institutional mechanisms by which such knowledge is formally transmitted (see Akinnaso 1992).

IFÁ AND Ẹ̀Ẹ̀RÌNDÍNLÓGÚN

The Yoruba are known to practise as many as five or six methods of divination (Bascom, 1969). However, the most important and reliable methods are those based on the manipulation of *ìkín* (ritually treated palm nuts); *ọ̀pẹ̀lẹ̀* (a divining chain); or *owó ẹ̀rọ̀ mẹ́ẹ̀rìndínlógún* (ritually treated cowrie shells) and the recitation of specific (oral) texts associated with particular configurations of these objects. Only two types of divination are text-based in this sense, namely *ifá* and *ẹ̀ẹ̀rìndínlógún* (also referred to as 'sixteen-cowrie' divination or, simply, 'sixteen cowries'; see Bascom 1980). The striking similarities between the two types (see Akinnaso 1992) make it possible to regard them as variations of the same system of divination. At the same time, however, each has unique characteristics which qualify it for separate treatment. For example, each type of text-based divination is practised within a distinctive cult. These cults are widespread, with practitioners in Nigeria, Benin Republic (formerly Dahomey), Porto Novo, Brazil and Cuba (see especially Bascom 1952, 1969; Peel 1990).

Ifá and *ẹ̀ẹ̀rìndínlógún* are similar (indeed, identical in some respects), one (*ẹ̀ẹ̀rìndínlógún*) being, in fact, a mythological, historical and structural derivative of the other (see Bascom 1980: 18–21; Akinnaso 1982, 1992). To a great extent, *ifá* and *ẹ̀ẹ̀rìndínlógún* texts share similar myths, stories and themes and employ similar methods of acquisition and performance. Together, they constitute a specialized body of knowledge and a system of social, emotional and pathological control, employing relevant historical and mythological precedents contained in the special divination corpus to be recited, chanted, or sung (as appropriate) by the diviner.

The basic differences are in the size of the corpus to be memorized and recited by the diviner, and the instruments and methods used in invoking the text to be recited in a given case. While *ifá* makes use of 256 (16 × 16) configurations (of the divining instrument), of which sixteen are basic, *ẹ̀ẹ̀rìndínlógún* makes use of seventeen configurations which parallel the sixteen basic *ifá* configurations (see Bascom 1980). Furthermore, while *ifá* uses *ìkín* as the instrument for invoking the appropriate text, *ẹ̀ẹ̀rìndínlógún* employs *owó ẹ̀rọ̀ mẹ́ẹ̀rìndínlógún* which gave the system its name. Interestingly, the number of palm nuts used in *ifá* is also sixteen, the same number of basic *odù* (i.e. a body of text consisting of numerous *ẹsẹ* [narratives]) in both systems. *Ifá* also makes use of the *ọ̀pẹ̀lẹ̀*, whereas *ẹ̀ẹ̀rìndínlógún* does not appear to have an alternative instrument. Moreover, *ifá* employs a divining bag (which is flattened out so that the *ọ̀pẹ̀lẹ̀* can be cast on it) and *opón ifá*, the divining tray, a specially carved wood board, symbolically decorated at the edges. The inner surface of this board is covered with *ìyẹ̀* (sacred powder), obtained specially from wood dust.

In *ifá*, appropriate graphic signs are made on the powdered tray, depending on the configurations of the *ìkín* or *ọ̀pẹ̀lẹ̀* which are cast on the flattened divining bag (for details, see Bascom 1969: Chapter 4;

Abimbola 1976: 26–32). In *ẹ̀rìndínlógún*, on the other hand, the sacred cowrie shells are cast on a basketry tray, woven in rectangular or circular fashion. Because wood dust is not used, there is no way of making signs on the tray as in *ifá*. Instead, the sixteen cowries are cast on the tray such that the cowries are themselves the signs. Although the following description is based on *ẹ̀rìndínlógún*, *ifá* follows basically the same procedure.

When the sixteen cowries are cast, one of seventeen possible configurations (from zero to sixteen) appears, depending on how many cowries fall with their 'eyes' up and how many fall with their 'eyes' down. The emergent pattern corresponds to an *odù*. For example, when there are eight cowries facing 'eye' up and eight facing 'eye' down, the configuration is an *odù* known as *Èjì Ogbe*, with which certain specified *ese* are associated. Once the *odù* has been determined by the first toss of the cowries, the diviner begins to recite the narratives associated with it until he is stopped by the client, who ordinarily selects the narrative that is relevant to her or his own case.

Basically, as in *ifá*, each *ẹsẹ* contains a complete narrative which is an account of a known historical or unknown mythological consultation, consisting of a named diviner, a named client, a specified problem, the diviner's recommendations including a list of sacrificial items, the client's reactions and their consequences. Thus, each complete narrative has a fixed structure and it is marked off from other narratives by a complete story of a given mythological or historical consultation sandwiched between a formulaic prologue and epilogue. The epilogue commonly contains moral exhortations and, sometimes, a meta-analysis of the narrative itself (for further details, see Bascom, 1980; Akinnaso, 1982).

Once the client gives some indication of the relevance of a recited narrative, the divining process goes into a session of 'simultaneity and sequencing' more or less as described by Parkin (1991). This phase is marked by a series of questions posed by the diviner to the client in a bid to identify the nature of her or his problem. However, this interrogative phase is highly structured. Usually, more specific information can be obtained through a process known as *ibò dídì*. This involves additional casts of the cowries and a choice between specific alternatives on the basis of the rank order of the seventeen *odù* (see Table 10.1). Choice is restricted to two alternatives, between 'left hand' and 'right hand'. The choice between more than two alternatives is made only by deciding between them in sequence and receiving 'Yes' or 'No' answers to specific questions. Predictions of outcome are also settled through *ibò*. In general, predictions fall into two categories: *ire* ('blessing' or 'good tidings') and *ibi* ('evil' or 'bad tidings'). Each category is composite and its members are ranked in order. Further inquiries can be made about the specific nature and recipient of the blessing or evil and what should be done to realize or avert the prediction.

Ìbò is an interesting process symbolizing the quest-for-knowledge motif

Table 10.1 The rank order of the *odù**

First rank**		Second rank		Third rank	
eji ogbe	(8)	owonrin	(11)	ika	(13)
ofun	(10)	osa	(9)	oturupon	(14)
irosun	(4)	odi	(7)	ofun kanran	(15)
ogunda	(3)	obara	(6)	irete	(16)
eji oko	(2)	ose	(5)	opira	(0)
okanran	(1)				
ejila sebora	(12)				

Notes: * Figures indicate the number of cowries lying 'eye' up.
** The ordering within each rank follows the pattern suggested by one diviner to William Bascom (Bascom 1980: 7).

that characterizes the entire divinatory process. Etymologically, the word *ibò* means secret, being a nominal derivative of the verb *bò*, 'to cover'. It is used in this nominal form, mainly as part of the esoteric lexicon of divination, where it means 'hidden object(s)'. *Ìbò* is represented by two small objects: the chest-bone of a small tortoise, designating a positive response; and a small pebble, designating a negative response. *Ìbò dídì* is the process of hiding, but also of uncovering, the objects. It is thus a type of problem-solving.

The client holds one of these objects in each hand and asks the god of divination to indicate by the configuration of the sixteen cowries which hand is selected. For example, a client who consults a diviner specifically to find out what is in store for him/her in the new year may stop the diviner after the latter has recited an *ęsę* that predicts *ire* to find out which of the five major folk categories of *ire* is being predicted. Is it *ire àikú* (longevity); *ire ajé* (money); *ire obìnrin* (women, i.e. wives); *ire ọmọ* (children); or *ire ibùjóòkó* (shelter or abode)? At this juncture, the client is presented with the objects of the *ìbò*. The client then holds them in both hands, whispers into them one of the five categories of *ire* about which specific information is required, separates the objects by keeping one within each closed fist and then, with fists still tighly closed, the client stretches her or his arms towards the divining paraphernalia in a gesture of readiness. Then the diviner throws the cowries and interprets the resulting configuration according to the guide provided in Table 10.2.

The right hand is indicated with a single cast if any of the seven first-ranked *odù* appears in the ensuing configuration. However, if any of the second-ranked *odù* appears, a second cast of the cowries is required. If one of the second-ranked *odù* appears on this second cast, then the right hand is selected; but if a first-ranked *odù* appears on the second cast, then the left hand is chosen. If, during the first or the second cast of the cowries, any of the third-ranked *odù* appears, then it is concluded that there is no answer. The entire process may then be repeated until there is an answer,

Table 10.2. Procedure for *ibò* selection

Cast	Odù	Result
First	first-ranked	right hand
	second-ranked	second cast required
	third-ranked	start all over again
Second	first-ranked	left hand
	second-ranked	right hand
	third-ranked	start all over again

be it positive or negative. A positive answer is produced when the object in the chosen hand is the tortoise's chest-bone; the answer is negative if the object is the small pebble. If, for example, a positive answer is produced at the end of the exercise, the client may want to have more specific information, e.g. about the specific recipient of the promised blessing. Will it be the client, a relative, a close friend? There is no theoretical limit to the number of fine-tunings nor to the *ibò* that can be performed at a given divination session.

Once the client is satisfied with the answers provided through the process of *ibò*, the next stage is to work out, again through *ibò*, details of the necessary sacrifice: what should be offered, to whom, where, when and how? The scope of the diviner's recommendations, of course, is constrained by the historical or mythological precedent contained in the relevant *ese*. Sacrifice, an obligatory feature of every divination session, is offered both to ensure the promised blessing (if the prediction is positive) or to avert evil (if the prediction is negative) and to ensure a cohesive link between the two poles of the cosmological order: plants and animals, often consumed by humans, are offered in sacrifice to ancestors and the gods. Sacrifices may be offered in the privacy of the client's home, at a prescribed *oríta*, a T-junction (such junctions have ritual, if not mythical, significance in Yoruba culture), at the village shrine, or in the diviner's yard, although the diviner's yard is often preferred, perhaps to ensure proper procedure and the efficacy of the sacrifice. All diviners have somewhere in their backyard the shrine of *Èsù* (*Ẹlẹgbara*), the trickster god, to whom most sacrifices supervised by the diviner are made, in part to enlist his co-operation in ensuring the efficacy of the sacrifice and in part to use him as the conveyor of the sacrifice to the recipients, varying from ritually significant trees (such as the iroko' tree) to ancestors and recognized divinities.

WHERE DOES THE DIVINER'S KNOWLEDGE COME FROM?

In the course of his career, a diviner typically accumulates a great deal of knowledge, a form of symbolic capital, which, in the absence of economic accumulation, is used as a means of controlling people (see Bourdieu 1977, 1991). Diviners also enjoy the further luxury of being able to convert their knowledge to economic and social capital, without necessarily exchanging it. As Auguste Comte once commented about language, the diviner's knowledge is thus a kind of wealth that is augmented, rather than diminished, by use. The critical question remains, however, as to how the diviner comes about this knowledge. Recent studies of Yoruba divination indicate that the diviner derives his knowledge from three main sources; namely, schooling, secular experience and consultations with clients (Akinnaso 1992).

The core of the diviner's specialized knowledge is derived from special schooling, averaging ten to fifteen years (see Bascom 1969, 1980; Abimbola 1976, 1977; Akinnaso 1982, 1992). To attend divination schools, the prospective learner must first be transformed from his status as a lay person to that of a medium through a special initiation ceremony, lasting several days (Bascom 1980; Akinnaso 1992). In the course of the subsequent training, the novitiate learns the configurations of the appropriate divining instrument and the *odù* associated with each configuration; memorizes the text, including the prescribed sacrifice, associated with each *odù*; and acquires appropriate socio-linguistic and rhetorical skills. He also learns the names of medicinal herbs and how to make necessary concoctions from them, etc. Moreover, he learns important aspects of Yoruba history, mythology, philosophy, medicine and religious practices. In addition to the transmission of esoteric knowledge, the curriculum also includes the deliberate transmission of professional ethics, values and attitudes appropriate to divinatory practice. Learning is both by deliberate instruction and by watching the master as he divines (see Akinnaso 1992, for details). As he masters the text, the novitiate also acquires exegetical skills, particularly how to interpret the text and use it in real circumstances.

After graduation, the diviner continues to learn more text and more herbs from either or both of two main sources. One is the periodic meetings of practising diviners, which function like professional conferences and seminars where diviners share experiences, exchange ideas and update their knowlegde. Abimbola (1976: 15) describes the nature and function of such meetings:

> In most communities *Ifá* priests also meet regularly once every month and once every year. The yearly meeting is observed as a festival which is known as Mọlẹ. . . . Perhaps the most interesting aspect of the annual Mọlẹ festival and the other congregational assemblies of *Ifá* priests is the chanting of *Ifá* texts which is referred to as *iyere*.

Another source of additional knowledge is a further apprenticeship to a diviner who has a larger repertoire of *odù* and *ẹsẹ* or specializes in attending to certain specific problems. As Bascom (1969: 86) reports for *ifá*, diviners arrange refresher courses for themselves 'by paying other diviners to teach them specific verses or medicines'. A diviner may have to travel far and wide in search of a suitable tutor, apprentice himself to the specialist for some time and pay for his tuition in cash or in kind. Maupoil highlights the extent and spatio-temporal dimensions of Yoruba divination training, by focusing on the training experience of a particular diviner:

> A diviner at Porto Novo in the mid-1930s was born in Ife in the 1870s and destined to Ifa at birth. At twelve, he was apprenticed to his uncle for four years and then to another babalawo at Ife. After further periods of apprenticeship, at Ibadan and Ogbomosho, [he went] back to Ife [aged] ca. twenty to assist the Awoni (King's diviners). He had now 'cast Ifa' for a client for the first time. Then [he went] to Ilesha for a year, where he learnt medical recipes and to Ijebu Ode for four years, working with a noted diviner, son of the King. [He later went] to Porto Novo in 1901 and then for six years [learned divination] at various places in Dahomey (Ketu, Abomey, Kalavi). Then [he went] to Abeokuta for a year and a half, where he learnt amulets and the use of leaves. He continued the study of amulets and Ifa at Lagos, finally marrying a fifth wife and settling as a diviner and amulet-maker at Porto Novo, in his forties.

> (cited and translated by Peel 1990: 343)

Although not every *ifá* diviner goes through this regimen, this diviner's experience illustrates the possibilities and draws attention to the fact he 'grows' as a social person (adding a fifth wife to his already large family) as he enriches his ritual knowledge and technical expertise.

Although the elaborate training eventually elevates the diviner's status to that of a ritual specialist, the above case reminds us that the diviner remains a social person as well and that his social roles in society provide an additional source of knowledge. In Idanre, my home town, where I have done most of my fieldwork, all the diviners, including my grand-father, were farmers in their own right, each with many wives and many children. They all belonged to apppriate *òtú* (age-grade associations) and participated actively in community affairs. Many of them were, indeed, local chiefs. In fact, as of 1993, the head chief of Isalu quarter, one of the three major traditional divisions of Idanreland, was a reputable diviner and a successful cocoa farmer who participated actively in the affairs of the Co-operative Produce and Marketing Society in his village and expe-rienced fluctuations in harvest and price like the other farmers. As a quarter chief, he administered virtually a third of Idanreland, providing spiritual and moral leadership, including the settlement of disputes. He was also, of necessity, a 'traditional' politician, with a prominent role in the traditional *ùghà* (Council of Chiefs) which meets every nine days in the King's palace. In addition to these traditional roles, he was also actively involved in the 'modern' democratic political process. For example, during the series of elections between 1990 and 1993, several meetings were held in his house to resolve conflicts among rival candidates within his quarter and even between members of different political parties from within and outside his quarter. I attended at least two such meetings in 1991.

Ifá diviners, like the Isalu head chief, are at a particular advantage in gathering socio-political information, because they have a strong professional association, characterized by an elaborate hierarchical structure, which in many respects parallels as well as complements the larger political organization (see Bascom 1969; Abimbola 1976; Akinnaso 1992). In Idanre, the King is the head of the association, although the power is normally delegated to the Lisa, the second-in-rank to the King, otherwise known as *Qbaà'de* (*qba òde*, i.e. the King outside [the palace] or, better still, the King of township affairs). The Lisa settles minor disputes and co-ordinates the activities of the other chiefs, especially during *ùghà* meetings. He ordinarily shares his knowledge of current affairs with the diviners during their periodic meetings and seeks their advice, especially at moments of crisis, on behalf of the King. The King, of course, can summon any diviner to the palace for consultation and advice. Any diviner can also voluntarily go to the King to offer free advice, to warn of possible danger ahead, or, sometimes, to use the visit as a smokescreen for gathering information about royal happenings.

Clients also provide a vital source of social knowledge, particularly in the answers they provide to the diviner's questions during the divination session. Since clients do not normally disclose the specific nature of their problems to start with, whatever they say or do not say during the consultation, their demeanour and attitudes, etc., provide important clues for the diviner. In situations where an enduring diviner–client relationship has developed, as was often the case in many village communities, it is not unusual for the diviner to have acquired a great deal of background information about his clients; such information could come in handy in future divination.

The above description points to a composite form of knowledge, deriving from ritual, social, economic and political experiences. Yoruba diviners draw on these multiple sources of knowledge not only in analysing social and pathological disorders but also in embellishing, recontextualizing and interpreting the text they recite (see below). Although a diviner is defined by society (for example, as *babaláwo* or *awolórìṣà* in Yoruba) and by anthropologists (as a diviner or as a ritual specialist), principally in reference to his ritual knowledge and role, it should be borne in mind that, in the course of divination, diviners typically appropriate and incorporate other forms of knowledge as if they all derived from the same transcendental source.

THE CONSULTATIONS MARKET AND THE OFFICIAL LANGUAGE

Theoretically at least, the whole of Yorubaland and even beyond provides the consultations market for diviners. In modern Yorubaland, this market is rather diffuse as diviners, local herbalists, *aláàdúrà* (spiritual) churches and (Western) medical doctors compete for clients. It is not uncommon for a seriously ill or otherwise disturbed person to seek *ìwòsàn* (restored health or equilibrium) from a combination of these sources. While outstanding diviners are often sought out by clients from all parts of Yorubaland, most diviners attend to clients from within their communities and their immediate environs. However, quite a number of diviners travel far and wide in search or service of clients or in search of knowledgeable diviners from whom they could learn more. The historical supremacy of *ifá* over *ẹẹ̀rìndínlógún*, its link with the traditional political system, and its overall popularity place *ifá* diviners at a particular advantage in securing clients.

Divination, like other forms of specialized knowledge, is an intellectual property (see Harrison 1992), characterized, as discussed in more detail elsewhere (Akinnaso 1985, 1992), by an 'official' language (see Bourdieu 1991) and a discourse of legitimation (see Lyotard 1984). As indicated above, this discourse is constituted in the Yoruba case by the divination corpus; a specialized rhetorical structure; a special technology of knowledge, the divining paraphernalia; and predictable ritual sequences, through which the corpus is accessed and occult realities revealed. These are the features which constitute the 'anteriority' or the 'archaic "before"' of Yoruba divination (see Feuchtwang 1993 and the application of these concepts to Taiwanese spirit-mediums). The orthodoxy of Yoruba divination is evaluated relative to these features.

Although some degree of collaboration and meaning negotiation between diviner and client are involved during the actual process of divination, the textualized nature of Yoruba divination puts the diviner in perpetual control, because he and not the client, is in command of the sacred text and the technology for accessing it. In a sense, this reliance on a relatively fixed text puts Yoruba divination in the same class as literate religions – Judaism, Christianity and Islam. To be sure, there are interesting differences and similarities of detail between oral and written religious texts. For example, although both types of text are subject to variable interpretations, literate religious texts (such as the Testaments and the Quran) are indisputably graphically fixed, whereas, it can be argued, oral religious texts (such as the *ifá* text) are not indisputably the same as the previous recounting, because they are subject to memory limitations and individual experience. It would appear that what is fixed about oral religious texts is not so much the content as the rhetorical structure, although in *ifá* and *ẹẹ̀rìndínlógún* deliberate efforts are made to replicate both structure and content during training; hence rote-learning features prominently in Yoruba divination pedagogy as in Quranic pedagogy.

Like the Quran, the 'official' or 'authorized' language of Yoruba divination would appear to be preordained, being dictated by the language of its sacred text. However, because it is an oral text, it is rendered in the various dialects of diviners from different parts of Yorubaland. What is 'normalized' or 'standardized' about the language is its rhetorical structure, which all diviners acquire during training. This rhetorical structure is characterized by the use of formulas and themes, semantic and syntactic parallelism, proverbs and tropes of various kinds, etiological explanations, archaic and esoteric lexicon, vocables and a recitational format, including the use of chants and songs (see Bascom 1969, 1980; Abimbola 1976, 1977; Akinnaso 1982, 1985). Provided that this rhetorical structure is preserved along with the main plot and theme of the narratives being recited, a great deal of improvisation occurs during performance, despite the emphasis on exact memorization during training and the diviners' insistence that their text is fixed. In real divination sessions, diviners often exploit such improvisatory possibilities to recontextualize and, sometimes, modify their memorized text, thus accommodating change into an otherwise fixed text.

THE LOCAL AND THE GLOBAL

For present purposes, I use the terms local and global, each in two conjunctive senses: local refers to events and practices originating in, and contained within, a circumscribed, local setting and the ritual discourses available to specialists within the community; global, on the other hand, refers to events and practices, such as an external religion, originating from outside and the ritual discourses of such practices.

Textual incorporation and (re)contextualization are among the processes by which the local and the global are integrated in Yoruba divination. Abimbola (1969: 96) has recorded a classic example of a diviner's creation and incorporation of a text reflecting a contemporary event of global significance, the Islamization of the Old Oyo Empire. This probably happened during the early half of the nineteenth century, when Islam had taken firm roots in many parts of Africa and was just spreading within the Oyo Empire, apparently with the support of the *Aláàfin*, the King of the Oyo kingdom, who himself eventually converted. The diviners did not like what was happening; when the occasion arose, they did not hide their displeasure. The opportunity came when a diviner was divining for the King. He injected the following prologue into one of the *ẹsẹ* he recited:

> *Wútùwútù yáákì,*
> *Wútùwútù yambele;*
> *Ká s'úré pàtàpìrà,*
> *Ká f'ẹwù àlàárì fọn'kun àmódi,*
> *Léèkeléèke eye ìmòle.*

> *Wútùwútù yááki,*
> *Wútùwútù yambele*;
> Running *pàtàpìrà*,
> Using *àlàári* clothing to clean *àmódi*'s nose,
> The egret [is] the Muslim's bird

The opening parallel construction is a series of semantically empty vocables, mimicking Arabic sounds, thus symbolically criticizing Muslim
converts for reciting Quranic texts whose meaning they do not know.
However, beyond the initial play on sounds, the condensed metaphor of
the third and fourth lines mocks Muslims for running (*s'úré* = *sá eré*) to
their place of worship like animals (*pàtàpìrà* imitates the footprints
of animals, particularly cows, as they run in a group) and accuses them
of using *àlàári* (a highly valued type of traditional clothing) to rub (*fon*)
àmódi's nose (*àmódi* is the Yoruba stereotype for someone whose nose
is perpetually filled with filthy mucus, or *ikun*). The historical reference
of this text, particularly the latter metaphor, is captured in Gbadamosi's
(1978: 5) account of the growth of Islam among the Yoruba:

> [Even before 1840], in the capital of the Oyo Empire, Islam was fairly
> well established. It had been introduced by Afaa Yigi, of Arab descent,
> probably during the reign of Alafin Ajagbo. This Arab had stayed in
> the palace, it is said, at the request of the Alafin; and it was around
> him that the nucleus of converts gathered.

It is easy to see that the *àlàári* in the diviner's lines is in fact the King,
who, by providing shelter to the Muslims, allowed himself to be used for
what the diviner considered to be the Muslim's 'dirty' (*ikun*) course.
However, in a witty, diplomatic closure, this serious message is disguised
by the colour metaphor in which the whiteness of the Muslim preacher's
(*ìmòle*) robe is associated with the white colour of the egret (*léèkeléèke*).
But, again, this metaphor hides another serious message: the ominous
status of the egret in Yoruba culture. The appearance of the egret portends
misfortune, especially death; the more of them there are during their
migratory season, the more widespread the misfortune they are believed
to portend. By associating the egret with the Muslims, the diviner was
predicting a future misfortune.

As events unfolded in Old Oyo, misfortune actually struck in the form
of the Afonja revolt against the *Aláàfin*. Afonja formed an alliance with
the Muslims both within the Oyo Empire and the Sokoto Caliphate to
the north, fought the *Aláàfin* and successfully won independence from
him, leading to the establishment of Ilorin. However, as Gbadamosi (1978:
9–10) reports, Afonja's Muslim supporters became ambitious, killed him
and took over power in Ilorin. Since that time, the Muslims have been in
control of power in Ilorin.

What is particularly interesting about the incorporation of this new material into an otherwise fixed text is that the new text takes the place of the formulaic prologue which has hitherto been considered fixed and unchangeable (see Bascom 1980; Akinnaso 1982). However, although the diviner has incorporated material reflecting current events in Yorubaland, he has conformed to the rhetorical structure of the canon. The structural similarities are very apparent between the text above and the following, also recorded by Abimbola (1977: 126), which introduces an established *ęsę* in *Òtúá Méjì* (one of *ifá*'s sixteen major *odù*):

> *Ayóóró ęnu;*
> *Ayòòrò ęnu;*
> *Ębìtì ęnu ò tàsé;*
> *Ęnu ofóró níí pofóró;*
> *Ęnu ofòrò níí pofòrò;*
> *Ęnu fórofòro níí pofòrò.*

The talkative mouth;
The mouth that talks at large;
The trap set by mouth never fails to catch victims.
It is the mouth of the talkative that kills the talkative;
It is the mouth of he who talks at large that kills he who talks at large;
It is talking too much that kills the talkative.

Like the newer text above, this older text begins with a parallel construction, not of vocables but of frozen, esoteric lexicon (*ayóóró* and *ayòòrò*), distinguished by tonal contrasts. These words and another pair, *ofóró* and *ofòrò* in lines four and five, are not established Yoruba words as such; rather, they are part of the sound symbolism and 'tonal plays' characteristic of *ifá* text (see Abimbola 1977). In this context, these 'words' have an onomatopoeic quality in that they describe what the mouth of a talkative person does as it spins out one word after the other. The *ęsę* in which this prologue occurs is itself an allegory on the danger of talking too much. The principal character of the allegory is the squirrel who builds his nest by the roadside. Despite the warning that he should not report everything he sees or knows to passers-by, he told of his wife who had just given birth to two young ones, inviting people to come and see their nest. On hearing this, some passers-by located the nest, took the young squirrels away and later ate them with pounded yam. The *ęsę* ends in a sarcasm that describes the final fate of the young squirrels: *Wón sì bá ọbę lọ* 'And they disappeared with stew.'

I myself witnessed another example of not only the incorporation of a new text but also the restructuring of the divinatory process to suit particular local conditions and clients. Following the failure of the SDP (Social Democratic Party) to win the chairmanship election in Idanre local government in Ondo state in 1991 (partly because of internal divisions within the party and partly because many community leaders, particularly the King and his chiefs, did not like the SDP candidate), and the local knowledge that the NRC (National Republican Convention) candidate who won the election had allegedly tendered a forged tax-clearance certificate (an obligatory prerequisite for successful candidacy) before the NEC (National Electoral Commission), the SDP submitted a petition to the Electoral Tribunal, seeking the nullification of the election. The King and his chiefs summoned several meetings aimed at persuading the SDP to withdraw the case from the Tribunal for at least two reasons. First, the case laid a dangerous precedent as this was the first time that the results of a local election were being contested in court. In particular, the King wanted to avert the animosities that often attended court litigations: according to local folk belief, *Ẹẹ ti kóòtù bò ya s'om'iye*: 'Siblings don't return from the court of law maintaining their previous bond of relationship.' Second, the King and many of his chiefs were anxious to prevent a possible legal victory for the SDP candidate, the expectation of victory being based on several factors – the SDP was in power at the state level; the state chairman was a close friend and supporter of the candidate; the rumours that the NRC candidate submitted false documents had become transmuted into fact in the course of their transmission. The persistence of the SDP in pursuing the case led both parties to adopt whatever means might lead to victory. One of the common means pursued by both parties was divination.

Since I was directly involved in the electoral process and the King's reconciliation meetings, I was particularly anxious to know what outcome divination would foretell. A friend (about 50 years old) and one of the leaders of the SDP in the community took me on a visit to a diviner near his house. He had earlier consulted this diviner on several occasions, before and after the elections. However, this visit was the first attempt to consult the diviner specifically on the possible outcome of the court case.

In preparing for the visit, we had purchased two bottles of Schiedam's Aromatic Schnapps and a huge keg of palmwine which were presented to the diviner by my friend. The visit was brief and to the point. The consultation, held in Idanre dialect of Yoruba, began thus:

> Client *(my friend)*:   Father of divination, I greet you. You will say that I have come again. You must be current about our present affairs. You said the election would be tough and, truly, it was. I have come to find out how this would turn out.
> Diviner *(shaking his head)*:   I tried my best to invoke *ifá* on that occasion, I really did. It's all right, I got your message. I will relay it to *ifá*. Will you wait, or will you come back, for the reply?

My friend and I consulted briefly. I wanted us to wait and witness the whole process; but my friend, who knew and trusted his diviner, advised otherwise. We subsequently left, agreeing to reconvene the following morning.

As soon as we showed up the following morning, the diviner immediately led us to his shrine. It was a dark, inner room in the house, with light barely coming in through a small, half-open window. After invoking *ifá*, by chanting the appropriate verses, he spent the next half-hour or so reporting his findings, gliding from one mode or genre to another. Three aspects of this report are of relevance here.

First, the diviner told us that the matter was difficult; there was no clear answer. However, there was no straightforward declaration to this effect. Rather, the diviner used a series of metaphors, anecdotes and stories to illustrate this point. The road, he said, had split into two; it was not clear which one to take. He then told the story of a man who once approached Orunmila (the archetypal diviner) and requested Orunmila to give him an axe with which to cultivate land (in narrating this story, the diviner chanted, sang and simply talked; what I provide here is a mere paraphrase of the main story). Orunmila told the man that there was only one axe and that another person had come to request it. If the first person performed the appropriate sacrifice, he might have the axe. Then the man asked if he too should go and perform a sacrifice but Orunmila would not tell him which sacrifice to perform. Three markets (i.e. three market-cycles of five days each) passed and the first man did not show up. Then the second man returned and asked which sacrifice to make so he could have the axe. Then Orunmila told him to look for the first man and ask him which sacrifice to perform. Next the first man arrived; he had not performed the sacrifice and Orunmila would not give him the axe. He was told the axe would be given to another person if the appropriate sacrifice was not performed. At this juncture the axe said, 'I don't want to leave Orunmila's house; and, if at all I do, I will only follow *Ògún* (the God of Iron).'

Another aspect of the diviner's report was a long socio-historical commentary about events in Idanreland and beyond in the last fifty years or so. In the course of this commentary, the diviner mentioned Awolowo and Akintola (past Yoruba political leaders in opposing camps); *òmìnira* (independence); *òṣèlú* (the local word for politician); *Demo* (nickname for the NNDP [Nigerian National Democratic Party]), Akintola's political party, whose activities led to the election crisis in western Nigeria which precipitated the first military takeover in 1966; *jóléjólé* (a reference to the burning down of the houses of prominent members of Akintola's party in Idanre during the crisis); *ìjoba Olóógun* (military government); etc. He also mentioned the protracted dispute between Idanre and Akure over territorial boundaries. The overall theme of the socio-historical commentary was crisis, past or imminent.

Finally, the diviner philosophized extensively on the role of *ìwé* (book; i.e. literacy) in Idanre affairs. Before the era of *alákòwé* (the literate ones) and *òṣèlú* (politicians), he argued, disputes were settled by the King. *Ìgbàgbó* (Christianity) brought *ìwé*, he added, while the *ajélè* (local term for the Divisional Officer during the colonial period) brought *olóòpá* (police) and *kóòtù* (court) to us at Oke-Idanre. Since that time, it has been one crisis after another.

My friend finally interrupted, asking the diviner what he thought we should do. His response was spontaneous – he would have to consult *ifá* again. At this juncture, the objects of the *ibò* were presented to my friend and several questions were raised, to which answers were provided in binary alternatives as in Mambila divination (Zeitlyn 1990). Should any sacrifice be offered to avert failure? What type of sacrifice? To whom should the sacrifice be offered? Will the present court case lead to a serious crisis? If so, what can be done to avert it, etc.? Each question was mediated by further divination, involving the recitation of appropriate narratives and the diviner's own reflections. This phase of the divination lasted over two hours, the most time being spent on the question of whether or not the court case would lead to a crisis. *Ifá* predicted a serious crisis and the diviner was trying to decipher from the verses which sacrifice to offer, not necessarily to prevent the crisis (it appeared inevitable) but to guarantee our personal safety.

This consultation clearly involved a diviner and a customary client. This patron-client relationship was evident from the start. Apart from explicit linguistic references, such as 'I have come again,' the cryptic way in which my friend indicated to the diviner that he had come for consultation easily betrays some shared knowledge between him and the diviner. In fact, the court case that prompted the consultation was not directly mentioned. Rather, it was referred to as 'this', which only makes sense with reference to the election in the preceding line over which the diviner was consulted and whose result was unfavorable, as predicted. Of course, clients are not obliged to state the specific problem which they want diviners to solve. The fact that my friend gave some indication at all further indicates the degree of familiarity and mutual trust between him and the diviner. Furthermore, divination is typically performed in the client's presence. However, in this case the major part of the consultation was done by the diviner alone, although with our consent. My friend confirmed that he had even written to the diviner before (from his farming outpost in a remote village), requesting him to divine on certain specific problems. However, the diviner's response to such written requests was never another letter. If divination indicated urgent action, the diviner would send someone to him.

What is more interesting about this consultation is the diviner's integration of ritual, historical, social and political knowledge in analysing the problem at hand. This highlights a perspective of divination best articulated by Peek (1991b: 194–5):

> As a means of acquiring normally inaccessible information, divination utilizes a non-normal mode of cognition which is then synthesized by

the diviner and the client(s) with everyday knowledge in order to allow the client(s) to make plans of action. ...

Divination never results in a simple restatement of tradition to be followed blindly. It is a dynamic reassessment of customs and values in the face of an ever-changing world. . . . [Divination provides] the context in which the old and the new, secular and sacred, real and ideal may be contrasted and resolved. It is through divination that a harmonious balance can be maintained in which a culture's most cherished values are adapted to the real world of continual flux.

However, it is not the case, as Peek (*ibid*.: 195) claims, that 'diviners can only report what they are told'. They do much more than that; they also interpret, and comment on, what they are told. The diviner in this case explained, when I visited him later, that divination is like reading a book written by another person. Each reader reads it his/her own way. This is an unusual acknowledgement of creativity by a practising diviner. But it is true that diviners are creative. Perhaps the most outstanding instance of this diviner's creativity was his injection of the following lines into an *ẹsẹ* he recited during the *ìbò* phase of the divination:

> *Ol'ífá d'ífá;*
> *Ol'ìgbàgbọ́ ka Bíbééli;*
> *Ìmọle ka Kùránù.*
> *Alákọwé k'ọwé;*
> *Alàghòrò í daa m'áso 'fun kò un,*
> *D'oun laa kọ́n 'Rósùn.*

> The diviner divines;
> The Christian consults the Bible
> The Muslim, the Quran.
> The literate writes;
> And the *àghòrò* priest requests white clothing,
> So he may be equipped to visit [worship] *Orósùn*.

These lines, marked by a series of grammatical parallelism, are replete with comparisons and historical allusions. The alternative approaches to problem-solving employed by traditional ritual specialists, *ol'ífá* (diviners) and *al'àghòrò* (*àghòrò* priests), are compared to those of *ol'ígbàgbọ́* (Christians), *ìmọle* (Muslims) and *alákọwé* (the literate ones). By referring to these alternative approaches, the diviner was drawing our attention to the fact that our 'opponent' (the other party to the court case) was seeking help from some of these quarters. More importantly, however, these references reflect the diviner's sensitivity to alternative paradigms in competition with his own.

To the best of my knowledge, no *ifá* verse contains these lines (although no diviner has a finite knowledge of the verses and no researcher can claim to have a finite record of such verses). As a native of Idanre and an active participant in the community's social, educational and political development for several years, it was easy for me to locate the source of the diviner's new lines in the community's past and present experiences. Moreover, these lines fit perfectly into Idanre people's vibrant oral culture, particularly the rich repertoire of puns, jokes, word-plays, language games, proverbs and 'invented' stories, many of which often contain critical commentaries on social, economic and political events. It may well be that the huge *ifá* corpus became larger and larger as it incorporated more and more stories, lines and observations from secular experience.

By the same token, aspects of the divination corpus have diffused into more mundane oral poetries and even ordinary conversational discourse. For example, the popular *ifá* counting mnemonics are also found, in various forms, in other genres, including *ìjálá* poetry, songs, children's language games and everyday conversation (see Fagborun 1990). Similarly, many proverbs and proverbial statements contained in the divination corpus are incorporated or adapted into other genres, including everyday language. Furthermore, some of the narratives, admonitions and etiological explanations contained in the divination corpus (see especially Bascom 1969, 1980) overlap with those commonly shared in folktales and sometimes transmitted directly to children by their parents. For example, the squirrel fable cited above provides the basis for the admonitory statement, *Má s'ẹnu fórofòro* (Don't run your mouth *fórofòro*), or 'Don't be talkative', that parents often address to their children. *Oríkì* (appelations, attributions, praise-songs), excellently analysed by Karin Barber (1991), also abound in the divination corpus, where they are applied to both human and non-human characters. The recitational format of divinatory speech and the attributive content of *oríkì* provide the basic framework for a more recent genre, *ewì* chants, performed on social occasions.

Whatever the direction of diffusion, the Yoruba people, particularly diviners, want to believe that the divinatory text provides the template for other genres of Yoruba discourse. This is not at all surprising, since the divinatory text is said to be a repository of Yoruba knowledge (see especially Abimbola 1976, 1977; Bascom 1969, 1980). However, it is precisely this fact which makes it possible for the text to admit new data. For how else could growth in Yoruba knowledge be acknowledged, if it is not incorporated into the divinatory text in some way?

DISCUSSION AND CONCLUSION

There are three striking similarities between the Oyo diviner's nineteenth-century text and the Idanre diviner's 1992 text. First, both of them make explicit references to at least one religion of conversion, Islam or Christianity, providing critical comments upon such religion. There has never been a peaceful rapprochement between divination and the literate religions in Yorubaland, nor has one religion been able to eclipse or assimilate the other. Indeed, Yoruba diviners have always been wary, sometimes scornful, of alternative systems of knowledge, particularly alternative religious systems. In Idanre, the opposition of diviners and other cultic priests to Christianity stretched over thirty years despite the colonial administration's establishment of a local police post in 1910 and a Native Court in 1915, precisely to suppress such opposition. It is not surprising, therefore, that in another part of Yorubaland 'the intertwined conversion histories of [two diviners,] Akibode and Masolowo, [were] drawn out over nearly a decade' (Peel 1990: 352). Surely, like Akibode and Masolowo, some Idanre diviners eventually 'converted' to Christianity (one of the diviners who divined for me when I was young and continued to divine until he died, was even baptized as Stephen, phonologically adapted to *Títíbìnì* in Idanre dialect). For them, however, 'conversion' only provided a medium for appropriation, a way to see how the Christian 'god' was worshipped and to take from Christianity whatever was considered useful to the diviner and his system of knowledge. In no time, parallels were being noted between Biblical and *ifá* texts (see, especially, Lijadu 1908), while arguments were also being raised about *ifá*'s anticipation of Christianity, or at least of Christian themes (Peel 1990: 365). This may well explain why most of the 'converted' diviners in Idanre never surrendered their divining paraphernalia and continued to consult *ifá* between church services. The point here is that Islam and Christianity did not spread into a sort of vacuum in Yorubaland but into a complicated context which provided counter-understandings. Within such a context, divination could be seen as setting limits to these external religions, recontextualizing them and providing critical comments upon them.

Another shared feature between the texts is thematic – they all developed out of an underlying concern about imminent danger, thus reinforcing *ifá*'s prophetic capacity to anticipate the future. In both cases, the diviner's apprehensions were confirmed by events. In Idanre, even before the Electoral Tribunal gave its ruling, the local government buildings were burned down, apparently in an attempt to destroy certain documents which were to be tendered before the Tribunal. Accusations and counter-accusations ensued between the opposing political parties, leading to antagonism between friends and relatives.

The third striking similarity between the *ifá* texts is the degree to which they are adapted to the established rhetorical structure of the divinatory text. In a sense, this stylistic adaptation is symbolic of the process by which themes, ideas and events are adapted into *ifá* texts and how the texts are in turn recontextualized to suit particular circumstances.

The foregoing analysis opens up new perspectives on issues of knowledge, power and authority on the one hand, and the theoretical problem of boundary delineation on the other. In particular, the findings indicate that more is known about a diviner's knowledge and powers when we move beyond his strictly ritual functions and mystical powers to how he incorporates contemporary concerns with dynamic process and dialogue in performing these functions. A focus on the processes of textual incorporation and thematic adaptation reveals an established system of hybridity, even in areas of specialized knowledge, such as divination. While the progression from knowledge through power to authority seems to fit perfectly well with Western notions of linearity, the processes by which religious knowledge becomes authority, by first being converted to power, in non-Western traditions remain a vexing problem for anthropologists. The canonical approach is to explain religious authority in terms of political authority (see, for example, Ahern 1981). Stephan Feuchtwang has recently tackled this problem and concluded that 'the performance of religious rituals confers and represents authority in their own right' (1993: 35). Underlying Feuchtwang's conclusion are the ideas that 'religious rituals are always anachronistic; whatever their social function, the anachronism is precisely what provides their symbolic power' (*ibid.*: 40) and, therefore, that 'the authority of religious representation rests in its rituals and myths of anteriority' (*ibid.*: 48). While this is generally true, it is only part of the story.

The above analysis shows that ritual specialists also derive symbolic power from the *perceived* relevance and contextuality of the rituals they perform. Indeed, not only ritual specialists but also gods are assessed on the basis of relevance and contextuality (see Barber's [1981] account of how Yoruba *òrìsà* worshippers make or unmake the *òrìsà* on this basis). In this perspective, knowledge of the mechanical process of divination or even of the divinatory text (the archaic before) does not make a diviner. A true diviner is one who has the ability, the creative potentials, to interpret misfortune or otherwise divine reality for others (see Middleton 1960; Whyte 1991). Whyte (1991: 170–1) specifically summarizes the importance of Nyole divination in terms of the diviner's creativity and the relevance of his predictions:

> In a cultural system where people's views of their society and their place within it are so closely tied to the interpretation of misfortune, divination plays a key role in formulating and reformulating the understanding that is the basis for social action. . . . What is more striking about Nyole divination is its vitality and flexibility as a mechanism for creating privileged definitions of persons and society.

The diviner's exegetical ability and the relevance of his interpretations and predictions are thus critical to a definition of his authority. What this implies is that the diviner's authority is not necessarily *given*, prior to the divination session; rather, it is *created* in the process of divination. This is perhaps why Bourdieu views the symbolic efficacy of religious language as rooted not so much in anteriorities but in social relations involving the complicity of those who are subjected to such language:

The symbolic efficacy of words is exercised only in so far as the person subjected to it recognizes the person who exercises it as authorized to do so, or, what amounts to the same thing, only in so far as he fails to realize that, in submitting to it, he himself has contributed, through his recognition, to its establishment.

(1991: 116)

Feuchtwang's incomplete assessment of religious authority may have resulted from undue reliance on *ideology* (texts, fixed structures, precedents and stories of cultic foundations). The above analysis shows that a focus on ideology must be integrated with an analysis of *practice* (including process and dialogue) in order fully to understand the nature and perception of religious authority. In addition, the social persona and creative potentials of ritual specialists must be acknowledged and admitted as data. Rasmussen (1992) has successfully demonstrated how such an integrated analysis revealed the true nature of Tuareg blacksmiths and marabouts, two types of ritual specialists whose roles are shown to be partly distinctive, partly complementary and partly overlapping, rather than polar opposites as previously conceived.

This analysis also reveals that typologies, such as those mentioned at the beginning of this chapter, tend to hinder not only the study of the creative processes by which boundaries are adjusted or dissolved, but also the dynamics of incremental growth in knowledge. Previous studies of Yoruba divination have failed to capture such dynamic processes, because they have focused either on the recording of specially elicited texts or on the reconstruction of historical documents, such as missionaries' diaries, which were in themselves already embedded in the writers' interpretive paradigms. (Peel [1990] successfully gets around these anterior interpretive constraints by recontextualizing missionary narratives within the general context of Yoruba religion and previous studies of *ifá* divination.) However, the diviner's creative potentials are released in actual divination sessions, particularly in dealing with established customers for whom they do not need to 'stage' a special performance. Such creativity, as Parkin (1991) has so well argued, is a necessary precondition for the dissolution of the various boundaries created by our typologies.

The creativity of ritual specialists is, however, subject to cultural and structural constraints (*ibid.*). I have demonstrated that, in the Yoruba case, the diviner's creativity is constrained by a variety of cultural and structural constraints, including the canonical text, its authorized language and rhetorical structure, the institutional mechanisms governing the acquisition of divinatory knowledge, and the professional sanctions governing divinatory practice. But it is precisely these constraints that the diviner creatively manipulates in order to achieve some measure of contextuality and Sperberian relevance which, in turn, reinforces the diviner's authority.

In the process, cultural certainties are reaffirmed, recontextualized and modified at the same time.

REFERENCES

Abbink, J. (1993) 'Reading the entrails: analysis of an African divination discourse', *Man* (n.s.) 28: 705–26.

Abimbola, W. (1969) *Ìjìnlè Ohun Enu Ifá: Apá Kejì*, Glasgow: Collins.

—— (1976) *IFÁ: An Exposition of Ifa Literary Corpus*, Ibadan: Oxford University Press.

—— (1977) *Ifá Divination Poetry*, New York: NOK Publishers.

Ahern, E.M. (1981) *Chinese Ritual and Politics*, Cambridge: Cambridge University Press.

Akinnaso, F.N. (1980) 'The sociolinguistic basis of Yoruba personal names', *Anthropological Linguistics* 22: 275–304.

—— (1982) 'The literate writes and the nonliterate chants: written language and ritual communication in sociolinguistic perspective', pp. 7–36, in W. Frawley (ed.) *Linguistics and Literacy*, New York: Plenum Press.

—— (1985) 'On the similarities between spoken and written language', *Language and Speech* 28: 323–59.

—— (1992) 'Schooling, language and knowledge in literate and nonliterate societies', *Comparative Studies in Society and History* 34: 68–109.

Barber, K. (1981) 'How man makes god in West Africa', *Africa* 51: 724–45.

—— (1991) *I Could Speak until Tomorrow: Oriki, Women and the Past in a Yoruba Town*, Edinburgh: Edinburgh University Press.

—— and Waterman, C. (1993) 'Traversing the global and local: *Fuji* and praise poetry in contemporary Yorùbá popular culture', paper presented at the IV ASA Decennial Conference, Oxford.

Barth, F. (1990) 'The guru and the conjurer: transactions in knowledge and the shaping of culture in Southeast Asia and Melanesia', *Man* (n.s.) 25: 640–53.

Bascom, W. (1952) 'Two forms of Afro-Cuban divination', pp. 169–79, in S. Tax (ed.) *Acculturation in the Americas*, vol. II, Chicago: University of Chicago Press.

—— (1969) *Ifa Divination: Communication between Gods and Men in West Africa*, Bloomington, IN: Indiana University Press.

—— (1980) *Sixteen Cowries: Yoruba Divination from Africa to the New World*, Bloomington, IN: Indiana University Press.

Bloch, M. (1986) *From Blessing to Violence: History and Ideology in the Circumcision Ritual of the Merina of Madagascar*, Cambridge: Cambridge University Press.

Boas, F. (1955) [1928] *Primitive Art*, New York: Dover.

Bourdieu, P. (1977) 'The economics of linguistic exchanges', *Social Science Information* 16: 645–68.

—— (1991) *Language and Symbolic Power*, Cambridge: Polity Press.

Bryant, J.M. (1986) 'Intellectuals and religion in Ancient Greece: notes on a Weberian theme', *British Journal of Sociology* XXXVII: 269–96.

Durkheim, E. and Mauss, M. (1967) [1903] *Primitive Classification*, Chicago: University of Chicago Press.

Fagborun, J.G. (1990) 'Yoruba counting verses: a linguistic approach to oral tradition', *African Languages and Cultures* 3: 167–80.

Feuchtwang, S. (1993) 'Historical metaphor: a study of religious representation and the recognition of authority', *Man* (n.s.) 28: 35–49.

Gajek, E. (1990) 'Christmas under the Third Reich', *Anthropology Today* 6: 3–9.

Gbadamosi, T.G.O. (1978) *The Growth of Islam among the Yoruba 1841–1908*, Atlantic Highlands, NJ: Humanities Press.

Hannerz, U. (1987) 'The world in creolisation', *Africa* 57: 546–59.

Harrison, S. (1992) 'Ritual as intellectual property', *Man* (n.s.) 27: 225–44.

Hooker, J.T. (1976) *Mycenaean Greece*, London: Routledge and Kegan Paul.

Hoskins, J. (1993) 'Violence, sacrifice and divination: giving and taking life in eastern Indonesia', *American Ethnologist* 20: 159–78.

Leach, E.R. (1968) 'Ritual', pp. 520–6, in L. Sills (ed.) *International Encyclopedia of the Social Sciences*, New York: Macmillan.

Lijadu, E.M. (1972) [1908] *Orunmila*, Ado Ekiti: Omolayo Standard Press.

Loewe, M. and Blacker, C. (eds) (1981) *Divination and Oracles*, London: George Allen & Unwin.

Lyotard, J.-F. (1984) [1979] *The Postmodern Condition: A Report on Knowledge*, trans. G. Bennington and B. Massumi, Manchester: Manchester University Press.

Middleton, J. (1960) *Lugbara Religion: Ritual and Authority among an East African People*, London: Oxford University Press.

Murphy, W.P. (1980) 'Secret knowledge as property and power in Kpelle society: elders vs. youth', *Africa* 50: 193–207.

Parkin, D. (1991) 'Simultaneity and sequencing in the oracular speech of Kenyan diviners', pp. 173–89, in P.M. Peek (ed.) *African Divination Systems: Ways of Knowing*, Bloomington, IN: Indiana University Press.

Peek, P.M. (ed.) (1991a) *African Divination Systems: Ways of Knowing*, Bloomington, IN: Indiana University Press.

—— (1991b) 'African divination systems: non-normal modes of cognition', pp. 193–221, in P.M. Peek (ed.) *African Divination Systems: Ways of Knowing*, Bloomington, IN: Indiana University Press.

Peel, J.D.Y. (1990) 'The pastor and the *babalawo*: the interaction of religions in nineteenth-century Yorubaland', *Africa* 60: 338–69.

Radcliffe-Brown, A.R. (1952) *Structure and Function in Primitive Society*, London: Cohen and West.

Rasmussen, S.J. (1992) 'Ritual specialists, ambiguity and power in Tuareg society', *Man* (n.s.) 27: 105–28.

Robertson-Smith, W. (1889) *Lectures on the Religion of the Semites*, Edinburgh: Black.

Sperber, D. and Wilson, D. (1986) *Relevance: Communication and Cognition*, Oxford: Blackwell.

Turner, V.W. (1974) *Revelation and Divination in the Ndembu Ritual*, Ithaca, NY: Cornell University Press.

Werbner, R.P. (1989) *Ritual Passage, Sacred Journey: The Process and Organization of Religious Movement*, Manchester/Washington, DC: Manchester University Press/Smithsonian Institution.

Whyte, S.R. (1991) 'Knowledge and power in Nyole divination', pp. 153–72, in P.M. Peek (ed.) *African Divination Systems: Ways of Knowing*, Bloomington, IN: Indiana University Press.

Zeitlyn, D. (1990) 'Professor Garfinkel visits the soothsayers: ethnomethodology and Mambila divination', *Man* (n.s.) 25: 654–6

11 Choking on the Quran

And other consuming parables from the western Indian Ocean front

Michael Lambek

A recent article on postmodern identity begins this way:

> According to anthropological folklore, in traditional societies, one's identity was fixed, solid and stable. Identity was a function of prede-fined social roles and a traditional system of myths which provided orientation and religious sanctions to one's place in the world, while rigorously circumscribing the realm of thought and behavior. One was born and died a member of one's clan, a member of a fixed kinship system and a member of one's tribe or group with one's life trajectory fixed in advance. In pre-modern societies, identity was unproblematical and not subject to reflection or discussion. Individuals did not undergo identity crises, or radically modify their identity. One was a hunter and a member of the tribe and that was that.
>
> (Kellner 1992: 141).

Leaving aside the question of whether by 'anthropological folklore' Kellner means to suggest that this is what anthropologists think or merely that this is what others take anthropologists to think, and leaving aside the clever way in which by invoking the word 'folklore' Kellner is able ironically to distance himself from the stereotype he proceeds to construct; leaving aside too that I am beginning my argument by means of a straw man, it is troubling that such a global picture of anthropology's 'other' should be so easily acknowledged today, especially one that is implicitly sexist and that lumps together all 'pre-modern' societies as a single type, epitomized here in the figure of the hunter and his [*sic*] tribe. In the light of this, at least one course for anthropology remains clear. We must continue to deconstruct this global prototypical 'other', to document and analyse the differences between other social fields[1] and within them – to speak, as it were, for difference. What makes this path difficult is that we must describe difference in a manner that neither idealizes nor essen-tializes it, that does not simply legitimate the understanding of difference with which we start.

In much contemporary thinking local is to global as pre-modern is to (post)modern, as singularity is to plurality, or unity is to diversity. Hence the assumption, evident in Kellner, that relative to ourselves, the members of 'pre-modern' societies enjoyed the privilege of full local certainty. My anecdotes from the western Indian Ocean challenge this. In problematizing the notion of the 'local' my argument takes two tacks. I question both the quality of the certainties found at the centres of the local and the quality of boundedness found at the margins. The answers to these questions turn out to be two sides of the same coin.

THE OVERLAY OF CERTAINTIES: HISTORICAL CONTINGENCY AND INCOMMENSURABILITY

It is often said that the stable model functionalism portrayed was but a reflection of the enforced stability of colonial imposition. It might be added that the certainty of functionalist arguments, and the certainty of the 'natives' as portrayed by the functionalists, were but refractions of the certainty of the colonizing mission itself and of science in the first half of the twentieth century. Now that Westerners have either lost that sense of certainty (if indeed we ever had it) about our mode of thought, about our identity and about the direction of our society, or have given in to one of a variety of fundamentalisms (which, by their very shrillness, betray the underlying anxiety they are designed to replace), it certainly behoves us to problematize the issue as well for those societies and times we like to set up in contrast to ourselves.

Without wishing to commit the opposite fallacy to Kellner's, namely constructing others entirely in our own image, we must nevertheless proceed to challenge the 'folklore' that paints the identities of others in ways that spark no recognition, save one of longing, in our own experience. Instead of essentializing the assumed certainty of other societies, we must recognize its precariousness. We must investigate how knowledge was and is organized; how and under what conditions certainty was and is collectively produced and challenged; what uncertainty prevailed and how this was concealed and mystified, or enjoyed; how identities were sustained but also negotiated, transcended and made the subject of play. At the least, we must distinguish between the certainty that is raised as an explicit credo or moral cry and the implicit certainty, the matter-of-factness that, in Bourdieu's famous words, 'goes without saying because it comes without saying' (1977: 167). It is certainty in the former, oppositional sense that concerns James (in the Introduction to this volume) in her reference to exclusive truth-claims. It is certainty in the second, implicit, uncontested, taken-for-granted sense that Kellner conjures up. However, a portrait of Kellner's sort does not really distinguish between the certainty of authoritative discourse ('reciting by heart') that is imposed from without, and the certainty of internally persuasive discourse ('retelling in one's own words') that is assimilated by the individual and expressed from within (Bakhtin 1981: 341ff., 424). In appearing to posit a unity between them, it begs the questions that must be at issue in any social field.[2] Hence the static, two-dimensional portrait of identity.

The vehicles, idioms and ideologies of certainty situated in any particular social context have to be analysed historically rather than simply classified.[3] Even when we conduct a synchronic analysis we have to recognize that the repertoire of knowledge available at any given time has its origins in diverse periods. The growth of knowledge is never simply cumulative or unilinear, with newer ideas and idioms replacing the old. Instead, there are a series of partial displacements, accommodations and contestations such that the whole is not a consistent, rational system (James 1988; Lambek 1993a).[4]

This point may be rephrased in the idiom of global and local. Many of the social fields in which anthropologists study have been located within the spheres of the 'great' (i.e. obviously translocal) religions, or of dynastic states or empires prior to Euro-American colonialism. In these contexts, relations of local to global are far more complex than a simple opposition precisely because they are of long standing. Similarly, Ranger (1993) has made a strong case for the complexity of local–global relations in the pre-colonial religions of Southern Africa. The various phases of such relations do not simply succeed but overlay each other in complex ways. In other words, while globalism may be a recent intellectual discovery or posture, a newly 'imagined community' (Anderson 1991), as a process or series of processes it is of long duration. Hence any local entity we study is likely to include incommensurable components derived from sources of varying historical and geographical distance.

BOUNDARIES: POSSESSIVE INDIVIDUALISM VERSUS OBJECT RELATIONS

Collective identity in the western Indian Ocean has not corresponded to the reified and exclusionary views of culture so widely appropriated today to articulate, legitimate and control identity, as one of so many discrete and equivalent units in the HRAF (Human Relations Area Files) or the United Nations. The example will help us to denaturalize this view of culture or nation that Handler (1988) has so compellingly analysed as a form of 'possessive individualism'. Indeed, I will venture to juxtapose to this a construction of boundaries that is more 'object-relational'.

A word of caution is necessary here. The point is not to portray social phenomena in psychological terms and certainly not in developmental ones (which, to be sure, is the primary emphasis of object relations theory).[5] Rather, in any social locus there is an interplay between the individual and the collective, such that metaphors drawn from each realm of experience are used to articulate the other (see Douglas 1966). This has the self-affirming, legitimating and naturalizing force that Sahlins (1976) has described for the relations between nature and culture in Western discourse. We project our social categories onto nature and then use nature to justify our social categories. So, too, in the realm of identity; we project our categories and impose our mode of relating onto the individual and then use him or her[6] to model and justify our social categories and collective relationships. This process, largely mystified to its agents, is one of the primary grounds for certainty at both the implicit, hegemonic and explicit, ideological levels. If collective identities and truths are legitimated in this manner, then we need both to reveal the particular metaphors, as Handler has done with nationalism, and to explore alternative models of the individual, whether drawn from foreign ethno-psychologies and practices or from the debates within the broad domain of psychoanalytic theorizing.[7]

According to Handler, 'Nationalism is an ideology about individuated being. It is an ideology concerned with boundedness, continuity and homogeneity encompassing diversity' (1988: 6). In this ideology:

> Individuals demonstrate their being, their individuality, through choice; choice is the creative manifestation of self, the imposition of self onto the external world. Property is what results from choices – products that exist in the external world yet remain linked through proprietorship to the self that created them. Thus the nation and its members 'have' a culture, the existence of which both follows from and proves the existence of the nation itself.
>
> (*ibid.*: 51)[8]

This model of possessive individualism bears not a little similarity to Freudian drive theory. While the latter is still highly salient in popular culture, it has largely been replaced in psychoanalytic theory (Mitchell 1988). In an object-relational view of identity it is the internalizing of others – other people – that takes precedence over the building of rigid boundaries around an individuated self.[9] Identity formation flows in both directions. The flux of projections and introjections ensures that some aspects of the developing self are likely to have originally been perceived or experienced as aspects of the primary other or others, and aspects of the other may have originally been felt as aspects of the self. On a psychological level, then, even the apparent boundaries of the individual do not separate him or her in any simple way from the rest of the world. Identity is defined not in terms of distinct or exclusive features – (cultural) property – but in terms of relative connection to the outside. An object-relational identity emphasizes sharing over difference, connection over separation, communion over boundaries and dependency over self-sufficiency (Benjamin 1988: 76). 'Insistent separateness' is viewed as a defence rather than a fact of nature (Chodorow 1989: 148–9). I argue that this model makes better sense of the western Indian Ocean material than does that of possessive individualism.

In sum, with our newly acute senses of history and of social differentiation and now of ostensibly global processes to temper our own certain knowledge that practice is culturally mediated, we have come (again) to recognize that culture cannot be viewed as a series of discrete, bounded, internally unified and consistent wholes for which systems and structures provide appropriate metaphors. Hence the notion of the 'local' must be problematized for all periods and all kinds of social fields. Similarly with 'certainty'. Indeed, a scrupulous attention to the vernacular, to borrow James and Johnson's (1988) suggestive term, becomes ever more critical in the face of globalisms, whether of the rhetorical or the material, the figurative or the literal varieties, if only to help ensure they do not become self-fulfilling.

BODIES AND TEXTS: THE CONFRONTATION OF ALTERNATE CERTAINTIES

I turn now to the social field that I know best, villages of Muslim Kibushy (northern Malagasy) speakers in the French-controlled island of Mayotte within the otherwise independent Comoro archipelago of the western Indian Ocean during the period 1975–92. Note already the multidimensional specification of 'local' context. Mayotte is not the sort of society Kellner had in mind; it is in part the product of mercantile relations, regional power struggles, colonialism, a marginal and waning plantation economy and so on. But then the point is, as Wolf (1982) and others have established, that such influences have shaped, to a degree, even the populations that appeared, on first ethnographic gaze, isolated or autonomous. It is difficult to imagine any society that is simply traditional, simply local. Because I cannot hope to examine all relations of context systematically within a single chapter, I take as my departure a series of small fieldwork incidents. All three contain an alimentary idiom that may serve as a key to boundary issues (Douglas 1966) as well as a ground for legitimating certainty (Lambek 1992). Hence another theme of the chapter lies in the distinction between objectified and embodied practices in localizing knowledge.

My first anecdote is offered to show that certainty itself is not unproblematic and may be multiple rather than unitary. Malagasy and Muslim ideas and practices have been jostling each other within the region for centuries. The acknowledgement of each by the other and the problematic relationship between them are continuously reproduced in minute practices such as the following (as extracted and revised from my fieldnotes):

August 5, 1985, 4 am. In the midst of a large spirit possession (*trumba*) ceremony a young woman named Athimary suddenly attracted a lot of attention when the spirit that was then possessing her began gagging and choking uncontrollably. I was worried that something was seriously wrong but people explained the problem. Athimary had been sick for a long time. They had applied spirit medicine but the spirit would never speak when it rose, so Athimary's mother decided to change the direction of the treatment and had an amulet made for her daughter and gave her many doses of *singa* medicine (liquid Quranic verses). This was now bothering her; it might be good medicine for a human being but it made the *trumba* [Malagasy spirit] very angry. Although the spirit had not yet spoken, the adepts could see what the trouble was. Indeed, the experience of having something stuck in the throat could not have been rendered more vividly.

Athimary's predicament was not original.[10] Like virtually everyone in Mayotte, she is a good Muslim; like many, she is on the road to becoming a spirit-medium. In order to avert the sort of trauma that befell Athimary, and so as not to expose their bodies to contestations between the various forms of knowledge and power, people remove their amulets before setting out to attend a spirit ceremony. At the same time, spirit-curers often prescribe amulets for their clients. What then is the nature of the opposition?

I want to make several brief points. First, what is local here is the conjunction of two traditions, each of which is widespread in the region and each of which spreads in its own particular way. Before the imposition of colonialism there was a flourishing regional network embedded in a much more extensive mercantile system. Mayotte was a small link in this network that joined the East African coast to Madagascar. Islam reached Mayotte as early as the 1400s.[11] Islam is a 'great transcontinental sodality' linked through a common sacred language (Anderson 1991: 36); it has neither a single centre nor specific boundaries. As Goody asks, 'In Islamic ... societies, what is the "whole?" ' (1968: 9). Islam is a text-based religion; its practice is 'textually mediated' and hence specfically extra-local in scope. It brings with it literacy, albeit of a restricted sort; and it also brought to Mayotte (if indeed it did not follow) a compendium of materials written in Arabic but not part of Islam *per se* (Lewis 1986). These materials include elements of astrology that can be traced back to Chaldean times (some of which are also found in the West); so-called 'magical' practices reputed to have elements of ancient Egyptian and Hebrew derivation (Blanchy and Said 1990); and humoral medicine which, as the result of both Islamic and Iberian mercantile activity and colonialism, has been a truly global, albeit pre-modern, phenomenon. The spread of these cultural features in earlier centuries is something that is too easily overlooked; it is simply ethnocentric and historically naive (chronocentric?) to assume that translocal phenomena only become significant in the contemporary period.[12]

The spread of Islam may be counterposed to practices stemming from the opposite direction, from the Sakalava polities of Madagascar. *Trumba* spirit possession is what remains in Mayotte of the Sakalava cult of the royal ancestors; it is centred on royal tombs in Madagascar. Living royalty and the explicit political ideas and forces of which the spirits continue to be a manifestation in Madagascar have disappeared from Mayotte but the otherness of possession, its explicit location outside the bounds of Islam, remains. Possession has provided a position from which local people have been able to interpret and contextualize Islam. In a sense, they have been fortunate to partake of two originally independent and hegemonic forms of knowledge and power, each with its own grounds of certainty and each able to put the other slightly off balance.[13] In each case, Islam and possession, people in Mayotte were able to imagine others at great distance from themselves enacting similar performances (see Anderson 1991).

Second, what the *trumba* refused to swallow is a text; but the act of choking, like its message, is not textually mediated. The truth of the Quran is indubitable and so is the presence of spirits. Both are rendered certain through local performance, but the factors conducive to certainty have a different weight in each case. Both the objectified written word and embodied acts can be powerful forms of legitimacy, means of ensuring certainty, but they operate according to different principles and exhibit different kinds of strains. The sacred text of the Quran is an 'authoritative discourse' that is originally imposed from without (Bakhtin 1981: 341ff.) and is available in precisely identical form, both simultaneously across space and over time, to everyone who has been able to study it. This consistency and at the same time exclusivity is a central part of a text's authority, its truth value. It is particularly evident with the Quran where uniformity is preserved to the degree that translations into vernaculars have not been acceptable (see Anderson 1991: 12ff.; Lambek 1993a).

The act of choking brings this privileged yet diffuse transhistorical and translocal presence to a precise moment in space and time. If the text asserts eternal truths, possession is context-bound; its existence is legitimated by the brute fact of having the body invaded by a foreign spirit. Any larger concerns are mediated by the immediacy of the experience, the unqualified here-and-now of the spirit within one's body or standing opposite one, taking over the body of a host one knows well. Full possession is dependent upon an 'internally-persuasive discourse' (Bakhtin 1981) that becomes a matter of being as much as knowing.[14] Possession gains its legitimacy from acts of displacement, public and discrete during moments of trance but also more private and temporally durable in the practice of taboos, responses to tabooed substances, and dream life. Possession is vigorously embodied, presenting a striking image to onlookers and a radical shift of experience for the host. Its legitimacy is manifest in bodily responses that appear clearly distinct from conscious will (Lambek 1992). Who can argue with the fact that one is choking?

Muslims read and recite texts, objectified knowledge handed down through a chain of scribes and voices and originally provided by a divine voice. Spirits must (re-)establish their own voices in each host, a process not yet complete in Athimary's case; they inaugurate their public careers by enunciating their names. Texts detach meaning from local sites of production and interpretation; they uncouple words from the ordinary constraints of speech, action and historicity (Ricoeur 1971). The meaning of possession, the legitimacy of each appearance of a spirit, must be established anew. And unlike texts, spirits speak and can be spoken to. The immediate context is always relevant.

It is easy to be extremely dualist about this. Yet Islam has its embodied, practical and disputational qualities as possession has its objectified ones. To take the latter first, speaking as or with spirits does share some of the more constraining features associated with texts; for example, spirits do not always respond when addressed (Lambek 1993b). Moreover, the identities of spirits (in terms of their formal properties such as name, dress, etc.) can remain relatively stable across diverse settings. In *trumba* possession the spirits signify, among other things, the power and the enduring nature of the Sakalava royal dynasty. Like written texts, spirits 'externalize social consciousness' (Smith 1990: 211).

Conversely, one of the most significant features of the Quran is that it is actively recited, not passively read. If spirits sometimes choke on the Quran, it would be fairer to talk about how often it is swallowed. The text is copied, taught, memorized, enunciated, listened to, performed as prayer and oath and on occasion dissolved in water and ingested. Each of these acts is unique and immediate. Yet at the same time, each is mediated by the identical text (Smith 1990). Swallowing the Quran is wholesale penetration, an act that immediately and intimately connects the recipient to the vast world and stable truth of Islam. It is both an embodiment of the text and a textualization of the body. This is what makes it a powerful medicine.[15]

Third, while Athimary's act can be understood as a form of resistance[16] and while resistance to the power of writing and to the authority of the written word can be found in a number of other contexts in Mayotte, it is important to understand the contours and limits of this resistance. The act of choking on the Quran is abrupt and forceful, a concise drama of rejection, yet it does not deny the validity of Islam. Indeed, the Quranic verses are said to be 'like fire' to the spirits; the spirits quickly pull away from them. However, as a spirit-curer explained it, some spirits, like some people, know how to recite liturgy (*midzor*). It is precisely these spirits who won't accept the verses as a means of settling them down; they know what is written and what the effects are likely to be. The most knowledgeable spirits are also the most dangerous, since they are the least susceptible to the ordinary techniques of containment and since they know how to subvert Islamic strategies. This play between the texts and spirits provides a space in which the strengths of each are recognized, in which the power of Islam is respected even as it is subverted. Moreover, a challenge that is entirely embodied in nature must be highly context-dependent rather than absolute or universal in scope; it holds only within a limited frame. The message is not that Islam is false or that the spirits are actively opposed to Islam but that they stand outside it. If spirits are not Muslims, the point is made that humans are.

This contrast between the text and the act of choking stands as an image for the global and local, the enduring and the immediate, the objectified and the embodied, the discursive and the non-discursive, the essence and the act. What Athimary's performance provides is a contextualization of Islam. It is an acknowledgement of the incorporation of Islam into local society and at the same time a demonstration that internalization has its limits. Moreover, it is a framed performance and partial and indirect in its claims. And far from illustrating the 'drunken savage' of Gellner's motif, possession has an ironic side that the earnest practice of Islam (or of any of the textually mediated missionizing religions) precisely lacks.

In sum, what is lived through here is the locally informed conjunction of two different forms of knowledge and practice stemming from two 'hegemonic' systems of quite different order. The local repertoire comprises both Islam and possession. Each is productive of a particular form of global–local relations[17] and produces its own form of certainty. While they do not often appear at the same moment or compete for the same act of commitment as in the case of Athimary, the certainty of each is compromised or at least contextualized by the presence of the other. Islam is explicitly harder on possession than the reverse, readier to pronounce exclusionary statements, and it is the dominant of the two (Lambek 1993a). But if Islam forms a portion of the practice and identity of every villager, possession makes up for this by its immediacy, its insidiousness and its recourse to irony. For example, while the *trumbas* choke on the Quran and enjoy flaunting Muslim convention, during the month of the Prophet's birth they also host a performance of the *Maulida* at the tomb (*mahabu*) of the Sakalava ruler who converted to Islam and who became the last and chief *trumba* in Mayotte after his death there. Muslim participants must overlook the fact that Islam rejects the identification of the *trumbas* as deceased human beings. Possession's localizing and contextualizing propensities bear similarities to the incorporative tendencies of society, to be discussed shortly.[18]

If neither possession nor Islam gains conclusive purchase over the other, they both lie at the heart of things. Culture in Mayotte is not then constituted as the manifestation of an inner essence, the elaboration of a central truth, a uniform cosmos, a system or structure, not even when conceptualized in terms of contradiction. Rather it is the conjunction of incommensurable ideas or discourses, i.e. those not 'able to be brought under a set of rules which will tell us how rational agreement can be reached ... where statements seem to conflict' (Rorty 1980: 316). This is not a matter of logical contradiction, since there is no neutral language or framework in terms of which the two discourses could be fully expressed;

invocation of one does not logically entail the other but nor does it rule it out. They address overlapping but somewhat different issues; each conceptualizes the world and the sense of problem somewhat differently. As distinct regimes of knowledge, the differences between Islam and spirit possession are not resolvable through logic because they cannot, except in extreme moments like ingestion and expulsion, be put in the same language. Yet their very incommensurability demands a mutual hermeneutics (see *ibid.*: 347); they can only meaningfully co-exist in such a way that each attempts to interpret the other, or rather, that their respective and mutual practitioners address their conjunction. The act of expelling the Quran is but one move in what has become a very long, subtle conversation. This may at times take the form of an argument but never of a logical refutation or the subsumption of one by the other. Indeed, even to speak of it as a conversation may be placing too great an emphasis on the discursive quality of the process.

BOUNDARY POLITICS DURING THE 1970S

Recipes of the global and the local

If swallowing the Quran has taken us to the centre of local culture, the following accounts reflect on the constitution of its boundaries. In 1975 a dish commonly served in Mayotte was manioc and unripe banana cooked in coconut cream. I recorded and started to use the name I heard it called: *gorbaly*. I don't recall exactly when I was enlightened about the use of the term. Perhaps it was when I heard a dish of rice referred to as *île par île* and queried the association. I had arrived in Mayotte a short time after the referendum in the colony of the Comores that was to decide its future. When the votes were tabulated it was clear that the vast majority of people from each of the other three islands in the archipelago wanted their independence from France, whereas the majority from Mayotte opted to stay part of the French system. Debate raged as to whether Mayotte could go its own way and stay apart from the emerging new nation, whether reckoning island by island could supersede the global count. Full of moral certainty and the political sentiments that were then sweeping anthropology, I assured the villagers that I too hated colonialism and shared their desire for independence. I was quite astonished to be told that such views would not be tolerated; unless I was able to remain silent on the subject I would be ejected from the village forthwith. Independence, the global reckoning that they pronounced *gorbaly*, was a recipe for economic disaster. From the point of view of the majority of small cultivators, the immediate power to be feared and resisted was the exploitative elite on the neighbouring islands who would come and seize their land. People would be left with nothing to eat but bananas, manioc and coconut, *gorbaly*. The culinary products were explicit metonyms of the political options and their expected outcomes. Should the vote be disaggregated *île par île* and local sentiment succeed in keeping the French in place, then there was a good chance the French would develop Mayotte. They might set up factories, build roads. And there would be rice on the table every night.

Here we have, in local idiom, alternative modern visions of the global periphery: modernization through benevolent assistance at 'catching up' versus autonomous 'nationhood'. Proponents of both positions selected their respective narratives in the spirit of hope for the future. However, while I saw this as a moral issue, the villagers voted on a pragmatic basis. People were willing to swallow dependency, many of whose negative features they well recognized, in wagering for land security and 'development'.[19]

So much for my first lesson in the politics of the global and local. But the moral of the story for us here has to do with the tremendous ambiguity of these concepts seen as alternatives. The *gorbaly* story poses the questions: which is the global and which is the local, for whom, and where are we positioned to know the difference? While 'global' was the scenario rejected by the majority of villagers in Mayotte, its implications were evaluated in highly 'local' terms. A global outcome – union with the other islands of the archipelago, independence like every other African state – it was foreseen, would run down the economy, such as it then was, forcing people to rely on the most local of their products, ones for which land was relatively easy to come by. The explicitly 'local' alternative, *île par île*, Mayotte for itself, has had more obvious globalizing consequences: rapidly increasing integration into the French political and world economic system and the total bypassing of the regional arena.

In what must be ranked as a major political victory, although it was contested by the neighbouring République Féderale Islamique des Comores and received bad press throughout Africa, it is the latter scenario that has largely come to pass. Some eighteen years after the referendum Mayotte remains a notorious political anomaly. In the discourse of post-colonial nationalism, France has shamefully failed to live up to its commitment to leave Mayotte and allow it to join the Comores. However, the French have responded to a greater or lesser degree to many of the demands of the party that advocated the *île par île* solution. Increased dependency and development have gone hand in hand. Roads, schools and clinics have finally been constructed. The economy is now based virtually entirely on wage labour and state benefits and subsidies. While I have no wish to defend the honour of France in this matter (and while developments are leading to new forms of nationalist sentiment, especially on the part of educated youths who realize that they have received both more and less than their parents bargained for), a French pull-out at the moment would radically disorient and impoverish the vast majority of the population and considerably undermine their hopes and projects.

How could all this be? Do the people of Mayotte simply march on their stomachs? Were they cynical or pragmatic to such a shameful degree as to sell their birthright for a mess of rice pottage? Were they naive enough to let themselves be co-opted by a few Creole leaders of the pro-French movement? Or is it that local constructions of identity operated according to a logic with which we are less familiar? Is it not perhaps food or the incorporative activities of digestion rather than birthrights and the individuated products of reproduction that serve most strongly to articulate the nature of identity? Is certainty not perhaps grounded more in acts than in states, in existence more than essence? Does not an object-relational model of identity fit the case better than one of possessive individualism?

ALLIANCE AS INCORPORATION

If the distinction between local and global does not serve to clarify the choices others make, one of the changes that is marked by the term globalism concerns our view of the world; we have come to see ourselves inextricably connected to local events in distant parts. And our moral queasiness rises. But we have to be careful not to project uncritically our unease on others. An analysis that presents others explicitly resisting us is reassuring, but the fact that it is 'politically correct' in our terms does not always make it an accurate rendering of others' positions.

The political strategy found in Mayotte during the 1970s bears more than a little similarity to long-standing techniques in which polities in the region, attempting either to impose domination upon or to escape from each other, roped in more distant allies – the French, the English and the Omanis – who were, of course, all too ready to exploit the situation. In the 1840s the Antankarana of northern Madagascar made a pact with the French in order to regain territory seized from them by the expanding Merina state based in the central highlands of Madagascar. To this day the Antankarana explicitly identify themselves as allies of the French. A key artefact of the kingdom is the dagger said to have been given to the monarch by Louis-Philippe in the 1840s; the Antankarana insignia combine an Islamic moon and star (conversion to Islam in the nineteenth century having been the fulfilment of a vow subsequent to a miraculous escape from the Merina) with the *tricolore*. The very name of the current Antankarana monarch, Isa Alexandre Tsimanamboholahy, indexes the interest in cultural *métissage* which indeed forms the basis of the ideology of his kingdom. The Antankarana regularly invite French diplomats to their rituals and they call upon the Consul for funds to renovate the royal residence. Assimilating European tourists and somewhat embarrassed anthropologists to their French allies, they readily include us as well.[20]

'Strategy' is a concept insufficient to portray these developments if it implies historical agency in a kind of moral vacuum. Strategies are rendered acceptable and reasonable, are selected and gain popular support, according to broader understandings of the world, implicit truths. Nor is strategy sufficient to account for the disinclination towards dogmatic positions. In northern Madagascar, where Muslims, Catholics, Protestants and non-believers (*tsy mivavaka*) live happily side by side, there is a kind of openness and tolerance of heterogeneity (which may include but rigidly circumscribe, exclusionary domains) that James in her original introductory remarks at the ASA Conference set up as a pole of her model. These societies partially incorporate others and are often willing to be partially incorporated so that boundaries are deliberately blurred.

In voting as they did, the people of Mayotte were not hampered by the sort of nationalist identity politics described by Handler (1988) that have become so common we tend to naturalize them. They looked forward rather than back. There was no nostalgia for a golden past but a hard-headed realism about the possibility of an impoverished future. Although the political split of the 1970s was highly exclusionary, brooking no internal opposition such as mine, the division was political in the purest sense, based on a single issue: whether to align with the Comores or with France. For a time party membership became the most salient basis of identity; families and villages were split in hurtful ways (Lambek and Breslar 1986) and subsequently reunited. What is noteworthy is that the divisions did not fall along ethnic or linguistic lines.[21] Indeed, ethnic differentiation was not particularly salient in Mayotte; collective identity was simply not objectified in this abstract manner. Both rice (*vary*) and bananas in coconut cream (*huntsy an vaniu*) were foods enjoyed equally by all sides. People identified themselves in the broadest possible but also the most concrete terms, as *ulun belu* (humans), *silamu* (Muslims), *ulu mainting* (Black people), or *ulu maskin* (the poor).[22] More narrowly, people were identified by locality of origin or current residence. Loyalty to and activity in the place of residence were at least as significant as any prejudice attributed to origins.[23]

Nor was the political division along explicitly religious lines. Indeed, while the Comoran elites claimed to have more direct links to the sources of Islamic authority than the majority of villagers, vernacular Islam also formed a major vehicle for pro-French activism. The fight for Mayotte was engaged in largely by women.[24] It was they who organized resistance to the Comorian regime, they who expressly challenged the French to stay and they who eventually celebrated victory. Their main means of organizing was an elaboration of the ceremonial exchange system in which villages invited each other to Islamic recitals. Political congresses were articulated on this basis as were more militant activities. So, on one memorable occasion women from around Mayotte gathered to protect a piece of road-building equipment from being removed to the Grande Comore and passed the time singing the Maulida (a popular Arabic composition commemorating the Prophet).

In sum, what is striking is the relative inattendance to boundaries and clearcut social divisions at all levels. Mayotte provides an illustration of a society based on incorporative principles in which residence and achievement have been far more significant than descent or ascription.[25] There were no discrete, named, descent groups and marriage was conceptualized as the incorporation of new adults – women and men – within the community rather than as an exchange or alliance between distinct units. The people of Mayotte were not xenophobic, nor did they have a highly developed consciousness of themselves as distinct; boundaries were not strongly marked. The political crisis of the 1970s led to the development of a Mahorais identity, yet it was one based less on autonomy than on merger with France.

When the referendum was won by the pro-French party and the French government acceded to the results, the women planted a French flag in the village and danced around it, then crowded into bush taxis and drove across the island singing. The mode of celebration at becoming 'French', the dances and songs performed by massed women, were 'local' or 'traditional' in kind, with no sense of anomaly, of inauthenticity or betrayal of origins. This is a portrait of cultural integrity rather than inferiority, cynicism or breakdown. As one young man put it to me in 1975 (my paraphrase):

> People here have lots of customs (*fomba*) and interests (*kabar*), far more than those of the Europeans (*vazaha*). After all, we take on all their customs and interests in addition to those proper to Islam. Many of us go on to study European customs in order to get good-paying jobs. But the French (*vazaha*) don't interest themselves in our customs. If the French know more things than we do, such as how to produce medicines, they should teach us. Once we learn, we will know more than they do, because we have Islam too.

The French viewed the political developments with bemusement. How could these people – who did not look or act French and who, for the majority, did not even speak French, nor therefore, think like the French – ever take their association with France so seriously, so literally? Nevertheless, their response too was quite literal, beginning with the infusion of universal primary education in French and leading to the development of an elaborate educational system. In 1992 it was with somewhat more justification from both sides (though still a great deal of ambivalence from the metropolitans) that the villagers responded to the question of their identity, '*Zahay favazaha*, We have become Europeans.'

AN ACT OF CONSUMPTION

The *gorbaly* story is about regional politics in which the region is rejected for a local/global solution. Global means, in a sense, the circumvention of

the immediately interlocal. In Western Europe this has entailed the transcending of national boundaries in favour of regions. In a place like
Mayotte it has meant the transcending of the region in favour of direct
links to a metropole.[26]

In the years following the referendum, the French greatly intensified
their investment in Mayotte, producing a radical cultural and economic
transformation. Much could be said regarding this brave new hetero-
topia.[27] For some there has been unprecedented opportunity. Others talk
about an inverted 'papaya world', *dunia papay*, taking their cue from a
tree in which the smaller fruit ride above the larger and older ones.
Ironically, given that the original pro-French vote had been partly impelled
by concern for rice land, one of the most striking indices of change is that
by 1992 rice cultivation had been entirely abandoned. A great deal of rice
is consumed but it is all imported. And for sale along with it is an enormous array of foreign foods.

The final anecdote brings us full circle, juxtaposing the increased penetration of capital and global commodities with the act of a spirit-medium.
In the household where I stayed we were served tender pieces of fried
chicken, quite different from the local poultry whose toughness had always
been offset by a delicious spicy sauce. The chicken was imported frozen
from South Africa and sold in the South African-owned supermarket (with
video monitors and automatic checkout) in town, as well as by local
merchants newly equipped with freezers. Knowing that his wife had long
been tabooed chicken by her *trumba* spirits and was even now submitting to a relatively recent taboo against goat meat, I asked my host what
she was eating.

'The same as we are,' he replied.

'What happened to her taboo against chicken?' I asked with astonishment.

'She is still tabooed *akoho* (chicken).'

'But this *is* chicken,' I said, naive as ever, assuming some misunder-
standing and worrying that if she were not warned it would have the same
unpleasant effects on his wife as did the local variety.

'Of course it is,' he whispered back, winking. 'But we call it *vorung*
(bird)!'

What are we to make of the woman's act? Is it a wholehearted
embracing, a swallowing whole, of the new global, capitalist relations of
consumption and an expression of freedom from past constraints? Is it a
dismissal of the new products as being, unlike the Quran, of too little
power or value even to merit a taboo? Is it an appropriation of the global
product on one's own terms, exhibiting, in true Malagasy fashion, the
power to maintain relevance by marking an absence (here the absence
of the taboo)? Is this but a form of 'experimental practice', 'the realm of
partial recognition, of inchoate awareness, of ambiguous perception'
(Comaroff and Comaroff 1991: 31, 29), one whose implications are still

as open to the actors themselves as they remain interpretively opaque to me? In hushing me perhaps my host is warning me not to prejudge the issue. Or are these questions merely the product of *our* discourse, frenzied attempts to impose significance on the simple act of eating a piece of store-bought chicken that is certainly more tender than the local variety?

At the least we can say that if the chicken is a foreign product, the decision to eat it is a local act, couched in a local idiom of acceptance and rejection of potent, polluting and neutral substances. So too are the indubitable results, whether satisfaction or nausea.

CONCLUSION

The globalization of individual discourses is complemented by the fact that the conjunction of any particular set of discourses is precisely a localized phenomenon. Rethinking cultures as the marked intersections of multiple discourses and the successive attempts to make local sense of such contingencies may be appropriate. 'Local culture' here is less an *a priori* than the complex sedimentary product of the spread of various discourses (see James 1988). So questions to ask include how diverse discourses are circulated and become articulated at local levels. To borrow a Marxist language, how do we talk about the articulation of modes of discursive production and consumption? And, given the fact that discursive diffusion is not a new phenomenon, how have the modes of articulation changed with new forms of objectification?

We have seen that Mayotte was a geographic locus, long part of a region viewed *île par île* rather than a bounded social whole, and characterized by a translocal spread of culture and weakly articulated boundaries. The constitution of identity in Mayotte did not fit the dominant global view of cultures as bounded entities in a universe of like objects or as the discrete contents of the packages so bounded. I suggest that it may be expressed as object-relational. I do not mean that identity in Mayotte was predicated on an explicit ideology of object relations, as Handler (1988) argues that nationalism is based on possessive individualism, but rather that such an approach provides a useful model for understanding local practice.

Two undoubtedly controversial lines of thought follow from this argument. If I were not acutely aware of the ironies of advocating the globalization of the local practice I have described here, I might go on to suggest that an object-relational model makes better analytic sense of cultural processes in general, even where it is manifestly not the model of the agents themselves. This could provide an avenue for replacing the bounded and ultimately essentialist uses of culture that were a part of the anthropological tool kit and that reappear in vulgar form in the rhetoric of both nationalism and multiculturalism. The objectification of distinct cultures is at best a kind of complicity with local acts, at worst the imposition of our framework. The borrowing by other discourses of this anthropologically authorized facticity compounds the distortion.

Second, object relations theory provides not just a different general model of identity but an account of why boundaries are more closed in some instances than in others. If Chodorow (1989) is correct that women are generally less concerned than men with defending boundaries, one might suspect that excessive concern with boundaries, 'insistent separateness', is largely a male problem (but compare Kristeva 1992). Drawing upon Malagasy gender relations and practices (unhappily not described here), one could suggest that 'object-relational' identity politics are likely to be associated with social fields in which gender distinctions are relatively unproblematic and in which women have a strong say. In other words, where men are not particularly defensive about demarcating their boundaries from women, they are less likely to be concerned about boundaries in general. This would help to illuminate the fact that exclusionary, fundamentalist politics are generally male-run and that they tend to make use of an abusive or constricting representation of women.

Needless to say, to polarize the alternatives in this way risks psychological reductionism and the essentialization of gender. It also ignores the significant political and economic forces, experiences and interests that impel the kinds of consciousness the models formulate. In any given historical instance many factors have to be taken into account. In the western Indian Ocean, object-relational forms of local identification may have had an affinity with both the prevalent mercantile activity and the tributary mode of production. Nor, in Mayotte, were they greatly challenged by the objectifying forces of colonialism, given the prior presence of Islamic literacy, the absence of Christian missionaries and the peripheralization of Mayotte within the Comores. The fact that class distinctions and the competition for resources were conceived to be more significant on an inter- rather than intra-island basis was another critical factor in the support for France. All this has begun to change with the serious attempt to educate a whole generation in French and with rapidly increased commoditization and subsequent class differentiation within Mayotte itself.

In Handler's (1988) depiction of the ideology of nationhood the claim to homogeneity is a central feature. The first anecdote was presented precisely in order to illustrate the heterogeneity of 'culture' in Mayotte. If it is problematic to see society composed of rigidly bounded units, the error is compounded when we identify each of them with a corresponding unitary culture or religion. Religion is at heart less a 'cultural system' than Geertz (1973) once imagined it. Bounded religious structures are the products of rationalization, born of various kinds of legitimating exercises, including textual inscription by anthropological scribes. Moreover, religious ideas work in contexts in which there are always alternatives present, other ideas, other practices, other truths, some of them possibly vying to be seen as the Truth. This is true even prior to the advent of writing or the challenges posed by the missionizing religions (see Ranger 1993).

Incommensurability is a central issue here. To say that it is characteristic of culture has two implications for this chapter. The first is that local certainty does not rest on the bedrock of deep, single or fully coherent structures but rather is the active product of shifting or balancing between outcrops.[28] The second is that culture can never be pinned down, never fixed. It must always be in motion, locked in 'internal' dialogue.[29] The problems that anthropologists have had in translating between cultures may not be all that different from the practical problems all of us have in articulating diverse forms of knowledge within our 'single' culture (and once one drops the sense of bounded units, the distinction is in any case only relative).

Perhaps one way to avoid the negative repercussions of analytic elegance is to change our conceptual apparatus from nouns to verbs, a procedure that Schafer (1976) has urged upon psychoanalysis and a distinction that harkens back in anthropology to Whorf's contrast of Hopi with Indo-European languages (Carroll 1956). It is to resurrect Leslie White's (1949) memorable dictum that 'culture is culturing'. When culture is reconstructed as verb rather than noun, it is no longer discrete or stable and hence cannot be 'captured'.

Consistent with the object-relational perspective and also with the shift from nouns to verbs (or structure to practice), difference from others, to the extent that it becomes an issue, might be phrased more in terms of negation – not being, having or participating in specific features that are characteristic of the outside world or particular outsiders – than in terms of unique, positive attributes, of what is essential and belongs exclusively to the inside. Taboos in Mayotte actively ground identity by establishing that internalization has its limits (Lambek 1992). The contexts of such differences range from the highly localized, indeed the personal, to the global, but they are not viewed as biological essences; people readily adopt taboos associated with the community or polity in which they choose to live.

It is not surprising that eating forms the connecting thread between my anecdotes since it is a kind of 'naturally symbolic act' by which to express and carry out internalization, the localizing of that which was global. Conversely, alimentary rejection is an act of boundary marking. My analysis has only piggy-backed on the indigenous form, providing a more abstract and far less embodied and active account. Eating and choking are not merely symbolic but indexical and performative and this adds to their impact; they serve to naturalize acceptance and resistance in the sense that the embodied consequences appear beyond their agents' conscious control.

In the end, it is the body itself that provides the primary index of the certain and the local; locality is defined by the presence of my body. Moreover, embodied acts can be neither mechanically reproduced (in Walter Benjamin's sense) nor reduced to objects of representation but only imitated, re-enacted by others; hence they are always at least indexical of locality and existence. Embodiment retains the potential for resistance precisely because it is incommensurable with the objectified forms in which most global commodities and ideas are circulated. Yet it would be a mistake to romanticize this. The body is also the vehicle through which what is originally external can become most fully incorporated and naturalized and through which and on which violence is perpetrated. Embodiment, as in the case of *trumba* possession or eating frozen chicken, is likely to be the expression not of freedom but of an alternative regime of truth. Conversely, then, reflective thought remains a significant form of resistance from embodied forms of domination. The profoundest moments of certainty may occur when embodied and objectified knowledge are mutually enhancing, exhilarating in the mystical peaks of the Sufi dance, or painful in the depths of anorexia. Most of the time we are caught in the flux between, in the uncertainties left us by the incommensurability of things but also in the space for movement this provides.

ACKNOWLEDGEMENTS

The research on which this chapter is based has been generously supported by the National Science Foundation, the National Geographic Society and especially the Social Sciences and Humanities Research Council of Canada who have also provided me with the time to write it. It was made possible by the hospitality of people in Mayotte. I have benefited from discussions with Paul Antze, Emmanuel Tehindrazanarivelo, Jean-Michel Vidal and Andrew Walsh, as well as with participants at the ASA Conference. My deepest appreciation to Janice Boddy and Jacqueline Solway for close critical readings of an early draft and to Wendy James for her diplomatic and insightful comments on a subsequent one. None of these people bears responsibility for the opinions expressed.

NOTES

1 Of course, I recognize with Ricoeur that 'there are just *others*, that we ourselves are an "other" among others' (from *History and Truth*, 1965, as cited by Owens 1983: 57).
2 This has been an issue in much thoughtful social science, ranging, for example, from Berger and Luckmann's dialectic (1966), through the Comaroffs' reworking of the play between 'hegemony' and 'ideology' (1991: 19–32).
3 Goody (e.g. 1968, 1986) provides a notable contemporary attempt to take up the programme with regard to writing. For an incisive critique see Bloch 1989. Both authors invoke Weber.
4 One need only think of the vagaries of English spelling or the composite nature of a celebration such as Christmas.
5 Object relations is an approach which stems from the work of British psycho-

analysts such as Fairbairn and Winnicott, themselves deriving ideas from Klein. It has its roots in Freud, whose theory of narcissism 'sustains the view that we are all incorporations and extensions of – take in and provide aspects of – one another' (Chodorow 1989: 147). For a recent synthesis see Mitchell 1988.

6 The models are often gender-inflected; paradoxically, given Chodorow's argument about women's openness relative to men, it is often the boundedness of women that is used to express the exclusivity of the community (e.g. Boddy 1989).

7 Object relations is a particularly compelling model because it sees the constitution of individual identity in relation to social context in somewhat the same self-fulfilling manner I have just described for ideology.

8 See also Nedelsky 1990 for an analysis of the pervasive discourse of boundedness in American legal and political thought.

9 I use the term object relational rather than simply relational to emphasize that the conceptual shift is not simply from entities to relationships but rather to the problematic nature of boundedness and to the ways 'betweenness' is brought 'within'.

10 Her dramatization, the scheduling and so on were entirely her own but I leave aside here the personal dimensions of the case.

11 Movement within the western Indian Ocean has been significant throughout the last millennium but its relative importance and ease have declined in recent decades. It is now quicker to reach Paris from Mayotte than it is to get to Zanzibar, or to order goods from a French mail order firm than to receive Islamic books or medicines from Mombasa.

12 At the same time, as James notes in the Introduction to this volume, the nature of the process changes. Indeed, what is striking in a place like Madagascar now is how the increase in international communication goes hand in hand with the breakdown of national communication. Thus in the summer of 1993, while people in the larger cities followed the day-to-day development of the Marseilles football scandal on television, those in many parts of the countryside waited weeks for the results of the national elections.

13 I grossly oversimplify here both because there are several forms of possession, from diverse sources and because Islam does not imply consensus nor is its position with regard to other social forces a unitary one. See Giles 1987 for the scope of East African possession. The question of Islamic consensus can be seen in terms of a fissure between the 'certain knowledge' constituted by the sacred texts and the 'contestable authority' of those who claim to speak on the texts' behalf. This is characteristic not only of Islam on the periphery (Lambek 1990b) but of Islam everywhere (e.g. Eickelman 1992; Fischer and Abedi 1990; Gilsenan 1982; Messick 1989) and, indeed, of any body of propositional knowledge (Asad 1988: 78).

14 The word 'discourse' may be problematic here; spirit possession certainly contains elements one would want to characterize as 'non-discursive'.

15 I subscribe to Rappaport's argument (1979) that certainty is the product of acts of commitment in which the discursive and the non-discursive are conjoined.

16 Boddy (1989) and Comaroff (1985) provide outstanding ethnographic analyses of embodied practices as forms of resistance.

17 Indeed each produces its own chronotope, a point I cannot develop here.

18 For more on the relationship of Islam and possession as forms of historical practice see Lambek (1993a: Chapter 2). Other dimensions of possession's contextualizing qualities are discussed in Boddy 1989.

19 Although Mayotte has been under French control since 1841, events prior to the referendum certainly did not encourage people to expect much good from

the French. Early colonialism was highly coercive and exploitative (Martin 1983; Shepherd 1980). For much of the twentieth century colonialism meant largely a political vacuum and economic stagnation at the local level.

20 These comments are based on research in progress conducted with Andrew Walsh.

21 There are speakers of dialects from two distinct language families in Mayotte: Kibushy (Austronesian) and Shimaore (Bantu). Ethnic background may have played a greater role in the political affiliations of functionaries than it did among villagers but this was more a matter of *de facto* political connections than of recourse to primordial sentiment. The lack of conflict over linguistic issues was striking to an anthropologist hailing from Québec but ought not to surprise the readers of Vail (1991). Ranger (1991) provides a concise account of the colonial interventions that led to the development of objectified linguistic boundaries.

22 To be sure, most of these terms served to distinguish local people from the French.

23 This openness varies somewhat, according to the status claims of the speakers.

24 Women were also the active force on the opposing side. In general, women were more certain of what they wanted than were men, or at least felt freer to assert their wishes. Contrary to widely diffused journalistic reports, there was then no sizeable Christian community on Mayotte.

25 On incorporative societies generally see Turner 1979. In Mayotte personal achievement led simultaneously to further incorporation within the group as self and other became increasingly interconnected and interdependent in practices such as virgin marriage (Lambek 1983), ceremonial exchange (Lambek 1990a) and spirit possession (Lambek 1988). Relevant factors in the underplaying of descent include the dislocations of the nineteenth century and the egalitarian ethos despite the need to hide slave ancestry. In general, however, there is a marked similarity to the principles of identity discerned for the Vezo, another Malagasy group living on the borders of a more hierarchical society (Astuti, 1995). Such a position may be characteristic of being subject to a tributary mode of production but it is also consistent with widespread features of Malagasy kinship and marriage practices.

26 Such a strategy of linking to a metropolis in order to avoid domination by regional elites is probably quite widespread. However, as Wendy James suggests (personal communication, 28 August, 1993), 'it is only islands which can pursue the thing very effectively, because of their undeniable territorial identity'.

27 See Vidal 1994.

28 This argument is elaborated in Lambek (1993: Chapter 12).

29 This is a point that some people know well. The Sakalava appear to shun explicitness and closure as polluting or death-like.

   Fingarette puts the limitations on cultural consistency much more sharply than I do but his lesson makes a fitting conclusion: 'If living life in terms of fallible, ultimately incoherent and self-contradictory concepts were impossible, suicide or paralysis would be the only possible reactions. But living such a life is not impossible: it is our fate. Humility is in order here, intellectual humility as well as moral and spiritual' (1991: 219).

REFERENCES

Anderson, B. (1991) *Imagined Communities*, London: Verso.

Asad, T. (1988) 'Towards a genealogy of the concept of ritual', pp. 73–87, in W. James and D.H. Johnson (eds) *Vernacular Christianity: Essays in the Social*

Anthropology of Religion presented to Godfrey Lienhardt, Oxford/New York: JASO/Lilian Barber Press.

Astuti, R. (1995), *People of the Sea*, Cambridge: Cambridge University Press.

Bakhtin, M.M. (1981) *The Dialogic Imagination*, ed. M. Holquist, trans. C. Emerson and M. Holquist, Austin, TX: University of Texas Press.

Benjamin, J. (1988) *The Bonds of Love*, New York: Pantheon.

Berger, P. and Luckmann, T. (1966) *The Social Construction of Reality*, Garden City, NJ: Doubleday.

Blanchy, S. and Mussa Said (1990) 'Inscriptions religieuses et magico-religieuses sur les monuments historiques à Ngazidja', *Etudes Ocean Indien* 11: 7–62.

Bloch, M. (1989) 'Literacy and Enlightenment', pp. 15–37, in K. Schousboe and M.T. Larsen (eds) *Literacy and Society*, Copenhagen: Akademisk Forlag.

Boddy, J. (1989) *Wombs and Alien Spirits: Women, Men and the zar cult in Northern Sudan*, Madison, WI: University of Wisconsin Press.

Bourdieu, P. (1977) *Outline of a Theory of Practice*, trans. R. Nice, Cambridge: Cambridge University Press.

Carroll, J.B. (1956) *Language, Thought and Reality. Selected Writings of Benjamin Lee Whorf*, New York: Wiley.

Chodorow, N.J. (1989) *Feminism and Psychoanalytic Theory*, New Haven, CT: Yale University Press.

Comaroff, Jean (1985) *Body of Power, Spirit of Resistance*, Chicago: University of Chicago Press.

—— and John Comaroff (1991) *Of Revelation and Revolution*, vol. 1, Chicago: University of Chicago Press.

Douglas, M. (1966) *Purity and Danger*, Harmondsworth: Penguin.

Eickelman, D. (1992) 'Mass Higher Education and the Religious Imagination in Contemporary Arab Societies', *American Ethnologist* 19(4): 643–55.

Fingarette, H. (1991) 'Comment and Response', in M. Bockover (ed.) *Rules, Rituals and Responsibility: Essays Dedicated to Herbert Fingarette*, LaSalle, IL: Open Court.

Fischer, M.M.J. and Mehdi Abedi (1990) *Debating Muslims: Cultural Dialogues in Postmodernity and Tradition*, Madison, WI: University of Wisconsin Press.

Geertz, C. (1973) 'Religion as a cultural system', in *The Interpretation of Cultures: Selected Essays by Clifford Geertz*, New York: Basic Books.

Giles, L. (1987) 'Possession Cults on the Swahili Coast', *Africa* 57(2): 234–57.

Gilsenan, M. (1982) *Recognizing Islam: An Anthropologist's Introduction*, London: Croom Helm.

Goody, J. (1968) *Introduction to Literacy in Traditional Societies*, Cambridge: Cambridge University Press.

——(1986) *The Logic of Writing and the Organization of Society*, Cambridge: Cambridge University Press.

Handler, R. (1988) *Nationalism and the Politics of Culture in Quebec*, Madison, WI: University of Wisconsin Press.

James, W. (1988) *The Listening Ebony: Moral Knowledge, Religion and Power among the Uduk of Sudan*, Oxford: Clarendon Press.

—— and D. H. Johnson (1988) 'Introductory Essay: On "Native" Christianity', pp. 1–12 in *Vernacular Christianity: Essays in the Social Anthropology of Religion Presented to Godfrey Lienhardt* (JASO Occasional Papers no. 7), Oxford/New York: JASO/Lilian Barber Press.

Kellner, D. (1992) 'Popular Culture and the Construction of Postmodern Identities', pp. 141–77, in S. Lash and J. Friedman (eds) *Modernity & Identity*, Oxford: Blackwell.

Kristeva, J. (1992) 'What of Tomorrow's Nation?' *Alphabet City* 2: 32–6

Lambek, M. (1983) 'Virgin Marriage & the Autonomy of Women in Mayotte', *Signs* 9(2): 264–81.

——(1988) 'Spirit Possession/Spirit Succession: Aspects of Social Continuity in Mayotte', *American Ethnologist* 15(4): 710–31.

——(1990a) 'Exchange, Time and Person in Mayotte', *American Anthropologist* 92(3): 647–61.

——(1990b) 'Certain Knowledge, Contestable Authority: Power and Practice on the Islamic Periphery', *American Ethnologist* 17(1): 23–40.

——(1992) 'Taboo as Cultural Practice among Malagasy Speakers', *Man* 27: 19–42.

——(1993a) *Knowledge and Practice in Mayotte: Local Discourses of Islam, Sorcery and Spirit Possession*, Toronto: University of Toronto Press.

——(1993b) 'Cultivating Critical Distance: Oracles and the Politics of Voice', *PoLAR, Political and Legal Anthropology Review* 16(2): 9–18.

—— and J. Breslar (1986) 'Ritual and Social Change: The Case of Funerals in Mayotte', pp. 393–410, in C. Kottak *et al.* (eds) *Madagascar: Society and History*, Durham, NC: Carolina Academic Press.

Lewis, I.M. (1986) 'The Power of the Past: African "Survivals" in Islam', pp. 94–107, in *Religion in Context: Cults and Charisma*, Cambridge: Cambridge University Press.

Martin, J. (1983) *Comores: quatres îles entre pirates et planteurs*, Paris: L'Harmattan.

Messick, B. (1989) 'Just Writing: Paradox and Political Economy in Yemeni Legal Documents', *Cultural Anthropology* 4(1): 26–50

Mitchell, S.A. (1988) *Relational Concepts in Psychoanalysis*, Cambridge, MA: Harvard University Press.

Nedelsky, J. (1990) 'Law, Boundaries and the Bounded Self', *Representations* 30: 162–89.

Owens, C. (1983) 'The Discourse of Others: Feminists and Postmodernism', in H. Foster (ed.) *The Anti-Aesthetic: Essays on Postmodern Culture*, Port Townsend, WA: Bay Press.

Ranger, T.O. (1991) 'Missionaries, Migrants and the Manyika: The Invention of Ethnicity in Zimbabwe', pp. 118–50, in L. Vail (ed.) *The Creation of Tribalism*, Berkeley, CA: University of California Press.

——(1993) 'The Local and the Global in Southern African Religious History', pp. 65–98, in R. Hefner (ed.) *Conversion to Christianity*, Berkeley, CA: University of California Press.

Rappaport, R. (1979) 'The Obvious Aspects of Ritual', pp. 173–221, in *Ecology, Meaning and Religion*, Richmond, CA: North Atlantic Books.

Ricoeur, P. (1971) 'The Model of the Text', *Social Research* 38: 529–62.

Rorty, R. (1980) *Philosophy and the Mirror of Nature*, Princeton, NJ: Princeton University Press.

Sahlins, M. (1976) *Culture and Practical Reason*, Chicago: University of Chicago Press.

Schafer, R. (1976) *A New Language for Psychoanalysis*, New Haven, CT: Yale University Press.

Shepherd, G. (1980) 'The Comorians and the East African Slave Trade', pp. 73–99, in J.L. Watson (ed.) *Asian and African Systems of Slavery*, Berkeley, CA: University of California Press.

Smith, D.F. (1990) *Texts, Facts and Femininity: Exploring the Relations of Ruling*, London: Routledge.

Turner, D. (1979) 'Hunting and Gathering: Cree and Australian', pp. 195–213, in D.H. Turner and G.A. Smith (eds) *Challenging Anthropology*, Toronto: McGraw

Hill Ryerson.

Vail, L. (1991) 'Introduction' to *The Creation of Tribalism*, Berkeley, CA: University of California Press.

Vidal, J.-M. (1994) 'L'Adolescence à Mayotte: Histoire, Changements et Paradoxes', Doctoral thesis, Université de Montréal.

White, L. (1949) *The Science of Culture*, New York: Farrar, Straus and Giroux.

Wolf, E. (1982) *Europe and the People without History*, Berkeley, CA: University of California Press.

Part IV

Epilogue: a professional dilemma?

'You know, we admire the English. They are a very "regular" people. But it's a shame you don't have any culture.'

(*Greek student to Roger Just*)

12 Cultural certainties and private doubts

Roger Just

> When it was a matter of wonder how
> Keats, who was ignorant of Greek,
> could have written his 'Hyperion',
> Shelley, whom envy never touched,
> gave as reason, 'Because he was Greek'.
> (W.S. Landor, *Imaginary*
> *Conversations*)

I

'Local knowledge' must be construed in a very particular way to present itself as a focus of anthropological interest in the 1990s – else one might seriously wonder what anthropology has been doing for the last seventy years. Malinowski did, after all, aver at the end of that much thumbed introduction to *Argonauts of the Western Pacific* that the final goal of ethnography was: 'to grasp the native's point of view, his relation to life, to realize *his* vision of *his* world' (Malinowski, 1961: 25; original emphasis [and original pronouns]).

In retrospect, of course, Malinowski's goal can be made to seem both impossibly optimistic and arguably wrong-headed. Could anyone really realize someone else's world and vision, especially when this was to be done with 'the subjective desire of feeling by what these people live' (*ibid.*)? And as ethnographers, would we really wish to? – for to go so mentally native might be to risk recreating the very incomprehension we had set out to dispel. But this is a mischievous quibble. Both morally and methodologically, Malinowski's was good advice; only of course what ethnography did, even when it was entitled *We the Tikopia*, was not to present 'the native's point of view' but to present a reconstruction of that view in 'our' terms: terms through which we had necessarily come to understand it; terms in which we were required to represent it; terms which constituted anthropology's 'own "making sense" of the diverse ways human beings "make sense" ', as Marilyn Strathern (1992: 7) now puts it. To labour the obvious, 'local knowledge', or at least knowledge gained in and of some particular locality, was always anthropology's business but it was always rendered into something else – academic discourse – that could be taken to function 'globally'. As for Malinowski, while he was assuredly a cultural relativist (hence his respect for 'the native's point of view'), he was also a great believer in 'science' – that is, in the possibility of the objective validity of the global discourse into which the local was translated.

What now allows the mischievous reading of Malinowski's good advice is the relative demise of our faith in science (our science) as global. 'Cultural translation', a phrase that took hold in the 1960s to refer to that 'making sense' of others' sense-making,[1] is now realized as no more than a cultural translation: the approximation of one local dialect in terms of another, rather than the accurate rendition of all local vernaculars into some superordinate language that could simultaneously preserve them and universalize them. For some, clearly, the realization has been more shocking (or belated) than for others. Frankly I don't think it much troubled Evans-Pritchard or Lévi-Strauss, to cite rather disparate ancestors.[2] And *a priori* the cultural relativity (historical contingency) of one's own intellectual apparatus (and its sustaining institutions) need be no more (or less) worrying than the abstract insolubles of moral relativism – while I suspect the practical solution is much the same: when in academia write as an academic. But if a crisis has lately been invoked,[3] the opportunism of latter-day naivety might be both too cynical and too simple an explanation. Certain discomfiting changes do seem genuinely to have occurred. Nor do they relate merely to an increased awareness of the intellectual relativity of one's own vantage point. As Professor Strathern suggests, they also relate to the appropriation by so many local discourses of that 'global' language we once took to be our own. A new universalism seems inherent even in the common parlance by which present localisms ward off, both politically and intellectually, all attempts at their encompassment. All cultures now have 'a culture'; all ethnic groups now have 'ethnicity'; all world-views now incorporate a 'world-view'; and every knowledge-system knowingly rejects the claim that it can be known and systematized except, it seems, in the terms it sets itself.[4]

All this can be a little disconcerting, especially when, as anthropologists, we might feel that cultures talking about 'culture', ethnic groups about 'ethnicity' and world-views about their 'world-view' are nevertheless not always talking about quite the same things as ourselves. At the very least the waters are muddier and one could be forgiven for yearning for simpler days when 'indigenous concepts' were on one side of the hermeneutic fence and 'analytic concepts' securely on the other. But my theme (rather than my argument) throughout what follows is that, in some cases at least, the disconcerting overlaying of local and global is not entirely new and the confusions generated not limited only to discerning academics of this particular *fin de siècle*. My case in point is Greece.

II

Andreas, who ran the *kapnopolio*, the tobacco-shop, in Spartohori, was a self-educated man. He had left school at about 12 years of age, but he was something of a reader, and he was certainly a talker and a thinker, and he held court every day in his tobacco-shop where the problems of the world were discussed – and some that were a touch more parochial. He was also a pessimist and a cynic and in 1977, during my first bout of fieldwork in Spartohori,[5] he once remarked to me, 'You know, Rogeri, two-and-a-half thousand years ago a Greek discovered electricity. We got it four years ago. What happened?'

Such questions can be disarming and Andreas' was not the only one of its kind addressed to me in Greece. In fact I don't know 'what happened', though without vanity I probably know more than most people. I suppose the rough answer is 'two-and-half thousand years of history' and everything that that entails. But such is not a particularly satisfying answer and certainly it was not a satisfying answer to Andreas' question which, after all, was more metaphysical (or possibly political, or possibly ethical) than it was empirical. Whatever sort of answer Andreas wanted (and I don't seriously think he was expecting one), it was not to be couched in terms of a blow-by-blow scholarly account of the socio-economic vicissitudes of Hellenism over two-and-a-half millennia. Rather, for Andreas, as for many members of the Greek population, the problem was one which, though assuredly 'historical' in form, actually denied history in its contemporary urgency. What Andreas wanted to know was how Greece could *simultaneously* be both the *fons et origo* of 'civilization' and, at least in 1977, marginalized as part of Europe's internal Third World. Greece's fame was Demokritos and all his noble peers; Spartohori's reality was a village without electricity until 1973.[6]

For Greece, or at least for the Greeks, there is thus little need to invoke the 'condition of postmodernity' or to reflect on the shifting grounds on which academic discourse now encounters ethnographic creatures of its own making in order to register both the juxtaposition of the global and the local and their problematic incommensurability. The point is that ever since the Renaissance, and arguably before, and with growing momentum during the eighteenth and nineteenth centuries, the global language of the West, the language of science, culture and 'civilization', with all its embedded reference points (Demokritos included), was thoroughly 'Hellenized'. Landor's Shelley could claim that Keats was Greek. But Greece itself remained on the periphery of much of what was done in its name. Witness a most trivial example, the term we coined for our own discipline; and yet in Greece 'anthropology' is a very recent academic development indeed.[7]

III

I do not wish to dwell overly on history, for in this case there is too much of it and I am in any case more concerned with present effects than historical causes; but a few examples (albeit monumental ones) may serve to give an impression of the historical overlaying of Hellenism's global forms on its local realizations – and impressions here are precisely the issue.

On the Citadel, the 'Old Fort', on Corfu there is a wonderful little church, the church of Ayios Yeoryios (St George). It is, however, like no other Orthodox church I know of in Greece, for it is built as a perfect Doric temple. And the reason it is not like other Orthodox Christian churches in Greece (which follow a canonical plan and embody in their architecture a canonical cosmology, both set down in the Byzantine period) is that it was not built by the Greeks as a Greek church but by the British as an Anglican church, the church, indeed, of St George, during the time when Britain held Corfu and the Ionian Islands as a Protectorate.[8] Perhaps, in its Hellenism, it somewhat departed from what more pious Anglicans could have wished; at least the traveller Anstead could sourly remark in 1863 that it was 'the model of a heathen temple, very classical at any rate, if not exactly adapted to its present use' (Anstead, 1863, cited in Young, 1973: 150). But if there are historical ironies involved in the construction of a Christian church as a 'heathen temple', from a Greek point of view there must be even more in the British having come to Greece to construct it. It is not, however, the sole example of such ironies.

Athens is one of the few European capital cities not to bear the marks of the great eighteenth-century Hellenic revival – and for obvious reasons. In the eighteenth century Athens was not a major European capital but a provincial town of the Ottoman Empire. Nevertheless there are three notable buildings in Athens that are classified by architectural historians as interesting, albeit late, examples of the neo-Hellenic style that had earlier swept through Europe. They are the University of Athens, the Hellenic Academy and the National Library, built between 1839 and 1892 – all built, that is to say, after Greece's independence. But again, they were not built by Greeks, for Greece's independence from the Ottomans was won at the price of submission to the Great Powers. The architects were thus a pair of Danes, the Hansen brothers,[9] commissioned to design these public buildings for Greece's new capital by another foreigner, Greece's equally new King, Otho, son of Ludwig of Bavaria.[10] Perhaps they chime with the ruins on the Acropolis that dominate the city and which were the inspiration of every European architect (though some would dispute their consonance, and 'pastiche' and 'academic' are words sometimes used);[11] but certainly they chime with little else. There is a gap of over 2,000 years between these buildings and their lofty paradigm. That in itself is perhaps not strange. Revivals are, after all, revivals. But what is odd – quite bizarre when one thinks on it – is that these buildings,

within sight of the Acropolis and intended to restate in however muddled
and overblown a fashion 'the glory that was Greece', are simultaneously
a foreign intrusion on Greek soil, the expression not of local taste and
local style but of the dominant European (indeed 'Western') fashion,
examples of which are to be found everywhere and earlier from Edinburgh
to New England.[12] But the opportunity for foreigners to 'build Greek' in
Greece must have been irresistible; and perhaps it did not seem even odd.
Colonialism arrived in the full fancy-dress of 'the native' ready to make
itself at home.[13]

IV

I have cited architecture merely to emphasize – though in substantial form
– the 'historical' irony that has become for modern Greece a 'cultural'
dilemma. But strictly speaking history is not the issue. One doesn't need
to be a Gibbon to know that empires decline and fall, powers wax and
wane. The sun has set pretty definitively on the British Empire (even the
Australians grumble about becoming a republic); more roads lead to
Washington these days than they do to Rome; and where now are the
Persians and the Medes? Lost glory is a common fate; so too is a rueful
nostalgia for it or a grandiloquent attempt to reclaim it. The peculiarity
of Greece's case is not that she has lost the cultural hegemony that once
was hers but that everyone else appears to have appropriated it; not that
foreign kings and foreign architects should have redesigned her capital
but that, as foreigners, they should have kindly done so in an Hellenic
style that had securely become 'their' style. Is Greece thus the borrower
or the lender?; the local source of global knowledge or its tardy imitator?
I was interested to see, in a recent trip to south Sulawesi, cast concrete
columns, still recognizably Corinthian, decorating the gardens of the
middle class in suburban Ujung Pandang – courtesy, I presume, of a
lingering Dutch influence. And it is worth remembering that when, at the
outbreak of the Greek War of Independence in 1821, the great expatriate
scholar, Adamantios Korais, sought assistance from Jean-Pierre Boyer, the
black President of newly independent Haiti (Clogg, 1985: 8), Boyer replied
not only in a language but in a form of discourse that was courtesy of the
French – and thereby thoroughly Hellenic:

> déjà les Grecs modernes comptent … des trophées dignes de Sala-
> mine. . . . Puissent-ils, semblables aux Grecs de l'antiquité, leurs ancêtres
> et sous les ordres de Miltiade qui les dirige, faire triompher, dans les
> champs d'une nouvelle Marathon, la cause sainte qu'ils ont entreprise
> pour la défense de leurs droits, de la religion et de la Patrie!
>
> (quoted in Clogg, 1985: 8)

> [already the modern Greeks can count … victories worthy of Sala-
> mis. . . . May they, like the Greeks of antiquity, their ancestors, and

under the command of Miltiades who leads them, make triumphant in the fields of a new Marathon the holy cause that they have undertaken for the defence of their rights, their religion and their Fatherland!]

Voices from the corners of other nations' erstwhile empires thus echo back to a Greece that had little knowledge of them (and which played no part in their creation) parodies of a history that is both hers and theirs.

One aspect of the dilemma was nicely apparent in the debate that occurred in the 1980s over Greek demands for the return of that most famous of Hellenic monuments, the Elgin marbles. I take no side in what is a complex political issue but the terms of its rhetoric are worth noting, for one of the less jaundiced arguments put forward by the British side, and one that attracted some support, was that the Elgin marbles were not a Greek heritage, or rather not an exclusively Greek heritage, because they belonged to the West as a whole. They were part of a common 'civilization' (it therefore following, somewhat less securely, that they were more accessible to civilization in the British Museum than on the Acropolis).[14] The problem for the Greek side and for the former Minister of Culture, Melina Mercouri, was that at one level this was a view they would want fully to endorse. Greek culture is not just Greek culture; the Parthenon is not just a Greek monument. Greek culture is in fact 'Culture' (just please also remember that it is Greek); the Parthenon is a world monument (only it's ours and would you mind giving the frieze back).[15] Here nationalism, which is by no means a peculiarly Greek vice, encounters a quite peculiarly Greek problem, for if one of the major aims of nationalism is to distinguish 'us' from 'them', how do you do that if the very measure of your fame is the degree to which your definitions of self have been appropriated by others? How, in short, are you to play the role of being exclusively universal?[16]

V

It would be easy to dismiss all this as a silly problem: silly because whatever Greece was in the classical period is not, and could not be, what it is today; silly because whatever the post-Renaissance West made of Greece, it was of the West's own making; silly because the contrast between global and local culture (science, knowledge) depends on a false reification of the global as something that could have an existence independent of its every local manifestation; silly because Keats wasn't Greek and, for that matter, Demokritos didn't discover electricity. But if such a problem genuinely presents itself to people, then anthropology must seriously entertain it. We are back, as we always must be, to Malinowski's injunction 'to grasp the native's point of view' – except that now the natives are awfully close to home and can put up a good case for owning it, and what in part they are talking about is 'us', who in any case often thought we were 'them', and in a language that we largely share. And so a few words about a few terms (my attempt to 'translate' a local vernacular into a global discourse whose provisionality is both revealed and assured by their common origins and continual evolution).[17]

'Culture' is of course the key word and Greek speakers of English make free use of it. But 'culture' (for once) is not a word of Greek derivation and in fact there is no particularly good word in Greek for it (see Tziovas 1989)[18] – or at least none that guards the careful (or perhaps vacuous) neutrality of anthropological usage. There are, however, several possible candidates – but it must be made clear that here we are dealing with words whose meanings have been anything but fixed and which are currently in some state of flux. It is not a question simply of finding a list of appropriate terms that might approximate to the English 'culture', or of noting the historical evolution of certain neologisms within Greek, formed and adopted to render something like 'culture'; the concepts that lie behind those terms are themselves evolving and changing (in just the same way as the signified of 'culture' has changed in English). Such definitions as I give below must therefore be taken as merely normative.

For 'culture', then, *koultoura* is one possibility but it is a relatively recent loan-word (coming into popular use in the 1970s) and refers either to 'high culture' (opera, theatre, the ballet, 'literature'), or else, by an even more recent but very significant extension, to the currently sanctified forms of folk-culture and popular culture. Thus *koultouriarides* is the term disparagingly used of members of the fashionable artsy-crafty/arty-farty set who are now as liable to wax lyrical over village weavings or urban low-life *bouzouki* music as they once were over *Don Giovanni*.[19] *Kallieryia* is another option, but again it clearly refers to 'high culture', for literally the word means 'cultivation', and what is more usually heard is the adjectival or substantive form, *kallieryimenos* i.e. 'a cultivated [person]'.

Historically, but only I think historically, two other words bear consideration: *pedia* (Ancient Greek *paideia*) and *vios*. Although *pedia* has always meant something like 'teaching, education, rearing, bringing-up'[20] and is now the standard word in modern Greek for 'education', the very breadth of the concept in classical antiquity made it a possible candidate in nineteenth-century Greece for a rendering of 'culture';[21] but, as Tziovas notes, the link with education has now made the equation difficult (1989: 333 n. 6). As for *vios*, it means basically 'life' and, in the absence of any specific term for 'culture', was used in the nineteenth century and into the twentieth century to refer to the life or behaviour of a people or group, and specifically to the Greek way of life (*ibid.*: 323). As a term for 'culture', however, its usage might at best be considered historically provisional.

Nowadays without doubt the commonest word in Greek for 'culture' (or rather, the word and concept that contend its space) is *politismos*; this, for example, is the word that forms part of the title of the ministry over which Melina Mercouri presided, 'Politismou ke Epistimon' – '[of] Culture

and Science(s)' (in its official English translation).[22] It is also the word
that, coupled with *Ellinikos* (Greek), forms part of the title of any number
of works on the nature and history of Greek culture. But – and this is a
major qualification – its rendering as 'culture' in English translation is
context-sensitive. When Adamantios Korais introduced the term into
Greek at the beginning of the nineteenth century, it was specifically to
render the French word *civilization* (*ibid.*: 322 and 333 n. 4)[23] and, both
etymologically and in common understanding, this is what it continues to
mean.[24] By the 1920s such a phrase as *laikos politismos* (popular civilization) could sporadically appear (*ibid.*: 324) but the term has never lost its
connotations of material and intellectual progress.[25] Even granted that
'The Ministry of Civilization and Science' would appear a little over the
top on headed note-paper and official invitations (as any educated Greek
would know), I thus still have my doubts that many Greek-speakers would
feel comfortable talking of Australian aboriginal *politismos* or Bedouin
Arab *politismos*. That would sound too close to a contradiction in terms
– though the possibility cannot be discounted, for in the end it will depend
on the intellectual and ideological position of the speaker.[26]

Indeed, it must be admitted that there are now two adjectives derived
from *politismos* – *politistikos* and *politismikos* – which are being extensively used to render 'cultural' in a relatively neutral way; but they are
both of very recent coinage and appear to have come about largely in
response to the very demands of translating English (etc.) 'cultural' and/or
of expressing that concept anew within a Greek context.[27] Moreover, the
very fact that they now do so in the context of such phrases as 'cultural
history' (*politismiki istoria*), 'cultural association' (*politistikos sindesmos*),
'cultural organization' (*politistikos organismos*), 'cultural foundations'
(*politistika idrimata*), 'cultural conservation' (*politismiki thorakisi*) and
even 'cultural park' (*politismiko parko*) – all part of the current global
'culture' discourse – makes one wonder whether in Greek these neologisms have not come into being at the very time when the ubiquity of
culture's usage has drained the term of useful meaning.[28]

Finally and still very much in common usage, there are a phrase and a
word which might appear to correspond reasonably well with the anthropological usage of 'culture': *ithi ke ethima*, which can, somewhat prob-
lematically, be rendered as 'customs and habits'; and *paradosi* which means
quite simply 'tradition' (whatever we may then take that to mean). *Ithi
ke ethima* and *paradosi* are used either interchangeably or in conjunction
to refer to the way of life of a people, and have the advantage of being
far more inclusive than either *koultoura* or *politismos*, for notions of 'high'
culture, or artistic production, or 'civilization' are (at least provisionally)
absent. And they can be, and are, used of peoples who, from a normative Greek perspective, would fall outside the boundaries of *politismos*
and who were not blessed with *koultoura*. Nevertheless *ithi ke ethima/
paradosi* still carry certain connotations and in practice are subject to some

sociological refinement. First, the words are still most commonly heard with reference not to foreign 'cultures' but to Greek culture, where they specifically emphasize the values, activities and practices of the 'folk', the *laos* (subject of that well-institutionalized study in Greece, *laographia*, 'folklore').[29] Second, with reference to Greek culture and in the hands of the literati and academic establishment who define the concept, *paradosi*, 'tradition', tends to become both holistic and unitary, while at the same time being very selectively constructed.

The phrase in common use is actually *i paradosi mas*, 'our tradition', and it is notable that with the possessive pronoun 'our' it always appears in the singular. As a part of national(ist) ideology, it thus conflates Greek culture into a singular entity and a common possession. Epirot kilts (*fustanelles*) and Cretan breeches (*vrakes*), or the allegedly Asia Minor *bouzouki*[30] and the Ionian Islands guitar (*kithara*), all become for promoters of Greek culture parts of the one 'tradition' whose boundary is simply set at 'Hellenism'. And what is done regionally is also done historically: the tradition is conceived of as a line of continuity from Homeric Greece to the present, so that Cretan folk-dances (or Macedonian folk-dances) are seen to be reiterating the same movements, styles, or at the very least fundamental 'spirit' that infused the choruses of the classical tragedians (thus opening the way, it should be noted, for an important link between *politismos*, 'high culture/civilization' and the folk-tradition). The selectivity of the *ithi ke ethima* to be included as part of this unitary folk-tradition then further distances it from what an anthropologist might understand as 'culture' (though not from what most ethnic nationalists elsewhere seem to be parading as its contents), for while folk-dances are certainly part of it, soccer is not; while retsina is, whisky isn't;[31] while monogamy is exalted, adultery and infidelity are ignored. In fact the better part of everyday life is not included and while the 'habits and customs' of the Greeks embrace all Hellenism over time and space, the 'tradition' remains both iconographic and prescriptive.

Whichever way one goes, then, and with due allowance made for the subtle redefining of terms that is taking place, to talk of 'culture' in Greek and in Greece and particularly about Greek culture, is to be drawn into a series of presuppositions about what 'culture' is that are not quite the same as those entertained by anthropologists. But they do – and in all fairness this must be stressed – share a common semantic (dare I say 'cultural'?) heritage with what used to be part of the West's 'global' language when 'culture' was 'civilization'. And within that particular 'tradition' (here words are seriously beginning to fail) Greek culture was deemed to lie at the roots of civilization. No wonder, then, that in some quarters there should be confusion.

So let me now return to the likes of Andreas in his tobacco-shop in Spartohori to explore reactions to this – but also to other quarters, for socially, economically, educationally, Greece is a highly differentiated society. Many of my Greek friends and acquaintances might read what I have written, shrug their shoulders and wryly agree – or even more wryly say much the same things themselves. Other Greeks might take it as a call to arms. If I have alluded to a 'Greek' cultural dilemma, it would be a dangerous mistake to think that there was a uniform Greek response to it. My contention is only that such a dilemma, ready-made by the global discourse that has externally constituted Hellenism, is one that all those who perceive themselves as Greek in some fashion confront.

VI

In Spartohori, as in many villages that I visited in Greece, the common claim made to me (a foreign student, after all, an 'educated' man) was, 'We have a history here, you know.' Not that the villagers pretended to know the history; they modestly left that to scholars and intellectuals. The cultural certainty was only that 'here' a history existed – though the implication was that in other places it did not, or not to the same degree.

In a curious way, of course, the villagers were right. If one conceives of history as what historians have written, as knowledge of the past rather than as the past itself (a notorious conception within anthropology, after all),[32] then all the villagers were doing was to reiterate the product of two closely allied assertions that Western historiography has so often made: Herodotus was the 'father of history', i.e. the first person to write it; and the history of Western civilization, which includes an historical consciousness and therefore something worth writing about, started with the Greeks. And, as I have suggested, the villagers' claim was made modestly enough. They did not count themselves scholars and intellectuals. Aware of much the same irony that prompted my friend Andreas' remark, they were merely seeking agreement from the foreign scholar who ought to know 'better than we do' of what they rightly took to be a commonplace. And since 15,000 kilometres away and as a result of British colonialism rather than Greek expansion, I had spent six years of my life reading Herodotus and studying that little pin-point of history to which everything nevertheless always referred itself back – a couple of hundred thousand people over a couple of hundred years more than two millennia ago – I was able to oblige in good faith. In fact all I was really required to do was to play my role within a sort of cosmic division of labour: 'We did it when we were at the height of our powers'; 'You are now in the position to appreciate better than we what it was we did.'

Only if I begged to demur, only if I tried to qualify this cultural certainty by (foolishly) querying the grounds of its construction, only if what might be called the 'at-least-we-were-there-first' method of coping with the present were challenged, would the dissonance between my education and the villagers' understanding become apparent. Then their dialect of the universal language began to sound oddly parochial. Greece's priority would be revealed not as a matter of reputation but of reality, not of fame but of fact. Greece genuinely had a 'past' when other nations didn't. When the retired high-school teacher in the neighbouring village of Katomeri (who often put me through my paces) asked what the English had been doing when the Greeks had been building the Acropolis, I muttered (not very knowledgeably) about Stonehenge, only to be told flat that England didn't have any history before 1066. And his was not an entirely uncommon point of view. The Greek taxi-driver from Sydney whom I met on my flight from Melbourne had already pointed out to me that whereas Greeks in Australia had two-and-half thousand years of history behind them, other Australians like myself had only two hundred. His history stretched back; mine was mysteriously truncated. And a couple of years ago, when the 'Macedonian question' was beginning to make news, one of Melbourne's Greek-language newspapers carried a cartoon clipped from the Athenian press depicting two figures, one male, dressed in a short tunic and wearing a 'classical Greek' helmet, the other female but with an ape-like face and wearing a baggy coat and the type of woman's hat that would make her iconographically represent the 'Anglo-Saxon' matron (whether in the image of the Queen, the Queen Mother, or Mrs Thatcher). The female figure, who clutches her handbag under her arm, has 'Australia' written on her coat; the male figure, who leans on his sword, carries a shield labelled 'Macedonian'. The caption (in Greek) says:

> *Macedonian*: My good woman, we have been Greeks for 3,000 years.
> *Australia*: My boy, how should I know anything about that? We were apes then.[33]

If history started with the Greeks, it follows that there must have been a time when non-Greeks had no history. And was I not, as a 'European', as an ex-classicist indeed, only getting back in very literal form what I had helped to create?

Such a reification of history (so that in some peoples' cases it can actually be absent) cannot, of course, be attributed to Greece's educated classes. Nevertheless, recognition of Greece's historical priority remains a common expectancy, even if it is conceived of in terms of cultural rather than ontological precedence. A furore was created in Greece in 1990 with the revelation of the contents of the then unpublished European Community-sponsored *Europe: a history of its peoples*, prepared under the direction of the French academic (and Annales School historian) Jean-Baptiste Duroselle. Greece and the Greeks were omitted! The shock was profound (justifiably so, in my opinion). It was one thing to admit that one might have been overtaken by history; quite another to discover that one had never been in the running. Had not the West always acknowledged Greece's pre-eminence? Was not European civilization the fruit of Greek civilization? 'A Europe of the Visigoths?!' gasped one Greek headline. But the reaction of *To Vima*, one of Greece's more serious newspapers, was more interesting. It featured an interview with Jean-Pierre Vernant, the great French ancient historian, anthropologist and, as *To Vima* remarked, philhellene. Vernant's comments were, as one would expect, judicious and in an interview slightly critical of Duroselle and certainly sympathetic to Greek sensibilities, Vernant stressed that Duroselle's history should not be taken as an 'official' history of Europe, for there could be no such thing. There were all sorts of histories: economic, social, political and *tou politismou*, 'of civilization [culture?]'. In printing an important interview with a leading European scholar on a delicate national issue, *To Vima* thus fulfilled its responsibilities to the intelligentsia of Greece. But – and think this not insignificant – the head-line for the interview was 'Many histories exist' and the passage from the interview extracted and italicized in quotation marks as a sub-heading read as follows:

> Certainly no-one can doubt the contribution of Ancient Greek civi-lization to the history of European civilization. However, the history of European civilization is not the history of Europe. And it is an egre-gious error to say that the history of Europe started at Marathon. What took place at Marathon was the battle of the Ancient Greeks against the Persians! Europe did not exist then.
>
> (*To Vima*, 3 June 1990 [my translation])

Quite so. But what *To Vima* had thus to emphasize to its relatively elite readership was precisely the fact that history was not a singular and natural entity; that it was a construct, a point of view; that history and 'civiliza-tion' were not necessarily the same thing; and that consequently it was at least possible for Europe and Europeans to construct themselves without Greece.[34] That was news.

VII

Since culture is tradition and tradition is history and history is civiliza-tion, historical certainties are cultural certainties (no apologies for the murkiness of the syllogism). Historical pre-eminence amounts to cultural pre-eminence and back in the village 'we have a history here' is matched by other claims – and other doubts. Spartohori had an acute conscious-ness of itself as a village removed from the niceties of urbanity. 'What do you expect,' commented my patron and protector, old Michalis, 'this is a village, isn't it? We don't have *politismos*; we don't even have toilets.'

An investigation of the historical diffusion of the bowled toilet might serve as an interesting index of the worldwide hegemony of European cultural forms (not to mention the spread of dysentery) but if Sparto-horiots felt themselves bereft on that particular ground, as Greeks they were assured on others. The 'at-least-we-were-there-first' syndrome was matched by a strong belief in the cultural superiority of whatever remained. Language was a case in point – and a case pointed to everywhere I went in Greece. Indeed, though I have never been able to trace their source, the uniformity of the examples cited from one end of Greece to the other makes me suspect that at some time they must have entered the pedagogical system. At all events, the following scenario would take place. I would address someone in not very good Greek. I would then be congratulated on my Greek – a congratulation, I soon realized, that reflected well on all parties, for it would immediately be followed by an expression of amazement that I could speak Greek at all since it was 'the most difficult language'. Unlike all other languages, for example, 'it has many words for the same thing'; and then, invariably, my interlocutor would point to the ground and say, 'What do you call that in English?'

'A stone,' I would glumly reply.

'Ah, yes but in Greek, you see, we have many words for it,' at which stage I would be treated to a list of near-synonyms that roughly matched the English 'stone': 'rock', 'boulder', 'gravel', 'yonnie', 'tor', etc. By way of slight variation, this was sometimes done with the word for 'bottle-cap' or 'cork' but the assertion remained the same: Greek had many words for the same object; other languages had only one. A complementary, but more sophisticated, version of the above seized on morphology and syntax rather than vocabulary and asserted that Greek was unique in having a grammar. It alone had gender, number, case, tense – the whole gamut of inflections that students of Greek, in Greece as much as anywhere else, have drummed into them and about which, in Greece, there has always been some room to argue.[35]

It must of course be admitted that experientially Greek claims make some 'local' sense. English may have as many (if not more) synonyms 'for the same thing' as Greek but largely because versions of it are spoken over a much wider area by far more people. Dialectal variation is still something which most Greeks encounter within a relatively small population and confined geographical area. As for grammar, the formal complexities of Greek may be no greater than those of German, or Russian, or Hindi, or certainly Finnish, and I know enough to know that no language lacks a grammar; but it is true that English and to a degree, say, French and Italian, are easier to 'pigeonize' than Greek if only because they lack a fully inflected morphology. Broken English is readily communicable; broken Greek not to the same extent – and in a tourist-ridden country, most Greeks are personally acquainted with that fact.

But beyond the Greek experience of other languages (and on the whole the Greeks are pretty good polyglots, especially when compared with their English-speaking counterparts) lies once again a consciousness of the historical and cultural centrality of Greek to 'European civilization': a centrality, I would argue, constructed in Europe by everyone from Petrarch (who knew no Greek) to Keats (who knew no Greek) – but which has come into being nonetheless. If it is known by the 'average person' in Greece that a very significant proportion of, say, contemporary (post-Renaissance) English words are Greek-derived (because learned persons borrowed them or made them up) and if it is also known that, however horrendously they pronounced it, until quite lately members of the European educated classes were all versed in (Ancient) Greek and some still are, then it is difficult to argue in Greece that the reasons for this have little to do with the intrinsic superiority of Greek: to argue, for example, that (despite whatever their masters might have said) little boys learned Greek at Eton because, for British historical reasons, it marked them as possessors of the cultural capital required of members of the British ruling class and not because they were necessarily the wiser statesmen for it; or that anthropology was called 'anthropology' not because English was semantically incapable of coining a word for the concept but because 'personstudy' would have sounded odd in the company of 'geography', 'geology', 'psychology' and all the other 'scientific' terms already part of an English language which, like most other European languages, was habituated to gloss its learned terms with the prestige of Latin and Greek.[36] In short, in Greece it is very difficult to argue that the strength of tradition (*paradosi*) lies in its ability to demand contemporary conformity (including an enthusiasm for soccer) rather than to provide access to some sublime past. Surely little English (and German and French) boys learned Greek because it was a richer, more expressive, more precise and indeed a more ancient language than theirs (why else bother?); surely English borrowed Greek terms because its own were deficient? Thus local common sense will always prevail against the deconstruction of global structures (if only because the global will only make sense when locally construed). It can be (inevitably must be) overlooked that *psycholoyia* is in (historical) fact a loan word from German or French,[37] despite the (equally historical) fact that *psyche* is standard Greek for 'soul' and always did mean something (subject of many learned articles) other than one's physical (Greek *phusis* – 'nature') being, or that *laographia* (Greek 'writing-about-the-people') was a conscious academic equivalent of 'folklore', despite the fact the word *laographia* really did exist in Greek-speaking Roman Egypt with the meaning of a poll-tax.[38] On the whole, it is easier to celebrate history if you substantially dispense with it.

VIII

But language is only part of a greater whole in what I might now term the 'despite-appearances-we-still-are-pre-eminent' tactic of cultural superiority. Spartohori, like most Greek villages, was extremely ambitious for its youth and, with immense and commendable sacrifice on the part of parents, many young Spartohoriots were sent to the university or to other tertiary institutes in Athens or elsewhere in Greece. Mostly they studied economics. In summer the students returned to the village and I came to know many of them well. They were as nice a bunch of young people as one could meet and sometimes I played cards with them in the coffee-shop. On one occasion one of them said to me, 'You know, we admire the English [amongst whom I was numbered]. They are a very "regular" (*taktikos*) people. But it's a shame you don't have any culture (*koultoura*). You only have two writers: Shakespeare and Oscar Wilde.' Under the circumstances I did not feel like pointing out that Oscar Wilde was Irish, but there is perhaps nothing like other people's chauvinism for sharpening one's own and I remember spending a sleepless night trying to recite from 'A' for 'Anonymous' onwards the roll-call of English authors.

Again, this particular view, though not perhaps warranted, is at least understandable, for Greece's contemporary literary output is extraordinarily impressive, especially given the size of the country. This century it has produced two Nobel Prize-winning poets and a couple of the finest twentieth-century poets who happen not to have been prize-winners. I doubt many people in the village were particularly conversant with Cavafy,[39] or Seferis, or Elitis or Ritsos and I doubt that my student friend was; but he would certainly have read some of their works, known their names and, more to the point, like any Greek he would have been conscious of Greece's contemporary literary reputation. That is a matter of general knowledge and justified national pride. Conversely, though I am unsure why Oscar Wilde should have been singled out as England's only other author,[40] Shakespeare, or at least knowledge of his existence, has become part of 'global general knowledge', one of the 'Western tradition's' reference points along with, let us say, Italy's Dante, Germany's Goethe and possibly Spain's Cervantes. But of English writers, only Shakespeare has been thus 'universalized'. Given the asymmetry between the contents of 'global (general) knowledge' on the one hand and my friend's local consciousness of contemporary Greek literary achievements on the other, it is perhaps not surprising that the contrast he made should have been so politely invidious. After all, though most British economics students would have heard of Homer, how many would know of Cavafy, Seferis, Ritsos, Elitis *et al.*?

But if in the end my friend's presumption did approach chauvinism, once again it is a chauvinism that comes lightly, almost naturally, as a result of Greece's appropriation by the rest of the West; nor does it depend on a knowledge of Cavafy, Seferis, Ritsos, Elitis *et al.* For if Herodotus has been made the father of 'history' (in general), Homer has been made the source of 'literature' (in general). And within the construction of global Western culture/civilization, there is not just Homer. There is Aeschylus, Sophocles, Euripides, Aristophanes, Hesiod, Pindar. . . . Limited to Shakespeare (and didn't he pinch from Plutarch?) – or Dante or Goethe or Cervantes – the rest of the world's contribution to the very canon it created starts to look a bit slim. In fact the invidiousness of the comparison stems not so much from a one-sided pitching of a local's knowledge of Greek achievements against other nations' entries in the global hall of fame, as from a face-value local reading of the global construct itself. And when what has been globally constructed can be locally claimed, a little chauvinism should come as no surprise.

IX

'Hellenism', 'the Western tradition', 'civilization' in any historical sense is of course, a construct. That is not to suggest that it is either vacuous or unreal; it is as real as the architecture it created, the poetry it inspired, or the lives of the people who subscribed to it. But it remains a construct nevertheless, quite as much as Orientalism with which, at moments, it shares remarkable affinities. The radical difference, of course, is that it is a construct about 'ourselves'; a theatre in which we, rather than 'others', have managed to play the fancy parts – while the dilemma for Greece has revolved around this central casting. Who are the 'we'?

As I have suggested, Greek reactions to this question have been various (as, indeed, have non-Greek reactions) and in this chapter I have illustrated only one of their directions:[41] the reappropriation by local Hellenism of global Hellenism; the plea that we should continue to acknowledge as a local reality the source of our global tradition – in short, the demand that we should remain true to our words. But we never have. As Professor Strathern (1992: 6) remarks, 'In the case of displacement, when the ground moves, the figures alter.' In the Greek case the figures altered long ago. It was the British who built their Doric temple; it was the Bavarians and the Danes who redesigned Athens; it was German professors who wrote treatises on Greek verbs.[42] And writers in the *Telegraph* and *Sunday Telegraph* still sneer at Greece as an unfit nation to own its own Parthenon frieze.[43] For 150 years Greece has had to struggle to reappropriate its heritage – to reclaim civilization for itself. But now the ground is shifting yet again.

In his recent *Culture and Truth: the remaking of social analysis* (1989), Renato Rosaldo relates with some passion the affair of the 'Western culture controversy' at Stanford, where first-year undergraduates were obliged to read a 'core list' of 'great books' from Homer through to Shakespeare and Voltaire in order to learn 'our heritage' before studying 'other' cultural traditions:

> Conflict erupted, however, when a significant number of students and faculty questioned the 'we' who was defining 'our heritage' as a shelf of books written in another time (before World War I) and in another place (ancient Athens and Western Europe).

(1989: x)

Well, so much for the Enlightenment (and personally I regret its passing);

but I am certain Rosaldo has his finger firmly on the pulse of change. Increasingly the problem for Greece will become not to prove that Greek civilization was in fact 'Greek' but to maintain that Greek civilization was in fact 'Civilization'. And as culture (???) increasingly overtakes civilization (*politismos*) as our common-market coinage, the danger for the Greeks is that the local may truly triumph over the global and Hellenism be deconstructed as a Western illusion to be reconstructed in a merely parochial form. The Elgin marbles may yet become just the Parthenon's frieze. Indeed, the process is already underway: hence Duroselle's history of Europe; hence Jean-Pierre Vernant's gentle admonitions; hence my own irritations as a sometime-classicist-turned-anthropologist with a definition of English (*sic*) culture in terms of Shakespeare and Oscar Wilde. And, since I started with Malinowski, will anyone ever again entitle a book *Argonauts of the Western Pacific*?! Which leads me, by way of a coda, to an anecdotal account of the place of anthropology in Greece.

In 1982, shortly after I took up the position of Assistant Director at the British School at Athens, there was a 'cocktail party' (at which beer, wine and spirits but never cocktails, were served) in the Director's 'Upper House'. During the proceedings I was approached by a woman (whose name I have genuinely forgotten) who congratulated me on my recent appointment. She was Greek and I had seen her many times, without ever having made her acquaintance, in Oxford in the Ashmolean Museum and the Taylorian Library. She asked me what period and field of Greek archaeology I was researching. As it happens, I am hard put to tell red-figure ware from black-figure ware but the mistake was understandable; my appointment to the British School as an anthropologist rather than as an archaeologist was a surprising one, not least to myself. I therefore explained that I was a social anthropologist and that my fieldwork had been in the village of Spartohori on the island of Meganisi. Rather perplexed, she said to me, 'You mean you are studying *us*?' I was hesitant. After all, I had not been studying urban middle-class Oxford-educated Greek archaeologists and thinking that it perhaps might aid my *bonae fides*, I asked whether she had ever read John Campbell's *Honour, Family and Patronage*. The answer was resoundingly 'yes' and that she thought the book ought to be burned. Shocked, I asked why; whereupon she explained to me, with apparent disregard for the contradiction, that Campbell's book (published in 1962) did not accurately represent 'modern Greece' and that in any case all that stuff about sexism and honour and the position of women was not anything any Greek needed to be told; they lived through it.

I regret to say I broke off the conversation but the memory of it has always intrigued me, since it encapsulates in particularly stark form one aspect of the dilemma which I have discussed. Consider her position. She was a Greek who had done her postgraduate degree in Greek archaeology at Oxford – and not just because the Arundel marbles happened to be housed in the Ashmolean. An Oxford degree secured her position within Greek academia better than a Greek degree. That could (I do not know with what degree of difficulty) be swallowed. But if it was necessary, or advisable, for a Greek to study Greece in England, at least that was because Greek civilization/culture was 'civilization/culture' (however displaced), to which the housing of the Arundel marbles bore testimony. The affront I caused, or which Campbell caused, was that we were not studying Greek *politismos*. Nor, in rural contexts, were we exactly studying *ta ithi ke ethima*. We were studying Greek villages as we might have studied (to the best of our less-than-dispassionate abilities) the Nuer or the Dinka or the Lele. We were studying 'other cultures' in which global 'culture' found no place. We had reduced the sublime to what was, by a particular accident of 'cultural translation', not only ridiculous but also offensive. From the Greek point of view, perhaps we had forgotten whence we came.

NOTES

1 I believe the phrase to be attributable to Evans-Pritchard, and certainly it appears (in a slightly different form) in his 1950 Marett Lecture 'Social anthropology: past and present'; but as an index of its currency, see, for example, the title of the 1971 volume of essays, *The Translation of Culture*, edited by T.O. Beidelman and presented to Evans-Pritchard in the year of his retirement.

2 From a 'postmodern' position, Lévi-Strauss is now considered to be one of the great 'totalizers', and such statements as 'I believe the ultimate goal of the human sciences to be not to constitute, but to dissolve man' (1966: 247) lend credibility to the view; but Lévi-Strauss' position was considerably more subtle, and essentially relativistic, as the following passage from the same essay (his argument with Sartre) makes clear:

> All meaning is answerable to a lesser meaning, which gives it its highest meaning, and if this regression finally ends in recognizing 'a contingent law of which one can say only: *it is thus*, and not otherwise' (Sartre, [1960] p. 128), *this prospect is not alarming to those whose thought is not tormented by transcendence even in a latent form*. For man will have gained all he can reasonably hope for if, on the sole condition of bowing to this contingent law, he succeeds in determining his form of conduct and in placing all else in the realm of the intelligible.
>
> (1966: 255–6, emphasis added)

3 I refer in general to the 'writing culture' authors: Clifford, Marcus, Fischer *et al.*; but see more specifically Marcus and Fischer 1986.

4 For a brilliant analysis of an example of the process of the universalization of 'culture' see Turner 1991. In this case, however, one might want only to applaud the activities of the Kayapo.

5 Fieldwork was conducted between 1977 and 1980 primarily in the village of Spartohori, on the tiny island of Meganisi, administratively part of the larger Ionian island of Lefkada (or Lefkas), Greece.

6 See Herzfeld (1987: 3). Herzfeld's general thesis in *Anthropology through the Looking Glass* concerning the relationship between anthropological knowledge and Greek identity is germane to my chapter as a whole, and of particular

relevance to the anecdote with which it ends.

7 The word 'anthropology' (*anthropoloyia*) is in common use in Greece, but refers to physical anthropology or to a branch of physiology. I refer to the development of social or cultural anthropology, which has been late. A Department of Anthropology was not created until the establishment of the new University of the Aegean in 1987, where to the best of my knowledge the subject is still not taught at undergraduate level. It should be noted, however, that under the direction of the late A. Kiriakidou-Nestoros, folklore studies at the University of Thessaloniki took a notably anthropological bent from the 1970s, and that a course in anthropology was also taught at the Pandios School of Economics in Athens in the early 1980s. Nor is there now any shortage of overseas-trained Greek anthropologists of Greece, many of whom are making substantial international contributions to the field.

8 Corfu and the other Ionian islands were constituted as a British Protectorate under the administration of a Lord High Commissioner between 1814 and 1864.

9 The university was built in 1839–42 by Christian Hanscn, the Hellenic Academy and the National Library rather later, in 1859 and 1887–91, to the designs of Theodore von Hansen.

10 Otho (1833–62) was 17 years old when he took the throne of Greece, one of six possible candidates considered by the 'Great Powers', i.e. France, Britain and Russia. See Dakin (1972: 61ff.).

11 See, for example, Rossiter (1977: 162). Hitchcock refers to the work of the Hansen brothers as 'Conventional essays in the international Greek Revival mode, here made somewhat ironical by their proximity to the great fifth-century ruins' (1958: 38). Their buildings are invidiously compared with a simpler example of the neo-Hellenic style, the Old Palace built for King Otho in 1835–6. This too was a 'foreign' construction, the work of Gartner, architect of the Ludwigstrasse in Munich (Hitchcock, 1958: 38; see Yarwood, 1976: 499).

12 This is not to suggest that Greek architects of the period were not also imbued with an 'imported' neo-Hellenism, for example Kaftanzoglou, Kleanthis and Kalkos. Interestingly, however, and in accord with the internationalism of their professional training, they also built in an Italianate style (Rossiter, 1977: 163; Hitchcock, 1958: 38–9).

13 Strictly speaking, Greece was not 'colonized', but from the Greek state's very inception it was subject to the authority of the Great Powers; and King Otho, for example, arrived with a full complement of Bavarian advisers and military officers.

14 Thus, for example, Godfrey Barker referred in the concluding words of his article in the *Daily Telegraph* (5 Nov. 1984) to 'art that is ancestral to us all'. His major argument, however, laced with quite extraordinary insult, was that 'this illiterate, resigned, enfeebled race [the Greeks], for two millennia a shadow of past Periclean glories' were not fit guardians for such treasures. More soberly, an article by Louis Ronze in the *Courier* (no. 87, Sept.–Oct. 1984, reprinted from *Jours d'Europe*) made the point that:

> Countries are not water-tight cultural compartments ... but a continuous culture in time and space. Consider the fact that a vast part of European art is directly inspired by Greece: Greek works, part of Europe's artistic heritage, are therefore equally at home in Paris, London, Berlin or Rome.

Roger Scruton, in *The Times*, 7 June 1983, went one better:

> The patrimony of Athens exists only partly in marble. The meaning of those marbles is to be found in literature, in law, in institutions, in public spirit.

... Who is heir to that spirit? Who adopted that literature, those laws, and those institutions?

Scruton's answer was 'Britain', or rather, Lord Elgin himself and the British Parliament of the time.

15 As Melina Mercouri said in an interview with Susan Crosland, 'The British say they have saved the Marbles. Well, thank you *very* much. Now give them back' (*The Sunday Times*, 22 May 1983). But the compression of the national and the universal can be illustrated, more or less at random, by the remarks of Andre Kazazis, then a Greek member of the Council of Europe's Parliamentary Assembly, in a quite temperate piece published in the *Courier* 87, Sept.–Oct. 1984:

> The Acropolis is the most perfect expression of Greek civilization at its height. Its monuments are witness to the triumph of the Greek mind over barbarian forces. ... This monument of classical architecture is an integral part of the day-to-day life of Greeks, particularly Athenians. Mutilated or moved elsewhere, it ceases to exist. It is and must be a monument to the European heritage.

Spotlight, the English-language fortnightly publication of the Greek Institute for Political Studies, was a deal more patriotic, and thereby mystically universalistic, in its comments:

> The meaning of the Acropolis for humanity is its presentation, on this specific holy rock, of the limitless potential of man. That is why it is a crime against humanity and civilization for even a little piece of stone to be removed from this place, which, to a point, is symbolic of the world as a whole.
>
> (*Spotlight*, 1 Dec. 1985)

16 I echo Herzfeld's rather nicer phrase, 'ecumenical ethnocentrism' (1982: 51), which he uses to describe the attitude of the nineteenth-century scholars Zambelios and Valvis.

17 I am grateful to Dr Stathis Gauntlett, who read and commented on an earlier version of this chapter and who directed me to a number of Greek sources to substantiate my argument.

18 In an article primarily concerned with the nature of Greek literary development, Tziovas points out that 'there is the absence of a basic concept of culture from the Greek lexical stock or its replacement by other concepts' (1989: 321).

19 The example is not hypothetical. A recent excursion to the Athens Opera with his small son to see a performance of *Don Giovanni* prompted N.K. Androulakis, Professor of Criminal Law at the University of Athens, to write a long piece in the Athenian newspaper, *To Vima* (6 Oct. 1991), entitled 'Don Giovanni and *tsifteteli* [belly-dancing]'. His criticism was of neither the singing nor the production, but of the audience. Where, puzzled Prof. Androulakis, had all the young people, the students, the intellectuals, and indeed the smart set and the 'upper class' gone, whose attendance at the opera had been a feature of his own youth? The answer was that they had all gone over to a new 'unified totalizing musicopoetic formation in which, higgledy-piggledy, Elitis [Nobel laureate poet] and *tsifteteli* [belly-dancing], Seferis [Nobel laureate poet] and turkogypsy song, have been muddled together, and this formation has spread and completely taken over Hellenic music' (my translation).

20 See Liddell and Scott's *Greek-English Lexicon* (9th edn., 1940, Clarendon Press) under *paideia*. The term is cognate with *pais*, 'a child'.

21 Note, for example, how (outside Greece) a classicist like Werner Jaeger could

entitle his monumental three-volume work on classical antiquity *Paideia: the ideals of Greek culture* (1945).

22 Melina Mercouri was Minister of Science and Culture from 1981 to 1989. She resumed office in October 1993, but as Minister of Culture. Mercouri died, a national hero, on 6 March 1994.

23 As Tziovas (1989: 322) notes, 'It is striking that ... 19th century [Greek] scholars were only minimally concerned with rendering into Greek the crucial term "culture" or "kultur", a concept that had begun to be used in Europe around the middle of the 18th century with a new meaning.' It should be noted, however, that in Europe 'kultur' and 'culture' did not quite refer to the contemporary anthropologist's 'culture', but rather to the intellectual (or 'spiritual') development of a people as opposed to the material (and political) progress of their 'civilization'.

24 The Greek etymology of *politismos* closely parallels the Latin etymology of 'civilization': *civis* (city) plus abstract noun ending; the stem *polit-* of *politis* (citizen) from *polis* (city) plus abstract noun ending.

25 In fact Dimitrakos' *Mega Lexikon Olis tis Ellinikis Glossis* (Great Dictionary of the Whole Greek Language, 1964) defines it as: 'a state of society in which man has definitively separated himself from the immediate influence of nature and has developed an ethical, spiritual and aesthetic life, in contrast to savages and barbarians' (my translation).

26 It should be remembered that 'civilization' in English used to be regularly coupled with 'Western' or 'British', or, when it was understood globally (and in evolutionary terms), with 'Mesopotamian' (as civilization's 'cradle'); the term now seems not so much to have been semantically redefined by anthropologists *et al.* as simply abandoned — in favour, again, of 'culture'.

27 Neither word appears in Dimitrakos' 1964 *Lexikon*, but both appear in the 1991 Patakis *Sinchrono Lexiko tis Neoellinikis Glossas* (Contemporary Lexicon of Modern Greek) where, however, they are very generally defined simply as relating to *politismos* or concerned with the development of *politismos*.

28 The usages above of the two terms, which appear to be almost interchangeable, are taken more at less at random from contemporary Greek newspapers and journals. *Politistikos organismos* (cultural organization), however, appeared in a 1982 government gazette.

29 See Herzfeld (1982) for the development of *laographia*.

30 The provenance of the *bouzouki* is disputed, but both the instrument and the music associated with it (*rebetika*) were at one stage considered 'asiatic', and were censored under the Metaxas regime as 'unhellenic'. See Gauntlett (1991: 14ff.). The *bouzouki* and *rebetika* are now very much in vogue. See note 19 above.

31 But for the popularity of whisky in Greece see Stewart (1991: 126).

32 Here Malinowski's work (and influence) can again be cited – see particularly the 1945 posthumous collection of essays. And the notion of 'historyless societies' had a long life.

33 The cartoon appeared in the Melbourne Greek-Australian monthly, *Omoyenia Pictorial*, Sept. 1988, but was by the famous Athenian cartoonist, Kostas Mitropoulos, and reprinted from the Athenian press. That Australia should have featured in the Athenian news at the time is explained by the fact that the Minister for Northern Greece had requested the Australian Prime Minister (then Bob Hawke) to change a chapter in the forthcoming Australian Bicentenary encyclopaedia *The Australian Peoples*, which included the Macedonians as a separate (non-Greek) ethnic group. The request was denied.

34 It should be made clear (as Vernant made clear) that the *Vima* interview took place before the actual publication of Duroselle's *History*. The English-

language version I have consulted does make mention of the Greeks (perhaps as a result of protests), but very scant mention. Chapter Four of the work is entitled 'Classical Antiquity: Greek Wisdom, Roman Grandeur', but its sub-headings give an idea of the direction taken: 'The Roman conquest', 'Roman law, the state, and the family', '*Civis Romanus sum*: consolidation and assimilation', 'The Roman vision of Europe' and 'Roman Europe: East and West' — not much to assuage Greece's feelings. As for the Byzantine Empire, it makes a brief appearance in Chapter Eight under the sub-heading of 'The break with Byzantium'!

35 The long history of the 'language question' in Greece, the various policy changes that have affected the Greek state's educational system, and in general the prescriptive nature of academic (and political) pronouncements on language, have meant that most Greeks are conscious of the possibility of contending forms. One can always have an interesting debate with an Athenian taxi-driver about the 'correct' form of the genitive case of *polis* (city) – a situation that has little parallel in most other Western capitals.

36 For what it is worth, *The Oxford Dictionary* gives 1542 as its earliest example of the English (*sic*) 'geographie'; 1795 for 'geology' in its current meaning; and 1748 for 'psychology' in a modern sense. All three terms also existed in earlier Latin and French forms from which the English forms were derived. In fact the term 'anthropology' has been around in English since the sixteenth century, though not with its current meaning.

37 *The Oxford Dictionary* notes that neither 'psychology' nor its related terms existed in [Ancient] Greek; the word was introduced in its Latin form in Germany in the sixteenth century. In all probability it would have come into modern Greek via German or French rather than English.

38 See Herzfeld's (1982: 110–12) admirable account of the complexities involved in the 'coining' of this term.

39 Cavafy was of course an Egyptian Greek, but would be included by anyone (except himself) as a Greek poet.

40 It has been suggested to me that, from a Greek perspective, Oscar Wilde appears quintessentially 'English' because of the notoriety of his homosexuality. This facet of the Englishman as 'other' may have wider currency; certainly French friends were also not surprised that Oscar Wilde should appear as a paradigm of English letters.

41 As Herzfeld has discussed, another avenue lies in the demotic anti-classical 'Romiossini' tradition. See particularly Herzfeld 1987.

42 It is perhaps worth noting that in a recent work on George Seferis, Beaton (1990) takes Seferis' acute awareness of Ancient Greece's appropriation by the West, and of Greece's uncritical attempts to reappropriate anything that 'looked Greek', as central to his interpretation of Seferis' *Mythistorema*. Beaton quotes from Seferis' essay, 'Dialogue on Poetry':

> But we, driven by the very best of intentions, burning with the desire to bring back to Greece whatever is Greek, wherever we caught sight of something that looked Greek, brought back without investigating further, thousands of alien values that of course had nothing whatever to do with our country. (1990: 92)

43 I take as a particularly noxious example Charles Moore's piece in the *Telegraph* 30 Jan. 1984, where he argues that the Elgin marbles should not be returned to 'the debased culture that now breeds amid the ruins of an ancient civilization'. In as much as such a statement bears serious consideration, it is at least interesting to note the antithesis created between 'culture' and 'civilization' – though with what wit I am not sure.

REFERENCES

Androulakis, N.K. (1991) 'Don Giovanni and *tsifteteli* [belly-dancing]', *To Vima* 6 Oct. 1991.
Barker, G. (1983) 'End of the marbles match', *Daily Telegraph* 5 Nov. 1983.
Beaton, R. (1990) *George Seferis*, Bristol: Bristol Classical Press.
Beidelman, T.O. (ed.) (1971) *The Translation of Culture*, London: Tavistock.
Campbell, J.K. (1962) *Honour, Family and Patronage*, Oxford: Clarendon Press.
Clogg, R. (1985) 'Sense of the past in pre-independence Greece', pp. 7–30, in R. Sussex and J.C. Eade (eds) *Culture and Nationalism in Nineteenth-Century Eastern Europe*, Columbus, OH: Slavica Publishers.
—— (1986) *A Short History of Modern Greece*, Cambridge: Cambridge University Press.
Crosland, S. (1983) 'Melina and the marbles', *The Sunday Times* 22 May 1983.
Dakin, D. (1972) *The Unification of Greece, 1770–1923*, London: Ernest Benn.
Duroselle, J.-B. (1990) *Europe: a History of its Peoples*, London: Viking.
Evans-Pritchard, E.E. (1962) [1950] 'Social anthropology: past and present', reprinted in E.E. Evans-Pritchard *Essays in Social Anthropology*, London: Faber & Faber.
Gauntlett, S. (1991) 'Orpheus in the criminal underworld: myth in and about rebetika', *Mandatoforos* 34: 7–48.
Herzfeld, M. (1982) *Ours Once More: folklore, ideology and the making of modern Greece*, Austin, TX: University of Texas Press.
—— (1987) *Anthropology through the Looking Glass*, Cambridge: Cambridge University Press.
Hitchcock, H-R. (1958) *Architecture: Nineteenth and Twentieth Centuries*, Harmondsworth: Penguin.
Jaeger, W. (1945) *Paideia: the Ideals of Greek Culture*, Oxford: Basil Blackwell
Kazazis, A. (1984) 'Thefts, donations or sales?', *Courier* 87 Sept.–Oct. 1984.
Lévi-Strauss, C. (1966) *The Savage Mind*, London: Weidenfeld & Nicolson.
Malinowski, B. (1961) [1922] *Argonauts of the Western Pacific*, New York: E.P. Dutton & Co.
Malinowski, B. (1945) *The Dynamics of Culture Change*, New Haven, CT: Yale University Press.
Marcus, G.E. and Fischer, M.M. (1986) *Anthropology as Cultural Critique: an experimental moment in the human sciences*, Chicago: University of Chicago Press.
Moore, C. (1984) 'Beware of bearing gifts to Greeks', *Telegraph* 30 Jan. 1984.
Omoyenia Pictorial Sept. 1988.
Ronze, L. (1983) 'Who owns the Venus of Milo?', *Courier* 81 Sept.–Oct. 1983, reprinted from *Jours d'Europe* (1983) June–July 299–300.
Rosaldo, R. (1989) *Culture and Truth: the remaking of social analysis*, Boston, MA: Beacon Press.
Rossiter, S. (1977) *Blue Guide: Greece*, London: Ernest Benn.
Sartre, J-P. (1960) *Critique de la raison dialectique*, Paris.
Scruton, R. (1983) *The Times* 7 June 1983.
Sinchrono Lexiko tis Neoellinikis Glossas (1991) Athens: Ekdosis Pataki.
Spotlight: a fortnightly publication of the Institute for Political Studies, 1 Dec. 1985.
Stewart, C. (1991) *Demons and the Devil*, Princeton, NJ: Princeton University Press
Strathern, M. (1992) 'Preliminary Observations', notes circulated to ASA IV Decennial Conference speakers.
Turner, T. (1991) 'Representing, Resisting, Rethinking', pp. 285–313, in G.W.

Stocking (ed.) *Colonial Situations: Essays on the contextualization of ethnographic knowledge*, Madison, WI: University of Wisconsin Press.

Tziovas, D. (1989) 'Residual orality and belated textuality in Greek literature and culture', *Journal of Modern Greek Studies* 7(2): 321–35.

Yarwood, D. (1976) *The Architecture of Europe*, New York: Hastings House.

Young, M. (1973) *Corfu and the Other Ionian Islands*, London: Jonathan Cape.

Name index

Abbink, J. 236
Abdelrahman, H.M. 21, 27, 28
Abdullahi, Khalifa 27
Abimbola, W. 235, 236, 238, 241, 243, 245, 247, 252
Ackerman, S.E. 116
Adams, W.Y. 24, 25
Ahern, E.M. 254
Ahmed, Martha Nasim 1
Akinnaso, F.N. 11, 235–8, 241, 243–5, 247
Al-Bashir, General Omar 21, 27–8
Al-Shahi, Ahmed 25
Almond, P.C. 207
Alter, R. 175
Alworung'a, King of Okoro Alur 46
Amin, Idi 50, 52, 53, 54, 56
Amin, Samir 18
Amital, Rabbi Yehudah 174
Ammerman, N.T. 97
Anderson, B. 17, 28, 260, 263, 264
Anderson, R.M. 101
Appadurai, A. 17, 34, 38, 162
Appiah, R.M. 97
Ariel, Y. 173, 175
Aristotle 135
Asad, T. 8, 9, 196
Atahiya, Ustaza 34, 36
Attar, Farid al-Din 150, 157
Ausbacher, Menachem 167
Averill, L.J. 93
Aviad, J. 175
Aviner, S. 173
Avinieri, S. 181

Baba Qasim 141
Baba Sali 166
Bakhtin, M.M. 107, 259, 264
Barber, K. 235, 252, 254

Barr, J. 96
Barth, F. 66, 79, 138, 236
Bascom, W. 236–8, 241, 243, 245, 247, 252
Basso, K.H. 162
Bauer, J. 171
Becker, A.L. 135, 139
Beeman, W. 70
Benjamin, J. 261
Benjamin, W. 175, 276
Benvenisti, M. 165, 166, 170, 179
Berger, Peter 220
Berkovitz, Dov 173–4, 180
Blanchy, S. 263
Blavatsky, Helena Petrovna 207
Bloch, M. 235, 236
Boas, F. 235
Boddy, J. 4, 19, 20
Bohannan, P. 55
Boudens, R. 196, 197
Bourdieu, P. 63–4, 241, 244, 254–5, 259
Bowes, A.M. 164
Boyer, Jean-Pierre 289
Bruner, E.M. 162
Bryant, J.M. 235
Buber, M. 182

Callinicos, Alex 10
Campbell, Bebe Moore 80
Campbell, John 301
Cannizzo, Jeanne 23–4
Caplan, L. 3, 5, 8, 95
Capper, J. 201, 204, 205, 206
Carroll, J.B. 275
Chandler, Raymond 74
Chandra Muzaffar 112
Chekal, Mark 82
Chodorow, N.J. 261, 274
Clogg, R. 289

Subject index

Acropolis 288–9, 290, 295
AIDS: Anii people (Bénin) 227; Uganda 54–5
alcohol: Alur 49–50; Anii 224
Alur 45–56; alcohol 49–50; Amin regime 50, 52, 53, 54, 56; divisions 46–8; ethnic identity 52–6; global knowledge 48–9, 54–6; Jok Memba 49; Nebbi Community 53; Nile as boundary 48; polarization of culture 51–2; resettlement in Bunyoro 50; World Wars 48
Anii people (Bénin) 215–28; AIDS 227; Bassila see Bassila; certainty 228; civic ritual 223, 225–6; competing authorities 227; disease 216–20; drinking water 216–18, 227; ecological destruction 220–21; Islamization 223–5; lost taboos 220–21, 225; modernization 227–8; spirits of nature (ukono) 221–3, 225
Antankarana 269
anthropological fieldwork 10–12
architecture 288–9
Ariel 176–7
asceticism 154–7
Association of Social Anthropologists (ASA) Decennial Conference (Oxford, 1993) 2–10
Athens 288–9
Australia 295

Bassila (Bénin): Assemblée générale 226; Islamization 221, 224; medicine 219; see also Anii people
beer-brewers see alcohol
Bénin see Anii people; Bassila
Buddhism: Burma 210; indifference to religious boundaries 197–200;

modernism 208–10; Protestant Buddhism 209–10; Sri Lanka 195–210; Thailand 209; Theravada tradition 198–9, 210
Buganda 50, 55–6
Bunyoro 48; settlement of Alur 50
Burma 210

Calvinism 196–7
Canada: nationalism 29–30; see also Toronto
capitalism: and racism 79–80; in Uganda 54–6
Ceylon see Sri Lanka
charisma: Protestant fundamentalism 100–105; Sufism 134
Christianity: Christian certainty 1, 88–107, 200; missionaries see missionaries; Pentecostalism 101–3, 105; urban Protestantism in south India 92–107; Yorubaland 252–3
colonialism: Greece 289; Mayotte 267–9, 274; Sri Lanka 208–10
common cold 216–17
constructivism, radical 220
Corfu 288
creolization 45–6, 54, 234–5
cultural translation 286
culture: folklorizing of tradition 22–3, 37; Greece 291–4; incommensurability 259–60, 275; possessive individualism 260–62; racist use of term 61–2, 78–9, 81–2

dakwah 112–33; activists 117–19; arts students 123–4, 126–8; development (phases) 113–16; discussion groups 121–2; education 119–33; science students 120–23, 125–6, 130; usrah